The History of the
Parshall Family

From the Conquest of England by William of Normandy, A. D. 1066, to the close of the 19th century.

By

James Clark Parshall, Esq.,

Counselor at Law, Author of the Barker Genealogy, James Parshall and His Descendants, etc.

It is the greatest of blessings in life to have had good ancestors.—Benj. Franklin.

Syracuse
1903.

TO MY FATHER

WILLIAM PARSHALL

WHOSE PRIDE IN HIS FAMILY AND WHOSE REMARKABLE KNOWLEDGE OF HIS ANCESTRY FIRST SUGGESTED TO ME THE COMPILATION OF THE PRESENT HISTORY AND

TO THE VENERABLE

ASA PARSHALL

OF CHEMUNG, N. Y.

TO WHOSE GENEROSITY THE FAMILY IS INDEBTED FOR ITS PUBLICATION, THIS WORK IS AFFECTIONATELY DEDICATED.

THIS EDITION IS LIMITED

TO THREE HUNDRED COPIES, OF WHICH THIS

IS No.______________

Index to Illustrations.

Preface.

The history herewith given to the family is the result of more than seven years' continuous labor, and has been carried on in the face of obstacles which have seemed at times nearly insurmountable.

A work of this character is necessarily more or less incomplete, but much valuable data regarding our family is herewith presented and may aid some subsequent historian in the preparation of a more complete work.

An opinion seems to have prevailed among some of the family that the work was intended as a source of personal profit to the author; this idea is wholly erroneous, it having been a constant expense since its commencement. The book has been from first to last a "labor of love" only.

The peculiar difficulties in the preparation of an American genealogy have been fully experienced in this work. The families are scattered from ocean to ocean, from lakes to gulf. Several are residents of foreign countries. They are often without records and still more often without sufficient interest in the work to give what aid they might. The "Family Bible" has too often been carried off by daughters and then lost to the family name.

The family is a small one and there is but one family bearing the name. The English branch appears to be wholly extinct. No member of the family has even been historical great, but the individual members of it have ever been characterized by industry, sobriety and scrupulous honesty. So far as the author's observation goes our name has never appeared in literature, with a single exception. In "The Deserter," by Harold Frederick, the hero is a boy, Job Parshall by name, though it may be stated that Job was *not* "the deserter."

Since the work was placed in the hands of the publishers. vexatious delays have occurred, which, however, were seemingly unavoidable. After the work had been fairly advanced, a serious illness of the author, which necessitated a still more serious operation, further delayed the work, but all obstacles have been successfully surmounted and the work is before you.

To the venerable Asa Parshall, of Chemung, N. Y., the family owes a debt of gratitude which it can never repay. Whatever credit may fall to the author for his work no less praise is due to "Uncle" Asa for his unflagging interest and finally to his generosity which has furnished a large part of the means necessary to the publication of the work. But for him my work would have gone for naught.

I have been greatly assisted in my work by a little volume, entitled The Parshall and VanEtten Families, by Mrs. Annie Parshall Davis, which treats of the descendants of Samuel^{5}. This little work was prepared by Mrs. Davis while suffering from an illness, which ultimately proved fatal, and while it necessarily contained many errors it has proved of immense assistance to the author in tracing this branch of the family.

The author also begs to acknowledge his indebtedness to Horace Field Parshall, of London, Eng., for financial assistance rendered to the work.

A number of blank pages of suitable paper have been bound in the work for a family record, and it is earnestly desired that each family strive to keep this record accurately for the benefit of some future historian of our race.

Trusting that my efforts as the historian of our family may be rewarded by your approbation, and that you may prove kindly critics, I beg to subscribe myself,

SYRACUSE, 16 May, 1903. Your affectionate cousin,

JAMES CLARK PARSHALL.

The Pershalls of England.

The name of "Pershale" appears upon the Roll of Battel Abbey as one of the leaders of that conquering host which accompanied William of Normandy to England and took part in the Battle of Hastings, 14 Oct. 1066. To perpetuate the glorious event the Conqueror caused to be erected a magnificent abbey which he munificently endowed and in it was hung a roll containing the names of those nobles and leaders who had fought in the battle. The roll bore this inscription:*

> **"Dicitur a bello, bellum locus hic, quia bello**
> **Angligenae victi, sunt hic in morte relicti:**
> **Martyris in Christi festo cecidere Calixti;**
> **Sexagenus erat sextus millessimus annus**
> **Cum pereunt Angli, stella monstrante cometa."**

And is followed by the names of the individuals, among whom is that of the Pershale referred to. This roll has long since perished, but a number of more or less authentic copies exist and most of these bear the name of Pershale. Burke, the great authority on heraldry, gives the name in his list, and Duschesne in a smaller list, so that the participation of our ancestor in the battle is at least as well authenticated as that of any other claimants to descent from the followers of the conqueror. The Norman

* Burke's Roll of Battel Abbey 4-8.

origin of the family is probably beyond question. It has always been so believed in America and the English family from which the American has sprung, claimed descent paternally from the Norman Counts of Corbeil. This appears to have been a tradition in the family handed down from generation to generation, but the evidence of its truth—if truth it be—has long since succumbed to the corroding hand of Time. We may, therefore, without doing great violence to the probabilities, conjecture a half-savage ancestor among the followers of the Norwegian Rollo, in his invasion and conquest of Normandy; others might be found among the fierce warriors who in the ninth and tenth centuries of our era devastated Europe with fire and sword. It is not impossible that another may have been of the crew of that hardy adventurer, who, defying wind and waves, turned his carved prow toward the setting sun and discovered America, five hundred years before Columbus had seen the light of day. Fierce as the wolves themselves and scarcely less wild, they knew neither pity nor remorse; fearlessly they faced death and met it with a fortitude begotten of their faith in their pagan gods, and of the eternal feasts and combats of Valhalla.

No records of the family apparently exist, covering the interval from the Conquest to the reign of King Edward III., when the family is found seated in Staffordshire, where it had doubtless been for many generations. The family is traced to Sir Richard de Pershall and I introduce in this place the lineage as given by Burke:*

Sir Richard de Pershall, son of Sir Richard Pershall, by Alice Swinnerton, his wife. He was a Knight and a person of great power in Staffordshire, having been high sheriff, an office in those days of great authority, 7 Edward III (1333) and from the 11th to the 15th (1337-1341) of the same King. He *m.* Margaret *dau.* and heiress of Hugh, Lord of Knighton, and thus added that manor to his possessions. He was succeeded by his son

Sir Adam de Pershall, who was sheriff 15 Edward III (1341), and who made a similar accession to his estate by marriage with two heiresses, the *daus.* of John Weston, Lord of Weston Lizard, in the County of Salop

* Burke's Extinct and Dormant Baronetcies 406; Visitation of Kent, 1619-1621, p. 179.

and John de Coverswall, of Bishop's Offley. By the former he had a son and heir

Sir Adam de Pershall, of Weston Lizard, whose grandson and heir another

Sir Adam Pershall, left two *daus.* his co-heiresses, viz.:

Margaret Pershall, who married Sir Richard Mytton and conveyed to him the estate of Weston Lizard.

Johanna Pershall, *m.* to W. de Birmingham.

By the latter he had a son

Sir Richard Pershall, who acquired a considerable fortune with his wife, Johanna, *dau.* and heiress of Reginald Chetwynde, of Chetwynde, and left a son and heir

Sir Thomas Pershall, Knight, living 4 Richard II (1376), who, by his first wife, Philippa, had two sons

Richard } who *m. temp.* Henry IV (1399-1413), two sisters, the *daus.*
Nicholas } of Hugh Malpas, of Checkley, and thus brought great estates into the family. Richard, the elder son, left two *daus. m. temp.* Henry VII (1485-1500), the elder Isabella, to Sir Thomas Grosvenor; and the younger, Jocosa, to W. Pigott, of Cheshire. Of Nicholas more presently.

Sir Thomas, by his second wife, Alice, *dau.* of Roger Knightley, of Knightley, in Staffordshire, left a son

Humphrey, of Over Tayne, father of

Richard, who *m.* Alice, *dau.* of Robert Knightley, Esq., of Goswell, and had a son

Humphrey, father of

Hugh Pershall, who by his wife Isabella, *dau.* and heiress of John Stanley, of Pipe, left three daughters, his co-heiresses, viz.:

Catherine, *m.* to Sir John Blount, Knt., of Kinlett, in Salop.

Isabella, *m.* to Richard Fane, of Tunbridge, in Kent.

Jocosa, *m.* Humphrey Wolrych, of Dudmaston, in Salop.

The second son of the first wife

Nicholas Pershall, by Helen, his wife, dau. and co-heiress of Hugh Malpas, left a son and heir

Hugh Pershall, Esq., the first of the family, who resided at Horseley, in the County of Stafford. He was sheriff 4 Henry VII (1489)[a] and by Julia, his wife, *dau.* of Sir Robert Corbet, of Moreton Corbet, had a son and heir.

a. Some years ago I read an extremely interesting anecdote of this same Sir Hugh Pershall, which, as I am unable to find it again to quote the book, I relate, with tolerable accuracy, from memory:

At the time of the invasion of the Duke of Richmond. so soon to become King Henry VII., Sir Hugh was in command of a town or city for the reigning King, Richard III., to whom our ancestor was loyal. Being summoned by the Duke to surrender, Sir Hugh gallantly swore that the Duke would have to pass over his body before he won an entrance to the town.

Perceiving, however, in a short time, that the cause of Richard was desperate, and the futility of resistance, he was fain to surrender and make

HUMPHREY PERSHALL, ESQ., of Horseley, who *m.* Helen, *dau.* of Humphrey Swinnerton, Esq., of Swinnerton Castle, and widow of Henry Delves, Esq., and had issue

JOHN, of Checkley.
RICHARD, whose son
HENRY, *d. s. p.*
William from whom descended
John Pershall, of Naples.

The eldest son and continuator of the family

JOHN PERSHALL, ESQ., of Checkley, m. Helena, *dau.* of John Harcourt, Esq., of Ranton, in the County of Stafford, and left a son and heir

RICHARD PERSHALL, ESQ., who *m.* Isabella, *dau.* and heiress of Thomas Rolleston, Esq., of Derbyshire, and had seven sons and two *daus.* The eldest son

THOMAS PERSHALL, ESQ., succeeded to the family estates, resided at Horseley. He *m.* Joanna, *dau.* of Sir Edmund Fettiplace, of Berkshire, and was succeeded by his son

JOHN PERSHALL, ESQ., of Horseley, in Staffordshire, who was among the first Baronets created by King James I, 25 Nov., 1612, and in four years afterwards was sheriff of the county. He *m.* Anne, *dau.* of Ralph Sheldon, Esq., of Beoly, in the County of Worcester, and had issue

THOMAS, his heir, born in 1596, who *m.* Bridget, *dau.* of Sir William Stafford Knt., of Blatherwick, and dying in the lifetime of his father left

JOHN, successor to his grandfather.
Bridget, *m.* to George, son of William Massey, Esq.
Anne, *m.* to Christopher Hawley, Esq.
Elizabeth, *m.* to Sir Robert Bosvile, of Bianno.
Lettice, *m.* to John Barber, gent. of Flashbrook.

Humphrey, ancestor of the Pershalls of Halne, to whose representatives the Baronetcy of Horseley is said to have passed at the decease of Sir Thomas Pershall, in 1712.
Ralph.
William (Sir), *m.* (1) Mary *dau.* of Richard Thimelby, Esq., and (2) Frances, *dau.* of Walter, Lord Aston.
John, *m.* Bridget, *dau.* of Robert Knightley, Esq., of Warwickshire.
Anne, *m.* to Sir Richard Fleetwood, Bath.
Elizabeth, *m.* to William Scot, Esq., of Sussex.
Dorothy, m. to William Stanford, Esq., of Perryhall.

his peace with Richmond. His oath, however, was not to be lightly violated, so he was obliged to resort to a singular expedient to avoid perjuring himself. Notifying Richmond that he was ready to surrender, and of the difficulties of the case, he opened the gate of the town, lay down on the ground and the Duke stepping carefully over him entered it with his followers. Whether he took part in the battle of Bosworth Field or not, I am unable to say, but that he subsequently rose in favor with the King is certain, for a few years later we find him Sheriff of Staffordshire, an office in those days of very great honor and authority.

Jane, *m.* to Richard Colvert, Esq., of Cockerem.
Katherine, *m.* to James Pool, Esq., of Wishall.
Margaret, *m.* to Richard Brent, Esq.
Frances, *m.* to John Stanford, Esq., of Sayford.

Sir John died 13 Jany., 1646, and was succeeded by his grandson

SIR JOHN, who *m.* in 1660, Frances, *dau.* of Col. Thomas Legh, of Adlington, in Cheshire, and dying in 1701, was succeeded by his son

SIR THOMAS PERSHALL, *m.* Miss Medcalf and had a son

John, who *m.* Charlotte, *dau.* of Thomas, Lord Colepeper, and died before his father in 1706, leaving two *daus.*, his co-heiresses, viz.:

Frances, *m.* to Thomas Ireland, Esq., of the County of Salop, and had a son.

Arabella, baptized in 1702, *m.* to John, third Earl Breadalbane.

Sir Thomas died in Feby., 1712, and since that time the Baronetcy has lain dormant.

In this place it seems to me pertinent to introduce an account of the efforts of a certain Rev. John Pearsall to show a connection existing between that family and the more aristocratic Pershalls.*

"In the year 1612, John Pershall, of Horseley, County Stafford, the descendant and representative of an ancient family, which is said to be paternally descended from the Norman Counts of Corbeil, was created a Baronet by James I. He *m.* Anne, *dau.* of Ralph Sheldon, of Beoly, in Worcestershire, and dying in 1646, was succeeded by his grandson, John Pershall, the only son of his son Thomas, who had died *v. p.* Sir John died in 1701, and was succeeded by his son Sir Thomas, on whose death without surviving male issue in 1712, the dignity is presumed to have become extinct.

"But about the year 1771, the Rev. John Pearsall, of Oxford, (formerly a schoolmaster at Highgate and afterwards at Guilford) the descendant of a respectable yeoman family, seated for many generations at Hawne and Witley, in the parish of Halesowen, changed the name which he and his ancestors had hitherto used, and adopted the style and designation of Sir John Pershall, Bart., alleging that the title had on the death of the above-named Sir Thomas Pershall, in 1712, passed to his (the Reverend gentleman's) grandfather, Thomas, the grandson of Humphrey Pearsall, who, he asserted, was the second son of the first Baronet of Horslev.

"To support these pretensions the surname of the grandfather, which had been originally engraved *Pearsall*, was altered on his tombstone at Halesowen to *Pershall;* and a tablet recording the births, marriages and deaths of sundry Pershalls of Hawne, (including Humphrey 'fil D'ni Joh'is de Horseley Hall in agro Staff. B'ti, who died in 1650, *aet* 51) was placed in Halesowen church.

"The Reverend Baronet had issue three surviving sons: 'Sir' John, who succeeded him, and died at his apartments in Chelsea Hospital, 21 Nov., 1820,

* VII. Herald and Gen. 270 etc.

in his 62d year. Sparry Pershall, born in 1760, who *m.* Anna Maria, *dau.* of Thomas Homer (by Patience, *dau.* of Richard Keelinge) and *d. s. p.*, 24 Dec., 1803; and Samuel, born 1761. The daughters were Anna Maria, born 1764, died 1765; and Elizabeth Maria, who was married to Sir Busic Harwood, Knt., M. D., and died in 1836, *aet.* 73.

"From Humphrey, third son of Humphrey, third, of Hawne (the alleged second son of the Horseley Baronet) Robert Lucas de Pearsall of Willsbridge, Co. Gloucester, is descended, and in Burke's *Landed Gentry* and *Royal Descents* the pedigree is traced from the Pershalls of Horseley.

"It is stated in these works that Humphrey Pershall of Horseley succeeded to the estate of the Halne or Hawn in the parish of Halesowen on the death (without issue in 1616) of his cousin John Pearsall;" but the exact connection of John of Hawne with the Humphrey of Horseley is not shown, and I am inclined to think that the so-called second son of Sir John was really descended from Humphrey Peyrsall, husbandman, who in 1562, obtained a lease of lands in Hawne for 1,000 years from Messrs. Blount and Tuckey, to whom the estate had been granted by John Dudley, Duke of Northumberland.

"Lawrence Pearsall, yeoman, dealt with the Witley estate in 1580, and Humphrey Pearsall of Hawne, yeoman, in 1616. The next of the family that I meet with is John Pearsall of Witley Barn, yeoman. His will is dated 1659; in it he mentions his *cousin* John Pearsall of Hawne, his wife Joan, his brother-in-law Thomas Carpenter, his son John and his three daughters Joan, Joice and Elizabeth.

"In 1671, the son of John was 'of Witley Barn, yeoman' the daughter Joan was then unmarried; Joice was the wife of Thomas Pennell, of Elmley Lovett, Co. Worcester, 'agricola;' Elizabeth, of Zachariah Birch, of Harbourne, Co. Stafford *nailor*.

"The name of Pershall no longer occurs in the roll of Baronets, but as the title is pronounced by Burke to be *dormant*, it is not improbable that it may at no distant day re-appear in the Baronetage.

"I do not mean to positively assert that the alleged descent of the Hawne family from the Pershalls of Horseley cannot be satisfactorily established, but I certainly do consider it sufficiently doubtful to merit a place in your list of doubtful pedigrees and Baronetcies.

"Certainly the social position of the Halesowen family was very different to that enjoyed by the Pershalls of Horseley, who matched with Sheldons, Staffords, Knightleys, Fleetwoods, &c., but what makes the matter still more suspicious is the tampering with tombstones, an act which cannot be too highly reprehended. I should be very glad, however, if this letter should elicit some information which would tend to establish what I cannot but consider a very doubtful claim."

Late in the reign of Elizabeth, and in the following reign of James I., an Edmond Pershall of London, a member of the Grocers' guild or corporation, acquired prominence, and I introduce in this place a brief sketch of him, which is compiled, I believe, from records of the Grocers' Company:

Pershall

ARMS: Argent a cross patee flory, on a canton gules a wolf's head erased of the field.

CREST: A wolf's head sable, holding in his mouth a marigold ppr.

Pashall--Pearshall--Piershall--Pershall--Peshall, etc., Edmond, grocer, 2. Sub.—; pd. £25. Admitted to Livery, May 24, 1596; paid £15 as his share of the levy of 1598; warden, 1609, when he had to pay the default of his brother warden, Timothy Bathurst, to the amount of £368; was senior warden in 1616. Westminster, March 29, 1615. Grant to Edmond Peshall and Edw. White of London, of the late imposition of 2s. per ℔ on tobacco imported for ten years paying to the King £3,500 the first year and £7,oco per ann. afterwards, with sole power to import tobacco and to name persons for selling the same, with a proviso of determination at six months' notice, if found prejudicial to the State.*

This Edmond Pershall was one of the sons in all probability of Richard who *m.* Isabella, *dau.* of Thomas Rolleston and had seven sons and two daughters, mention of whom is made on a preceeding page. I find the following description of Edmond, son of Richard, which seems to render it probable that he was identical with the Edmond of London.

Edmundus Pershall iam sup'tstes apud Bromley in co Cautij. *m.* Maria filia Lauceloti Bathurst nuper aldermanus Lond. *Issue:* Robertus Pershall de Lincolne Inne fil p'mogenitus aet 20 An et Amplius; Edmundus fil. 2 aet 18 An et Amplius; Thomas fil. 3 aet 15 An; Maria aet 8 Annos.†

The inference from this is clear as to *why* he paid "the default of his brother warden, Timothy Bathurst, to the amount of £368."

I think it extremely probable that James the Emigrant was a grandson of this Edmond, or of one of his brothers.

* Genesis of the U. S., 962.
† Visitation of Kent, 1619-1621, p. 179.

James Parshall, the Emigrant.

FAMILY I

JAMES[1] [1], was born, beyond a doubt, in England, probably about the middle of the seventeenth century. There are no records extant showing the exact date, but the fact that he died about twenty-three years after his marriage indicates that he had not, in all probability, reached a very advanced age. He *d.* at Southold, Suffolk County, N. Y., 15 Sept., 1701,* *m.* probably at Easthampton, Suffolk County, about 1678, Elizabeth, only *dau.* of David and Mary (Lerringman) Gardiner, of Easthampton.†

Children‡

2 I. Mary[2] *b.* abt. 1679.
3 II. Israel[2] *b.*—Mch., 1680. FAM. II.
4 III. David[2] *b.* 1683. FAM. III.
5 IV. Benjamin[2] prob. *d. inf.*
6 V. Margaret[2] *m.* 1710, Caleb Howell.§

The first record of him that we have is a deed, under date of Dec. 12, 1679, by which it appears that he was at that time a resident of the Isle of Wight, or Gardiner's Island, as it is now known, and which was included within the limits of the township of Easthampton. As this deed is the earliest known record in which his name is mentioned I reproduce it here in full:

* Rec. Probate Court; Early L. I. Wills, 227.
† Moore's Index of S'old; II. S'old Town Rec. 266; Id. 438; Early L. I. Wills, 226.
‡ I. Doc. Hist. of N. Y. 453.
§ Salmon Record.

"This indenture made ye twelfth of December in the two and thirtyeth yeare of ye reighn of our Soveraigne Lord Charles ye Second by the grace of God King of England &c and in ye yeare of our Lord Christ one thousand six hundred seventy-nine Between John Yongs Senr of the Towne of Southold on the one part and James Parshall of ye Ile of Whight in New England on the other part Witnesseth that the said John Yongs for and in consideration of a full satisfaction to me payd have granted and sould and by these presents doe grant and sell unto the said James Parshall, the first division of Acquabauk being five lotts of upland which the sd Yongs purchased of Joseph Horton and John Tucker, butting and bounding as followith—To the North Sea or Sound North—and to the East the land of Mary Wells, and to the sd John Yongs his late division West:—Also five lotts of meadow lying and being on the South side the River and on the East side of the deepe Kreek butting and bounding as followeth—on the North west to a tree marked in manner of a crows foot to a pine tree marked with ye sd Yongs his mark South Est. To have and to hold &c.

"In witness whereof I the sd John Yongs have hereunto sett my hand and seale the day and yeare first above written.

"John Yongs"

"Witnesses
Benjamin Yongs
Thomas Osman"
"Entered ye 22d of the 1 Moth 1679
Pr Benjamin Yo: Rdr"*

It was prior, in all probability, to the date of this deed that he had married his wife. It is of record that his eldest son, Israel, was born in Mch. 1680, and there is every probability that his *dau.*, Mary was older than her brother. Her name is mentioned first in contemporary records which would be absolutely inexplicable on any other hypothesis. This would indicate a date hardly later than 1678 for his marriage. The parents of Elizabeth Gardiner were married, 4 June, 1657,† hence she could not have been more than 20 years of age at the time of her marriage, and may have been two or three years younger. Her parents had three sons beside the daughter Elizabeth, but as the dates of their birth are not of record, we have no means of knowing whether she was the eldest child. As to the age of James, we can only conjecture: It is not probable that he was more than 40 at the time of his marriage and he was probably

* I. S'old Town Rec. 379 &c.
† II. Sav. Gen. Dict. 225.

considerably younger. The males of the early generations of the family in America seem to have died comparatively young, and it is probable that at the time of James' death, he had not reached his sixtieth year. His eldest son died at 58; his second son at 43; his third son probably in childhood, and the only one of his grandsons of whom we can speak with certainty, died at about 50 years of age. I believe the birth of James may safely be placed between 1640 and 1650.

That he was of English ancestry and a descendant of the family mentioned in the preceding chapter is morally certain. The family was a small one and the similarity of name leaves no room for doubt on the subject. There is a tradition in one branch of the family (the descendants of Jonathan[3]) that the ancestor was a Hugenot refugee, but this is untenable. The very fact that the tradition is confined absolutely to this one branch is sufficient to disprove it. The Hugenot strain in this branch, if any, doubtless came through marriage with the daughter of some of the Hugenot refugees who had settled in Orange County, N. Y., where this branch of the family located at an early period.

Elizabeth Gardiner, wife of James, was the only daughter of David Gardiner, Esq., second proprietor of Gardiner's Island, and grandaughter of Capt. Lion Gardiner, the founder of the family which bears his name and the first proprietor of the estate. David, her father, was educated in London, where, 4 June, 1657, he married Mary Lerringman, a widow, of St. Margarets, Westminster.* He died very suddenly at Hartford, Conn., whither he had gone, probably on public business, 10 July, 1689.† His grave was discovered in 1836, in the ancient burying ground back of the Congregational Church at Hartford, and bears this inscription:

* II. Sav. Gen. Dict. 225.
† Grave at Hartford, Ct.; Conn. Hist. Col. 59.

"HERE LYETH THE BODY OF MR. DAVID GARDINER
OF GARDINER'S ISLAND DECEASED IVLY 10, 1689
IN THE FIFTY FOVRTH YEAR OF HIS AGE.
WELL, SICK, DEAD IN ONE HOVRS SPACE.
"Engrave the remembrance of Death on thy heart
When as thov doest see how swiftly hovrs depart"*

Her grandfather, Lyon, or Lion, as he wrote it, born in 1599,† of English parentage, was an engineer in the service of the Prince of Orange in the Netherlands. On 11 Aug., 1635, with his wife, and a single female servant, Elizabeth Colet, and eleven other male passengers, he embarked at London in a small vessel, the Bachilor, of only 25 tons burthen, and reached Boston, 28 Nov., in the same year.‡ In possession of the Gardiner family, on Gardiner's Island, is an old Bible, on a blank page of which is written, in the handwriting of Lion Gardiner, the following:

"In the year of our Lord, 1635, the 10th of July, came I, Lion Gardiner and Mary my wife from Worden, a town in Holland, where my wife was born, being the daughter of one Diricke Willemson, deureant; her mother's name was Hachir, and her Aunt, sister of her mother, was the wife of Wouter Leanerdson, old burger Muster, dwelling in the hostrade, over against the Bruser in the Unicorne's head; her brother's name was Punce Garretson, also old burger Muster. We came from Worden to London, and from there to New England, and dwelt at Saybrook fort four years—it is at the mouth of Connecticut river—of which I was commander, and there was born to me a son, named David, 1636, the 29th of April, the first born in that place, and in 1638 a daughter was born, named Mary, 30th of August, and then I went to an Island of my own, which I had bought and purchased of the Indians, called by them Monchonack, by us, Isle of Wight, and there was born another daughter, named Elizabeth, the 14th September, 1641, she being the first child of English parents that was born there."*

He commanded the fort at Saybrook during the Pequot War and was a man of great energy and force of character. He died late in 1663. The following is a description of his tomb at Easthampton:

* Conn. Hist. Col. 59; II. Sav Gen. Dict, 225.
† Grave at Easthampton.
‡ II. Sav. Gen. Dict. 226.

"On a sunny knoll in the old burial ground of Easthampton, (L. I.) amid blue-eyed grass and cinquefoil, rises the granite tomb of the first English planter within the limits of the present State of New York. On the slab beneath the roof whose pediments bear the escutcheon of his family, lies in helmet, cuirass, and greaves, the effigy of Lion Gardiner. On the plinth is inscribed, on the four sides, a brief summary of his life:

"'An officer of ye English army and an Enginery of ye Master of Workes Fortification of ye Leaguers of ye Prince of Orange in ye Low Countries. In 1635 he came to New England.

"'In service of a Company of Lords and Gentlemen He build'd and command'd Say Brook Forte

"'After completed his terme of service he moved in 1639 to his Island of which he was sole owner. Born 1599, he died in this towne in 1663.'"*

It appears to have been several years after the purchase of the land at Aquebogue, before James finally removed to Southold. The rate lists of 1683 do not contain his name, but in the census of Southold taken in 1686,† it appears that he was then a resident of that place; his family consisting of "six white males, two white females, three male slaves, and two female slaves." The names of the different members are not given. The census of 1698,‡ however, gives the names of James and his family as follows:

James Pershall
Margaret Pershall
Mary Pershall
Israel Pershall
David Pershall
Benjamen Pershall
Margarett Pershall Junjs.

Whether the name of Margaret is an error for Elizabeth or was the name of a second wife, evidence fails to disclose. I strongly incline to the former hypothesis. We have no record of the death of Elizabeth, nor of a second marriage of James. Elizabeth was living June 26th, 1690, as the following receipt to the executors of her father's estate will show:

* Early Long Island, 216.
† XXXIII. N. Y. Col. Mss. 94.
‡ I. Doc. Hist. of N. Y. 453.

"Receipt and release of James Parshall of Southold to John, David and Lyon Gardiner dated 26th June 1690, for ninety pounds current mony as a legacy and for any other sum due Elizabeth Parshall his wife, and daughter of David Gardiner late deceased.

"Witnesses
Joseph Griffin
Stephen Baily
Entd pr Benj: Yo. Rdr.

mark of
JAMES X PARSHALL

"I do also hereby engage, in case of a nonpayment of the sd above obligation never to exact or desire any more than ninety pounds, as my wife's and my full proportion of the estate of my father in law Mr David Gardiner deceased.

"Witness my hand and seal 26th June 1690.

"Memorandum: If the sd Estate shall be wasted or destroyed by robery or fire before the obligation of ninety pounds be performed then I am to bear my proportion of what shall be wasted or destroyed—June 26th 1690—

mark of
"JAMES X PARSHALL

"Entd pr Benj: Yo. Rdr—"*

His will, made in 1692, a little more than two years after the receipt set forth on the preceding page, mentions his wife, but without naming her. I insert that extremely interesting document in this place:

"In ye name of God Amen—Southold this 14th. of Oct. 1692 I James Parshall of the town of S'hold in ye County of Suffolk upon Long Island in ye Province of N. York being weak in body but of sound memory do ordain & establish these presents to be my last will & testamt in manner & form following—First—I bequeath my soul to Jesus Christ my merciful Redeemer & my body to ye earth by decent burial in ye last assured hopes of its resurrection again at ye last day & as to my outward estate all my just debts being first paid & funeral charges allowed for by my executors I do will & dispose as followeth—Impmis I do give and bequeath unto my two sons Israel & David all my accommodations of both upland & meadow to them & their heirs forever equally to be divided between them two only my eldest son Israel is to have the eastermost side of this my accommodation of upland in Occabauke with all the improvements thereon that is to say my dwelling house barn outhouses fences orchards & improved lands—also my will is that all my implements of husbandry & arms be equally divided between my sd two sons. 2ly I do give & bequeath to my beloved wife one bed with all the furniture thereunto belonging—4ly I do give & bequeath her choice of my Indian Girls also my will is that my wife enjoy one room of my dwelling house & half my orchard during her widowhood and no longer— 5ly I do give and bequeath to my eldest daughter

* II. S'old Town Rec. 266.

Mary one bed with all ye furniture thereunto belonging Also I give unto my sd daughter my other Indian Girl— 6ly my will is yt all ye rest of my estate shall be equally divided between my wife & all my surviving children— 7ly My will is yt & if my two grown Indian slaves do serve faithfully five years (that then and not else they shall be free) Lastly—My mind & will is yt my beloved brothers in law John Gardiner & David Gardiner together with my friend Mr. Thomas Mapes be executors to this my last Will & testamt. And I do advise them to put out my two sons to such trades as they shall incline to learn for the confirmation hereof I have hereunto set my hand & fixed my seal in Southold this 14 day of Oct in ye year of our Lord God, 1692.

JAMES PARSHALL [Seal] *

"Signed sealed published & declared before us
"Evan Davise
Samuel Swazy
Tho. Mapes"

The following minute of the proceedings on the probate of the foregoing instrument is also of record:

"By the tenor of these presents know ye yt on ye 28 day of Oct. 1701 at ye manor of St. Georges in ye County of Suffolk before ye Honoble Coll William Smith Judge of the Prerogative Court in ye sd County was proved & approved ye last will & testamt of James Parshall late of S'hold in ye sd County deceased on ye 15 day of Sept. 1701 who by his sd will did nominate and appoint his brothers in law John & David Gardiner & Thomas Mapes his executors—and ye administration of the goods & chattels of ye sd deceased was granted to ye sd David Gardiner & Thomas Mapes."*

A careful perusal of this will makes it appear probable that all the children of James, mentioned in the Census of 1698, were born prior to the date thereof. Benjamin probably died in childhood as no records of him are extant. The bare mention of his name in the Census of 1698 is all that is known of him. The Census of 1698, also contains the last record of his eldest daughter Mary, "Margaret Junjr," married Caleb Howell in 1710,† after which she also disappears from the records.

James was "a gentleman," in the sense in which the word was used in Colonial times, and a man of considerable means, which he probably brought with him from England. The following, relative to James, appears in a work relating to Long Island:

* Early L. I. Wills of Suffolk Co. 226.
† Salmon Rec.

"Israel and David Parshall were sons of James Parshall, who married Elizabeth, the only daughter of David Gardiner, who lived on the Pesapunck Neck, at Mattituck, and afterwards became the second proprietor of Gardiner's Island. Of the Parshalls we have no account. James, who styles himself 'Gent of the Isle of Wight,' with his wife figures conspicuously in the settlement of his father-in-law's estate.

"He owned and occupied large tracts of land at Aquebogue, lived upon the North Road, and left his estate to his sons Israel and David. The name of Parshall is not now, we believe, to be found in Southold, or even in Riverhead Town."*

As a curiosity, rather than as possessing any particular genealogical value, I insert the following quaint deed of an Indian girl:

"Know all men by these presents that I James Paresall belonging to Southold in ye County of Suffolk on ye Island of Nassaw yeoman have sold and delivered unto John Parker of Southampton fuller an Indian Garle aged about eight years daughter of one Dorcas an Indian woman, which said Sarah was my slave for her life time; and I doe by these presents sell her ye sd Sarah unto him the said John Parker dureing her naturall life, to be unto him ye said Parker his heires and assigns as his or their proper estate; and I doe bind myself my heirs, executs and administrats to make good ye sale of ye above Indian gairle to him ye said Parker his heirs and assigns; and I doe acknowledge to have received of him ye said Parker for and in consideration of said Indian garle as full satisfaction, the full and just sum of sixteen pounds current money of the province.

"In witness whereof I have hereunto sett my hand and seale this 27th day of March 1698.

"Witnesses
Joseph Moore
Samuel Clark—

his
JAMES I PEARSALL
mark

"Entd May ye 10th 1712"†

The place of burial of James is unknown, though doubtless it is some ancient cemetery in or near Southold. No stone marks his final resting place. The place of his sepulcher is as problematical as that of Moses. The cemetery at Mattituck, where his sons Israel and David lie buried was not opened until 1715, some fourteen years after the death of James, hence it is not probable that he rests there. The following from an unpublished manu-

* II. S'old Town Rec. 438.
† Id. 179 &c.

script by the Rev. Mr. Craven, pastor of the Presbyterian church at Mattituck, though relating only to the cemetery at that place will be of interest in this connection:

Mattituck Burying Ground.

In 1809, the Burying Ground was already nearly one hundred years old, and many were its occupants. Some were probably buried here in 1715, the very year it was given to the parish. No stone in it bears an older date than 1723, but this is not strange, for all the stones had to be brought from a distance, most of them from England, at considerable expense. Those strange, little blue slate gravestones of the last century cost more comparatively than fine marble monuments to-day. *Not one half* the graves, perhaps not *one third,* are marked. There are thirty-five stones placed earlier than 1750. There are twenty-five that mark the graves of men and women whose lives dated into the 17th century. It is not improbable that men and women born before Southold Town was settled in 1640, *lie in unmarked graves* in Mattituck churchyard."

It should be a matter of keen regret that the first ancestor of our family in America lies in a forgotten grave.

The Second Generation

FAMILY II.

ISRAEL^{2} Capt. [3], (*James*^{1}) eldest son of James and Elizabeth (Gardiner) Parshall, *b.* probably Gardiner's Island, 1680; *d.* Aquebogue, Suffolk Co., N. Y., 18 Apl., 1738, "in the 58th year of his age;"* *m.* (1) 4 Dec., 1702,† Joanna Swezey (*b.* about 1678; *d.* 22 Feby., 1724; age 47 years 3 mos.)"*

[*Aquebogue, N. Y.*]

Children‡

7 I. Joanna^{3} *b.* about 1703; *d.* 31 May, 1733; "age 30 years;" *m.* 15 Mch., 1722, Christopher Youngs.** *Issue:*§

- i. James^{4} (Youngs) *m.* 5 May, 1748, Mehitabel Benjamin.
- ii. Christopher^{4} (Youngs) *m.* 1744, Anne Wells.
- iii. Joanna^{4} (Youngs) *m.* 16 Apl., 1753, Daniel Wells.

8 II. James^{3} *d.* 9 Apl., 1719.**

9 III. Elizabeth^{3} *b.* 27 June, 1705;†† *d.* 23 Feby., 1793;†† *m.* 28 Oct., 1724,** Joseph Davies (*b.* 22 Mch., 1702; *d.* 26 Sept., 1790.††) *Issue:*‡‡

---

* Grave at Mattituck; Sal. Rec.; Moore's Index 108.
† Sal. Rec.; Moore's Index 108.
‡ Will of Israel Parshall, XIII. N. Y. Wills, 296; Moore's Index 108.
§ Fam. Rec. Pos. S. Young, Jr., N. Y.
** Salmon Record.
†† Bible Rec. Joseph Davies pos. Mrs. Sarah C. Post.
‡‡ Will of Joseph Davies, from a copy in my pos. It does not appear where the orig. is recorded. Prob. among N. Y. Wills.

i. Joseph[4] (Davies) *b.* 1735-6; *d.* 1 May, 1814, "in the 78th year of his age."*
ii. Israel[4] (Davies).
iii. Timothy (Davies) *b.* 21 Sept., 1750.†[a]
iv. Experience[4] (Davies)
v. Amy[4] (Davies)
vi. Elizabeth[4] (Davies)
vii. Jemimah[4] (Davies)
viii. Keziah[4] (Davies)

10 IV. Keziah,[3] *m.* 12 Jany., 1727, Joseph Mapes‡ (*d.* 1771, "aet 83") *Issue:*§
i. Keziah[4] (Mapes) *m.* Thomas Reeve.
ii. Joseph[4] (Mapes) *m.* — Apl., 1749, Elizabeth Davies.**
iii. Jabez[4] (Mapes) *d. inf.*
iv. Joanna[4] (Mapes) *m.* Peter Hallock.
v. Jabez[4] (Mapes) *d. s. p.*
vi. James[4] (Mapes)
vii. Phineas[4] (Mapes)
viii. Anne[4] (Mapes)

a. Timothy Davies, or Davis, as the name is spelled by his descendants, was of Welsh extraction, *b.* Brookhaven, Long Island, 21 Sept. 1750; *m.* (1) Elizabeth Jayne (*b.* 21 Sept., 1757). *Issue:* *i.* Parshall, *b.* 23 Apl., 1779; *ii.* Asenath, *b.* 31 May, 1781; *iii.* Joseph Nash, *b.* 31 Mch. 1783; *iv.* Israel, *b.* 6 Jany. 1785; *v.* Joanna, *b.* 24 June, 1787; *vi.* Timothy, *b.* 25 Feby. 1790; *vii.* Elizabeth, *b.* 8 Mch. 1792; *viii.* Tabatha, *b.* 1794. He *m.* (2) 5 Dec. 1795, Mary Hallock, and had *issue:* *ix.* Maria Jayne, *b.* 18 Oct. 1797; *d.* 5 Jany. 1877; *m.* 30 Jany. 1823, John Clark (*d.* 28 Jany. 1861) *s.* John and Elizabeth (Corwin) Clark;** *gd. s.* John and Rachel (Soper) Clark; *gt.-gd. s.* Thomas and Elizabeth (—) Clark; *gt.-gt.-gd. s.* Thomas and Mary (—) Clark.†† Mrs. Sarah Clark Post, of Greenport, Suffolk Co., N. Y., is a *dau.* of John and Maria Jayne (Davies) Clark; and it is to her kindness of heart, coupled with a keen enthusiasm for genealogical research, that I am indebted for these records of the descendants of Elizabeth Parshall, as well as for much other extremely valuable data. The old Davies family Bible is in her possession, but a page containing very early records has been torn from it and unfortunately lost, hence my inability to give fuller data of this family.

---

* Grave at Mattituck.
† Bible Rec. Joseph Davies, pos. Mrs. Sarah C. Post.
‡ Salmon Record.
§ Will of Joseph Mapes, XXXV. N. Y., Wills, 216.
** Corwin Gen. 57.
†† Bible Rec. of John Clark, pos. Mrs. Sarah C. Post.

11 v. Israel,[3] *b.* probably 1708-12. FAM. IV.

12 VI. Jemima,[3] *m.* 17 May, 1730, Jonathan Terry* (*d.* 18 Nov., 1753).*

13 VII. Experience,[3] *m.* 11 Nov., 1736, Daniel Reeve.* *Prob. Issue:*[a]

Israel, *m.* (2) 26 May, 1726, the widow Mary Terry,* who survived him,** and is probably the Mary Parshil who, 9 June 1752, became one of the incorporators of a new Church Society at Mattituck.†

Connected by ties of consanguinity and marriage with many of its oldest and best families; possessed of abundant means; a gentleman in the sense in which the word was then understood, Israel Parshall was one of the most prominent men of his day in Southold. To the very considerable landed estate which he had received from his father, he added from time to time until he became, probably, one of the largest landowners in the township. In 1715, he appears as a private in "Ye Soffolk Regt. *Anno Don* 1715, Henry Smith Col., Joseph Wickham Lieut. (Col.), William Smith Major."†† Subsequently, in all probability he became Captain of the Southold Company, for toward the latter part of his life he is invariably referred to in contemporary records as "Capt." Israel Parshall. His will,** dated 23 June, 1737, proved, 22 May, 1738, mentions his "wife Mary." To his son

a. In the History of the Strong Family‡ it is stated that Joshua Brown *m.* the *wid.* Experience Reeve, who was Experience Parshall. I find no authority whatever to substantiate this statement. A Joshua Brown did *m.* 19 June, 1749, a *wid.* Experience *Terry.** A Daniel Reeve *m.* 26 Aug. 1734, Sarah Owen,* so it is clear there were at least two Reeves bearing the name of Daniel, one of whom *d.* at Albany, 13 Dec. 1746,* and letters of administration were granted to his *wid.*,§ but which of the two Daniels it was who *d.* I am quite unable to say.

* Salmon Record.
† Mattituck Ch. Rec.
‡ Hist. Strong Fam. I. 652.
§ Prob. N. Y. Wills.
†† Rept. State Historian I. 508; Col. N. Y. Hist. Mss. 428.
** Will of Israel Parshall, XIII. N. Y. Wills, 296; Moore's Index 108.

Israel he leaves his real estate, and to his daughters Jemima Terry, Elizabeth Davis, Keziah Mapes and Experience Reeve and to his son-in-law Christopher Youngs, he leaves £50 each. His son James, who was beyond question the eldest son, had died long before the making of the will, and consequently is not mentioned. Israel[2] is the ancestor who, according to the tradition current among the descendants of his nephew Jonathan, fled from France after the revocation of the Edict of Nantes, and this tradition has been embalmed in a so-called history.* Israel was born 1680, and the revocation of the Edict occurred 18 Oct., 1685, or when he was about five years of age. It is as clear and certain as anything within the range of human knowledge that Israel Parshall was born, lived and died on Long Island.

FAMILY III.

DAVID[2] [4], *(James[1]) b.* probably Gardiners Island, Suffolk Co., N. Y., ——July, 1682; *d.* Aquebogue, 25 Jany., 1725-6; "age 43 years and six months;"† *m.* about 1704, his cousin Mary,‡ *dau.* David[a] and Martha (Youngs) Gardiner (*b.* 1685; *d.* suddenly, 19 Apl., 1725, "age 40 years").†

Children:

14 I. David[3] *b.* probably 1705. FAM. V.

15 II. Mary[3]** *b.* 1707; *d.* 19 July, 1779; *m.* 3 Nov., 1726 Deacon Nathaniel Wells, *Issue:*

a. David Gardiner was the son of David and brother of Elizabeth Gardiner, wife of James.‡ Martha Youngs, his wife, was the *dau.* of Col. John,‡ and grand dau. of Rev. John Youngs.§ The first clergyman at Southold. He was *b.* England, 1597-8; *d.* Southold, L. I., 24 Feby., 1671-2; *m.* 1622, Joan Herrington, of Southold, England.§

---

* Ruttenber & Clark's Hist. of Orange Co. 240 etc.
† Grave at Mattituck; Sal. Rec.; Moore's Indexes.
‡ Moore's Indexes; Gardiner Gen.; Wm. Wells Fam. of S'old 265; Will of David Gardiner, N. Y. Wills.
§ IX. Am. Ancestry, 80; Corwin Gen. 161.
** Wm. Wells Fam. of S'old, 265.

i. Nathaniel[4] (Wells) *b.* ——Oct., 1729.
ii. Mary[4] (Wells) *b.* 1733; *d.* 26 Jany., 1805; *m.* 21 Nov., 1751, John Wells.
iii. James[4] (Wells) *b.* about 1735.
iv. Abigail[4] (Wells) *b.* 1738; *d.* 19 Oct. 1755.
v. Bethiah[4] (Wells) *b.* about 1740; *m.* 1764, William Luce.
vi. Sarah[4] (Wells) *b.* 1743-4; *m.* William Downes.
vii. Manly[4] (Wells) *b.* 1746.
viii. Nathaniel[4] (Wells) *b.* 1751.

16 III. Sarah[3] *m.* 1726, Joshua Hallock.*
17 IV. Abigail[3] *b.* *m.* 1 Nov. 1739. Barnabas Horton.*
18 V. Jonathan[3] *b.* probably about 1715-16. FAM. VI.
19 VI. Bethiah[3]† *b.* 19 Feby., 1724;‡ *d.* Morristown, N. J.; *m.* (1) 21 Feby., 1743, Rev. David Youngs.‡

Issue:

i. David[4] (Youngs) *b.* 19 Aug., 1745.
ii. Hannah[4] (Youngs) *b.* 13 June, 1747; *m.* (1) David Wheeler; *m.* (2) Capt. Enoch Beach.
iii. Ephriam[4] (Youngs) *b.* 26 Oct., 1749.
iv. James[4] (Youngs) *b.* 22 Jany., 175—; *m.* his step sister Ruth Halsey.

m. (2) Capt. Benjamin Halsey, of Morristown, N. J., probably *no issue.*

David, like his brother Israel, was a large land owner in Southold, and was probably one of the wealthiest men in the community where he resided. He appears to have been of a more retiring disposition than his brother and took a less conspicuous, if not less active part in the affairs of the town. He also appears as a private in the Southold Militia Co., in 1715.

* Salmon Record.
† Thos. Halsey and His Descendants in Am. 51.
‡ Bible Rec. Rev. David Youngs.

His will, dated, 24 Jany., 1725-6, and proved 16 Mch., 1725-6, is as follows:*

"In the name of God, Amen. The 24th day of January, in the year of our Lord, 1726, I, David Parshall, of Southold, in the County of Suffolk, and Colony of New York, husbandman; being very sick and weak in body but of perfect mind and memory * * * * * * this my *Last Will and Testament.*

Imprimis: I give and bequeath to my eldest son, David Parshall, the one-half of my land that I now live upon. The outermost side & also the land one half of my undivided Land with my Eastermost piece of Meadow Ground at Sawmill Brook Lying between Israel Parshall on the East side and Joseph Brown the West side & my half of all the rest of my Meadow ground.

Secondly, I will & bequeath to my youngest son Jonathan Parshall, the one-half of my land that I now live upon. The west half also the one-half of my undivided Land & my Meadow Ground not given before.

Thirdly, I give & bequeath to my youngest son Jonathan Parshall, Sixty pounds in Current money of New York, my will is that the said £60 shall be put to use at the discretion of my Executors while my said son shall come to the age of 21 years.

Fourthly: I give & bequeath all the rest of my estate after my lawful debts are paid unto all my children equally to be divided between them at the discretion of my Executors.

Further my will is that if any of my Daughters shall die before marriage then their part shall be divided equally between the rest of my daughters who are the survivors.

Lastly: I constitute & ordain my brother Israel Parshall, Samuel Swezey & John Wells my only & sole executors of this my last Will & testament.

(Signed) DAVID PARSHALL

In presence of
Samuel Wells
Christopher Youngs Sen.
Peter Simmonds Junr.

He appears to have been greatly attached to his wife, whose untimely death he survived but a few months.

* Will of David Parshall, N. Y. Wills, Lib. X., p. 157 (old p. 161).

The Third Generation

FAMILY IV.

ISRAEL[3] [11], (*Israel[2] James[1]*) *b.* probably Aquebogue, Suffolk Co., N. Y., about 1708-12; *m.* 16 Nov., 1732, Bethia Case.*

Children:

20 I. James[4] *b.* about 1733-5. FAM. VII.
21 II. Israel[4] *b.* 6 Oct., 1736.† FAM. VIII.
22 III. Phineas.[4a]
23 IV. Benjamin[4] *b.* 12 Sept., 1744.‡ FAM. IX.
24 V. Jesse.[4]
25 VI. Delilah[4]§ *m.* ———Terry. *Issue:*

i. Deliverance[5] (Terry) *m.* Israel Parshall (see FAM. XVII.) Probably others.

26 VII. Bethiah[4] *m.* 1 Mch., 1749-50, David Wells.*
27 VIII. Jemima[4] *m.* 1750, James Webb.*
28 IX. Joanna[4] *m.* 1751-2, Joshua Wells.*
29 X. A child[4] *d.* 17 Nov., 1748.*
30 XI. A son[4] *d.* 18 Dec., 1751.*

a. Phineas Parshall was a soldier of the Revolution, serving in the 3d

---

* Salmon Record.
† Grave at Chemung, N. Y.
‡ Bible Rec. pos. Dr. Geo. H. Parshall.
§ Griswold Rec. pos. Asa Parshall, Chemung, N. Y.

The existing records of Israel Parshall are of the most meager description. It is clear, however, that he remained for about twenty years after his marriage a resident of the town of Southold. On 6 Apl., 1749, he sold to Jonathan Youngs, for a consideration of £400, "a certain parcel of land situate in the first division of Aquebogue lands, at the place called Long Swamp, bounded N. by the Sound, S. by the Kings highway called the North Rhoad, E. by Christopher Youngs, and W. by Christopher Youngs, Jun.[2]"* This being probably all the realty then held by him, and after the death of his son, 18 Dec., 1751,† he probably removed to Orange Co., N. Y., where many of his neighbors, friends and relatives had preceded him. He may have been the Israel Parshall, who, 14 Feby., 1756, witnessed the will of Samuel Gale, of Goshen,‡ and he probably was the one who at the Census of Slaves, 1755, was returned under "The Number of all the Negro that's belonging Vnder Captain John Wessnor, of floriday"§ as the owner of one male negro slave. This would seem to indicate that he was then a resident of the Precinct of Florida, in that County. He probably *d.* or removed from the county before the breaking out of the Revolutionary War, as his name does not appear in any of the records of that period. No will, purporting to be his, has been discovered, so that there exists no positive evidence as to his children. The names, however, of James and Israel, were hereditary in his line and the impossibility of their being sons of any one else makes it altogether probable that they were his. A record in possession of the

Regt. Orange Co. Militia.** He was a resident of Orange Co., N. Y., at the breaking out of the war and signed the Association to support Congress.†† He afterwards removed to Cherry Valley, Otsego Co., N. Y., where he made his home and died there in the early part of the 19th Century. Whether he married and left issue, I have no means of knowing; I have been unable to gain the slightest information regarding him beyond that disclosed by the Revolutionary records.

* II. S'old Town Rec. 465.
† Salmon Record.
‡ Calendar of Wills, 1626-1838, 159.
§ III. Doc. Hist. of N. Y. 850.
** N. Y. in The Rev., 255.
†† I. Col. of N. Y. Hist. Mss. 11.

descendants of Israel[4] states that he (Israel[4]) "had brothers James, Phineas, Benjamin and Jesse."* It seems to me that the evidence on this point, though slight, is not the less conclusive. The evidence, however, as to the daughters is less strong. The record referred to above states that "he (Israel[4]) had a sister Delilah." As to the others, their ages, approximated from the dates of their marriage makes it impossible that they could have been daughters of David,[2] David[3] or Jonathan.[3] There appears to be little room for doubt on the subject.

FAMILY V.

DAVID[3] [14], (*David*[2] *James*[1]) *b.* probably at Aquebogue; *d.* about Jany., 1760[a]; *m.* —— Dec., 1736, Sibyl, *dau.* Capt. Ephriam and Sarah (Herrick) White,† (*b.* about 1716; *d.* Patchogue, Suffolk Co., N. Y., 8 July, 1812, age 96 years).‡ [*Aquebogue, N. Y.*

Children:§

31 I. David[4] *b.* about 1737-8. FAM. X.

32 II. Desire[4] *m.* 19 Jany., 1755, Daniel Downs.**

33 III. Elias[4] *b.* about 1746. FAM. XI.

34 IV. Sibyl.[4b]

35 V. George[4] *d.* 29 July, 1755, ("drownded").**

a. The Will of David3 bears date 11 Mch., 1759; proved 28 Feby., 1760. He must have *d.* between these dates. Probably about Jany., 1760. All his children are mentioned by name in the Will, except George, who had died some years previously. It will be noted that the line of descent from James1 through David2 and David3 is proven by Wills and other documents of unimpeachable authenticity.

b. "Seles" Parshall *m.* 12 Nov., 1764, Joshua Howell.** This may have been Sibyl.4

---

* Griswold Rec. pos. Asa Parshall, Chemung, N. Y.
† Salmon Record; Howell's Hist. of Southampton, 400.
‡ Grave at Patchogue, N. Y.
§ Will of David Parshall, N. Y. Wills, Lib. 22, p. 150 (old p. 135).
** Salmon Record.

36 vi. Mehitabel[4] *b.* 27 Oct., 1750; *d.* 4 Apl., 1837; *m.* Phineas, *s.* David and Deborah (Wells) Corwin (*b.* 11 Sept., 1749; *d.* 24 Dec., 1828),* Issue.*

i. George[5] (Corwin) *b.* 10 Nov., 1768.
ii. James[5] (Corwin) *b.* 25 May, 1773.
iii. Sibyl[5] (Corwin) *b.* 25 May, 1773.
iv. Mehitabel[5] (Corwin) *b.* 29 May, 1777.
v. Sarah[5] (Corwin) *b.* 29 July, 1779.
vi. Bethia[5] (Corwin) *b.* 27 May, 1782.
vii. Phineas[5] (Corwin) *b.* 22 Aug., 1788.
viii. Desire[5] (Corwin) *b.* 6 Apl., 1788.
ix. Fanny[5] (Corwin) *b.* ——May, 1791.

37 vii. James[4] *b.* ——Sept., 1754. Fam. XII.
38 viii. John[4] *b.* 5 May, 1757. Fam. XIII.

To fix, even approximately, the date of David's birth, is a matter of considerable difficulty. From the circumstance that his father, David,[2] speaks in his will of his youngest son, Jonathan, being "under age," we are led to infer that at the time the will was drawn (Jany., 1726) David was of age, or very nearly so, which would make the date of his birth not later than 1705. But he married Dec., 1736, at which time he would necessarily have been 31 years of age, which, for the time, seems almost incredible. Marriages then were usually contracted very early in life, men marrying at from eighteen to twenty-two years of age. Moreover his wife was born in 1716, and such a discrepancy was also unusual. On the whole, however, the former date seems to me the more probable.

His will,† dated 11 Mch., 1759, proved 28 Feby., 1760, mentions all his children by name. I insert an epitome of the will in this place:

---

* Corwin Gen. 180
† Will of David Parshall, N. Y. Wills, Lib. 22, p. 150 (old p. 135).

I, David Parshall, of the town of Southold, . . . Yeoman . . to my oldest son David Parshall all land Northward of the New Road & Meadow at Sawmill Brook—To my second son Elias Parshall all my lands which lyeth between the North Rode & the South Rode where I now live, with all the buildings upon the same & also all that West Meadow—upon the North side of Peconeck River (allows his wife the improvements of it until he shall come of age)—To 3d son James Parshall land Southward of the South Rode and the Meadow adjoining to the said land & all the buildings which stand upon it. Land bounded upon the East by the lands of Nathan Perry; South by Samuel Wells, West by Isaiah Tuthill & North by Kings Rode allowing his mother my now wife the improvement until he come of age. To youngest son John Parshall £100, when he shall come of age. To my daughter Desire Downes £5. To my daughter Sebil Parshall £30, to my dau. Mehitabel £30 when eighteen or day of marriage. To my wife Sebil Parshall——?

Exrs. Wife Sebil & Son David.

Dated 11 Mch. 1759 *Proved* 28 Feby. 1760.

His widow, Sibyl, subsequently *m.* ——— Havens, and after his death made her home with her son Elias, at Patchogue, N. Y., where she *d.* at the extreme age of 96 years.

A silver snuff box, which belonged to David[3] is now in possession of Mr. Oliver A. Dutcher, of Cobleskill, N. Y., a great-grandson.

FAMILY VI.

JONATHAN[3] [18], (*David[2] James[1]*) younger son of David[2] stated in his father's will* (dated, 24 Jany., 1726) to be under 21 years of age; *m.* 4 Oct., 1739, Elizabeth Booth.†

Children:‡

39 I. Jonathan[4] *b.* 9 Nov., 1740. FAM. XIV.
40 II. David.[4] FAM. XV.
Perhaps also

---

* N. Y. Wills; Lib. 10, p. 157 (old p. 161).
† Salmon Record.
‡ Ruttenber & Clark's Hist. of Orange Co., N. Y., pp. 240-1.

41 III. Charles (Dr.)[4a]
42 IV. Caleb.[4a]
43 V. Thomas.[4a]

It appears that Jonathan left Long Island and went to Orange County, N. Y., where, in 1737, he purchased an estate of 607 acres of land in the Township of New Windsor. Returning to Long Island in 1739, he married and returned with his wife to his estate. Here she died and he deeded his estate to his sons, Jonathan and David, and went to Pittsburg, Pa., where he died.*[b]

His homestead was located in that part of the town known as "Little Britain," which was large and of indefinite extent, reaching one way from the Village of New Windsor to the town line of Montgomery, and in the other from Washingtonville to south line of Newburgh and Montgomery.† He lived on the old public highway leading from Neelytown to New Windsor, which ran centrally through the whole town‡

As an illustration of the loose manner in which much so-called history is written, I quote the following:

a. Dr. Charles Parshall was born probably in Orange County, N. Y., and is said to have located in Harrisburg, Pa. I have been unable to find any other trace of him. Caleb and Thomas Parshall were living in Pennsylvania and were taxpayers there. Thomas in Turbett Tp., Northumberland Co.,§ and Caleb in Derry Tp., Cumberland Co., from 1778 to 1786.**

b. Jonathan Parshall was living in Derry Tp., Cumberland Co., Pa., 1779-1782.†† On 12 Nov., 1770, he also "obtained a warrant for a survey of 110 acres, 153 perches" of land in Cumberland Co., Pa.‡‡ In all human probability this was Jonathan.3 Whether or not he finally went to Pittsburg, there is no authority beyond Ruttenber and Clark History cited. It would appear from this that his wife must have died and he have left Orange Co., N. Y., prior to 1770.

* Ruttenber & Clark's Hist. of Orange Co., N. Y., pp. 240-1.
† Eager's Hist. Orange Co., N. Y., p. 630.
‡ Id. 620.
§ XX. Pa. Archives (3d. Series) 145, 679.
** XXIV. Id. 744.
†† XIX. Pa. Archives (3d. Series) 676.
‡‡ XX. Id. 145, 679; XXIV. Id. 745.

"Parshall was one of the oldest families in New Windsor."

"Israel Parshall, the ancestor in Orange Co., was driven from France with the Hugenots after the Edict of Nantes, located on the east end of Long Island at Black River where he lived and died. Jonathan, his son, bought 607 acres of land belonging to the Markham tract, in 1737, occupied it for a while but after death of his wife went to Pittsburgh, Pa., where he died. He deeded his New Windsor estate to his 2 sons, Jonathan & David, both of whom passed their lives on the property. Jonathan married Jemima Terry & had 4 sons & a dau. of whom Moses was the third child. He also lived and died on the old homestead."*

The revocation of the Edict of Nantes occurred 18 Oct., 1685, at which time Israel[2] was about five years of age. That he was born, lived and died in this country is beyond a doubt. He is named in his father's Will† and his father was here several years certainly *before* the revocation of the Edict. Moreover, James Parshall *was not* a Frenchman nor a Huguenot. In all probability Israel[3] lived at some time in Orange Co., and left descendants there. This history being written a century or more later, the two families were confounded. That Jonathan[3] was the son of David[2] is proven by the Will of the latter,‡ in which he is distinctly named. The tradition of Huguenot ancestry has always prevailed in this branch of the family and in this one only. I can only account for it on the theory that they intermarried with some of the Huguenot families, who had settled in this country. The Terrys, I believe, were of French and probably Huguenot descent, and the wife of Jonathan,[4] according to this history, was a Terry, though another authority states that she was a Knapp.

---

* Ruttenber & Clark's Hist. of Orange Co., N. Y., pp. 240-1.
† Early L. I. Wills, 236.
‡ N. Y. Wills; Lib. 10, p. 157 (old p. 161).

The Fourth Generation

FAMILY VII.

JAMES[4] [20], (*Israel*[3] *Israel*[2] *James*[1]) *b.* Suffolk Co., N. Y., 1733-1735; *d.* ; *m.* .

Children:

44 I. Samuel[5] *b.* 20 Mch., 1757. FAM. XVI.
Probably others.

The records of James are of the most meager description. It is certain, however, that he had removed to Orange Co., N. Y., prior to the breaking out of the Revolutionary War. He signed the Association to support the Continental Congress, at Goshen Precinct, Orange Co., N. Y., 21 June, 1775.* He also appears to have been elected Ensign of the Chester Company, of the West Orange Regt.† He also appears as "one of the scouts, who served Apl., 5-6, being two days in conveying certain tory prisoners from Warwick Mountain to Kings Town" (probably Kingston).‡ That he served through the Revolution is certain, but as there was another James Parshall (*b.* 1762), who served in the latter part of the War, it is not always possible to determine from the official records one from the other. It is believed that he removed after the close of the War to Western New York,

* Col. of N. Y. Hist. Mss. I. 11.
† Id. 144.
‡ Id. II. 77.

and located in or near Palmyra, Wayne Co., but as the other James Parshall above referred to, located in the same place the difficulty of distinguishing them is increased. With him, came to Western New York, a sister, who had previously married ———Terry, and whose daughter, Deliverance, subsequently became the wife of his brother Israel's son Israel. A very old lady, Mrs. Zuby Griswold, a granddaughter of his brother Israel, made a statement in 1870, which was reduced to writing and is preserved in the records of this branch of the family,* as follows:

"Israel Parshall had three brothers, Jesse, of Orange Co., James, who died in the Lake Country and Benjamin who died young. I saw only James. There was also one sister Delilah."

There is no direct evidence that Samuel was the son of James, but the question does not seen to admit of much doubt. None of the other sons of Israel[3] were old enough to have had a son in 1757, except Israel, and we have the complete list of his children from records of undoubted authenticity. He was certainly not a son of David,[3] for David mentions all his sons by name in his Will. He was not the son of Jonathan,[3] for Jonathan was living in Orange Co., in 1757, and it is certain that Samuel was born on Long Island and probably grew to manhood there. Moreover, we have a pretty accurate list of Jonathan's sons from family and other authentic records. I have in my possession a copy of a letter written by James Parshall [306], great grandson of Samuel[5], to Asa Parshall [150], a grandson of Israel,[4] dated Titusville, Pa., 3 Nov. 1877, in which the writer says: "I have heard my mother mention the names of friends the same as you mention—Asa, Israel, Jesse, and others; also of relatives at Canandaigua Springs, N. Y." The evidence, though circumstantial, seems to be nearly conclusive. Samuel *must* have been either a son or brother of James[4] and that he was the latter is in the last degree improbable.

* Griswold Rec. pos. Asa Parshall, Chemung, N. Y.

*FAMILY VIII.**

ISRAEL[4] [21] *(Israel[3] Israel[2] James[1]), b.* Long Island, 7 Oct. 1736; *d.* Chemung, N. Y., 18 Fby. 1827;† *m.* prob. Orange Co., N. Y., abt. 1753, Ruth Howell (*b.* Long Island, 22 June, 1733; *d.* Chemung, 1808).†

Children:

45 I. Joanna[5]‡ *b.* Orange Co., N. Y., 16 Feby. 1754; *d.* Chemung, N. Y., 19 Mch. 1850; *m.* Orange Co., N. Y., 1775, Benjamin *s.* Benjamin and Anna (Blaine) Burt (*b.* Warwick, Orange Co., N. Y., 9 Mch. 1750; *d.* Chemung, 10 May, 1826). *Issue:*

- i. Benjamin[6] (Burt).
- ii. Keziah[6] (Burt) *m.*—Bentley.
- iii. Isabel[6] (Burt).
- iv. Ruth[6] (Burt) *m.* Asa Burnham.
- v. Beldon[6] (Burt) *d.* 23 Oct. 1864, age 71 yrs.
- vi. Elizabeth[6] (Burt).
- vii. David[6] (Burt) *b.* Lycoming, Pa., 16 Apl. 1786.[a]
- viii. Israel Parshall[6] (Burt) *b.* Chemung, N. Y., 19 Mch. 1801.[b]

a. A sketch of David Burt and his descendants may be found in Towner's History of Chemung Co., N. Y.

b. Israel Parshall Burt *m.* North Chemung, N. Y., 16 Dec., 1824, Polly, *dau.* Isaac and Mary (———) Hammond (*b.* North Chemung, 24 July, 1804; *d.* Ridgbury, Pa., — Oct., 1865). *Issue:* i. Alfred[7]; ii. Mijaneau[7]; iii. Sally[7]; iv. John[7]; v. Mary Jane[7]; vi. Joanna[7]; vii. Frances[7]; viii. Esther.§ On the one hundredth anniversary of his birth the venerable Israel P. Burt walked to the polls and voted and afterwards visited a photographer and sat for his picture. Shortly after he spent a week in New York as the guest of the N. Y. Journal. He still retains his faculties apparently unimpaired and bids fair to outlive many of the younger generations.*

---

* Fam. Recs. pos. Asa Parshall.
† Grave at Chemung.
‡ Towner's Hist. Chemung Co. N. Y.
§ Pers. Statement.

46 II. Gerusha^{5} *m.* Joseph Shoemaker.

47 III. Israel^{5} *b.* 1760. FAM. XVII.

48 IV. David^{5} *b.* 20 Aug. 1762. FAM. XVIII.

49 V. Deborah^{5} *b.* 1765; *m.* Joseph Scott.

50 VI. Lydia^{5} *m.* ——— Annis; *m.* 2 ———Cooley.

51 VII. Asa^{5} *b.* 26 Mch. 1770. FAM. XIX.

52 VIII. Keziah^{5} *m.* Benjamin Hulse, of Chemung, N. Y.

53 IX. Ruth^{5} *m.*

54 X. Anna^{5} *b.* Williamsport, Pa., 2 Apl. 1778; *d.* Chemung, N. Y., 28 Feby. 1827; *m.* Chemung, N. Y., 1798, Thomas, *s.* Thomas and Mercy (Lamb Keeney (*b.* Hartford, Ct., 28 Sept. 1776; *d.* Crooked Creek, Pa., 1 Sept. 1853). *Issue:*

i. Mercy^{6} (Keeney) *b.* 1802.
ii. Parshall^{6} (Keeney) *b.* 1804.
iii. Elijah^{6} (Keeney) } *b.* 30 Jany. 1806.[b]
iv. Elisha^{6} (Keeney) }
v. Jesse^{6} (Keeney) *b.* 1808.
vi. Alvira^{6} (Keeney) *b.* 1810.
vii. Ransom^{6} (Keeney) b. Syracuse, N. Y., 5 Apl., 1812.[c]
viii. Anna^{6} (Keeney) *b.* 1816.
ix. Thomas^{6} (Keeney) *b.* 1819; *d.* 1 Oct. 1898.

55 XI. Jesse^{5} *b.* abt. 1779. FAM. XX.

a. Mercy Keeney *d.* — July, 1889; *m.* — Mch., 1832, Simon Snyder Chamberlain. *Issue:* i. Simon Snyder^{7}; ii. Anna M.^{7} *m.* — Feby., 1856, Philo Warren. *Issue:* *i. Byron Snyder*^{8} *(Warren)*†

b. Elisha Keeney *d.* about 1876; Elijah *d.* 1856; *m.* Lucy McArthur and had *issue:* i. Rebecca^{7}; ii. Alexander^{7}; iii. Parshall^{7}; iv. Almira^{7}; v. Sophronia^{7}, and six others who died youth or infan.†

c. Ransom Keeney *m.* Middlebury, Tioga Co., Pa., 27 Dec., 1834, Rhoana, *dau.* Peter and Abigail (Orcott) Huntsinger (*b.* Butternut Tp., Otsego Co., N. Y., 15 Dec., 1819; *d.* Middlebury, Pa., 17 Dec., 1895). *Issue:* i. Rosalthe^{7} *b.* 18 Feby., 1836; ii. Coraline^{7} *b.* 6 May., 1838; *d.* 24 Oct., 1843; iii.

† Pers. know. Ransom Keeney.

Israel Parshall was born on Long Island, subsequently removed to Orange Co., N. Y., where his eldest child, a daughter was born in 1754. He afterward, but at what time is uncertain, removed to Pennsylvania, where he is found with his two eldest sons, at the breaking out of the Revolutionary War. He was a Second Lieutenant, 3d Co., 2nd Battalion, Northumberland Co. (Pa.) Associators, Col. James Potter, 24 Jany., 1776.* It appears from Tax List and other documentary records that he was a resident of Muncy Tp., Northumberland Co. (Pa.), 1783-1787. It is probable that he was then engaged in farming, as he is found assessed for 600 acres of land, with live stock, &c. He also appears to have owned a saw mill and various other property, both real and personal.†

He was among the earliest settlers of the town of Chemung, Chemung Co., N. Y., coming there from Pennsylvania, about 1789. At the treaty with the Indians held at Newtown (now Elmira) in 1790, he was present with his son Asa. A year later he received a deed (dated 22 Jany., 1791, signed by Gov. Clinton) for Lot No. 10, in said town. This lot was situate on Chemung River about 10 miles below the present City of Elmira; here he cleared a farm and spent the remainder of his life.‡ His death was the result of an accident. He started alone to ride a colt to a sugar camp on a winter day. The colt returned alone. Search being immediately instituted, he was found lying by the roadside insensible, and succumbed to the shock and exposure shortly after. It was conjectured that he was thrown from his

Angela[7] *b.* 17 Oct., 1839; *d.* 16 Sept., 1889; iv. Adelbert[7] *b.* 14 June, 1841; *d.* 2 July, 1879; v. Beatrice[7] *b.* 9 Apl., 1843; vi. Shuman[7] *b.* 24 May, 1845; *d.* 30 Apl., 1868; vii. Mortimer[7] *b.* 19 June, 1848; viii. Helentha[7] *b.* 11 Oct., 1850; *d.* 10 June, 1853; ix. Cassimer[7] *b.* 30 Aug., 1853; x. Sidney[7] *b.* 19 Dec., 1856; xi. Luella[7] *b.* — Oct., 1858. Rhoanna Orcott was a grandniece of Dolly Payne, wife of James Madison fourth president of the United States. Her sons Shuman and Adelbert served in the War of the Rebellion, Co. F, 11th Pa. Cav.§

---

* XIV. Pa. Archives (2d. Series) 319.
† XIX. Pa. Archives (3d Series) 561, 625, 782.
‡ Towner's Hist. of Chemung Co., N. Y.
§ Personal Statement.

horse. He is described by a granddaughter as being "a small man, weighing not more than 125 pounds," but possessed in an eminent degree that rugged vitality which is such a distinguishing characteristic of our race.

FAMILY IX.

BENJAMIN[4]* [23], (*Israel*[3] *Israel*[2] *James*[1]), *b.* 12 Sept., 1744; *d.* N. Y. City, 11 Nov., 1796; *m.* (1) ——— ———.[a]

Children:

56 I. Israel.[5] FAM. XXI.
57 II. James Carlisle,[5] *b.* 2 May, 1769. FAM. XXII.

m. (2), 20 Apl. 1786,* Mrs. Hannah Clark[b] (*b.* 28 Sept., 1746; *d.* N. Y. City, 24 Oct., 1824).*

Children:

58 III. Benjamin[5] *b.* 29 June, 1788. FAM. XXIII.

FAMILY X.

DAVID[4] [31], (*David*[3] *David*[2] *James*[1]) *b.* probably Aquebogue, Suffolk Co., N. Y.; *d.* Aquebogue, N. Y.; *m.* Elizabeth Sweezy.† [*Aquebogue, N. Y.*

a. It is possible that the first wife of Benjamin was a Carlisle. The name is characteristic of this branch of the family and his son James was the first who bore it.
b. Hannah Clark at the time of her marriage to Benjamin Parshall was a widow with two daughters, Hannah *b.* 11 Feby., 1770; Martha *b.* 22 Aug., 1774. Hannah, Jr., *m.* her step brother, James C.*

---

* Bible Rec. 57 pos. Dr. Geo. H. Parshall.
† Pers. know. 180; Corwin Gen. 176, erroneous given "James" Parshall.

*Children:**

59 I. Esther[5]† *m.* (1) Nathan, *s.* Nathan and Elizabeth (Hudson) Tuthill (*b.* Mch., 1770). *Issue:*

i. Nathan[6] (Tuthill).
ii. Elizabeth[6] (Tuthill) *b.* — Oct., 1792; *d.* 4 July, 1882; *m.* David Benjamin.
iii. Caleb Halsey[6] (Tuthill).
iv. Roxanna[6] (Tuthill).
v. Hannah[6] (Tuthill).
vi. Harriet[6] (Tuthill).
vii. Laura O.[6] (Tuthill).

m. (2) Daniel Terry. *Prob. issue.*

60 II. Sarah[5] *b.* about 1765; *d.* 15 Sept., 1852; age 87 years; *m.* Daniel Tuthill, of Speonk, N. Y.; (*d.* 8 Mch. 1845, age 87 years.‡ *Issue:*

i. Elizabeth[6] (Tuthill) *b.* 6 Sept. 1795; *d.* Niagara Co., N. Y., 6 Nov., 1855; *m.* 12 July 1817, Parker *s.* John and Julia (Hedges) Corwin.‡ Probably others.

61 III. Bethia[5]§ *m.* (1) Abraham King (*b.* 4 Nov., 1765; *d.* 26 July, 1801). *Issue:*

i. Gamaliel[6] (King)[a] *b.* 1 Dec., 1795; *d.* 6 Dec., 1874; *m.* Catherine Snow, 19 June, 1819.

m. (2) ——— Griffin, *prob. issue.*

62 IV. George[5] *b.* 1772. FAM. XXIV.

a. For descendants of Gamaliel King, see Mallman's Shelter Island.

* Pers. Know. 180.
† Mallman's Shelter Island, 200.
‡ Corwin Gen. 176.
§ Pers. know. 180; Mallman's Shelter Island, 293.

David was probably the last Parshall who lived at Aquebogue. The Census of 1776, shows that he and his brother Elias were the only ones then remaining. His death marked the final passing away of a family, which had been prominent in Southold Tp. for more than a century.

FAMILY XI.

ELIAS[4] [33], (*David*[3] *David*[2] *James*[1]) *b.* 1746; *d.* Bayport, L. I., 20 June, 1823, age 77 years;* *m.* 9 Mch., 1769, Anna, *dau.* Christopher and Anna (Wells) Youngs† (*b.* 18 Apl., 1751 *‡ *d.* Bayport, 6 Oct., 1824 *).

Children:

63 I. Anna[5]§ *b.* ————; *d.* Sayville, N. Y., 30 Apl., 1845; *m.* Isaac Howell (*b.* 1767; *d.* 28 Sept., 1839). *Issue:*

i. Jennie[6] (Howell) *m.* John Hawkins.
ii. Phebe[6] (Howell) *b.* 20 Mch., 1793.[a]
iii. Emily[6] (Howell) *m.* Isaac Corey.
iv. Daniel[6] (Howell) *m.* Nancy Terry.
v. Eliza[6] (Howell) *m.* David Corey.

a. Phebe Howell *d.* Sayville, N. Y.; *m.* Blue Point (L. I.) N. Y., 16 Oct., 1813, Reuben, *s.* Mathew and Elizabeth (Morris) Edwards (*b.* Sayville, 26 Mch., 1788; *d.* Sayville, 10 June, 1863). *Issue:* i. Elizabeth[7] (Edwards); *b.* 24 Aug., 1817; *m.* Jacob Smith; ii. Anna[7] (Edwards) *b.* 8 Mch., 1821; *m.* Edward Brown; iii. Reuben[7] (Edwards) *b.* 4 Feby., 1826; *m.* Henrietta Roe; iv. Phebe[7] (Edwards) *b.* Sayville, 8 Apl., 1829; *m.* Sayville, 4 Feby., 1851, Charles Z., *s.* Zebulon and Lucinda (Avery) Gillette (*b.* Blue Point, L. I., 12 Jan., 1827). *Issue:* i. Ida F.[8] (Gillette); ii. Charles E.[8] (Gillette); iii. Inez[8] (Gillette); iv. George[8] (Gillette); v. Margaret[8] (Gillette); vi. Lucillia P.[8] (Gillette).§

---

* Grave at Patchogue.
† Aguebogue Ch. Rec.
‡ Bible Rec. Christopher Youngs.
§ Fam. Rec. pos. Mrs. Phebe E. Gillette, Sayville, N. Y.

64 II. Elias[5] *b.* 11 Sept., 1771. FAM. XXV.
65 III. David[5] *d. inf.*
66 IV. David[5] *b.* — Dec., 1777. FAM. XXVI.
67 V. Polly[5]* *b.* 31 Aug., 1775; *m.* Jesse Reeve (*b.* 13 Dec., 1777*). *Issue:*

i. Huldah Maria[6] (Reeve) *b.* 11 Mch., 1801; *m.* ——— Lane.
ii. Polly Parshall[6] (Reeve) *b.* 29 Sept., 1802; *m.* ——— Coles.
iii. Hannah Carll[6] (Reeve) *b.* 19 Oct., 1805; *m.* ——— Horton.
iv. Lewis[6] (Reeve) *b.* 14 Apl., 1807.
v. David[6] (Reeve) *b.* 6 Feby., 1809.
vi. Hamilton[6] (Reeve) *b.* 6 Apl., 1811.
vii. Daniel Parshall[6] (Reeve) *b.* 4 May, 1813.
viii. Eliza Anne[6] (Reeve) *b.* 22 Sept., 1815; *m.* Lewis Hammond.
ix. Jesse Worthington[6] (Reeve) *b.* 10 Sept., 1818.
x. Hiram Riley[6] (Reeve) *b.* 2 May, 1820.

68 VI. Charity[5] *d. inf.*
69 VII. Charity† *b.* East Haddam, Conn., 6 Jany., 1782; *d.* Patchogue, Suffolk Co., N. Y., 7 May, 1869; *m.* Bayport (L. I.), N. Y., 7 Dec., 1802, Capt. Isaac Brown (*b.* Bridgehampton, L. I., 22 Apl., 1877; *d.* Patchogue, 15 Oct., 1854). *Issue: (All b. Bayport).*

i. Daniel[6] (Brown) *b.* 4 Nov., 1808.[a]

a. Daniel Brown *d.* 15 Sept., 1901; *m.* South Haven, L. I., 29 Dec., 1831, Hannah Ann, *dau.* Nathaniel and Fanny (Woodhull) Hawkins, Jr., (*b.* South Haven, 24 Sept., 1810; *d.* Patchogue, 1 Oct., 1886). *Issue:* i Frances

---

* Bible Rec. 67 from a copy in my pos.
† Fam. Rec. and pers. know. Clarissa Adaline Miller (now deceased) and her dau. Mrs. Clara Chichester.

ii. Clarissa Adaline[6] (Brown) *b.* 17 Mch., 1816.[a]

70 VIII. Lewis[5] *b.* 1783. FAM. XXVII.

71 IX. Daniel[5] *b.* 1787; *d.* 5 Nov., 1813, in the 26th year of his age.

72 X. Hannah[5] *b.* 23 Dec., 1794; *d.* Sayville, L. I., 22 Feby., 1880; *m.* Sayville, 28 Dec., 1816, Justus Overton (*b.* Coram, L. I., 6 Sept., 1795; *d.* Bayport, 7 Jany., 1835). *Issue:*

i. Ency[6] (Overton).
ii. Elias Parshall[6] (Overton).
iii. Huldah Catherine[6] (Overton).
iv. Anna[6] (Overton).
v. Sarah Jane[6] (Overton) *b.* Bayport, 8 Oct., 1827.[b]

Elias Parshall was a ship builder during the greater part of his life. He probably resided at Aquebogue until after the close

C.[7] *b.* 9 Jany., 1833; ii. Ellen R.[7] *b.* 15 Mch., 1838; *d.* 11 Dec., 1861; *unm.* Capt. Brown was the owner of a coasting vessel and followed the sea until about 60 years of age.†

a. Clarissa Adaline Brown *d.* Patchogue, 21 Jany., 1901; *m.* Bayport, 20 Apl., 1836, Charles Wheeler, *s.* James Smith and Abigail (Ketcham) Miller. *Issue:* i. Charles Edwin[7] (Miller); ii. Leander Parshall[7] (Miller); iii. Philander Brown[7] (Miller); (ii. and iii. twins); iv. James Isaac[7] (Miller); v. Eugene Atwood[7] (Miller); vi. Daniel Brown[7] (Miller); vii. Adrian Merton[7] (Miller); viii. Clara Celeste *b.* Patchogue, 7 Mch., 1853; *m.* Patchogue, 13 Feby., 1884, George Lewis Chichester (*b.* Brooklyn, 28 Dec., 1852) *s.* Daniel and Ann Eliza (Howman) Chichester; ix. Daniel Lewis[7] (Miller); x. Lillian Augusta[7] (Miller). The author acknowledges his indebtedness to Mrs. Chichester for records of Charity Parshall and her descendants, and for much other valuable data.†

b. Sarah Jane Overton, *m.* Sayville, N. Y., 28 Dec., 1848, Buell, *s.* Joshua and ——— (Avery) Tuthill (*b.* 28 June, 1822; *d.* Sayville, 23 Dec., 1900). *Issue:* i. Emily Frances[7] (Tuthill); ii. Albert Buell[7] (Tuthill); iii. Elias Parshall[7] (Tuthill) *b.* Sayville, 13 Sept., 1855; *d.* Sayville, 27 Jany. 1890; iv. Henry Howard[7] (Tuthill).*

* Fam. Rec. and pers. know. Mrs. Sarah Jane Tuthill.
† Fam. Rec. and pers. know. Clarissa Adaline Miller (now deceased), and her dau., Mrs. Clara Chichester.

of the Revolutionary War. It appears from the Census of 1776,* that he was then a resident of Southold Tp., and it is probable that he was during the War. In 1779, he was obliged, with others, to flee from the Island to escape the persecution of the British force, as appears from the following:

"At a meeting of the Governor and Council of Safety at Windham the 21st of September 1779

"*Present* His Excellency the Governor
Honble Matthew Griswold
Elipht Dyer Wm Williams } Esqrs
Wm Pitkin Nathl Wales }

"On motion of Elias Parshall, of S.hold on Long Island, representing that he is a friend to the United States, that he had lately built on said island a small vessel of about 20 tons, for trade; that by means of the threats and usage from the enemy, within whose power the inhabitants of said island are, he dared not remain longer on said island, and has therefore brought over part of his family and effects on board of said vessel to this State, which are now in the river at East Haddam, and moving for liberty of landing and safe protection for said effects for his own benefit; and further shewing that Matw Welles of said South Hold, a friend to the States, has also come over from said island in said vessel, with his family and effects, for the same occasion and for safety: Resolved, that the said Parshall be permitted to land his said goods and effects within this State, and that they shall and may remain safe & free from any arrests, in his own care, unless and until other order shall be given concerning them; provided that said effects and goods be under the inspection of Colo. Jabez Chapman, who is to examine and see that no articles are introduced from the enemy and contrary to law, and to make report to his Excellency the Governor in the premises. And the said Parshall is also permitted to bring over the rest of his family, and to be reported accordingly."*

Subsequently he removed to Patchogue, where he had a ship yard. He also was the owner and captain of a merchant vessel with which he made regular trips between New York and the West Indies. This vessel he commanded in person until after the marriage of his daughter Charity to Capt. Brown, when he retired from active command and was succeeded by his son-in-law. On one occasion his vessel was attacked by pirates, whom he defeated after a vigorous resistance. A set of silver buttons

* II. Records of State of Conn. 396 etc.

given him by his passengers to commemorate the event are still in possession of his great-granddaughter, Mrs. Louretta Neff, of Masontown, Pa.

The Wills of Elias Parshall* and his wife* are as follows:

In the Name of God Amen the Eighth day of May in the year of our Lord one thousand eight hundred and twenty one I Elias Parshall of the town of Islip County of Suffolk and State of New York feeling the decays of the body but of sound mind and memory But knowing the uncertainty of life and the certainty of death I do therefore make this my last will and testament that is to say Principally and first of all I give and recommend my soul into the hands of God who gave it and my body I commit into the earth to be buried in a decent Christian burial at the discretion of my executors Nothing doubting but at the general resurrection I shall receive the same again by the mighty power of God And as touching such worldly estate as it hath pleased God to bless me with in this life I give, devise, and dispose of the same in the following manner and form. *First* I order all my just debts should be paid and Likewise funeral Charges out of my estate I give and bequeath unto my beloved wife *Anna* Parshall all my household furniture to dispose of as she shall think proper together with the whole of my other estate during her natural life the whole to be disposed of as she the sd Anna Parshall shall think proper and further whatever of said property shall remain after the decease of the said Anna Parshall and all Necessary Expenses Paid except the said houshold furniture, the one equal quarter I give and bequeath to my Beloved grandchildren Lewis Parshall, Daniel Parshall, and Josiah Parshall the sons of my son Lewis Parshall Deceased to be equally divided between them when they shall arrive at the age of Twenty one years and in case of either of their decease to go to the survivor or survivors. The other three quarters to be disposed of as she the said Anna Parshall shall think proper at her decease. Lastly I do hereby nominate constitute and appoint my well beloved wife Anna Parshall and my son in law Isaak Howell to be the executrix and executor to this last will and testament and I do hereby utterly revoke and make void all other wills and testaments ratifying and confirming this my only last will and testament in witness whereof I have hereunto set my hand and my seal this day and years above written Signed sealed published pronounced declared by the said Elias Parshall as his last will and testament in presence of us the subscribers.

ELIAS PARSHALL (L S)

Zebulon Gillett John Hawkins

Daniel Howell.

---

* Records Suffolk Co. (N. Y.) Surrogate's Office.

In the name of God Amen I Anna Parshall of the Town of Islip County of Suffolk and State of New York, being at present feeble in Body but of sound disposing mind and memory, calling into view the mortality of my body do make and ordain this my Last Will and Testament, in manner and form following (viz) First of all I give and recommend my immortal soul into the hands of God who at first gave it, hoping for acceptance thereof only for the sake of Jesus Christ. My body I recommend to the earth to be buried in decent manner at the discretion of my friends expecting to receive it again by the mighty power of God at the morning of the general resurrection and as touching my worldly estate I give and dispose of it in the following manner. *Item* I do give and bequeath unto my daughter, Anna Howell, one great bible, one broadcloth cloak and two silver tablespoons. *Item* I do give and bequeath unto my daughter Polly Reeve two silver tablespoons. *Item.* I do give and bequeath unto my daughter Charity Brown two silver tablespoons *Item* I do give and bequeath unto my daughter Hannah Overton one bed, bedstead underbed and cord, also my largest iron pot, one brass kettle, one coverlet, one Dutch blanket and six silver tea spoons *Item* All the remainder of my household furniture Beds, bedding and clothing I do give and bequeath unto my said four daughters Anna, Polly, Charity and Hannah to be equally divided between them. *Item* I do give and bequeath unto my granddaughter Clarissa Adaline Brown the sum of twelve dollars *Item* I order all my just debts and funeral charges to be paid as soon as may be after my decease, and afterwards all the remainder of my property which will then be left I do give and bequeath unto my three daughters aforesaid, (viz) Anna, Polly and Hannah to be equally divided between them. Lastly I do hereby nominate constitute and appoint my son in law Isaac Howell, together with my friend William Beale Executors to this my last Will and testament, and I hereby revoke and disannul all former wills by me made and executed and declare this to be my last will and testament. In witness whereof, I the said Anna Parshall have hereunto set my hand and seal the twenty sixth day of July in the year of our lord one thousand eight hundred and twenty four. Signed, sealed published and declared by the said Anna Parshall to be her last will and testament in presence of

Wm C. Smith
William Beebe } Witnesses

her
ANNA X PARSHALL (L S)
mark

State of New York
County of Suffolk } ss.
Surrogate's Office

I do hereby certify that the foregoing are true copies of the last Wills and testaments of Elias Parshall and Anna Parshall, respectively, late of the town of Islip, in the County of Suffolk, deceased, as recorded in Liber E. of Records of Wills in this office; that the will of the said Elias Parshall, decd. was admitted to probate & recorded, and Letters Testamentary thereon issue to Isaac Howell the executor therein named on the 7th day of October, 1823; and the will of the said Anna Parshall decd. was admitted to probate & recorded, and Letters Testamentary thereon issued to Isaac Howell & William Beale the executors therein named, on the 26th day of October 1824.

In testimony whereof I have hereunto set my hand, and affixed the Surrogate's Seal of office at Bridgehampton in the said county, this 15th day of February, 1851.

A. T. ROSE, *County Judge*
Acting as Surrogate

FAMILY XII.

JAMES[4] [37], *(David[3], David[2], James[1]) b.* — Sept., 1754; *d.* 24 Apl., 1834, age 71 yrs., 7 mos.*; *m.* (1) Deborah Clark, on L. I., abt. 1779.†

Children:

73 I. James[5] *b.* 30 Nov. 1780. FAM. XXVIII.
74 II. Israel[5] *b.* 14 Sept. 1783. FAM. XXIX.
75 III. Miner[5] *b.* 10 Apl. 1787. FAM. XXX.

m. (2) Mrs. Dorothy (Longbotham) Bostwick[a] (*b.* Nov. 1755; *d.* 22 Mch. 1836.‡

Children:

76 IV. Deborah Clark[5],§ *b.* Middlefield Center, Otsego Co., N. Y., 27 July, 1796; *d.* Middlefield, 6 Sept. 1873; *m.* 31 Dec. 1864, Peleg Coffin (*d.* Middlefield, aged 86 yrs.). *No issue.*

a. Dorothy (Longbotham) Bostwick at the time of her marriage to James Parshall was the widow of James Bostwick, by whom she had two children, Richard (Bostwick) and Nancy (Bostwick); the latter of whom *m.* —— Quackenbush.

---

* Grave at Middlefield, N. Y.
† Pers. know. 218.
‡ Fam. Rec. pos. 230.
§ Fam. Rec. and pers. know. Mrs. Ruth Ann Cleveland.

77 v. George[5] *b.* 3 Mch. 1798. Fam. XXXI.

78 vi. Gilbert[5] *b.* 3 Mch. 1800. Fam. XXXII.

79 vii. David[5] *b.* 29 Nov. 1803. Fam. XXXIII.

80 viii. Lucy[5]* *b.* 22 Aug. 1806; *d.* Tompkins, Dela. Co., N. Y., 12 July, 1884; *m.* 12 Nov. 1828, Ferdinand (*b.* 30 Aug. 1806; d. 10 Nov. 1893), *s.* Ebenezer and Ruth (Driggs) Ingalls, of Middlefield, N. Y. *Issue:* (All *b.* Middlefield, N. Y.)

i. Mary Ann[6] (Ingalls) *b.* 28 Feby. 1830[a].
(Trout Creek, Dela. Co., N. Y.)

ii. Thompson Parshall[6] (Ingalls) *b.* 30 Aug. 1832.[b]

iii. Ralph Wilbur[6] (Ingalls) *b.* 20 Sept. 1835.[c]

iv. James Parshall[6] (Ingalls) *b.* 13 May, 1839.[d]

v. Israel Parshall[6] (Ingalls) *b.* 18 Oct. 1841; *d.* Middlefield, 20 Mch. 1844.

a. Mary Ann Ingalls *d.* Masonville, Dela. Co., N. Y., 3 Aug., 1870; *m.* Middlefield, N. Y., — Jany., 1849, Orlando Jones (*b.* Herkimer, N. Y., 1828; *d.* Middlefield, 1877); *Issue:* i. Elbert[7] (Jones); ii. Lucy[7] (Jones) *m.* ——— Buel; iii. Ellen[7] (Jones) *m.* ——— Burrows; iv. William Parshall[7] (Jones); v. Charles[7] (Jones); vi. Fanny[7] (Jones) *m.* ——— Briggs; vii. Cora A.[7] (Jones) *m.* ——— Drain; viii. Grace[7] (Jones) *m.* ——— Stage; ix. Evelyn[7] (Jones) *m.* ——— Widman; x. Orlando[7] (Jones).*

b. Thompson Parshall Ingalls *d.* Masonville, 9 Feby., 1890; *m.* Middlefield, — Dec., 1857, Adriel, *dau.* Stephen and Charity (Quackenbush) Deyo (*b.* Middlefield, 1855; *d.* Masonville, 13 Feby., 1890). *Issue:* i. Emma Deyo *m.* William S. Burrows.*

c. Ralph Wilbur Ingalls *m.* Middlefield, 4 July, 18—, Jane, *dau.* Moses and Cynthia (Granger) Buel. *Issue:* i. Albert[7]; ii. Augusta Ann[7] *m.* ——— Cornell; iii. Fidora Root[7]; iv. DeWitt Clinton[7]; v. Almira[7]; vi. Lucy May.[7]*

d. James Parshall Ingalls *d.* Masonville, 16 Mch., 1899; *m.* Middlefield, Adaline, *dau.* Nelson and Jemima (Finck) Southworth (*b.* 24 Dec., 1837; *d.* Masonville, 20 Sept., 1892). *Issue:* i. Caroline[7]; ii. Clarence P.[7]; iii. George Wilbur[7]; iv. Alphonzo Parshall[7]; v. Floyd Jason[7]; vi. Nathan[7]; vii. Dexter[7]; viii. Nelson Ferdinand.[7]*

* Fam. Rec. and pers. know. Mrs. Ruth Ann Cleveland.

vi. William Ebenezer[6] (Ingalls) *b.* 3 Nov. 1845.[a]
vii. Ruth Ann[6] (Ingalls) *b.* 24 July, 1849.[b]

James Parshall was a soldier of the Revolution. "He is recorded as a sergeant in the company commanded by Capt. Samuel Sackett, belonging to the Fourth Regiment of the New York line or Continentals, which regiment was under the command of Col. Henry B. Livingston, also that in the said record the said James Parshall is recorded as having enlisted June 1, 1777, for the war; also that the regiment was employed in active service in the Revolutionary War."† He served until 2 Dec., 1779, when he was granted a furlough, and went to Saybrook, Ct., where his family then was. While there he joined an expedition "for the purpose of detecting and suppressing a plundering party." He was captured in Gardiner's Bay by a British sloop of war and carried prisoner to New York where he was confined on the prison ship Scorpion until the following June. He underwent such hardships while in confinement that he was unable to rejoin his regiment."‡ Many interesting anecdotes of James have been related to me by my uncle, the late John A. Parshall, of Delhi, Delaware Co., N. Y., a grandson of James, who had often listened to his grandfather's relation of his adventures in the Revolution. James was a re-

a. William Ebenezer Ingalls *m.* Hartwick, Otsego Co., N. Y., 24 Dec. 1861, Cordelia, *dau.* Ira and ——— (Windsor) Murdock (*b.* Hartwick, 1843). *Issue:* i. Lester Luverne[7] *m.* Jennie Clark.*

b. Ruth Ann Ingalls *m.* Tompkins, Dela. Co., N. Y., 13 Dec., 1871, Jason *s.* Erastus Parker and Jane (Jinkins) Morse (*b.* Roxbury, Dela. Co., N. Y., 2 Dec., 1839; *d.* Masonville, 21 Sept., 1875). *No Issue.* *m.* 2d Tompkins, N. Y., 19 Nov., 1879, Orrin Goodrich *s.* James Forman and Clarissa (Goodrich) Cleveland (*b.* Kortright, Dela. Co., N. Y., 14 Dec., 1829). *Issue:* all *b.* Kortright, N. Y.) i. Silas Ferdinand[7] (Cleveland) *b.* 16 Sept., 1880; ii. Grover Altamont[7] *b.* 4 Sept., 1883; *d.* Kortright, 3 July, 1896; iii. Orrin Jason[7] *b.* 11 Apl., 1888; *d.* Kortright, 1 May, 1890; iv. Sarah Martha[7] *b.* 8 Aug., 1893.*

---

* Fam. Rec. and pers. know. Mrs. Ruth Ann Cleveland.
† Military Register, p. 81, in custody of the Regents of the University of the State of N. Y.
‡ Assembly Papers, Rev. Soldiers and Claims 22, p. 253.

markably fine penman and was often called upon to act as a sort of drum-head secretary to Gen. Washington. He was one of the guards over the unfortunate Major Andre before his execution. He accompanied Gen. Sullivan on his Indian Campaign and helped to build the dam at the foot of Otsego Lake. He was at Saratoga when Burgoyne surrendered and at the Battle of Monmouth, where, he says, many of the soldiers actually died of thirst, it being a very hot day. He was at Valley Forge, and endured all the hardships of that memorable winter. He was a man of herculean strength and was wont to boast with pardonable pride that in the Army, where wrestling was the principal amusement of the soldiers, *he never found but one man who could throw him*. After the death of his first wife, he removed to Cherry Valley and shortly after to Middlefield Center, where he cleared a farm, returned to Long Island on horseback and brought back his children and his second wife in the same fashion. The first house in which he lived in Middlefield Center was a log cabin, which was standing a few years ago, and, I presume, is yet.

FAMILY XIII.

JOHN[4] [38],* *(David[3], David[2], James[1])* *b.* Aquebogue, L. I., 5 May, 1757; *d.* Middlefield, N. Y., 10 Sept. 1838; *m.* Phebe Coddington (*b.* 28 Mch. 1759; *d. n.* Utica, N. Y., 10 Oct. 1822) of Newburg, N. Y. [*Middlefield Center, N. Y.*

Children:

81 I. *Sibyl*[5]† *b.* 15 Feby. 1780; *d.* at Addison, Steuben Co., N. Y.; *m.* Gordon Smith. *Issue:*†
[*Addison, Steuben Co., N. Y.*

* Bible Rec. 28 pos. Mrs. Rosamond Barry.
† Fam. Recs. and pers. know. Permelia McGown.

i. Clarissa[6] (Smith).
ii. Gordon[6] (Smith).
iii. John Parshall[6] (Smith).
iv. Daniel Tompkins[6] (Smith).
v. Sabrina[6] (Smith).
vi. Phebe[6] (Smith).

82 II. John[5] *b.* 2 June, 1782; *d.* 13 Jany. 1872; *unm.* [*Middlefield Center, N. Y.*

83 II. Phebe[5]* *b.* Middlefield Center, 1 Aug. 1784; *d.* Somerset, Niag. Co., N. Y., 10 Apl. 1859; *m.* Stephen Johnson. *No issue.* [*Somerset, Niag. Co., N. Y.*

84 IV. Mehitabel[5] *b.* 25 Sept. 1786; *d.* 14 Feby. 1821; *m.* ——— ———. *Issue:* [*Middlefield, N. Y.*

248 i. David Sidney[6a] *b.* 14 Apl. 1814. FAM. IC.

85 v. Elina[5]† *b.* 10 Dec. 1788; *d.* Cherry Valley, N. Y., 1 May, 1880; *m.* Asa Glazier (*b.* 1785; *d.* 1851). *Issue:* (All *b.* Cherry Valley, N. Y.) [*Cherry Valley, N. Y.*

i. Mehitabel[6] (Glazier) *b.* 23 Feby. 1811.[b]
ii. John[6] (Glazier).
iii. Elias[6] (Glazier).
iv. Polly N.[6] (Glazier).
v. Benjamin[6] (Glazier).
vi. Statira[6] (Glazier), *m.* ——— Wales.
vii. Arlina[6] (Glazier).

a. David Sidney adopted his mother's name (Parshall), hence it has seemed advisable to treat him in this work as a Parshall.

b. Mehitabel Glazier *d.* Cherry Valley, N. Y., 23 Jany., 1899; *m.* Cherry Valley, 6 Oct., 1829, William D., *s.* John and Mary (Clark) Spencer (*b.* Cherry Valley, 24 Dec., 1808; *d.* Cherry Valley, 21 Dec., 1890). *Issue: (All b. Cherry Valley, N. Y.)* i. Mary[7] (Spencer);

* Fam. Recs. and pers. know. Permella McGown.
† Bible Rec. 38, and Fam. Recs. pos. Hon. Edgar A. Spencer.

86 vi. Permilla[5] *b.* 19 Jany. 1792; *d.* Middlefield Center, 10 Oct. 1838; *unm.*

87 vii. Elias[5] *b.* 9 Feby. 1794. Fam. XXXIV.

88 viii. Maria[5]* *b.* Newburg, N. Y., 18 Mch. 1796; *d.* Cooperstown, N. Y., 21 Apl. 1869; *m.* Middlefield Center, N. Y., 7 Mch. 1820, James McGown. *Issue:*
[*Middlefield, N. Y.*

i. Margaret Adelia[6] (McGown) *b.* 28 May, 1821.[a]
[*Lyons, N. Y.*

ii. John Parshall[6] (McGown) *b.* 19 Oct. 1823; *d.* 1825.

iii. Permilla[6] (McGown) *b.* 31 Jany. 1826. *Unm.*
[*Cooperstown, N. Y.*

ii. Douglas W.[7] (Spencer); iii. Selina[7] (Spencer); iv. Asa[7] (Spencer); v. Josephine[7] (Spencer); vi. Martha[7] (Spencer); vii. Oliver[7] (Spencer); viii. Hester[7] (Spencer); ix. Phebe[7] (Spencer); x. Hon. Edgar A. (Spencer), Justice of the Supreme Court of the State of New York, *b.* 23 Nov., 1847; *m.* Gloversville, N. Y., 30 Sept., 1879, Frances, *dau.* Alanson and Mary (Sexton) Hosmer (*b.* Gloversville, 23 Nov., 1848). *Issue: i. Effa Hosmer*[8]*; ii. Alanson Hosmer*[8]; *iii. Mary Josephine*[8] *d. inf.;* xi. Jane L.[7] (Spencer); xii. William C.[7] (Spencer).†

a. Margaret Adelia McGown, *d.* Lyons, N. Y., 4 Aug., 1862; *m.* Putneyville, N. Y., — Apl., 1844, William, *s.* Nahum and Hannah (Brown) Burnett (*b.* Marbletown, N. Y., 22 Nov., 1816; *d.* Wayne, Mich., 12 Dec., 1896) *Issue:* i. Spencer Densmore[7] (Burnett) *b.* Lyons, 5 Aug., 1846; *m.* Geneva, N. Y., 1877, Hattie Day. *No issue;* ii. Maria Hannah[7] (Burnett) *b.* Lyons, 22 Oct., 1874), *m.* Galen, N. Y., 11 Feb., 1874, John Smart. *Issue: i. Emma May*[8] (*Smart*); iii. Charles Rupert[7] (Burnett) *b.* 15 Feb., 1850; *m.* Lyons, 15 Dec., 1875, Julia Ann, *dau.* Thomas and Harriet Crawford (Sturrat) Hunter (*b.* Lyons, 31 May, 1853). *Issue: i. Edith Verne*[8] *b. Newark, N. Y., 6 Aug., 1878; ii. Clarence Thomas*[8]; iv. Zillah Ennis[7] (Burnett) *b.* Lyons, 4 June, 1856; *m.* Newark, 18 Jany., 1872, James *s.* Zeizar and Nancy (Gamore) DeVall; (*b.* Arcadia, N. Y., 5 Dec. 1848). *Issue: i. Jennie L.*[8] *(DeVall);* v. Margaret[7] (Burnett) *b.* Lyons, 4 May, 1860; *d.* Detroit, Mich., 16 Jany., 1898, William McKay. *Issue: i. George*[8] *(McKay); ii. Roy*[8] *(McKay); iii. John Henry*[8] *(McKay)*.‡

* Bible Rec. 88, and Fam. Recs. pos. Permilla McGown.
† Fam. Recs. and pers. know. Hon. E. A. Spencer.
‡ Fam. Recs. pos. Charles R. Burnett.

iv. Mary Helen[6] (McGown) *b.* 19 Oct. 1828.[a] [*Cooperstown, N. Y.*

v. Elias Parshall[6] (McGown) *b.* 7 May, 1831; *d.* 4 Dec. 1888; *m.* Mary Bowen.

vi. Esther Ann[6] (McGown) *b.* 16 May, 1834.[b]

vii. Maria Josephine[6] (McGown) *b.* 7 May, 1837.[c] [*Quincy, Mich.*

viii. David Jefferson[6] (McGown) *b.* 19 Dec. 1839.[d] [*Cooperstown, N. Y.*

89 IX. Delia[5] *b.* Middlefield Center, N. Y., 26 July, 1799; *d. unm.*

90 X. Desiah[5]† *b.* Middlefield Center, N. Y., 8 Nov. 1800; *d.* Middlefield Center, 4 July, 1889; *m.* 20 Sept. 1827, Peter Dutcher (*d.* 22 Mch. 1885). *Issue:*

i. Calista V.[6] (Dutcher) *b.* 21 July, 1828; *d.* 6 May, 1863, *unm.* [*Middlefield, N. Y.*

ii. Varance[6] (Dutcher) *b.* 23 Sept. 1830; *d.* 8 Sept. 1843.

iii. David Jefferson[6] (Dutcher) *b.* 25 Feby. 1832; *d.* 5 Mch. 1832.

a. Mary Helen McGown *m.* 14 June, 1854, Hiram Mallory (*d.* 18 June, 1855). *No issue.**

b. Esther Ann McGown *m.* Cooperstown, 22 Feby., 1856, James Munn. *Issue:* i. Charles William[7] (Munn) *b.* Cooperstown, 12 Apl., 1857; ii. Arthur Elias[7] (Munn) *d.* 17 May, 1903.*

c. Maria Josephine McGown, *m.* Cooperstown, 5 Dec., 1894, George W., *s.* Prazilla and Matilda (Irwin) Woodworth (*b.* New York, 30 Oct. 1841).‡

d. David Jefferson McGown, *m.* Cooperstown, 29 Feby. 1879, Mary, *dau.* Thomas and Sarah (Wilson) Murphy (*b.* Longford, Ireland, 27 May, 1842). *Issue:* *i.* Wilson Elias[8] *b.* 20 July, 1882; *ii.* Frederick Hamilton[8] *b.* 11 Jany., 1885.‡

* Fam. Rec. and pers. know. Permilla McGown.
† Bible Rec. 38, and Fam. Recs. pos. Oliver A. Dutcher.
‡ Pers. statement.

iv. John Parshall[6] (Dutcher) *b.* 19 July, 1834.*
[*Santa Cruz, California.*

v. Oliver Andrew[6] (Dutcher) *b.* 15 Nov. 1836.*
[*Cobleskill, N. Y.*

vi. Celestia Regina[6] (Dutcher) *b.* 14 Mch. 1839.*
[*Middlefield, N. Y.*

vii. Laverna Mary[6] (Dutcher) *b.* 24 Dec. 1840.*
[*Gloversville, N. Y.*

viii. Alvin Peter[6] (Dutcher) *b.* 1 Oct. 1842; *d.* 22 June, 1858.

ix. Jennie Ellen[6] (Dutcher) *b.* 7 Jany. 1846.*
[*Schenectady, N. Y.*

a. John Parshall Dutcher, *m.* Randolph, Catt. Co., N. Y., 20 Mch. 1866, Cora Jane, *dau.* Florentine Fayette and Sophronia Delia (Dopkins) Mighells (*b.* Buffalo, N. Y., 25 Dec. 1842). *No issue.**

b. Oliver Andrew Dutcher, *m.* East Springfield, Otsego Co., N. Y., 25 Dec. 1865, Susan, *dau.* Thomas and Sarah (Stockley) Francis (*b.* East Springfield, 1 Oct. 1841). *Issue:* *i.* Ralph Egbert,[7] *b.* Middlefield Center, 17 Aug. 1871; *m.* South Kortright, Delaware Co., N. Y., 3 Oct. 1900, Harriet Lydia, *dau.* Silas Waddell and Ascenath Maria (English) Stoutenburgh (*b.* Harpersfield, Delaware Co., N. Y., 26 Sept. 1870).*

c. Celestia Regina Dutcher, *m.* Cherry Valley, N. Y., 19 Jany. 1873, Edwin Robert, *s.* Nathan and Mary (Seward) Tripp (*b.* Decatur, N. Y., 27 Jany. 1827). *Issue:* (All *b.* Middlefield Center, N. Y.) *i.* Bertha Lula[7] (Tripp), *b.* 16 Feby. 1875; *m.* Johnsonville, N. Y., 1 Feby. 1894, Hiram K., *s.* William E. and Harriet E. (Miller) Hoyt (*b.* Syracuse, N. Y., 28 Jany. 1866). *Issue:* *i. Hazel Lula*[8] *(Hoyt), b. Middlefield Center, 18 Mch. 1896; ii. Mildred Calestia*[8] *(Hoyt), b. Rochester, N. Y., 18 Oct., 1897;* *ii.* Byron Henry[7] (Tripp) *b.* Apl. 1878.*

d. Laverna Mary Dutcher, *m.* Cherry Valley, N. Y., 2 Sept. 1860, Simon *s.* Elijah and Hannah (———) Bennett (*b.* Middlefield, 11 June, 1838). *Issue:* *i.* Letitia J.[7] (Bennett), *b.* Otsego Co., N. Y., 15 June, 1861; *m.* Gloversville, N. Y., 10 June, 1881, Henry, s. George and Kate (———) Lewis (*b.* Gloversville, 18 Mch. 1859). *Issue:* *i. Charles P.*[8] *(Lewis); ii. Maude A.*[8] *(Lewis);* *ii.* Willard Oliver[7] (Bennett) *b.* Middlefield, 7 Mch. 1864; *m.* Gloversville, 26 Apl. 1886, Margaret, *dau.* Thomas and Catherine (——) O'Neil (*b.* Gloversville, 2 Oct. 1868). *Issue:* *i. Thomas Elmer*[8]*; ii. Laverna Willard*[8]*; iii. Leon*[8]*;* *iii.* Frank D.[7] (Bennett), *b.* Gloversville, 27 Apl. 1873.*

e. Jennie Ellen Dutcher, *m.* Middlefield Center, 18 Aug. 1868, Rev. S. W., *s.* Cornelius and Anna (Hoffman) Young (*b.* Seward, N. Y., 1 Apl. 1839). *Issue:* *i.* Dora D.[7] (Young) *b.* Middlefield Center, 27 June, 1870; *m.* Ven-

* Pers. statement.

x. Egbert William[6] (Dutcher) *b.* 3 Apl. 1848.[a]
[*Prescott, Ariz. Ter.*

91 xi. David Jefferson[5] *b.* 10 Feby. 1803. FAM. XXXV.

John Parshall was a soldier of the Revolution.‡ He enlisted in the Spring of 1876 in the Suffolk County Company, commanded by Capt. Reeve, and served about five months; re-enlisted in the company commanded by Capt. Conklin, and served as a carpenter at Newburg, Orange County, N. Y., for one year. On the 5th of May, 1778, he enlisted at Newburg in the company of Capt. Walker, under whom he served for about nine months. It was during this time that he took part in the Battle of Monmouth. In 1779 he was attached to the Newburg company, and was called on to render short tours of duty, as occasion demanded. In the Spring of 1780 he again enlisted as a volunteer in the company of Capt. Drake of Newburg and served about three months, participating in a battle with the Indians, near Fort Plain, N. Y. He also appears to have served for a short time in a Connecticut regiment. On October 16th, 1832, he applied for a pension which was granted for actual service in the Revolutionary War. He seems to have re-

ango, Pa., 2 Apl. 1890, Edward Leonard, *s.* William A. and Martha (Brookhouser) Patterson (*b.* Utica, Minn., 8 Feby. 1867); *ii.* Jennie Belle[7] (Young) *b.* Cedars, N. Y., 28 June, 1873; *m.* Orleans Corners, N. Y., 27 Apl. 1898, Rev. William E., *s.* Frederick B. and Mary Ann (Heasley) Crouser (*b.* New Lebanon, Pa., 13 June, 1871). *Issue: i. Clarence Francis L.*[8] *(Crouser)*; *iii.* Clarence G.[7] (Young), *b.* Poestenkill, N. Y., 30 Nov. 1877; *m.* Orleans Corners, N. Y., 1 Sept. 1897, Violet I., *dau.* Stephen and Henrietta (Coleman) Adams (*b.* Elmwood, Ill., 13 Mch. 1878).*

a. Dr. Egbert William Dutcher, *d.* Preston, Ariz., 24 Sept. 1898; *m.* Center Village, N. Y., 9 Oct. 1878, Ida Anna, *dau.* Allison Orlando and Julia E. (Knox) Smith (*b.* Allegany, N. Y., 27 Sept., 1855). *Issue: i.* Emma Ida,[7] *b.* Nineveh, N. Y., 25 May, 1880; *ii.* Egbert Knox,[7] *b.* Alleghany, N. Y., 3 May, 1885. Dr. Dutcher met his death in a heroic effort to save a lady from a burning building.†

---

* Pers. Statement.
† Fam. Recs. and pers. know. Emma Ida Dutcher.
‡ Recs. U. S. Pension Office; Muncell's Hist. of Suffolk Co., N. Y.; XV. Col. Hist. of N. Y. 216; N.. Y. in The Rev. 166; Conn. Soldiers and Sailors in The Rev.

mained in Newburg after the War until about 1803, when he removed to Middlefield, Otsego County, N. Y. Here he purchased a tract of wild land of 175 acres which had upon it a small log cabin in which he lived for some years. By tireless industry on the part of himself and his family, the heavy forests were cleared away; good substantial buildings were erected and at the time of his death he had acquired considerable property. The house and some other out-buildings were burned some years ago, but the barns are still standing.

FAMILY XIV.

JONATHAN^4 [39], *(Jonathan^3, David^2, James^1) b.* 9 Nov. 1840;* *d.* prob. Little Britain, Orange Co., N. Y., 5 Oct. 1816;* *m.* Jemima Knapp (*b.* 23 Mch. 1738; *d.* 4 Apl. 1825).*

*Children:**

92 I. James^5 *b.* 26 Sept. 1762. FAM. XXXVI.
93 II. Nathan^5 *b.* 24 June, 1766. FAM. XXXVII.
94 III. Lydia^5 *b.* 7 June, 1773; *d. s. p.* and *unm.*, 2 Jany., 1862.
95 IV. Moses^5 *b.* 16 Nov. 1777. FAM. XXXVIII.
96 V. Jesse^5 *b.* 18 June, 1780. FAM. XXXIX.

Jonathan lived and died upon the farm which his father had owned in Little Britain, Orange County, N. Y.† He appears to have been a prominent man in the place. "He held office" from 1763 to 1770,‡ though the nature of it is not specified. He was a soldier of the Revolution, serving in the 2d Regiment, Ulster County Militia.§

---

* Bible Rec. 89, pos. Geo. H. Parshall, Palmyra, N. Y.
† Ruttenber & Clark's Hist. Orange Co., N. Y.
‡ Eager's Hist. of Orange Co., N. Y. 622.
§ N. Y. in The Rev. 193.

FAMILY XV.

DAVID[4] [40], *(Jonathan[3], David[2], James[1]) b.* ———; *d.* ———; *m.* ———.

*Children:**

97 I. David[5] *b.* 13 Mch. 1784. FAM. XL.
98 II. Sally[5], *d. s. p. unm.*
99 III. Nancy[5] *b.* 19 Apl. 1789; *d.* 17 May, 1846; *m.* 4 May, 1805, Ezra Keeler. *Issue:*

i. Ebenezer[6] (Keeler).
ii. Goldsmith[6] (Keeler).
iii. Berthia[6] (Keeler), *m.* ——— Robinson.

David, like his brother Jonathan, lived and died upon the farm which his father had owned in Little Britain.† He also served in the Revolution, having been a private in Col. Graham's Regiment of Levies,‡ in the 4th Regiment of Orange County Militia,§ and in the 2d Regiment, Orange County Militia.**

* Fam. Recs. pos. Miss Nancy J. Robinson, Newberg, N. Y.
† Ruttenber and Clark's Hist. Orange Co.
‡ N. Y. in the Rev. 85 .
§ Id. 166.
** Id. 261.

The Fifth Generation

*FAMILY XVI.**

SAMUEL[5] [44], *(James[4], Israel[3], Israel[2], James[1])* *b.* Long Island, N. Y., 20 Mch. 1757; *d.* Ellsworth, O., abt. 1827; *m.* (1) Sarah ——.

[*Ellsworth, O.*

Children:

100 I. James[6] *b.* 6 June, 1779. FAM. XLI.
101 II. Samuel[6] *b.* 6 July, 1781. FAM. XLII.

m. (2), Long Island, N. Y., Rachel Stratton (*b.* L. I., 30 Mch. 1765; *d.* Ellsworth, O., abt. 1848).

Children:

102 III. Sarah[6]† *b.* Brooklyn, N. Y., 29 July, 1787; *d.* — Mch. 1873; *m.* Springfield, O., 18 July, 1806, David Rose (*b.* 7 Oct. 1783; *d.* 16 Oct. 1857). *Issue:*

i. Jesse[7] (Rose) *b.* 30 May, 1807.[a]
ii. Robert[7] (Rose) *b.* 20 Jany. 1809.[b]

a. Jesse Rose, *d.* 1867; *m.* 27 Jany. 1831, Esther Packard. *No issue.* *m.* (2) 18 Sept. 1866, Malvina Howard.†

b. Robert Rose, *m.* 15 Jany. 1835, Almyra Edsall, *d.* 2 Jany. 1865). *Issue:* *i.* Sarah M.,[8] *b.* 8 July, 1838; *ii.* Henry B.,[8] *b.* 8 July, 1838; *m.* Libbie Moher-

---

* P. and VanE. Fams. and pers. know. Lucinda Rose.
† Id. and pers. know. Rachel Rose Adams.

iii. Samuel^{7} (Rose) *b.* 6 Sept. 1811.[a]
iv. David^{7} (Rose) *b.* 20 July, 1813.
v. Rachel^{7} (Rose) *b.* 8 Jany. 1816.[b]
vi. William^{7} (Rose) *b.* 8 Apl. 1818.[c]
vii. Thomas^{7} (Rose) *b.* 29 Feby. 1820.[d]
viii. Ezra^{7} Dr. (Rose) *b.* 28 Feby. 1822.[e]
ix. Sarah Ann^{7} (Rose) *b.* 25 Oct. 1824.
x. Susan^{7} (Rose) *b.* 29 July, 1826.[aa]
xi. James^{7} (Rose) *b.* 12 Oct. 1829.[bb]

103 IV. Elizabeth^{6} *b.* 6 May, 1789; *m.* Jacob Cook. *Issue:*

i. John^{7} (Cook).
ii. Samuel^{7} (Cook).
iii. Rachel^{7} (Cook).
iv. Katharine^{7} (Cook).
v. Jacob^{7} (Cook).
vi. Socrates^{7} (Cook).

man; *iii.* Oscar A.^{8} *b.* 29 Mch. 1840; *m.* Minnie Morehead; *iv.* Mary A.^{8} *b.* 5 Aug. 1844; *v.* Ogden S.,^{8} *b.* 5 Apl. 1850, *m.* Flora Shinn; *vi.* Wallace E.^{8} *b.* 1 June, 1859.†

a. Samuel Rose, *m.* Antoinette Webb, of Ellsworth, O. *No issue.*†

b. Rachel Rose, *m.* 27 Sept. 1838, Henry Adams. *Issue: i.* Moses P.^{8} (Adams) *b.* Ellsworth, O., 9 Dec. 1841; *m.* Zanesville, O., 29 Dec., 1870, Lida Stephens. *Issue: i. Henry^{9} b. Kokomo, Ind., 21 Sept. 1871; ii. Leland^{9} b. Cleveland, O., 8 July, 1873; iii. Virginia^{9} b. Delaware, O., 29 Dec. 1880; ii.* Thomas^{8} (Adams) *b.* 8 June, 1844; *d.* Pittsburg, Pa., 5 Oct. 1890; *m.* Pittsburg, Pa., 7 June, 1870, Anna Caulburg. *Issue: i. George^{9} b. 20 Aug. 1884.**

c. William Rose, *d.* 12 Apl. 1870; *m.* 1843, Mary A. Tow, of Penfield, O. *Issue:* Harmon H.^{8} *b.* 7 Mch. 1844; *m.* 9 Apl. 1865, Susan Arner. *Issue: i. Louis^{9}; ii. Frederick^{9}; iii. Charles^{9}; ii.* Emory G.^{8} *b.* 4 July, 1846; *iii.* Alice^{8} *b.* 9 Apl. 1849; *d.* 8 Sept. 1859; *iv.* William E.^{8} *b.* 7 June, 1859.†

d. Thomas Rose, *m.* 2 Mch. 1848, Maria Babit. *Issue: i.* Luther^{8} (Dr.) *b.* 2 Dec. 1848; *m.* 5 Feby. 1874, Amanda Wilson; *ii.* Lottie^{8} *b.* 16 Oct. 1850; *m.* 1 Aug. 1870, Charles Mervin. *Issue: i. Royal^{9} (Mervin) b. 13 June, 1873; ii. Grace^{9} (Mervin) b. 19 Feby. 1876; iii.* Rachel^{8} b. 16 May, 1853; *iv.* David^{8} *b.* 27 Mch. 1855; *m.* 29 Apl. 1875, Rebecca Smith.†

e. Ezra Rose (Dr.), *m.* (1) Sarah Orr. *Issue: i.* Joshua^{8}; *ii.* Henrietta^{8}; *iii.* John^{8}; *iv.* Sarah^{8}; Dr. Rose *m.* (2), ——— Hall, a *wid.*†

aa Susan Rose, *m.* Simeon Keefer, *Issue: i.* Thomas^{8} (Keefer); *ii.* Ezra^{8} (Keefer); *iii.* Annette^{8} (Keefer); *iv.* Charles^{8} (Keefer).†

bb James Rose, *m.* 3 Oct. 1855, Ann Rummel.†

---

* Pers. statement.
† Fam. Recs. and pers. know. Rachel Rose Adams.

104 v. John[6] *b.* 24 June, 1791. FAM. XLIII.
105 vi. William[6] *b.* 15 Nov. 1794. FAM. XLIV.
106 vii. Daniel[6] *b.* 9 June, 1796. FAM. XLV.
107 viii. Thomas[6] *b.* 21 July, 1798. FAM. XLVI.
108 ix. David[6] *b.* 17 Oct. 1800. FAM. XLVII.
109 x. Jacob[6] *b.* 15 Mch. 1803. FAM. XLVIII.
110 xi. Nancy[6] *b.* 18 May, 1806; *m.* Samuel Wilday.
111 xii. Moses[6] *b.* 10 Jany. 1810. FAM. IL.

Samuel appears to have removed with his putative father to Orange County, N. Y., prior to the breaking out of the Revolutionary War, for it is a matter of record that he was living, with his father, in Goshen Precinct, in that county in 1775, when he was a private in Capt. Phenihas Rumsey's company, and signed the Association to support Congress.* On the 19th of September, 1775, he and others, then members of a Goshen company, signed a petition to revoke the commissions of the Captain and Lieutenant of the company to which they then belonged, on the ground, as stated, that their election had been procured by fraud and deceit.† Later he appears as a private in Capt. Marvin's company in Col. Drake's regiment, and the muster roll of this company, still extant, dated 26th of November, 1776, shows that on the 27th of August, preceding, he was reported absent from his company,‡ though the reason therefor is not stated. This muster roll is the last record in which the name of Samuel appears, and it is not to be found in the records of any State so far as I have been able to discover. That he was employed in a powder mill, in Maryland, during the greater part of the War, is absolutely certain. His granddaughter, Mrs. Lucinda Rose, when a girl, lived in the family of her grandparents and has frequently listened to thrilling tales of his experience in the mill, as related by her grandmother after the death of Samuel himself. It was during the War,

* XV. Col. Hist. of N. Y. 216.
† I. Col. of N. Y. Hist. Miss. 151.
‡ Id., 500.

probably about 1778, that he married his first wife. She died after the birth of her second child, probably about 1782, or 1783, and on Samuel's return home, immediately after the close of the War, he married in Brooklyn, about 1786, his second wife, Ruth Stratton. He remained in Brooklyn, in all probability, for a number of years, for several of his children were born there. From Brooklyn he returned to Orange County, thence to Beaver, Pa., then to Springfield, O., and finally located in Ellsworth Tp., Mahoning County, O. Here in the primeval solitude he cleared a farm, erected buildings, including a substantial house, and brought up his large family of children. He died about 1827; his wife about 1848.

---

*FAMILY XVII.**

ISRAEL[5] [47], (*Israel[4], Israel[3], Israel[2], James[1]*) *b.* 1760; *d.* ———; *m.* Deliverance Terry, his cousin.

[*Palmyra, N. Y.*

Children:

112 I. Israel[6] *b.* 1782. FAM. L.
113 II. Terry[6] *b.* 29 Jany. 1795. FAM. LI.
114 III. John[6] *d. s. p. unm.*
115 IV. Deborah[6] *m.* ——— Bradner.
116 V. Lydia[6] *m.* ——— Gibbs.
117 VI. Anna[6] *m.* ——— Farr.
118 VII. Ruth[6] *m.* ——— Nash.
119 VIII. Elsie[6] *d. s. p. unm.*
120 IX. Elizabeth[6] *m.* ——— Griswold.
121 X. Lois[6].

* Fam. Recs. and pers. know. Mrs. Jane Paige.

Israel probably removed with his parents from Orange County, N. Y., to Northumberland County, Pa., shortly before the breaking out of the Revolutionary War and resided there until about 1790, when he removed to New York State. He served as a soldier in the Revolution and appears, 13th of March, 1776, as an ensign in the 7th Battalion, Northumberland County Associators, Col. James Potter.* We also find that "Israel Parshall made an application for pension on January 14th, 1833, at which time he was 73 years of age, and resided at Palmyra, N. Y. In his application he alleged that he first enlisted at Loyal Lock, Penna., and served as a private, corporal and sergeant in companies commanded by Captains Newman, Hammond, Hepburn and Westfall, and in regiments commanded by Colonels Martin and Hartley. Length of service not stated. There is an affidavit on file in his claim showing that a brother, David Parshall, served with him."† He appears on the Tax Lists as a resident of Muncy Tp., Northumberland County, Pa., from 1783 to 1787.‡ It is inferred that at this time he was married, from the fact that his brother David is uniformly referred to in contemporaneous records as a "single man." It was probably about 1790 when he finally removed to Palmyra, N. Y., locating there on a farm given to him by his father-in-law. The mother of Deliverance Terry(wife of Israel) is said to have been a sister of Israel.[4] There is a tradition in the family that Deliverance was born in an Indian wigwam during the progress of a fierce battle between the whites and Indians. An Indian woman cared for her and her mother, and protected them from the rage of the redskins. "Delivered" her in fact from the awful peril in which she stood, and hence the name conferred upon her. Israel finally removed to Michigan with several of his children and died there at the advanced age of about eighty years.

* XIV. Pa. Archives (2d Series) 326.
† Recs. U. S. Pension Office.
‡ XIV. Pa. Archives (3d Series) 561, 625, 707.

*FAMILY XVIII.**

DAVID[5] [48], *(Israel[4], Israel[3], Israel[2], James[1])* *b.* 20 Aug. 1762; *d.* Canandaigua, N. Y., 25 June, 1836; *m.* Canandaigua, N. Y., Sarah Cronover (*b.* 3 Sept. 1769; *d.* Lockport, N. Y., 1 Mch. 1856).

Children:

122 I. Deborah[6] *b.* 21 Apl. 1788; *d.* 29 Dec. 1876; *m.* Israel Parshall. See FAM. II.
123 II. Daniel[6] *b.* 14 Nov. 1789.
124 III. Sarah[6] *b.* 6 Nov. 1790; *m.* ——— Gilbert.
125 IV. Ira[6] *b.* 5 Aug. 1792. FAM. LII.
126 V. Lucretia[6] *b.* 29 Jany. 1794; *m.* ——— Goodell.
127 VI. Asa[6] *b.* 15 May, 1796. FAM. LIII.
128 VII. David[6] *b.* 15 Apl. 1798. FAM. LIV.
129 VIII. Lucy[6] *b.* 22 Mch. 1800; *m.* ——— Nichols.
130 IX. Samuel[6] *b.* 30 Mch. 1802.
131 X. Israel[6] *b.* 8 Jany. 1804.
132 XI. Ruth[6] *b.* 23 Dec. 1805; *m.* George B. Chase.
133 XII. Amasa[6] *b.* 14 Oct. 1808; *d.* 11 Nov. 1885; *m.* Jane Boyd.
134 XIII. William[6] *b.* 14 Feby. 1811; *d.* 1 Aug. 1879; *m.* Laura Harrington.

David in all probability removed with his father and elder brother to Pennsylvania, before the breaking out of the Revolutionary War, as his name appears with theirs in various Tax Lists, as a "single man."† He, too, served in the Revolution

* Fam. Recs. pos. John D. Parshall; Bible Rec. 125 pos. Geo. H. Parshall.
† XIV. Pa. Archives (3d Series) 525, 625, 709.

as a private soldier.* He is referred to in Pennsylvania official records as "a Pennsylvania pensioner residing in New York;"† "from which it also appears that he died 1st of March, 1833, aged 71 years."† Physically David is said to have been a small man, like his father, but of vigorous constitution and possessed of great physical strength.

FAMILY XIX.‡

ASA^{5} [51], *(Israel^{4}, Israel^{3}, Israel^{2}, James^{1}) b.* 26 Mch. 1770; *d.* Chemung, N. Y., 23 Mch., 1848; *m.* 22 Jany., 1797, Susannah, *dau.* Thomas and Mercy (Lamb) Keeney (*b.* Hartford, Ct., 5 Mch. 1781; *d.* Chemung, 19 Oct. 1865).

Children:

135 I. Isaac^{6} *b.* 5 Feby., 1798; *d. s. p.* 21 Feby., 1858; *m.* 13 Apl. 1825, Sarah Luther (*d.* 15 Oct. 1871).

136 II. Amzi^{6} *b.* 6 June, 1799. FAM. LV.

137 III. Mercy^{6} *b.* 21 Mch. 1801; *d. s. p.* 21 Feby. 1882; *m.* 13 Sept. 1842, Samuel Grennell.

138 IV. Ruby^{6} *b.* 26 Nov. 1802; *d.* 30 Mch. 1811.

139 V. Benjamin^{6} *b.* 21 June, 1804; *d.* 10 Jany. 1866; *m.* Rowena Soper, 27 Nov. 1832. *No issue.*

140 VI. Thomas Keeney^{6} *b.* 24 Mch. 1806. FAM. LVI.

141 VII. Ransom^{6} *b.* 23 Mch. 1808. FAM. LVII.

142 VIII. Luther^{6} *b.* 22 Mch. 1810. FAM. LVIII.

143 IX. Elizabeth^{6} *b.* 28 Oct. 1811; *d.* 16 Dec. 1854; *m.* Henry Roberts, 7 Jany. 1830.

144 X. Israel^{6} *b.* 4 May, 1815. FAM. LIX.

145 XI. Asa^{6} *b.* 9 Apl. 1813; *d.* 25 Jany. 1814.

---

* XXIII. Pa. Archives, 472.

† Id.

‡ Fam. Rec. pos. 150.

146 xii. Susannah[6]* *b.* Chemung, 4 June, 1817; *d.* Owasso, Mich., 6 Dec. 1889; *m.* Chemung, 14 Dec. 1834, Guy Nelson, *s.* Guy N. and Susan (——) Roberts (*b.* 11 Jany. 1813; *d.* Pontiac, Mich., 13 Dec. 1889). *Issue:*

i. Isaac Parshall[7] (Roberts) *b.* Green Oak, Liv. Co., Mich., 4 Oct. 1835.[a] [*Eaton Rapids, Mich.*

ii. Sarah R.[7] (Roberts) *b.* Oceola, Mich., 20 Jany., 1838.[b] [*Clarkston, Oakland Co. Mich.*

iii. Mary Maria[7] (Roberts) *b.* Oceola, 27 July, 1842.[c] [*Detroit, Mich.*

iv. Delia Etta[7] (Roberts) *b.* 19 May, 1849; *d.* 9 May, 1863.

v. Clarence[7] (Roberts) *b.* 3 Feby. 1851; *d.* 13 Apl. 1868.

vi. Derwent[7] (Roberts) *b.* 5 Oct. 1857; *d.* 17 Feby. 1862.

a. Isaac Parshall Roberts, *m.* Byron, Shiawassee Co., Mich., 22 Feby., 1857, Teena Harriet, *dau.* Garrett and Mary Ann (Bradley) Morse (*b.* Byron, Mich., 17 Jany., 1839). *Issue:* *i.* Trent Isaac[8] *b.* Goodrich, Gen. Co., Mich., 13 Feby. 1865; *d.* 25 July, 1865.†

b. Sarah R. Roberts, *m.* Oak Grove, Liv. Co., Mich., 21 Feby. 1854, Clark B., *s.* Marcus and Polly (Clark) Hart (*b.* Triangle, N. Y., 3 June, 1830; *d.* Vernon, Shiawassee Co., Mich., 8 May, 1879). *Issue:* *i.* Guy Nelson[8] (Hart), *b.* Oak Grove, Liv. Co., Mich., 1 Apl. 1856; *m.* Oregon, Lapeer Co., Mich., 24 Sept. 1884, Ida Maria, *dau.* Daniel and Mary Ann (Smith) Ovaitt (*b.* Troy, Oak. Co., Mich., 31 Aug. 1856). *ii.* Alice Mary[8] (Hart) *b.* Duplain, Clint. Co., Mich., 10 Feby. 1862; *m.* Owosso, Mich., 12 June, 1883, Edward A., *s.* George and Frances (——) Urch (*b.* Westbury, Somersetshire, Eng., 15 June, 1849).†

c. Mary Maria Roberts, *m.* Goodrich, Gen. Co., Mich., 1 May, 1864, John *s.* Samuel and Ruth (Hillman) West (*b.* Newark, N. Y., 20 Feby. 1838). *Issue:* *i.* Myrta Delia[8] (West) *b.* Corunna, Mich., 29 Dec. 1867; *m.* Clarkston, Mich., 18 Sept. 1889, Seward Elmer, *s.* Reuben N. and Elizabeth (Polhemus) Clark (*b.* Springfield, Oak. Co., Mich., 10 Jany. 18—). *Issue:* *i. Mary West[9] (Clark) b. Cincinnati, O., 4 June, 1892.*†

* Fam. Rec. and pers. know. Isaac P. Roberts.
† Pers. state.

147 XIII. Ruth[6]* *b.* Chemung, N. Y., 10 Feby. 1819; *m.* Chemung, 18 Oct. 1838, Richard, *s.* John and Levina (Mitchell) Inscho (*b.* L. I., 5 Feby. 1816; *d.* Tioga, Pa., 20 Jany. 1857). *Issue:* (All *b.* Jackson, Tioga Co., Pa). [*Tioga, Pa.*

i. Susan Keeney[7] (Inscho) *b.* 9 Nov. 1839.[a] [*Easton, Md.*

ii. John Luther[7] (Inscho) *b.* 11 Apl. 1844.[b] [*Tioga, Pa.*

iii. Jesse Parshall[7] (Inscho) *b.* 14 May, 1846.[c] [*Elmira, N. Y.*

iv. William Wallace[7] (Inscho) *b.* 5 Aug., 1851.[d] [*Canoe Camp, Pa.*

a. Susan Keeney Inscho, *m.* Jackson, Tioga Co., Pa., 29 Dec. 1864, Seth J., *s.* Samuel B. and Margaret (Westbrook) Snell. *Issue:* *i.* Cora Belle[8] (Snell) *b.* 21 Oct. 1865; *m.* 5 Oct. 1886, Edward A. Norton. *Issue:* *i. Rena May[9] (Norton) b. Mansfield, Pa., 28 Aug. 1887; ii. Ernest Seth[9] (Norton) b. Elkland, Pa., 12 Mch. 1891;* *ii.* Rose May[8] (Snell) *b.* 17 Jany. 1869; *m.* 5 Feby. 1890, Bayard Cahill (*d.* 7 Sept. 1892). *Issue:* *i. Fred. S.[9] (Cahill), b. Hillsboro, Ind., 6 Feby. 1892;* *m.* 2d, 23 Jany. 1895, William H. Clough. *Issue:* *ii. Ruth Virginia[9] (Clough) b. Berkley, Va., 16 Nov. 1896;* *iii.* Lizzie Lovina[8] (Snell) *b.* 8 Sept. 1872; *m.* 2 Jany. 1895, Millard G. Davis. *Issue:* *(All b. Chapel, Md.) i. Frank Snell[9] (Davis) b. 11 Oct. 1895; ii. Roy Elmer[9] (Davis) b. 6 Oct. 1898;* *iv.* Elmer Kress[8] (Snell) b. 1 May, 1874; *v.* Frank Richard[8] (Snell) *b.* 8 Apl. 1875, *d.* 11Aug. 1885; *vi.* Jesse Inscho[8] (Snell) *b.* Tioga, Pa., 22 Nov. 1876.*

b. John Luther Inscho, *m.* Tioga, Pa., 13 Feby. 1868, Mary, *dau.* Cephas and Lucia O. (Kelly) Miller (*b.* East Smithfield, Bradford Co., Pa., 5 Oct. 1848). *Issue:* *i.* Lena Maude,[8] *b.* 25 July, 1870; *m.* 12 Sept. 1900, Rev. William Charles McCormack, Ph. D.; *ii.* Ida May[8] *b.* 6 June, 1875; *d.* 17 June, 1882.*

c. Jesse Parshall Inscho, *m.* Caton, N. Y., 14 Oct. 1880, Clara A., *dau.* George W. and Phebe (Gregory) Brown (*b.* Caton, N. Y., 13 Feby. 1859). *No issue.**

d. William Wallace Inscho, *m.* Tioga, Pa., 11 Mch. 1873, Catherine Fuller (*b.* New York, 5 June, 1853). *Issue:* *i.* Hattie Mabel[8] *b.* 14 Apl. 1875; *m.* 22 June, 1898, Edward Robson. *Issue:* *i. Harold Edward[9] (Robson) b. 22 Apl. 1900;* *ii.* Ernest Parshall[8] *b.* 20 June, 1877; *m.* 15 Aug. 1900, Mary Jones; *iii.* Thomas Floyd[8] *b.* 20 Oct. 1879; *iv.* Nora Bell[9] *b.* 15 Sept. 1884;

* Personal statement.

v. Ruth Louisa[7] (Inscho) *b.* 8 Apl. 1853.[a]
[*Mansfield, Pa.*

vi. Mary Ella[7] (Inscho) *b.* 10 June, 1857.[b]
[*Big Flats, N. Y.*

vii. Eva Belle[7] (Inscho) *b.* 4 May, 1863.[c]
[*Tioga, Pa.*

148 xiv. Louisa[6]* *b.* Chemung, 24 Oct. 1820; *m.* Chemung, — Nov. 1849, John, *s.* John and Hannah (Smith) Bovier (*b.* Southport, N. Y., — Jany. 1816; *d.* Southport, 11 Feby. 1863). *Issue:* (All *b.* Chemung, N. Y.)

i. Asa Parshall[7] (Bovier) *b.* 23 Apl. 1851.[d]

ii. Flora Edneth[7] (Bovier) *b.* — Aug. 1859.[e]

m. (2) Southport, N. Y., 3 Nov. 1864, Robert Bruce, *s.* Simon and Jennie (Fish) Van Gorder. *No issue.*

v. Jesse Harrison[8] *b.* 29 Mch. 1888; *vi.* Frank Howard[8] *b.* 30 Oct. 1891; *vii.* Ruth Salina[8] *b.* 5 Nov. 1898.*

a. Ruth Louisa Inscho, *m.* Tioga, Pa., 1 Feby. 1871, T. F., *s.* Asa and Elizabeth (Williams) Rolason (*b.* Beemerville, N. J., 18 Aug. 1845). *Issue:* Lynn E.[8] (Rolason) *b.* 14 Nov. 1875; *d.* 15 Nov. 1879.*

b. Mary Ella Inscho, *m.* Tioga, Pa., 21 Aug. 1877, Dr. John Wilbur, *s.* Chester and Eliza (Hulslander) Stewart (*b.* Jackson, Tioga Co., Pa., 23 Mch. 1852). *Issue:* *i.* Richard Lee[8] (Stewart) Caton, N. Y., 21 Sept. 1878; *ii.* Clarence Wilber[8] (Stewart) *b.* Caton, 29 Jany. 1881; *iii.* Lulu Belle[8] (Stewart) *b.* Caton, 16 Aug. 1883; *iv.* Eliza May[8] (Stewart) *b.* Big Flats, N. Y., 2 Jany. 1888.*

c. Eva Belle Inscho, *m.* Tioga, Pa., 22 Nov. 1882, Charles, *s.* William T. and Eliza D. (Culp) Rhodes (*b.* 21 May, 1861). *Issue:* *i.* Bertha Aletha[8] (Rhodes) *b.* 11 Dec. 1883; *d.* 14 Sept. 1889; *ii.* Gertrude Blanche[8] (Rhodes) *b.* 16 Sept. 1885; *iii.* Ralph Waldo Emerson[8] (Rhodes) *b.* 23 Apl. 1888; *iv.* Richard Inscho[8] (Rhodes) *b.* 23 July, 1892.*

d. Asa Parshall Bovier, *m.* Southport, N. Y., 22 Feby. 1877, Emma, *dau.* Hammond and Harriet (Smith) Mathews. *Issue:* John Hammond[8] *b.* 26 Aug. 1886.*

e. Flora Edneth Bovier, *d.* Elmira, N. Y., 26 Jany. 1891; *m.* Elmira, — Jany. 1881, Isaac B., *s.* A. J. and Sally (Bonnell) Coykendall (*d.* Elmira, 5 Nov. 1899). *Issue:* *i.* Louisa Ednah[8] (Coykendall) *b.* 20 Feby. 1883.†

* Personal statement.
† Fam. Recs. and pers. know. 148.

149 xv. Jesse[6] *b.* 30 Mch. 1822. FAM. LX.

150 xvi. Asa[6] *b.* 20 Apl. 1825. FAM. LXI.

151 xvii. Lemira[6]* *b.* Chemung, 27 Aug., 1826; *m.* 24 Dec., 1851, George Baldwin, *s.* Henry and Catherine Beidleman) Snell (*b.* Chemung, 16 Nov. 1820). *Issue:* (All *b.* Chemung, N. Y.)

i. Alida Jane[7] (Snell) *b.* 11 Aug., 1854.[a] [*Chemung, N. Y.*

ii. Kate Anna Belle[7] (Snell) *b.* 12 June, 1857.[b] [*Chemung, N. Y.*

iii. Nora Louisa[7] (Snell) *b.* 5 Nov., 1858.[c] [*Chemung, N. Y.*

iv. George Baldwin[7] (Snell) *b.* 8 Oct., 1863.[d] [*Chemung, N. Y.*

v. John Henry[7] (Snell) *b.* 24 Apl., 1867.[e] [*Elmira, N. Y.*

FAMILY XX.†

JESSE[5] [55], (*Israel*[4] *Israel*[3] *Israel*[2] *James*[1]) *b.* about 1779; *d.* Centerfield, Ontario Co., N. Y., 1856; *m.* Mary Van Gorder. [*Centerfield, Ont. Co., N. Y.*

a. Alida Jane Snell, *m.* Chemung, 20 June, 1882, Fletcher W., *s.* Gordon and Rhoda (Greatsinger) Snell (*b.* Chemung, 17 Feby., 1850).*

b. Kate Anna Belle Snell, *m.* Chemung, 21 Dec., 1881, Philip Heermans, *s.* Niles Frost and Sarah Ann (Heermans) Wynkoop (*b.* Chemung, 25 Sept. 1854). *Issue:* *i.* Roy Baldwin[8] (Wynkoop); *ii.* Fletcher Snell[8] (Wynkoop); *iii.* Sarah Kathleen[8] (Wynkoop).*

c. Nora Louisa Snell, *m.* Chemung, 18 Jany., 1882, Charles Sumner, *s.* Ebenezer and Emily Jane (Burlingame) Gere (*b.* North Chemung, 21 June, 1857). *Issue:* *i.* Verna Emily[8] (Gere); *ii.* Myra Marguerite[8] (Gere).*

d. George Baldwin Snell, *m.* Chemung, 18 Sept. 1889, Elizabeth, *dau.* Daniel Deyo and Margaret (Gere) De Witt (*b.* Chemung, 7 Oct. 1865).*

e. John Henry Snell, m. Elmira, N. Y., 18 Dec. 1895, Edith, dau. Charles Edwin and Edith (Fielding) Hutchinson (*b.* Elmira, 11 June, 1873). *Issue:* *i.* Charles Baldwin.[8]*

---

* Personal statement.

† Fam. Recs. and pers. know. 441 and 442.

Children:

152 I. William.[6]
153 II. Amos.[6]
154 III. Samuel.[6]
155 IV. Daniel[6] *b.* about 1808. FAM. LXII.
156 V. Jesse[6] *b.* about 1810. FAM. LXIII.
157 VI. Elisha[6] *b.* — Oct., 1811. FAM. LXIV.
158 VII. Rufus[6] *b.* 2 Nov., 1814. FAM. LXV.
159 VIII. John[6] *b.* 22 Feby., 1822. FAM. LXVI.
160 IX. Otis Kimble[6] *b.* 18 Jany., 1823. FAM. LXVII.
161 X. Charles.[6]

There are but few records of Jesse Parshall extant. He appears to have lived for the greater part of his life in or near Canandaigua, N. Y., removing finally to Centerfield, Ontario Co., N. Y., where he died. Of his sons William, Amos, Samuel and Charles, I can find no trace.

---

*FAMILY XXI.**

ISRAEL[5] [56], (*Benjamin[4] Israel[3] Israel[2] James[1]*) *b.* 1760-1765; *d.* about 1818; *m.* Elizabeth Weeks.

Children:

162 I. Benjamin Carlisle[6] *b.* 17 May, 1803. FAM. LXVIII.
163 II. Elizabeth[6]† *b.* New York City, 31 Oct., 1818,; *d.* Utica, N. Y., 9 Oct., 1871; *m.* New York City, 1 Oct., 1838, George *s.* George and Margaret (Culbertson) Kincaid (*b.* Scotland, 12 Oct., 1819; *d.* Utica, N. Y., 27 Mch., 1893) *Issue:* (All *b.* Utica, N. Y.) [*Utica, N. Y.*

* Fam. Recs. and pers know. 478.
† Fam. Recs. and pers. know., Mrs. Chas. B. Kincaid.

i. James Carlisle Parshall[7] (Kincaid) *b.* 20 May, 1840.[a] [*Utica, N. Y.*

ii. George Andrew[7] (Kincaid) *b.* 25 Sept., 1842.[b] [*San Mateo, Cal.*

iii. Charles Benjamin[7] (Kincaid) *b.* 21 May, 1845.[c] [*Utica, N. Y.*

iv. Mary Easter[7] (Kincaid) *b.* 27 Oct., 1849.[d] [*Campbell, Santa Clara Co., Cal.*

v. William Morris,[7] Rev. (Kincaid) *b.* 16 Jany., 1856.[e] [*Honolulu, H. I.*

Israel Parshall was a soldier of the Revolution, enlisting in a Gloucester Co., N. J., regiment.‡ He was discharged in New

a. James Carlisle Parshall Kincaid, *m.* Utica, N. Y., 24 Aug. 1864, Elizabeth Lucretia, *dau.* Alrick and Laura E. (Squier) Hubbell (*b.* Utica, N. Y., 4 Aug. 1841). *Issue:* *i.* Alrick George[8] *d.*; *ii.* Frederick William[8]; *iii.* James Carlisle Parshall[8], Jr., *d.*; *iv.* Robert Carlton.[8]*

b. George Andrew Kincaid, *m.* Utica, N. Y., 13 June, 1866, Hattie P., *dau.* Zenas M. and Julia A. (Smith) Howes (*b.* Hampton, Oneida Co., N. Y., 5 May, 1846; *d.* Utica, 5 Jany. 1886). *Issue:* *i.* George H.[8] *b.* 1867; *ii.* Zenas M.[8] *b.* 1869; *iii.* Elizabeth I.[8] *b.* 1871; *iv.* Adelbert M.[8] *b.* 1873; *d.* 1876; *v.* Wales Buel[8] *b.* 1876.*

c. Charles Benjamin Kincaid, *d.* Utica, 26 May, 1898; *m.* Utica, 7 Aug. 1867, Hannah E., *dau.* Edward and Miriam (Davis) Hughes (*b.* Utica, 3 Sept. 1846). *Issue:* *i.* Thomas Ashley[8] *b.* 28 Nov. 1868; *ii.* Miriam Elizabeth[8] *b.* 27 Oct. 1874; *iii.* Amelia Cash[8] *b.* 23 May, 1876; *m.* ——— Cummings.†

d. Mary Easter Kincaid, *m.* Utica, 1 Oct. 1873, Robert Browner, *s.* Reuben and Louisa (———) Cash (*b.* Leroy, N. Y., 20 May, 1845). *No issue.**

e. Rev. William Morris Kincaid, *m.* (1) Cortland, N. Y., 14 Dec. 1875, Emily Melinda, *dau.* Thomas and Julia (———) Purinton (*b.* Buffalo Creek, W. Va., 8 July, 1852; *d.* Cortland, N. Y., 13 Apl. 1877). *Issue:* *i.* Emily Purinton[8] *b.* Cortland, 10 Apl. 1877; *d.* Cortland, 28 Aug. 1877; *m.* (2) Santa Ana, Cal., 18 Mch. 1882, Ellen, *dau.* Archibald Thomas and Delia (Latham) Douglas (*b.* New London, Ct., 27 Oct. 1855). *Issue:* *ii.* Anna Douglas[8] *b.* 18 Feby. 1882; *iii.* Douglas Archibald[8] *b.* 23 Aug. 1884; *iv.* Mary[8] *b.* 14 Sept. 1886; *d. s. p.*; *v.* William Veritas[8] *b.* 26 Apl. 1895.*

* Personal statement.
† Statement Mrs. Chas. B. Kincaid.
‡ State of New Jersey, Office of Adjutant General, Trenton, April 13, 1901. It is certified, that the records of this office show that Israel Parshall served as a Private, Minute Man, in the Gloucester County New Jersey Militia, during the Revolutionary War. Alexander C. Oliphant, Adjutant General. [Seal.]

York City, at the disbanding of Washington's Army. No records show the regiment in which he served or length of service. Nothing, in fact, beyond the mere mention of his name. It is probable, however, that he served in the latter part of the War.

---

*FAMILY XXII.**

JAMES CARLISLE[5] [57], (*Benjamin*[4] *Israel*[3] *Israel*[2] *James*[1]) *b.* Halifax, N. C., 2 May, 1769; *d.* ————; *m.* 6 June, 1789, Hannah Clark (*b.* prob. Orange Co., N. Y., 11 Feby., 1770).

Children:

164 I. Submit[6] *b.* 22 Apl., 1790; *d.* 26 July, 1791.
165 II. Lydia[6] *b.* 13 Dec., 1791; *d.* 13 Sept., 1792.
166 III. Hannah[6] *b.* 20 Aug., 1793; *d.* 9 July, 1794.
167 IV. Matilda[6] *b.* 5 May, 1795; *d.* 15 Dec., 1810.
168 V. Abner Page[6] *b.* 2 May, 1797; *d.* 22 Aug., 1798.
169 VI. Susan[6]† *b.* July, 1799; *d.* 8 Nov., 1880; *m.* William Quail. *Issue:*

i. James Timony[7] (Quail) *b.* 18 Nov., 1825.[a]
ii. Eliza E.[7] (Quail) *b.* 18 Nov., 1825. *m.* —— Blanck.
iii. William[7] (Quail).
iv. Charles[7] (Quail).
v. George[7] (Quail).
vi. Caroline[7] (Quail). *m.* —— Connor.

a. James Timony Quail, *d.* Brooklyn, 8 May, 1898; *m.* (1) New York, 27 Mch. 1848, Isabella, *dau.* William and Bridget (Reily) Lynd (*b.* New York, 27 Sept. 1827, *d.* N. J., 19 Jany. 1871). *Issue: (All b. New York),* *i.* William Charles[8] *b.* 22 Jany. 1850; *m.* Ireland, 25 Jany. 1876, Helena,

---

* Bible Rec. 57, possession Mrs. Caroline Connor.
† Fam. Rec. and pers. know., James T. Quail.

170 VII. James[6] *b.* 30 Nov., 1801; *d.* Buenos Ayers, 10 June, 1829.

171 VIII. Caroline Matilda[6]† *b.* N. Y. City, 15 Apl., 1804; *d.* N. Y., City, 9 June, 1883; *m.* N. Y. City, 26 Nov., 1827, Benjamin Franklin *s.* Sands and Susan (Potter) Ferris (*b.* Westchester, N. Y., 9 June, 1806). *Issue:* (All *b.* New York.)

i. William Hawkins[7] (Ferris) *b.* 13 Dec., 1828.
ii. Caroline Matilda[7] (Ferris *b.* 20 June, 1831.[a]
iii. Josephine A.[7] (Ferris) *b.* 21 Feby., 1835.

172 IX. William[6] *b.* 1 Jany., 1807.

173 X. Priscilla[6] *b.* 2 Apl., 1809; *d.* 20 Sept., 1809.

174 XI. Charles[6b] *b.* 2 Aug., 1810; *d. s. p.* 8 June, 1851.

m. (2) Mrs. Isabella (Pugsley) Oliver.

Children:

175 XII. Mary.[6]

XIII. A son *d. inf.*

dau. Maurice and Margaret (Connelly) Cummings (*b.* Ireland, 24 Dec. 1859). *Issue:* *i. John Francis[9] b. 15 Aug. 1887; ii. Frances Gertrude[9] b. 13 Dec. 1897*; *ii.* James Timony[8] *b.* 5 Oct. 1852; *m.* City Island, N. Y., 8 May, 1881, Cornelia Jane, *dau.* Isaac Cole and Emily (Banta) Van Allen (*b.* City Island, 13 June, 1854). *Issue: i. Wallace Isaac[9] b. Brooklyn, 23 Dec. 1882*; *iii.* George Washington[8] *b.* 12 June, 1855; *m.* Brooklyn, 23 Apl. 1883, Catherine, *dau.* John and Mary (Lang) Stryker (*b.* Brooklyn, 3 Feby. 1860). *Issue: i. George John[9] b. 25 Mch. 1885; ii. Harriet Isabella[9] b. 26 Feby. 1896.* James Timony[7] Quail *m.* (2) Brooklyn, 1866, Harriet Louise, *dau.* Thomas and Mary (———) Hoadley (*b.* Tuckahoe, Ala., 1838). *Issue:* *iv.* John Wallace Blanck[8]; *v.* Charles.[8]*

a. Caroline Matilda Ferris, *m.* Stamford, Ct., 14 Jany., 1850, Charles William, *s.* Horace and Ann (Miller) Waterbury (*b.* Stamford, Ct., 18 Jany. 1819; *d.* Stamford, 26 June, 1866). *Issue:* (All *b.* Stamford, Ct.), *i.* William Ferris[8] (Waterbury) *b.* 1 Mch. 1851; *m.* Greenwich, Ct., 20 Dec. 1877, Harriet Lucinda, *dau.* George F. and Harriet (Weed) Kenworthy. *Issue: i. Howard Roder[9] (Waterbury) b. 7 Jany. 1881; ii. Mildred Adele[9] (Waterbury) b. 12 Sept. 1887*; *ii.* Charles Parshall[8] (Waterbury) *b.* 20 Jany. 1855; *iii.* Edwin Horace[8] (Waterbury) *b.* 12 Aug. 1858; *iv.* Walter Scott[8] (Waterbury) *b.* 5 Nov. 1860; *v.* Caroline Parshall[8] (Waterbury) *b.* 27 Apl. 1863.†

b. Charles Parshall was one of the most prominent Wall Street men of

* Fam. Recs. and pers. know. James T. Quail.
† Fam. Recs. and pers. know. Wm. F. Waterbury.

*FAMILY XXIII.**

BENJAMIN[5] [58], (*Benjamin*[4] *Israel*[3] *Israel*[2] *James*[1]) *b.* N. Y. City, 29 June, 1788; *d.* Charleston, S. C., 13 Oct., 1816; *m.* N. Y. City, 16 Nov., 1811,† Mary, *dau.* of Conrad and Sorchie (Vail) Hotto (*b.* N. Y. City, 9 July, 1790; *d.* Morrisania (now N. Y. City), 12 Dec., 1869).

Children:

176 I. George Hotto[6] *b.* 16 Oct., 1812. FAM. LXIX.
177 II. James Lawrence[6] *b.* 14 Feby., 1815. FAM. LXX.

Receiving a common school education and learning the shoemakers' trade, he started in business for himself in New York City. Meeting with reverses in his business, he went to Charleston, S. C., hoping to improve his affairs. Here he opened a shop and store and was successful from the start. His wife and sons were preparing to follow him thither, when he died suddenly of a fever. His letters to his wife are filled with expressions of affection, for mother, wife and children. He was a man of irreproachable character, of high ideals, and noble purposes. He enlisted in a N. Y. Regt. in the War of 1812, but was not called into actual service.

FAMILY. XXIV.‡

GEORGE[5] [62], (*David*[4] *David*[3] *David*[2] *James*[1]) *b.* Riverhead, Suffolk Co., N. Y., — ———, 1772; *d.* Northville, Suff.

his day. He appears in the New York City Directory, 1846, as a member of the firm of Beebee & Parshall, Bullion Brokers, with office at 22½ Wall Street. He left a large fortune at his death.

* Fam. Rec. pos. Dr. Geo. H. Parshall.
† XVI. N. Y. Gen. and Biog. Rec. 86.
‡ Fam. Rec. and pers. know. 180.

Co., 15 Oct., 1825, age 53 years; *m.* Aquebogue, 22 Nov., 1806, the Widow Abigail (Wells) Terry (*b.* 7 May, 1788; *d.* So. Jamesport, Suff. Co., N. Y., 27 May, 1872).

[*Northville, Suff. Co., N. Y.*

Children:

178 I. David Terry[6] *b.* 18 Aug., 1807. FAM. LXXI.

179 II. Caleb Halsey[6] *b.* 21 Aug., 1809. FAM. LXXII.

180 III. Belinda Delia[6]* *b.* Northville, 4 June, 1814; *m.* Trumansburg, Tompkins Co., N. Y., 7 Nov., 1835, Israel Franklin *s.* of John and Martha (Emmons) Robinson (*b.* Riverhead, 16 June, 1812; *d.* So. Jamesport, 11 Apl., 1891). *Issue:*

[*So. Jamesport, Suff. Co., N. Y.*

i. Terry Parshall[7] (Robinson) *b.* 15 Nov., 1836.[a]
ii. Dewitt Clinton[7] (Robinson) *b.* 5 Mch., 1839.[b]
[*Penn Yan, N. Y.*
iii. Abigail Jane[7] (Robinson) *b.* 22 Jany., 1842.
iv. Ann Eliza[7] (Robinson) *b.* 31 May, 1847.
v. Miranda Adelia[7] (Robinson) *b.* 25 Oct., 1849.[c]
vi. Charles Franklin[7] (Robinson).

a. Terry Parshall Robinson, *d.* Forty Fort, Pa., 18 Feby. 1898; *m.* Huron, O., 7 Sept. 1862, Cathena, *dau.* Charles S. and Elizabeth (Boyd) Chapman (*b.* Riley, Sandusky Co., O., 31 Jany. 1837; *d.* Danbury Tp., Ottawa Co., O., 18 Nov. 1892). *Issue:* *i.* Howard Franklin[8] *b.* Buffalo, N. Y., 1 Oct. 1866; *d.* Danbury Tp., O., 8 Aug. 1889, *unm*; *ii.* Otis Chapman[8] (Dr.) *b.* Rochester, N. Y., 29 Dec. 1868; *m.* Hartsgrove, Ashtabula Co., O., 26 June, 1895, Ruth Mabel, *dau.* David Elmer and Lucy Dimmick (Babcock) Hurlburt (*b.* Hartsgrove, O., 2 Nov. 1871). *Issue: i. Russell Hurlburt[9] b. Windsor, Asht. Co., O., 20 Dec. 1896; ii. Ruth Natalie[9] b. Hartsgrove, 14 Apl. 1899.*†

b. Dewitt Clinton Robinson, *m.* Waterloo, N. Y., 16 Aug. 1864, Frances Eugenia, *dau.* Joel and Betsy E. (———) Williams (*b.* Waterloo, 20 Aug. 1843). *No issue.**

c. Miranda Adelia Robinson, *m.* So. Jamesport, N. Y., 13 Apl. 1873, William A. Slater. *Issue;* *i.* Ruth Vandeverr[8] (Slater).*

* Personal statement.
† Fam. Recs. and pers. state. Dr. Otis C. Robinson.

181 IV. Amanda Melvina[6]* *b.* Jamesport, L. I., 13 May, 1815; *d.* Friendship, Adams Co., Wis., 31 Oct., 1866; *m.* *n.* Milwaukee, Wis., 11 Oct., 1847, George, *s.* of John and Mary (Phillips) Boardman (*b.* Greene, N. Y., 10 July, 1819; *d.* Wheaton, Kan., 13 Nov., 1879). *Issue:*

i. George Parshall[7] (Boardman) *b.* 14 Nov., 1848.[a] [*Lakeport, Cal.*

ii Oscar Terry[7] (Boardman) *b.* 29 June, 1851.[b] [*Kelceyville, Cal.*

182 V. George Lorenzo[6] *b.* about 1818. FAM. LXXIII.

183 VI. Abbie Jane[6]† *b.* 20 Apl., 1824; *d.* Franksville, Wis., 10 Feby., 1897; *m.* Farmer, N. Y., — ——, 1845, Gilbert Adams, (*b.* Orange Co., N. Y., 1823; *d.* Franksville, Wis., 24 Jany., 1881). *Issue:* (All *b.* Franksville, Wis.)

i. George Parshall[7] (Adams) *b.* 27 Aug., 1846; *d.* Tombstone, Ariz., — July, 1886.

ii. Terry Gilbert[7] (Adams) *b.* 3 Mch., 1847; *d.* 12 June, 1902.[c]

a. George Parshall Boardman, *m.* 31 Dec., 1876, Sarah *dau.* Frederick and Catherine (Carmen) Wait (*b.* Columbia Co., Wis., 4 Dec. 1858). *Issue:* *i.* Oscar George[8] *b.* 29 Mch. 1878; *m.* 12 June, 1900, Jessie, *dau.* John and Blanche (Ormiston) Griffiths.*

b. Oscar Terry Boardman, *m.* Knights Landing, Cal., 7 Oct. 1876, Viola J., *dau.* Otis Ballou and Emma J. (Foster) Lapham (*b.* Rome Tp., Dane Co., Wis., 23 Feby. 1853). *Issue:* *i.* Wilfred Lapham[8] *b.* 9 July, 1878; *ii.* George Parshall[8] *b.* 2 June, 1880; *iii.* Otis Ballou[8] *b.* 25 July, 1882; *iv.* Eva Sarah[8] *b.* 6 Oct. 1889.*

c. Terry Gilbert Adams, *d.* 12 June, 1902; *m.* Caledonia, Racine Co., Wis., 18 Sept. 1872, Ella Eliza, *dau.* Lewis and Achsah (Miles) Sears (*b.* Caledonia, 16 Mch. 1852). *Issue:* *i.* Jessie Medora[8]; *ii.* George Gilbert[8]; *iii.* Carrie L.[8]†

---

* Fam. Rec. and pers. know. Geo. P. and Oscar T. Boardman.
† Fam. Rec. and pers. know. Terry G. Adams.

FAMILY XXV.*

ELIAS[5] [64], (*Elias[4] David[3] David[2] James[1]*) *b.* Southold, Suffolk Co., N. Y., 11 Sept., 1771; *d.* McClellandtown, Fayette Co., Pa., 13 Feby., 1856; *m.* (1) Morris Co., New Jersey, Jane Tingley.

Children:

184 I. Nathaniel[6] *b.* 31 Dec., 1791. FAM. LXXIV.
185 II. Eliza[6] *m.* ——— Spitznagle.
186 III. John[6] *b.* 2 Nov., 1795. FAM. LXXV.
187 IV. Jane[6]† *b.* probably N. J., 2 Nov., 1795; *d.* *n.* Uniontown, Pa., 18 Dec., 1886; *m.* German Tp., Fayette Co., Pa., 8 Apl., 1813, Bernard Dannels (*b.* 17 Mch., 1786; *d.* Luzerne Tp., Fayette Co., Pa., 1866).
Issue:

i. Elias[7] (Dannels) *b.* 7 Jany., 1814; *d. inf.*
ii. Madison[7] (Dannels) *b.* 24 Feby., 1815.
iii. John[7] (Dannels) *b.* 12 Feby., 1817.
iv. Henry[7] (Dannels) *b.* 20 Mch., 1819.
v. George Parshall[7] (Dannels) *b.* 9 Apl., 1821.
vi. Martha Louise[7] (Dannels) *b.* 7. Apl., 1823.
vii. Bernard[7] (Dannels) *b.* 17 Apl., 1826.
viii. Esaias[7] (Dannels) *b.* 10 Feby., 1828.
ix. Elizabeth[7] (Dannels) *b.* 5 June, 1830.
x. Allen[7] (Dannels) *b.* 29 May, 1832.

---

* Fam. Recs. pos. 533.
† Bible Rec. and pers. know. Rev. E. W. Dannels.

Elias Bergshall

xi. Ellis Woodward[7] Rev. (Dannels) *b.* 21 July, 1834.[a] [*Fultonham, O.*

xii. William Wood[7] (Dannels) *b.* 1837.

xiii. Nelson[7] (Dannels) *b.* 18 Feby., 1839.

xiv. Mary Matilda[7] (Dannels) *b.* 15 Feby., 1847.

188 v. Elias[6] *b.* 3 Aug., 1797. Fam. LXXVI.

189 vi. James[6] *b.* 3 Aug., 1797. Fam. LXXVII.

m. (2) Anna, dau. Frederick Strubel.

Children:

190 vii. Anna[6]* *b.* Fayette Co., Pa., 22 Mch., 1811; *d.* Putnam Co., O., 17 Mch., 1875; *m.* Fayette Co., Pa., 24 June, 1829, John, *s.* Jacob and Eve (Everly) Deffenbaugh (*b.* Fayette Co., Pa., 26 Oct., 1806; *d.* Putnam Co., O., 14 Jany., 1886). *Issue:*

i. Nancy[7] (Deffenbaugh) *b.* 26 Mch., 1831; *m.* Geo. L. Evans.

ii. Jacob[7] (Deffenbaugh) *b.* 2 Aug., 1833.[b] [*Columbus Grove, O.*

iii. William[7] (Deffenbaugh) *b.* 19 Nov., 1835; *d.* 10 Jany., 1837.

a. Rev. Ellis Woodward Dannels, *m.* Sharon, O., 1 Nov. 1855, Ruth, *dau.* John and Anna (McKee) Caldwell (*b.* Caldwell, O., 18 May, 1827). *Issue:* *i.* Clara Anna[8] *b.* Rural Dale, O.; *d.* Stockport, O., 25 Nov. 1895; *m.* 25 Oct. 1888, Elmer N. Dye; *ii.* Judson[8] *b.* Rural Dale, O., Mich. 1867; *d.* 28 Apl. 1867.†

b. Jacob Deffenbaugh, *m.* (1) Susannah, *dau.* Samuel and Elizabeth (Gander) Clevenger (*b.* 1837; *d.* Kalida, O., 26 July, 1860). *No issue.* *m.* (2) Putnam Co., O., 6 Oct. 1864, Mary M., *dau.* Jesse C. and Lydia (———) Darbyshire (*b.* Fayette Co., O., 5 May, 1845). *Issue:* *i.* Olive May[8] *b.* 21 Mch. 1866; *d.* 11 Jany. 1895; *m.* 5 Nov. 1885, ——— ———; *ii.* Lydia Ann[8] *b.* 2 Sept. 1868; *m.* 6 Mch. 1889, ——— ———; *iii.* Samuel Milton[8] *b.* 6 Oct. 1871; *m.* 19 Feby. 1895, ———; *iv.* Jessie Eliza[8] *b.* 12 Feby. 1879; *m.* 19 Aug. 1902, ——— ———.†

* Fam. Recs. and pers. know., Jacob Deffenbaugh.

† Pers statement.

iv. Joseph[7] (Deffenbaugh) *b.* 22 Oct., 1837. [*Kalida, O.*

v. Albert Gallatin[7] (Deffenbaugh) *b.* 2 Feby., 1840. [*Rimer, O.*

vi. Amanda Ann[7] (Deffenbaugh) *b.* 2 Apl., 1842; *m.* — Jany., 1862, John A. McKinley. [*Rimer, O.*

vii. Lewis Milton[7] (Deffenbaugh) *b.* 27 Nov., 1844.

viii. Emily Jane[7] (Deffenbaugh) *b.* 10 June, 1847; *m.* 28 June, 1866, Samuel Keirns. [*Columbus Grove, O.*

ix. John Henry[7] (Deffenbaugh) *b.* 11 Dec., 1849. [*Rimer, O.*

m. (3) Mrs. Mary (Brown) Grove. *No issue.*

Elias Parshall was born in the same house as his father. He removed from Long Island to Morris Co., N. J., and subsequently to Fayette Co., Pa., where he spent the remainder of his life and where many of his descendants still reside. He engaged in milling and flat boating to New Orleans, returning by way of New York. For several years he kept a hotel in Masontown, Pa., and carried on a shoe factory, bringing his leather across the mountains from Maryland and Virginia in a wagon. A man of rare talent for business and affairs, he laid the foundation of the fortune which his descendants have ever since enjoyed. (*See portrait.*)

FAMILY XXVI.

DAVID[5]* [66], (*Elias[4] David[3] David[2] James[1]*) *b.* Patchogue (L. I.), N. Y., — Dec., 1777; *d.* Wheeling, W. Va., 11 Dec., 1850; *m.* (1) probably Long Island, Abigail L'Hommedieu (*d.* Long Island, 1800-1805).

---

* Fam. Recs. and pers. know. 197.

Children:

191 I. Linda[6] *b.* 1800; *m.* Jacob Sprinkler. *Issue:*

i. Annie[7] *m.* Prosser or Presser, and lived in Birmingham, a suburb of Pittsburg, Pa.

ii. Elizabeth[7] *d.* fall of 1844.

And several sons.

m. (2) Uniontown, Pa., — Apl., 1806, Agnes, *dau.* James and Mary (Dickey)[a] Carlow (*b.* Uniontown, 6 Apl., 1788; *d.* Triadelphia, W. Va., 17 June, 1857).

Children:

192 II. Anna[6]* *b.* Uniontown, Pa., 30 June, 1808; *d.* Triadelphia, W. Va., 15 Nov., 1881; *m.* Short Creek, W. Va., 1828, Thomas Henderson (*b.* 1792; *d.* 1869). *Issue:*

i. James Parshall[7] (Henderson) *b.* 2 Apl., 1832; *d.* 15 Sept., 1876.

ii. Mary Ann[7] (Henderson) *b.* 15 Nov., 1834; *d.* 4 Dec., 1834.

iii. William[7] (Henderson) *b.* 3 Dec., 1835.

iv. Melissa Ann[7] (Henderson) *b.* 8 July, 1838.

v. Nancy Emeline[7] (Henderson) *b.* 2 Feby., 1841.[b]

vi. Thomas[7] (Henderson) *b.* 29 Apl., 1843; *d.* 6 Oct., 1861.

vii. Anna Martha[7] (Henderson) *b.* 29 Nov., 1845; *d.* 22 Nov., 1879; *m.* ——— Wells.

viii. David Hervey[7] (Henderson) *b.* 5 Dec., 1849.

193 III. James Carlow[6] *b.* 15 Sept., 1812. FAM. LXXVIII.

194 IV. David Youngs[6] *b.* — Dec., 1816. FAM. LXXIX.

a. Mary Dickey was a *dau.* of ——— Dickey and Agnes Stinton, a *dau.* of Lord Stinton, of Scotland.

b. Nancy Emmeline Henderson, *m.* West Alexander, Pa., 23 Aug. 1869, Thomas Henderson, a cousin.*

Fam. Rec. and pers. know. Nancy Emeline Henderson.

195 V. John Budd[6]* (Dr.) *b.* Uniontown, Pa., 3 Aug., 1819; *d.* Cincinnati, O., — Aug., 1872; *m.* 1857, Caroline Elizabeth Tucker, *dau.* Rev. ———— Craig (*d.* Cincinnati, 1868). *No issue.*

196 VI. Mary Catherine[6]* *b. n.* Wheeling, W. Va., 15 Sept., 1822; *d.* Triadelphia, W. Va., 12 Apl., 1855; *m.* Wheeling, 22 Nov., 1849, John, *s.* Moses and Mary (Wallace) Ferrell (*b. n.* Short Creek, W. Va., 3 Dec., 1821; *d.* Triadelphia, 24 Oct., 1876). *Issue:*

i. Mary Agnes[7] (Ferrell) *b.* 4 June, 1851.[a]
ii. Martha Jane[7] (Ferrell) *b.* 8 Mch., 1855.

197 VI. Sarah Lenfesty[6]* *b.* Wheeling, W. Va., 15 May, 1825; *m.* West Alexander, Pa., 13 July, 1859, John Ferrell (*See* 196). *Issue:*

i. Moses Seymour[7] (Ferrell) *d. inf.*
ii. Celeste Isabelle[7] (Ferrell) *b.* 6 Oct., 1862.
iii. Annie Caroline[7] (Ferrell) *b.* 21 Dec., 1866.

FAMILY XXVII.

LEWIS[5]† [70] (*Elias*[4] *David*[3] *David*[2] *James*[1]) *b.* about 1783; *d.* 5 Nov., 1813, "in the 30th year of his age;" *m.* Hannah, *dau. of* Nathaniel and Hannah (Wells) Hudson (*b.* 25 Apl., 1787; *d.* 12 Jany., 1847).

Children.‡

198 I. Lewis.[6]
199 II. Daniel.[6]
200 III. Josiah[6] *d. inf.*

a. Mary Agnes Ferrell, *m.* West Alexander, Pa., 7 July, 1868, Frank, *s.* Frank and Jennie (Moss) Muldoon (*b.* Little Wheeling Creek, W. Va.,

---

* Fam. Rec. and pers. know. 197.
† Mallman's Shelter Island; Grave at Patchogue, N. Y.
‡ Will of Elias Parshall, p. 40.

The following is an account of the manner in which Lewis Parshall and his brother Daniel met their death:

"MELANCHOLY OCCURRENCE.—Rarely, indeed, has it been our painful duty to record a more melancholy occurrence than one which recently took place in that part of Brooklin called Fire Place. On the evening of Friday, the 5th instant, eleven men, belonging to that village, went to the South Shore with a seine for fishing, viz: William Rose, Isaac Woodruff, Lewis Parshall, Benjamin Brown, Nehemiah Hand, James Horner, Charles Ellison, James Prior, Daniel Parshall, Harry Horner and John Hulse. On Saturday morning the affecting discovery was made that they were all drowned. It is supposed the whole party embarked in one boat, and went out to the outer bar, a distance of two miles from the shore, and which at low water is in some places bare, but that by some accident the boat was stove or sunk, and the whole party left to perish by the rising of the tide, which, at high water, is eight or ten feet on the bar. The boat came on shore in pieces, and also eight bodies. The six first named have left families. Long will a whole neighborhood lament this overwhelming affliction, and the tears of the widow and orphan flow for their husband, father and friend."*

FAMILY XXVIII.

JAMES† [73], (*James*[4] *David*[3] *David*[2] *James*[1]) *b.* 30 Nov., 1780; *d.* Clarksville, Otsego Co., N. Y., 15 Apl., 1850; *m.* 14 Feby., 1803, Lucy (Shove) Nichols[a] (*b.* 8 Sept., 1780; *d.* 5 Apl., 1852). (All *b.* Ricetown, Otsego Co., N. Y.)

Children: (All *b.* Ricetown, Otsego Co., N. Y.)

201 i. Clark D.[6] *b.* 12 Sept., 1804. FAM. LXXX.

9 Apl. 1843; *d.* Triadelphia, W. Va., 9 Aug. 1878). *Issue: i.* John D.[8] (Muldoon) *b.* 21 Oct. 1871; *ii.* Mary Gertrude[8] (Muldoon) *b.* 21 Feby. 1874; *iii.* Frank Hunter[8] (Muldoon) *b.* 21 Feby. 1874; *iv.* George Frazier[8] (Muldoon) *b.* 24 July, 1878. *m.* (2) — Nov. 1879, Prof. John C., *s.* David and Nancy (———) Frazier. *Issue: v.* Daisy Carothers[8] (Frazier) *b.* 12 Nov. 1880; *vi.* Jennie McClurkin[8] (Frazier) *b.* 8 Feby. 1883.*

a. Lucy (Shove) Nichols was the *wid.* of John Nichols, whom she *m.* 1 Jany. 1800. They had one child—a son—John Hugh Kelse Nichols, *b.* 8 June, 1801; *d.* 1 Aug. 1827, unm.†

---

* Long Island Star, 17 Nov. 1813.
† Bible Rec. 73, pos. Mrs. Helen M. Comstock.

202 II. Miner Cornwall[6] *b.* 15 Aug., 1806. FAM. LXXXI.

203 III. Daniel Shove[6] *b.* 12 Jany., 1809. FAM. LXXXII.

204 IV. Dorothy[6]* *b.* 12 Jany., 1809; *d.* Middlefield, N. Y., 19 Apl., 1849; *m.* 19 Dec., 1827, Robert C., *s.* of John and Margaret (O'Brien) Crandall (*b.* 3 Aug., 1803; *d.* ———). *Issue:*

i. Mary Ann[7] (Crandall) *b.* Westford, N. Y., 25 Nov., 1828.[a]
ii. Levi[7] (Crandall) *b.* 23 Apl., 1830.[b]
iii. Horace[7] (Crandall) *b.* 6 June, 1834.
iv. James[7] (Crandall) *b.* 27 Nov., 1836; *d.* — Oct., 1899.
v. George[7] (Crandall) *b.* 10 Dec., 1839.
vi. Irene[7] (Crandall) *b.* 5 May, 1842.[c]
vii. Curtis[7] (Crandall) *b.* 11 Oct., 1849.

205 V. Anson Cornwall[6] *b.* 1 Aug., 1811. FAM. LXXXIII.

a. Mary Ann Crandall, *m.* Westford, Otsego Co., N. Y., 11 July, 1849, James, *s.* Cornelius and Margaret (———) Lane (*b.* Milford, Otsego Co., 19 Nov. 1825). *Issue:* *i.* Fred M.[8] (Lane) *b.* 3 Nov. 1851; *m.* Milford, 26 May, 1875, Belle Elizabeth Jane, *dau.* Walton and Harriet (Luther) Stickney; *ii.* Revilo Parshall[8] (Lane) b. Westford, 12 Mch. 1859; *m.* Cooperstown, N. Y., 15 Oct. 1891, Julia Evaline, *dau.* Oliver R. and Mary (Jewett) Butler.†

b. Levi Crandall, *m.* 16 Dec. 1857, Elizabeth, *dau.* William and Sally A. (Rich) Marks (*d.* 1 Jany. 1903). *Issue:* *i.* Fred[8] *b.* 27 Dec. 1865; *m.* Hartwick, Otsego Co., N. Y., 20 Sept. 1893, Belle Wrigley; *ii.* Grace[8] *b.* 31 Mch. 1874; *m.* 19 July, 1893, Charles M. McLean.†

c. Irene Crandall, *m.* Plymouth, N. Y., 21 Dec. 1856, Lewis, *s.* Dudley and Anna (Church) Tallett (*b.* Otselic, N. Y., 23 Sept. 1837). *Issue:* (All *b.* Otselic, N. Y.), *i.* Jennie Dolly[8] (Tallett) *b.* 28 Sept. 18—; *m.* ——— Billings. *Issue:* *i. Moshier[9] (Billings)*; *ii. Walter[9] (Billings)*, *m.* (2) Norwich, N. Y., 5 Feby. 1898, Walter W., *s.* Norman and Sarah (Wheeler) Felt (*b.* Earlville, N. Y., 23 Jany., 1857); *ii.* Effie Anna[8] (Tallett) *b.* 7 Feby. 1868; *m.* Middlefield, N. Y., 31 Dec. 1885, Benjamin Gilbert, *s.* Mortimer Brown and Lucy S. (North) Hicks (*b.* Middlefield 14 Sept., 1857). *Issue:* *i. Claudine Mildred[9] (Hicks)*; *ii. Kenneth Bernard[9] (Hicks)*; *iii. Lewis Benjamin[9] (Hicks)*.†

* Fam. Rec. and pers. know. Levi Crandall, and Mrs. Mary A. Lane.
† Pers. statement.

206 VI. Elizabeth[6]* *b.* Middlefield, N. Y., 3 Sept., 1813; *d.* Middlefield, 19 Feby., 1854; *m.* 28 Mch., 1833, Edward Knapp. *Issue:*

i. Elbert (Knapp) *d. s. p.* and *unm.*

207 VII. Lucy Shove[6]† *b.* Middlefield, 15 Sept., 1815; *d.* Middlefield, 20 Oct., 1888; *m.* Middlefield, 26 Jany., 1840, Jacob, *s.* of Jacob and Margaret (Wickham) VanHuzen (*b.* Middlefield, 16 Oct., 1815). *Issue:*

i. James Parshall[7] (VanHuzen) *b.* 19 June, 1841.[a]
ii. Helen Parshall[7] (VanHuzen) *b.* 8 Oct., 1843; *d.* 24 Mch., 1844.

208 VIII. Alfred Ford[6] *b.* 19 Apl., 1817. FAM. LXXXIV.
209 IX. James Nichols[6] *b.* 3 July, 1819. FAM. LXXXV.
210 X. Deborah Clark[6] *b.* 3 July, 1819; *d.* 7 Aug., 1819.
211 XI. Revilo Ford[6] *b.* 30 Aug., 1822. FAM. LXXXVI.

FAMILY XXIX.‡

ISRAEL[5] [74], (*James[4] David[3] David[2] James[1]*) *b.* 14 Sept., 1783; *d.* Cherry Valley, N. Y., 24 June, 1848; *m.* Deborah, *dau.* of John and Rhoda (Hull) Thompson (*b.* Cherry Valley, 31 Mch., 1790; *d.* Cherry Valley, 6 Nov., 1847).

[*Cherry Valley, N. Y.*

a. James Parshall Van Huzen *m.* Middlefield, 10 June, 1862, Cornelia D., *dau.* J. Nelson and Lucy A. (Rich) Marks (*b.* Cherry Valley, N. Y., 27 Sept., 1844). *Issue:* (All *b.* Middlefield, N. Y.) *i.* Ella E.[8] *b.* 7 Apl., 1863; *m.* Athens, Pa., 29 Dec., 1880, Erastus Chandler *s.* James J. and

* Fam. Rec. and pers. know. Mrs. Mary Ann Lane.
† Fam. Rec. and pers. know. James P. Van Huzen.
‡ Fam. Rec. and pers. know. Jerome C. Dutcher.

Children: (All *b.* Cherry Valley, N. Y.)

212 I. Jesse[6] *b.* 22 Dec., 1807. FAM. LXXXVII.

213 II. Deborah Clark[6]† *b.* 6 June, 1809; *d.* Havana, N. Y., 4 Sept., 1884; *m.* Cherry Valley, 16 Feby., 1832, Philo, *s.* of Ruloff and Eleanor (Reno) Dutcher (*b.* Cherry Valley, 16 Sept., 1805; *d.* Cooperstown, N. Y., 16 Nov., 1848). *Issue:*

i. Israel Parshall[7] (Dutcher) *b.* 12 Nov., 1832; *d.* 6 Dec., 1849.

ii. Mary Ann[7] (Dutcher) *b.* Cherry Valley, N. Y., 19 Nov., 1836.[a] [*Montour Falls, N. Y.*

iii. James Hetherington[7] (Dutcher) *b.* 12 Mch., 1838; *d.* 8 June, 1864.

iv. Jerome Clark[7] (Dutcher) *b.* Cherry Valley, N. Y., 28 Sept., 1841.[b] [*Montour Falls, N. Y.*

214 III. Mary[6] *b.* 3 Sept., 1813; *d. s. p.* and *unm,* Cherry Valley, 23 May, 1849.

215 IV. James[6] *b.* 19 Dec., 1815. FAM. LXXXVIII.

Lavantia (Brown) Allen (*b.* Cooperstown, N. Y., 22 May, 1856). *Issue:* *i. Majorie Collins*[9] *(Allen) b. 20 Nov., 1897;* *ii.* William Nelson[8] *b.* Dec., 1864; *d.* Middlefield, 4 Sept., 1886, *unm.; iii.* Edwin Marks[8] *b.* 10 Nov., 1867; *d.* Middlefield, 23 Aug., 1869; *iv.* Carrie Marks[8] *b.* 2 Apl., 1871.*

a. Mary Ann Dutcher *m.* Cooperstown, N. Y., 18 May, 1857, Alonzo G. *s.* Lyman and Hannah (Irish) Ball. *Issue: i.* Charles Benjamin[8] (Ball) *b.* Cedar Falls, Ia., 8 July, 1858; *m.* Havana, N. Y., 15 June, 1886, Cora V., *dau.* Jesse and Abigail (Roberts) Stoddard. *Issue: i. Hattie B.*[9]; *ii. Velma*[9]*; iii. Lyman S.*[9]; *ii.* Hattie Emma[8] (Ball) *b.* Cooperstown, 3 Dec., 1860; *m.* Havana, 13 Jany., 1881, Albert Clark *s.* George and Catherine (Shewman) Frost (*b.* Millport, N. Y., 29 July, 1854). *Issue: i. Kate B.*[9] *(Frost); ii. Mary G.*[9] *(Frost); iii. Bernice*[9] *(Frost) iv. Clara L.*[9] *(Frost).*†

b. Jerome Clark Dutcher *m.* Havana, N. Y., 7 July, 1868, Mariette, *dau.* Hiram and Jane (Thompson) Lewis (*b.* Havana, 7 Jany., 1848) *Issue: i.* Mary Ella[9] *b.* Havana, 21 May, 1871; *m.* Corning, N. Y., 4 Mch., 1896, Wilford Mills *s.* Charles C. and Phebe J. (Reynolds) Goodell (*b.* New York, 6 Sept., 1868). *Issue: i. Ruth D.*[9] (Goodell); *ii. Helen C.*[9] *(Goodell).**

---

* Personal statement.
† Fam. Rec. and pers. know. Jerome C. Dutcher.

216 v. Rhoda[6] *m.* William Fitzgerald. *No Issue:*

217 vi. Clarissa Harlow[6]* *b.* 16 July, 1820; *d.* Washington, D. C., 31 Oct., 1893; *m.* Cherry Valley, 12 Dec., 1844, Delos, *s.* of Allen and Susanna (Cleveland) Granger (*b.* Lawrence, Schuyler Co., N. Y., 2 June, 1822; *d.* Eau Clair, Wis., 8 Aug., 1894). *Issue:*

i. Israel Parshall[7] (Granger) *b.* 29 Apl., 1846.
ii. Mary[7] (Granger) *b.* 25 July, 1847.[c] [*Eau Clair, Wis.*
iii. Delos[7] (Granger) *b.* 18 July, 1849. [*Ferndale, Cal.*
iv. William Edward[7] (Granger) *b.* 26 Jany., 1851. [*Eau Clair, Wis.*
v. Ora[7] (Granger) *b.* 8 June, 1856. [*Eau Clair, Wis.*
vi. Thydora[7] (Granger) *b.* 21 July, 1857.
vii. Charles[7] (Granger) *b.* 21 Dec., 1858. [*Dunnville, Wis.*
viii. Clorinda[7] (Granger) *b.* 2 Aug., 1861.
ix. Clarissa[7] (Granger) *b.*

FAMILY XXX.‡

MINER[5] [75], (*James*[4] *David*[3] *David*[2] *James*[1]) *b.* Long Island, 10 Apl., 1787; *d.* Pierstown, N. Y., 1 May, 1845§; *m.*

c. Mary Granger *m.* Chippewa Falls, Wis., 22 June, 1878, N. De L. *s.* N. P. and Charlotte (Dibble) Turner (*b.* Meredith, Dela. Co., N. Y., 24 Jany., 1848). *No issue.*†

* Cleveland Gen. 1542; Granger Gen. 260; pers. know. Mrs. Mary G. Turner.
† Personal statement.
‡ Fam. Rec. pos. the Author.

13 June, 1815, Speedy, *dau.* of Abel[a] and Elizabeth (Loomis) Clark (*b.* Pierstown, 22 Jany., 1791; *d.* 13 Mch., 1850)‡

Children: (All *b.* Pierstown, Otsego Co., N. Y.)

218 I. James Clark^6 *b.* 13 Apl., 1816; *d. s. p. unm.*, 19 June, 1842.
219 II. John Abel^6 *b.* 25 Sept., 1818. FAM. LXXXIX.
220 III. Robert Asahel^6 *b.* 14 July, 1820. FAM. XC.
221 IV. William^6 *b.* 15 May, 1822; *d.* 18 Aug., 1823.
222 V. William^6 *b.* 7 Nov., 1823. FAM. XCI.
223 VI. Ambrose Clark^6 *b.* 28 Apl., 1827; *d.* 19 Dec., 1845.
224 VII. Elizabeth H.^{6} *b.* 18 Aug., 1829; *d.* 25 June, 1835.
225 VIII. Abel Clark^6 *b.* 12 Sept., 1834; *d.* Syracuse, N. Y., 13 Feby., 1872; *m.* Syracuse, N. Y., 17 Oct., 1861, Kate Adele, *dau.* Austin Brooks and Catherine (Kimberly) Webber (*b.* Vernon, N. Y., 22 May, 1836; *d.* Syracuse, N. Y., 13 Nov., 1874).† *No issue.*

[*Syracuse, N. Y.*

a. Abel Clark was *b.* 24 Nov., 1765, *s.* Jared *b.* 1729, *s.* Nathaniel *b.* 1693, *s.* Daniel *b.* 1654, *s.* Hon. Daniel Clark, of Windsor, Conn. *b.* 1622; *d.* 1712. He was a tanner, currier and shoe maker by trade. Soon after attaining his majority and a little capital he removed from Connecticut to Cooperstown, bought a piece of land in Pierstown and built a tannery, shop and log house, then returning to Connecticut, he married his wife and started for Cooperstown the next day on horseback, with his wife and all his household effects on a pannier behind. Speedy was the first child, born in the log cabin which is still standing. The other children were Sherman, *b.* 10 Nov., 1792; *d.* 30 Mch., 1857; *m.* — Sept., 1825, Eliza Peck, of Conn.; Daniel Abel *b.* 21 Jany., 1794; *d.* 21 Feby., 1815; Erastus *b.* 2 Mch., 1795; *d.* 20 Oct., 1828, *unm.*; Eliza *b.* 22 Aug., 1797; *d.* 10 Dec., 1870; *m.* — Mch., 1828, Richard White; Betsey *b.* 18 Aug., 1802; *d.* 10 Jany., 1819; Huldah *b.* 20 Sept., 1804; *d.* 26 Mch., 1853; *m.* 28 Feby., 1822, Ira A. Thurber (*d.* 22 Aug., 1882); Marcia M., *b.* 8 Mch., 1807; *d.* 23 Oct., 1861; *m.* Tilly Littlejohn; Joseph L. *b.* 24 Apl., 1809; *d.* — Mch., 1900; *m.* 24 Oct., 1836, Mary E. Thorn, of New York, (*b.* — Oct., 1812; *d.* 25 May, 1895); George *b.* 13 Aug., 1811; *d.* 18 Jany., 1825; Daniel Abel (2) *b.* 31 Aug., 1815; *d. s. p.* 16 June, 1840; *m.* 28 July, 1839, Henrietta Harvey. Betsey Loomis, wife of Abel Clark, was *b.* Goshen, Conn., 1772; *d.* Pierstown, 5 Feby., 1853.*

---

* Fam. Rec. and pers. know. Jos. L. Clark.

† The data relative to Kate Adele Webber is from Fam. Rec. pos. Miss Fannie C. Moses of Detroit, her niece.

‡ Grave at Cooperstown, N. Y.

*FAMILY XXXI.**

GEORGE[5] [77], (*James[4] David[3] David[2] James[1]*) *b.* Middlefield, Otsego Co., N. Y., 3 Mch., 1798; *d.* Middlefield, 29 Dec., 1869; *m.* Middlefield, 9 Dec., 1824, Fanny, *dau.* of Daniel and Elizabeth (Springstead) Cummings (*b.* Middlefield, 29 June, 1804; *d.* Middlefield, 7 Aug., 1882).

Children: (All *b.* Middlefield, Otsego Co., N. Y.)

226 I. DeWitt Clinton[6] *b.* 12 Dec., 1825; *d.* Middlefield, 5 Dec., 1854; *m.* 28 May, 1854, Clarinda, *dau.* of Benjamin and Catherine (Shields) Pitts. *No issue.*

227 II. Peter[6] *b.* 24 Nov., 1827. FAM. XCII.

228 III. Levi[6] *b.* 23 June, 1830; *m.* 27 Mch., 1859, Catherine P. Hopkins.[a]

229 IV. Daniel[6] *b.* 24 Apl., 1833. FAM. XCIII.

230 V. George Washington[6] *b.* 4 Apl., 1837. FAM. XCIV.

231 VI. Frances Elizabeth[6] *b.* 5 Mch., 1842; *d.* 31 July, 1844.

232 VII. Charlotte Rexeville[6]† *b.* 27 Sept., 1844; *m.* Middlefield, 17 May, 1865, Aaron D., *s.* of Fahron and Harriet (North) Coffin (*b.* Middlefield, 26 Oct., 1844). *Issue:* (All *b.* Middlefield, N. Y.)

i. Luella[7] (Coffin) *b.* 17 Dec., 1867.[a]
ii. Gilbert[7] (Coffin) *b.* 29 Mch., 1869.[b]

a. Luella Coffin *m.* Oneonta, N. Y., 26 Oct., 1892, Rufus John *s.* John L. and Elizabeth (Wickoff) Torrey (*b.* Bowerstown, N. Y., 29 Dec., 1867). *Issue:* (all born at Oneonta, N. Y.) *i.* Travilla Harriet8 (Torrey) *b.* 5 Sept., 1894; *ii.* Dewey Rufus8 (Torrey) *b.* 21 July, 1898.†

b. Gilbert Coffin *m.* Buffalo, N. Y., 27 Nov., 1897, Belle, *dau.* Alonzo and Avis (Fitch) Cummings (*b.* Geneva, O., 3 Sept., 1877). *Issue:* i. Gladda Harriet8 *b.* Austinburg, O., 27 June, 1899.†

* Fam. Rec. and pers. know., 230.
† Pers. statement.

iii. George Parshall[7] (Coffin) *b.* 17 Mch., 1878.*

233 VIII. Dorothy Ann[6]† *b.* 13 Apl., 1849; *m.* Middlefield, 5 May, 1869, Frederick Augustus, *s.* of Barnabas Manning and Elizabeth (Pitts) Gilbert (*b.* 25 Apl., 1848). *Issue:*

i. Percy Parshall[7] (Gilbert) *b.* 20 Oct., 1873; *d.* Oneonta, 30 June, 1891, *unm.*

George Parshall received a common school education and passed his life as a farmer. He was a man of great reserve and of mental attainments, unusual to his walk in life. In social and political life he took no part, though he was a consistent Whig and later a Republican. (*See portrait*).

FAMILY. XXXII.†

GILBERT[5] [78], (*James*[4] *David*[3] *David*[2] *James*[1]) *b.* Middlefield, Otsego Co., N. Y., 3 Mch., 1800; *d.* Middlefield, 26 Sept., 1889; *m.* Middlefield, 30 Jany., 1828, Abbie, *dau.* of Paul and Anna (Todd) Coffin (*b.* Chatham, Columbia Co., N. Y., 8 Apl., 1805; *d.* Middlefield, 4 Jany., 1883).

Children: (All *b.* Middlefield, Otsego Co., N. Y.)

234 I. Farrand Coffin[6] *b.* 12 Dec., 1828. FAM. XCV.

235 II. James Giles[6] *b.* 7 Feby., 1830. FAM. XCVI.

236 III. Adriel[6] *b.* 13 Sept., 1831. FAM. XCVII.

237 IV. Anna Ophelia[6] *b.* 8 May, 1833; *m.* Middlefield, 31 Aug., 1853, John H. Conrad (*b.* Middlefield, 30 July, 1828). *No issue:*

a. George Parshall Coffin *m.* Oakfield, N. Y., Maude, *dau.* James and Lizzie (————) Murray (*b.* Bergen, N. Y., 24 Mch., 1881).*

---

* Personal statement.
† Fam. Rec. and pers. know., 237.

GEORGE PARSHALL

238 v. Albert Orlando[6] *b.* 17 Apl., 1835. FAM. XCVIII.
239 vi. Alphonso G.[6] (Capt.) *b.* 5 Mch., 1840; *d.* Dec., 1864.[1] *unm.*
240 vii. Henry Clay[6] *b.* 19 Aug., 1844. FAM. XCIX.

---

*FAMILY XXXIII.**

DAVID[5] [79], *(James[4], David[3], David[2], James[1])* *b.* Middlefield, Otsego Co., N. Y., 29 Nov. 1803; *d.* Danby, Tompkins Co., N. Y., 12 Apl. 1876; *m.* Middlefield, 27 Oct. 1825, Lucinda, *dau.* of Levi and Elizabeth (Whiteker) Granger (*b.* Middlefield, 29 June 1804; *d.* Danby, 21 Sept. 1891).
[*Danby, Tompkins Co., N. Y.*

Children:

241 i. Elizabeth Lavanche[6] *b.* 5 Aug. 1826; *m.* Danby, 26 Nov. 1845, Ayers D., *s.* of David and Elizabeth (Ayers) Cortright (*b.* Danby, — Nov. 1820. *Issue:* (All *b.* Danby, N. Y.)

i. Elbert[7] (Cortright) *b.* 19 May, 1848; *d.* abt. 1900. [*Swartwood, N. Y.*
ii. David[7] (Cortright) *b.* 17 Dec. 1853; *unm.* [*Halsey Valley, Tioga Co., N. Y.*

242 ii. Mary Eliza[6] *b.* 19 May, 1828; *d.* Danby, 9 Apl. 1863; *m.* Danby, 16 Feby. 1848, Leroy S.,[a] *s.* of Rev.

a. Capt. Leroy S. Hewitt was a type of the Christian gentleman. At his Country's call he went to the front and laid down his life upon the altar of his Country. He seems to have had a premonition of his fate for when leaving home he sang:
"Earthly home, ado, ado. Earthly friends, farewell to you."
They proved to be his last words to his family, for with the closing line:
"Friends and loved ones, weep no more; meet me on the other shore."
He left them. They never saw him again.

* Fam. Recs. compiled by Mary E. Mettler.

Thomas and Dorcas (Winney) Hewitt (*b.* 8 Feby. 1824; killed at Savage Sta., Va., 8 July, 1862). *Issue:*

i. Ida[7] (Hewitt) *b.* 17 Mch. 1853; *d.* 7 Dec. 1853.

243 III. Dorothy[6] *b.* 24 July, 1830; *m.* Danby, N. Y., 5 June, 1851, John J., *s.* of Jonathan and Sarah (Masterson) Mettler (*b.* Danby, 23 Sept. 1827; *d.* Danby, 22 Nov. 1900). *Issue:*

i. Charles Franklin[7] (Mettler) *b.* 28 Nov. 1853. [*Danby, N. Y.*

ii. Lucinda[7] (Mettler) *b.* 6 Feby. 1856. *Unm.* [*Danby, N. Y.*

iii. James Leroy[7] (Mettler) *b.* 25 Sept. 1858. [*Elmira, N. Y.*

iv. Addie[7] (Mettler) *b.* 26 July, 1863. [*Spencer, N. Y.*

v. Carrie[7] (Mettler) *b.* 4 Jany. 1868 [*West Danby, N. Y.*

vi. Mary E.[7] (Mettler) *b.* 30 June, 1876. *Unm.* [*Danby, N. Y.*

244 IV. Elbert C.[6] *b.* 22 Feby. 1833; *d.* 18 Mch. 1838.

245 V. Gilbert[6] *b.* 30 Aug. 1835. FAM. C.

246 VI. Elephas[6] *b.* 15 Mch. 1839. FAM. CI.

247 VII. Olivia Theresa[6] *b.* Danby, N. Y., 3 Aug. 1841; *d.* Halsey Valley, N. Y., 2 Feby. 1872; *m.* Ithaca, N. Y., 10 July, 1863, Frank, *s.* of Townsend and Sarah (Shepherd) Mabee. *Issue:*

i. Mary[7] (Mabee) *b.* 17 Apl. 1866.

ii. Jesse[7] (Mabee) *b.* 5 Apl., 1869; *d.* Mch., 1884.

David Parshall removed about 1830 to Danby, N. Y., but soon returned to Middlefield. A few years later, however, he returned with his family and settled upon the farm now owned by his son, Gilbert. The country at this time was a primeval wilderness; neighbors were few and far between. The comforts, and even the necessaries of life, were only to be had at great expense and by hard labor. For some time after his arrival at Danby the family lived in a log cabin, which was destroyed by fire some years ago. With infinite labor he cleared his farm, brought up his family and lived to see the wilderness transformed into a garden; to see the drudgery of farming become a pleasure by the invention of labor-saving machinery; the mowing machine, the reaper and binder take the place of the scythe and cradle. A kind and affectionate husband and an indulgent father, he did not allow his life to be all work, but was ever ready for a frolic with his children. His wife was a woman of saintly disposition who won the love and esteem of all whose privilege it was to know her.

---

*FAMILY XXXIV.**

ELIAS[5] [87], *(John[4], David[3], David[2], James[1]) b.* Newburg, N. Y., 1 Feby. 1794; *d.* 4 Sept. 1870; *m.* Polly, *dau.* Isaac and Elizabeth (———) Green† (*d.* 23 Aug. 1833, in the 34th year of her age).†

Children:

249 I. Stephen Tillson[6] *d.* 13 Apl. 1841, age 21 yrs.

m. (2) Mary, *dau.* of James Campbell, of Cherry Valley, prob. at that place.‡

---

* Bible Rec. 38 pos. Mrs. Rosamond Barry, and pers. know., 251 and 252.
† Grave at Middlefield Center, N. Y.
‡ Pers. know. 251 and 252.

Children:

250 II. Mary[6]* *b.* Cooperstown, N. Y., 1 Apl. 1836; *m.* Cooperstown, 8 Mch. 1869, James *s.* John and Mary (Saunders) Cummings (*b.* Fly Creek, Otsego Co., N. Y., 5 Apl. 1818; *d.* Milford, N. Y., 14 Mch. 1891). *Issue:* [*Capitan, N. M. Ter.*

i. Arthur (Cummings).

251 III. James Everette[6] *b.* 2 Aug. 1839. FAM. CIII.

252 IV. Anna[6]* *b.* Middlefield, N. Y., 20 Feby. 1844; *m.* Cooperstown, 12 May, 1853, Donn, *s.* of Borand and Anna (Yates) Van Vechten (*b.* *n.* Fonda, N. Y., 1827; *d.* Johnstown, N. Y., 20 Jany. 1886). *No issue.*

253 V. Henry E.[6] *b.* 26 Nov. 1850. FAM. CIV.

FAMILY XXXV.

DAVID JEFFERSON[6]† [91], *(John,[4] David,[3] David,[2] James[1]) b.* Middlefield Center, Otsego Co., N. Y., 10 Feby., 1803; *d.* Lake Geneva, Wis., 5 Nov. 1843; *m.* Middlefield Center, Sarah Rightor (*b.* 5 June, 1803; *d.* Lake Geneva, Wis., 11 Dec. 1880). [*Lake Geneva, Wis.*

Children:

254 I. Agnes[6]‡*b.* Middlefield, N. Y., 23 Feby. 1827; *d.* Ovid, N. Y., 28 Nov. 1875; *m.* Lake Geneva, Wis., Joseph, *s.* of John and Cynthia (Kinne) Dunlap (*b.* Pultney, Steuben Co., N. Y., 3 Feby. 1823). *Issue:* [*Ovid, N. Y.*

---

* Personal statement.
† Bible Rec. 91 pos. 659.
‡ Fam. Rec. and pers. know., Joseph Dunlap.

i. Adella[7] (Dunlap) *b.* 8 Apl. 1846; *d.* 10 Dec. 1898.
ii. Emma[7] (Dunlap) *b.* 21 Dec. 1847.
iii. Harriet A.[7] (Dunlap) *b.* 31 Dec. 1849; *d.* 26 July, 1875.
iv. Hulbert[7] (Dunlap) *b.* 3 Oct. 1851.
v. Frank[7] (Dunlap) *b.* 1 June, 1854; *d.* 20 Oct. 1876.
vi. Charles[7] (Dunlap) *b.* 22 Dec. 1857.
vii. George[7] (Dunlap) *b.* 3 Sept. 1860; *d.* 10 Oct. 1863.
viii. Jennie[7] (Dunlap) *b.* 12 Aug. 1863; *d.* 1 Mch. 1877.

255 II. John[6] *b.* 24 May, 1829. FAM. CV.

256 III. Phebe Ann[6]* *b.* prob. Middlefield, N. Y., 14 May, 1831; *d.* Peoria, Ill., 3 Apl. 1852; *m.* Geneva, Wis., 20 June, 1849, Harriman, *s.* of Benjamin and Nancy (Morse) Couch (*b.* West Boscomen, Merrimack Co., N. H., 20 May, 1825). *Issue:*

[*Peoria, Ill.*

i. A child, *d. inf.*

257 IV. Harriet Amelia[6]† *b.* prob. Middlefield, N. Y., 4 May, 1832; *d.* New Lisbon, Wis., 4 Mch. 1875; *m.* Lake Geneva. Wis., 29 Oct. 1849, Henry, *s.* of Edward and Harriet (Gardner) Macomber (*b.* Clearfield, Pa., 12 July, 1827; *d.* New Lisbon, Wis., 11 May, 1898). *Issue:*

i. Annie Belle[7] (Macomber) *b.* 27 July, 1852.[a]

[*New Lisbon, Wis.*

a. Anna Belle Macomber *m.* New Lisbon, Wis., 17 Nov., 1875, Richard Francis *s.* Richard Francis and Ann Elizabeth (Dibb) Champney (*b.* Holderness, Eng., 1 Apl., 1851). *Issue:* i. Joseph Henry[8] (Champney) *b.* 31

* Fam. Rec. and pers. know. Harriman Couch.
† Fam. Rec. and pers. know., Mrs. Anna Belle Champney.

ii. Martha Jane[7] (Macomber) *b.* 31 Mch. 1851; *d.* 3 May, 1852.
iii. Edward Clarence[7] (Macomber) *b.* 30 Apl. 1857; *d.* 10 Jany. 1883.
iv. William Deforest[7] (Macomber) *b.* 8 Mch. 1859; *d.* 16 Oct. 1900.
v. Burton Henry[7] (Macomber) *b.* 11 Sept. 1872.

FAMILY XXXVI.†

JAMES[5] [92], *(Jonathan[4], Jonathan[3], David[2], James[1]) b.* Long Island, 26 Sept. 1762; *d.* Palmyra, N. Y., 24 Mch. 1826; *m.* Little Britain, Orange Co., N. Y., Elizabeth Todd.

Children:

258 I. John[6] *b.* 15 Aug. 1789. FAM. CVI.
259 II. Joseph[6] *b.* 8 May, 1791. FAM. CVII.
260 III. Rebecca[6] *m.* ——— Hicks. *No issue.*
261 IV. Lydia[6] *m.* ——— Gibbs. *Issue:* Two sons.

FAMILY XXXVII.‡

NATHAN[5] [93], *(Jonathan[4], Jonathan[3], David[2], James[1]) b.* 24 June, 1766; *d.* Palmyra, N. Y., 12 Jany. 1836; *m.* 19 Oct. 1806, Mary Ann, *dau.* of James Galloway (*b.* 19 Oct. 1788; *d.* Palmyra, 18 June, 1852).

Aug., 1876; ii. Harriet Elizabeth8 (Champney) *b.* 18 Oct., 1878; iii. Richard Edward8 (Champney) *b.* 27 Nov., 1881; iv. Mary Elizabeth8 (Champney(*b.* 29 Oct., 1885; v. Ruth Myrle8 (Champney) *b.* 20 Aug., 1889; vi. Glen Allen8 (Champney) *b.* 19 Nov., 1892.*

---

* Personal statement.
† Fam. Rec. and pers. know., James J. Parshall.
‡ Bible Rec. in pos. Geo. H. Parshall; Fam. Recs. and pers. know. Lisette Parshall.

Children:

262 i. Elizabeth[6] *b.* Palmyra, N. Y., 5 Feby. 1808; *d.* Lyons, N. Y., 26 Jany. 1873; *m.* Lyons, 8 Jany. 1828, Cullen Foster. *Issue:* [*Lyons, N. Y.*

i. Graham Parshall[7] (Foster) *b.* 28 Feby. 1829.[a]

ii. Mary Elizabeth[7] (Foster) *b.* 11 Apl. 1831.[b] [*Lyons, N. Y.*

iii. Augusta Adele[7] (Foster) *b.* 30 June, 1833.[c] [*Binghamton, N. Y.*

iv. De Witt Parshall[7] (Foster) *b.* 10 Oct. 1837.[d] [*Lyons, N. Y.*

v. William Cullen[7] (Foster) *b.* 24 Nov. 1839. [*Binghamton, N. Y.*

vi. Cassius Barton[7] (Foster) *b.* 5 Jany. 1845; *d.* 16 Mch. 1892. *Unm.*

vii. Marianna Woodward[7] (Foster) *b.* 23 Mch., 1850.[e]

a. Graham Parshall Foster *d.* San Francisco, Cal., 3 Apl., 1876; *m.* New Bedford, Mass., 19 June, 1854, Mary Jane, *dau.* Patrick and Priscilla (Benson) Fitzgerald (*b.* New Bedford, Mass., 21 Nov., 1829). *Issue:* i. William Henry[8] *b.* New Bedford. 23 Mch., 1855; *m.* St. Helena, Cal., 19 May, 1886, Lizzie Kennedy Poulson; ii. George Graham[8] *b.* Sodus, N. Y., 2 Oct., 1867; *m.* San Jose. Cal., 26 Mch., 1893, Martha Lenora Newman; iii. Hendee[8] *b.* Sodus, N. Y., 21 Nov., 1869; *d.* San Francisco, Cal.,—Mch., 1877.*

b. Mary Elizabeth Foster *m.* Lyons, N. Y., 7 Dec., 1858, Levi *s.* William Bashford (*b.* Cold Spring, N. Y., 27 Jany., 1813; *d.* Los Angeles, Cal., 22 Mch., 1899). *No issue.*†

c. Augusta Adele Foster *m.* Lyons, N. Y., 26 May, 1853, William Henry *s.* Samuel and Susan (Stafford) Hecox (*b.* Skaneateles, N. Y., 10 Aug., 1815; *d.* Binghamton, N. Y., 17 Jany., 1891). *Issue:* i. Elizabeth Augusta[8] (Hecox); ii. Louise[8] (Hecox); iii. William Henry[8] (Hecox).†

d. DeWitt Parshall Foster *d.* Lyons, N. Y., 14 Dec., 1891; *m.* Lyons, 25 Oct., 1871, Albertine, *dau.* Ira and Martha (Lamb) Mirick (*b.* Lyons, 15 July, 1845). *Issue:* i. Cullen Mirick[8] *d. inf.*; ii. Isabelle Mirick[8]; iii. DeWitt Parshall[8]; iv. Albert[8]; v. Frederick Elton[8]; vi. Alexander.[8]†

e. Marianna Woodward Foster *m.* Lyons, 22 Jany., 1874, Frederick Phelps *s.* Daniel Ebenezer and Harriet Jones (Denis) Browne (*b.* Joliet, Ill., 12 Oct., 1847).†

---

* Fam. Rec. and pers. know., Mrs. G. P. Foster.
† Pers. statement.

263 II. Maria[6] *b.* 22 June, 1810; *d.* 13 July, 1815.
264 III. DeWitt[6] *b.* 25 Mch. 1812. FAM. CVIII.
265 IV. Hendee[6] *b.* 8 Dec. 1814. FAM. CIX.
266 V. Oren[6] *b.* 24 Jany. 1817; *d.* 17 Sept. 1826.
267 VI. Schuyler[6] *b.* 27 July, 1819. FAM. CX.

FAMILY XXXVIII.

MOSES[5] [95], *(Jonathan[4], Jonathan[3], David[2], James[1]) b.* Little Britain, Orange Co., N. Y., 16 Nov. 1777;* *d.* Little Britain, 25 Apl. 1818;* *m.* Ruth Miller.†

Children.†

268 I. Jemima[6] *m.* Dr. Drury. *Issue:*

i. Darwin[7] (Drury).

FAMILY XXXIX.‡

JESSE[5] [96], *(Jonathan[4], Jonathan[3], David[2], James[1]) b.* Orange Co., N. Y., 18 July, 1780;* *d.* Geneva, N. Y., 27 Oct. 1844;§ *m.* Nancy Bowers, prob. Orange Co. (*b.* 13 June, 1786; *d.* 23 Oct. 1865).‡ [*Seneca Castle, N. Y.*

Children:

269 I. Ezra K.[6] *d.* 29 Mch. 1888. FAM. CXI.
270 II. John B.[6] *b.* 28 Oct. 1808. FAM. CXII.
271 III. Charles Humphrey, *b.* 2 Mch. 1814. FAM. CXIII.

---

* Bible Rec. 39, pos. 687.
† Ruttenber & Clark's Hist. Orange Co., (N. Y.)
‡ Fam. Rec. and pers. know., 275.
§ XXXVI. N. E. Hist. and Gen. Reg., 200.

272 IV. Eliza^{6} prob. *d. inf.*
273 V. Susan^{6} prob. *d. inf.*
274 VI. Marjorie Bowers^{6} *d.* Hopewell, N. Y.; *m.* Christopher Price. *Issue:*

i. John^{7} (Price) *d.* 16 Feby. 1875.[a]

275 VII. Mary Jane^{6} *b.* New Windsor Tp., Orange Co., N. Y., 16 Sept. 1826. *Unm.* [*Palmyra, N. Y.*

FAMILY XL.†

DAVID^{5} [97], *(David^{4}, Jonathan^{3}, David^{2}, James^{1}) b.* Little Britain, Orange Co., N. Y., 13 Mch. 1784; *d.* Walden, Orange Co., N. Y., 10 May, 1832; *m.* Walden, N. Y., 11 Feby. 1806, Christiana, *dau.* James Kidd[b] (*b.* 21 July, 1784; *d.* Walden, N. Y., 9 July, 1851). [*Walden, Orange Co., N. Y.*

Children: (All *b.* Little Britain, Orange Co., N. Y.)

276 I. Milton^{6} *b.* 1 Dec. 1806; *d.* 15 Sept. 1815.
277 II. Elizabeth Kidd^{6} *b.* 1 Apl. 1809; *d.* Little Britain, 24 Sept. 1839; *m.* Walden, N. Y., 3 Jany. 1833, Andrew, *s.* of William and Christine (Clark) Whigam. *Issue:*

a. John Price *m.* 3 Nov., 1854, Julia, *dau.* Ebenezer and Mary (Minner) Carr (*b.* Slab City, Niagara Co., N. Y., 3 Dec., 1839). *Issue:* i. John Manly^{8} *b.* Hopewell, N. Y., 7 Aug., 1855; *m.* Manchester, N. Y., 21 Sept., 1875, Mary Adelaide, *dau.* Alfred and Mary Ann (Lowe) Smith (*b.* Manchester, N. Y., 4 Dec., 1857). *No issue;* ii. Mary Lamb^{8}; iii. Charles Martin^{8}; iv. Julia Alice.^{8}*

b. James Kidd was a miller and invented the bolting of buckwheat flour. He drove a supply wagon from Walden, Orange Co., N. Y., then known only as "The Falls," to Washington's Army in New Jersey. His father came from Ireland and settled in Orange County.

---

* Fam. Rec. and pers. know., John Manly Price.
† Fam. Rec. and pers. know., 277, 279 and 282.

i. David Parshall[7] (Whigam) *b.* 20 Dec. 1832.[a]
ii. Ann Elizabeth[7] (Whigam) *b.* 7 Feby. 1836.[b]
iii. George[6] (Whigam) *d. inf.*

278 III. James Kidd[6] *b.* 7 Mch., 1812; *d.* 27 June, 1812.
279 IV. James Milton[6] *b.* 11 Apl., 1813. FAM. CXIV.
280 V. Caleb[6] *b.* 24 Nov., 1815. FAM. CXV.
281 VI. Catherine Ann[6]* *b.* 26 June, 1817; *d.* ——— 1902; *m.* Walden, N. Y., 1 Sept., 1838, William, *s.* of Elisha and Mary (Topping) Raynor (*b.* Morriches, Suffolk County, N. Y., 5 Jany., 1807; *d.* Jacksonville, Ills., 27 Nov., 1890). *Issue:* (All *b.* Bellport, Suffolk Co., N. Y.). [*Jacksonville, Ills.*

i. Mary Elizabeth[7] (Raynor) *b.* 23 Sept., 1839.[c] [*Jacksonville, Ills.*
ii. William Edgar[7] (Raynor) *b.* 1 Oct., 1841.[d] [*St. Louis, Mo.*
iii. David Parshall[7] (Raynor) *d. s. p.* 23 Jany., 1848.

a. David Parshall Whigam *d.* East Coldenham, N. Y., 23 Oct., 1868; *m.* Coldenham, N. Y., 16 Jany., 1862. Mary King, *dau.* John and Mary (King) Crowell (*b.* Coldenham, 18 June, 1839). *No issue.* His widow *m.* William Howell, East Coldenham, N. Y.*

b. Ann Elizabeth Whigam *m.* Lemuel Lewis, *s.* Moses Jordan and Nancy (Mays) White (*b.* Franklin City, Pa., 5 Oct., 1838). *No issue.**

c. Mary Elizabeth Raynor *m.* Pleasant Plains, Ills., 26 Nov., 1863, Eliphalet Smith *s.* Trueworthy S. and Rachel Moor (Taylor) Gordon (*b.* New Hampton, N. H.. 10 Sept., 1831; *d.* Denvel, Col., 19 Oct., 1880). *Issue:* i. Clara Raynor8 (Gordon) *b.* Springfield, Ill., 6 Mch., 1866; *m.* Jacksonville, Ill.. 10 Apl., 1889, Martial Henry *s.* Martial Henry and Martinette (Rawlings) Havenhill (*b.* Ottawa, Ill., 4 Dec., 1863). *Issue: i. Lillian9 (Havenhill) b. Jacksonville, Ill., 26 Jany., 1890.*†

d. William Edgar Raynor *m.* St. Louis, Mo., 24 Aug., 1865, Rosalie Elizabeth, *dau.* Howard and Jane Matilda (Hurlburt) Chamberlin (*b.* Pittsfield, Mass.. 16 Oct., 1845). *Issue:* i. William Eugene8 *b.* St. Louis, Mo., 15 July, 1866; ii. Emma8 *b.* St. Louis, Mo., 18 Jany., 1870; iii. Howard Charles8 *b.* Eatontown, N. J., 22 July, 1875.*

* Fam. Recs. Compiled by E. N. Raynor.
† Fam. Recs. and pers. know. Mrs. M. H. Havenhill.

iv. Eugene Nicoll[7] (Raynor) *b.* 15 Oct., 1847.[a]
[*Champaign, Ills.*

282 VII. Fanny Bethia[6]* *b.* 16 Aug., 1821; *d.* Tallula, Ills., 13 Mch., 1899; *m.* Walden, N. Y., 17 May, 1853, Rev. Samuel Brittia, *s.* of Moses and Mary Ayers (*b.* 13 Aug., 1811; *d.* Tallula, Ills., 15 Dec., 1887). *Issue:*

i. Moses Depue[7] (Ayers) *b.* 4 July, 1854.[b]
[*Alice, Tex.*

ii. William Edgar[7] (Ayers) *b.* 9 Dec., 1855.[c]
[*Chicago, Ills.*

iii. Sarah Hunt Roy[7] (Ayers) *b.* 1 Oct., 1857.[d]
[*Chicago, Ills.*

iv. Gilbert Parshall[7] (Ayers) *b.* 21 Jany., 1859.[e]
[*Tallula, Ills.*

v. Charles Elting[7] (Ayers) *b.* 2 Feby., 1861; *d.* 22 Mch., 1861.

a. Eugene Nicoll Raynor *m.* Jacksonville, Ill., 10 Dec., 1873, Florence, *dau.* Augustus E. and Annie Elizabeth (Diller) Ayers (*b.* Jacksonville, Ill., 3 Jany., 1853). *Issue:* i. Clara Mae[8] *b.* Jacksonville, Ill., 6 Sept., 1874; *m.* Champaign, Ill., 1 Jany., 1896, Earnest Thomas *s.* Henry Washington and Henrietta Maria (Earnest) Rickard (*b. n.* Springfield, Ill., 13 Oct., 1872); ii. Annie.[8]†

b. Moses Depue Ayers *m.* Smiley, Gonzales Co., Tex., 15 June, 1881, Alice Maude Mary, *dau.* William and Elizabeth (Lane) Carpenter (*b.* Cambridge, Eng., 24 June, 1861). *Issue:* i. Sadie Pennie[8] *b.* 8 Apl., 1882; ii. Frankie Alice[8] *b.* 9 Dec., 1883; iii. Alberta Lee[8] *b.* 19 Nov., 1885; *d.* 20 May, 1887; iv. Samuel Roy Depue[8] *b.* 14 Aug., 1887; *d.* 31 July, 1897; v. Howard Eugene[8] *b.* 18 Sept., 1890; vi. Bessie Isabelle[8] *b.* 21 Mch., 1893; vii. Florence Bethia[8] *b.* 7 Jany., 1898.*

c. William Edgar Ayers *m.* 14 Jany., 1886, Mattie, *dau.* George McClong and Hannah Emily (Corson) Hand (*b.* Menard Co., Ill., 1 Sept., 1862). *Issue:* i. A son[8] *b.* and *d.* 8 Feby., 1887; ii. Stella Parshall[8] *b.* Menard Co., Ill., 11 Nov., 1888; iii. Alice Electa[8] *b.* Chicago, 21 May, 1891.*

d. Sarah Hunt Roy Ayers *m.* 2 Feby., 1888, Joshua Stevenson.*

e. Gilbert Parshall Ayers *m.* Refugio, Tex., 6 Dec., 1882, Penelope A., *dau.* Thomas C. and Mary C. (Busby) Heard (*b.* Refugio, Tex., 27 Jany., 1861; *d.* Refugio, 14 Feby., 1884). *No Issue.* *m.* 2d Petersburg, Ill., 15 Oct., 1895, Myra B., *dau.* Watson and Isabella (Grove) Sinclair (*b. n.* Ashland, Ill., 23 Apl., 1868). *Issue:* i. Arthur G.[8] *b.* Tallula, Ill., 10 May, 1898.

---

* Fam. Recs. compiled by E. N. Raynor.
† Pers. statement.

vi. Bayard Eugene[7] (Ayers) *b.* 11 Mch., 1868.[a]
[*Chicago, Ills.*

283 VIII. Sarah[6]* *b.* 21 Apl. 1823; *d.* Denver, Col., — Nov., 1890; *m.* 19 Sept., 1848, Augustus Brown Goodale (*b.* Greenpoint, L. I., N. Y., 25 Feby, 1826). *Issue:*
[*Port Jervis, N. Y.*

i. Augustus Bayard[7] (Goodale) *b.* 29 July, 1850.[b]
[*Port Jervis, N. Y.*

ii. Charles Elbert[7] (Goodale) *b.* 6 Mch., 1853.[c]

iii. Sarah[7] (Goodale) *b.* 6 Jany., 1857.[d]
[*Denver, Col.*

iv. Elizabeth (Goodale) *d. inf.*

284 IX. David Bayard[6] *b.* 11 Aug., 1826. FAM. CXVI.

a. Bayard Eugene Ayers *m.* Chicago, 20 Nov., 1896, Florence, *dau.* Samuel and Esther Sarah (Hilton) Croft (*b.* Liverpool, Eng., 27 July, 1867). *Issue:* i. Alfred Hilton8 *b.* Chicago, 1 May, 1898; ii. Mildred Bernice8 *b.* 31 Oct., 1901.*

b. Augustus Bayard Goodale *m.* Port Jervis, N. Y., 3 Dec., 1875, Alice Bennet. *Issue:* i. Edna Bayard.8*

c. Charles Elbert Goodale *m.* Bessie Cross. *Issue:* Augustus.8*

d. Sarah Goodale *m.* Port Jervis, N. Y., Frank Skinner.*

* Fam. Recs. compiled by E. N. Raynor.

The Sixth Generation.

*FAMILY XLI.**

JAMES[6] [100], *(Samuel[5], James[4], Israel[3], Israel[2], James[1])* *b.* prob. Long Island, 6 June, 1779; *d.* Milton, O.; *m.* prob. Springfield, O., Margaret, *dau.* Jacob Baht (*d.* abt. 1850). [*Milton, O.*

Children:

285 I. Sarah[7] *b.* 19 Mch., 1802; *m.* Daniel Van Etten.

286 II. Elizabeth[7] *b.* 29 July, 1803; *m.* Robert Porter.

287 III. Samuel[7] *b.* 15 Apl., 1805. FAM. CXVII.

288 IV. Jacob[7] *b.* 20 June, 1806. FAM. CXVIII.

289 V. James[7] *b.* 5 Dec., 1810; *m.* Hannah Foos; *d. s. p.*

290 VI. Hezekiah[7] *b.* 8 Apl., 1812; *m.* Maria Shaeffer.

291 VII. Margaret[7]† *b.* Petersburg, O., 18 Aug., 1816; *m.* Milton, O., 29 Jany., 1841, John, *s.* John and Dorothy (Clihonts) Hartzell (*b.* Lancaster Co., Pa., 25 Oct., 1792; *d.* Deerfield, O., 1 Sept., 1873). *Issue:* (All *b.* Deerfield, O.) [*North Benton, O.*

i. Annie[8] (Hartzell) *b.* 29 Oct., 1841.[a]

a. Annie Hartzell, *m.* Deerfield, O., 9 May, 1861, Jared Miller, *s.* Adam and Mary (Davis) McGowan (*b.* Smithtown, O., 29 Mch., 1835; *d.* Deerfield, 18 Dec., 1875). *Issue:* i. Lila Ada[9] (McGowan) *b.* 4 Apl., 1862; ii. Margaret[9] (McGowan) *b.* 11 July, 1864; iii. Mary A.[9] (McGowan) *b.* 6 Sept., 1866; iv. John Hartzell[9] (McGowan) *b.* 15 July, 1869; v. Gertrude Anise[9] (McGowan) *b.* 9 Nov., 1872; vi. Bertha Alice[9] (McGowan) *b.* 9 Nov., 1872.

---

* P. and Van E. Fams.; Fam. Rec. pos. 291.
† Pers. statement.

ii. Mary[8] (Hartzell) *b.* 22 Jany., 1843.[a]

292 VIII. Susannah[7] *b.* 15 Mch., 1818; *m.* Joseph Porter.
293 IX. Isaac[7] *b.* 16 Dec., 1819. FAM. CXIX.
294 X. Nancy[7] *b.* 15 Nov., 1820; *m.* David Crays.
295 XI. Rachel[7] *b.* 14 May, 1821; *m.* Aaron Porter. (?)
296 XII. John[7] *b.* 12 June, 1823; *d. s. p.*
297 XIII. Clinton[7] *b.* 4 Jany., 1825; *m.* Katharine Kale.

---

*FAMILY XLII.**

SAMUEL[6] [101], *(Samuel[5], James[4], Israel[3], Israel[2], James[1])* *b.* prob. Long Island, 6 July, 1781; *d.* Tidioute, Pa., 1840; *m.* Poland, Ohio, Elizabeth, *dau.* of Henry Goucher (*b.* Poland, O., 20 Mch., 1783; *d.* Tidioute, Pa., 9 Mch., 1866).
[*Tidioute, Warren Co., Pa.*

Children:

298 I. Henry[7] *b.* 1 Feby., 1807; *d. unm.*
299 II. John Munnell[7] *b.* 23 Feby., 1809. FAM. CXX.
300 III. Rhoda Ann[7] *b.* 22 Jany., 1811; *d.* Tidioute, Pa.; *m.* James, *s.* of Arthur Magill (*b. n.* Sayerstown, Pa., 1804; *d.* Tidioute, Pa., 3 Mch., 1891). *Issue:*
[*Tidioute, Pa.*

i. William Joshua[8] (Magill) *b.* 29 Dec., 1828.
ii. Elizabeth[8] (Magill) *b.* 13 Sept., 1833.
iii. James Luther[8] (Magill) *b.* 5 Aug., 1841.
iv. Gibreath Irvin[8] (Magill) *b.* 1 Dec., 1849.
v. Richard[8] (Magill) *b.* 1853; *d. s. p.*

a. Mary Hartzel, *m.* Deerfield, O., 25 Sept., 1871, Marcus, *s.* Thompson and Anna (Curtis) Bosworth (*b.* Braceville, O., 1 Feby., 1839). *Issue:* i. Delmer Willis[9] (Bosworth) *b.* 14 Aug., 1872; ii. John Thompson[9] (Bosworth) *b.* 10 June, 1875.†

---

* P. and Van E. Fams.; Fam. Rec. pos. Mrs. Esther A. Smith, Oberlin, O.
† Pers. know., 291.

301 iv. Elizabeth[7]* *b.* 12 Dec., 1812; *d.* Tidioute, Pa., 17 Jany., 1887; *m.* Deerfield, Pa., 14 June, 1832, Robert Harrison Henry (*b.* Erie Co., Pa., 31 July, 1805; *d.* Tidioute, Pa., 13 Jany., 1864). *Issue:* [*Tidioute, Pa.*

i. Elizabeth Jane[8] (Henry) *b.* 18 May, 1838.
ii. Livingston Grandin[8] (Henry) *b.* 29 Oct., 1844.

302 v. Samuel[7] *b.* Trumbull Co., O., 14 Nov., 1814. FAM. CXXI.

303 vi. Nancy[7]* *b.* Niles, O., 13 Nov., 1817; *d.* Williamstown, W. Va., 28 Feby., 1899; *m.* Tidioute, Pa., 12 June, 1837, Joseph, *s.* Joshua and Polly (McIntyre) Richardson (*b.* Frysburg, Me., 29 June, 1812; *d.* Oberlin, O., 9 Feby., 1884). *Issue:* [*Tidioute, Pa.*

i. Esther Ann[8] (Richardson) *b.* 5 May, 1838.[a] [*Oberlin, O.*
ii. Elizabeth Parshall[8] (Richardson) *b.* 5 Sept., 1840; *m.* — Jany., 1862, C. A. Dier.
iii. Sarah[8] (Richardson) *b.* 9 Sept., 1843; *d.* 1852.
iv. John Parshall[8] (Richardson) *b.* 18 Oct., 1845; *d.* 1851.
v. Charles Snow[8] (Richardson) *b.* 11 Aug., 1848.
vi. Nancy Jane[8] (Richardson) *b.* 10 Mch., 1851; *m.* — July, 1871, M. C. Carnahan.

304 vii. George Stranahan[7] *b.* 14 Jany., 1820. FAM. CXXII.

a. Esther Ann Richardson *m.* Warren, Pa., 22 Feby., 1855, Milton *s.* Solomon and Ann (Avery) Smith (*b.* Hartsgrove, Asht. Co., O., 30 July, 1830). *Issue:* i. Oren Joseph[9] (Smith); ii. Livingston Edward[9] (Smith); iii. Nellie Esther[9] (Smith); iv. Ulellah Nancy[9] (Smith); v. Marion Darius[9] (Smith).†

---

* P. and Van B. Fams.; Fam. Recs. and pers. know. Esther A. Smith; Richardson Mem. 179.
† Pers. statement.

305 VIII. Jeanette Stratton[7]* *b.* Tidioute, Pa., 22 Feby., 1822; *m.* Tidioute, Pa., — Dec., 1843, James, *s.* William and Rebecca (McIlvain) Kinnear (*b.* Juniata Co., Pa., 22 Jany., 1814). *Issue:* [*Tidioute, Pa.*

i. Charlotte Priscilla[8] (Kinnear) *b.* 7 Oct., 1844; *m.* David S. Thompson.

ii. Josephine[8] (Kinnear) *b.* 13 July, 1846; *m.* Marshall P. Getchell.

iii. James Marion[8] (Kinnear) *b.* 16 Aug., 1848; *d.* 11 July, 1849.

iv. William Filmore[8] (Kinnear) *b.* 27 July, 1850; *d.* 25 Oct., 1860.

v. James Wesley[8] (Kinnear) *b.* 2 Aug., 1859.

306 IX. James[7] *b.* 19 Sept., 1827. FAM. CXXIII.

FAMILY XLIII.†

JOHN[6] [104], *(Samuel[5], James[4], Israel[3], Israel[2], James[1]) b.* 24 June, 1791; *m.* Susan Everhart.

[*Ellsworth, Mahoning Co., O.*

Children:

307 I. Jacob Cook[7] *b.* 16 Dec. 1812. FAM. CXXIV.

308 II. A *dau.* who *m.* and had *issue,* but of whom all trace is lost.

---

* Pers. statement.

† P. and Van S. Fams.; Fam. Recs. pos. Rev. Heman F. Parshall.

*FAMILY XLIV.**

WILLIAM[6] [105], *(Samuel[5], James[4], Israel[3], Israel[2], James[1])* *b.* 15 Nov., 1794; *d.* Leesburg, Pa., 18 Sept., 1851; *m.* Jane McMurry (*d.* Leesburg, Pa., 15 Aug., 1869).

Children:

309 I. Joseph[7] *b.* 17 Aug., 1821. FAM. CXXV.
310 II. Samuel[7] *b.* 27 Oct., 1824. FAM. CXXVI.
311 III. James Alexander[7] *b.* 11 Dec., 1827. FAM. CXXVII.
312 IV. Mary[7] *d.* Mich., 1874; *m.* Mercer Co., Pa., 1838, John Rudolph (*d.* California, 1892). *Issue:*

i. Samuel[8] (Rudolph) *d.*
ii. Hannah[8] (Rudolph) [*California.*
iii. John[8] A. (Rudolph)[a] [*Leesburg, Pa.*
iv. William[8] (Rudolph) *d.*

FAMILY XLV.†

DANIEL[6] [106], *(Samuel[5], James[4], Israel[3], Israel[2], James[1])* *b.* prob. Orange Co., N. Y., 9 June, 1796; *d.* Waverly, Ia., 7 May, 1870; *m.* (1) 4 Sept., 1818, Margaret VanEtten (*d.* 15 May, 1825).

a. John A. Rudolph *m.* Leesburg, Pa., 1868, Ruth Axtell. *Issue:* i. William Grant[9] *b.* 31 Jany., 1870; ii. Venus Myrtle[9] *b.* 12 Jany., 1872; iii. John Melville[9] *b.* 21 Nov., 1873; iv. Ira Sankey[9] *b.* 15 Sept., 1875; v. Earl Stanley[9] *b.* 14 Apl., 1884.

* P. and Van E. Fam.; Fam. Recs. and pers. know., Mrs. Wm. A. Munnel, Banbury Pa.
† P. and Van E. Fams., and Fam. Rec. and pers. know., 313.

Children: (All *b.* Milton, O.)

313 I. Lucinda[7]* *b.* 4 Oct., 1819; *m.* Youngstown, O., 4 Nov., 1841, John, *s.* Jesse and Susan (Everhart) Rose (*b.* Ellsworth, O., 24 Sept., 1819; *d.* winter of 1901-2). *Issue:* (All *b.* Oberlin, O.)
[*Oberlin, O.*

i. Euphratia[8] (Rose) *b.* 15 Aug., 1842; *d.* 12 Apl., 1851.
ii. Daniel Eugene[8] (Rose) *b.* 27 Oct., 1844. [*New York.*
iii. Ezra Norris[8] (Rose) *b.* 25 Jany., 1852.
iv. Olin[8] (Rose) *b.* 1 May, 1855. [*Oberlin, O.*

314 II. Annie[7]† *b.* 28 Apl., 1821; *d.* Salem, O., 24 Jany., 1882; *m.* Berlin, O., 1839, James, *s.* Joseph, Davis. *Issue:*

i. Ada L.[8] *b.* 17 Mch., 1840; *m.* ——— Buck.
ii. Florence E.[8] *b.* 20 Oct., 1852; *m.* ——— Ruth. [*Newcastle, Pa.*

315 III. Sarah[7]† *b.* 9 Mch., 1823; *d.* Milton, O., 14 Aug., 1845; *m.* Milton, 5 May, 1843, John Noland. *Issue:*

i. Mary Ann[8] (Noland) *b.* 23 Feby., 1844.[a]

a. Mary Ann Noland *d.* New Lyme, O., 1 Apl., 1867; *m.* Green, O., 23 Feby., 1861, Prentice *s.* Martin and Angelina (Smith) Kee (*b.* Green, O., 29 Oct., 1839). *Issue:* i. Martin Deforest[9] (Kee) *b.* Green, O., 10 Aug., 1862; *m.* Cortland, O., 16 Apl., 1892, May A., *dau.* George R. and Abbie (Owen) Wilber (*b.* Cortland, O., 22 May., 1867); ii. Mary De Etta[9] (Kee) *b.* Greensburg, O., 18 Oct., 1864; *m.* Jefferson, O., 8 Dec., 1891, Ralph *s.* Jabez and Helen (Rood) Dodge (*b.* Lenox, O., 3 Feby., 1863). *Issue: i. Florence May[10] (Dodge) b. 23 June, 1895;* iii. Angelina Jane[9] (Kee) *b.* New Lyme, O., 31 Mch., 1867; *d.* Oberlin, O., 4 Aug., 1872.‡

* Pers. statement.
† Pers. know. Florence E. Ruth.
‡ Fam. Fam. Rec. and pers. know., Martin DeF. Kee, Warren, O.

316 IV. Margaret[7]* *b.* 25 Apl., 1825; *d.* Southington, O., 8 Oct., 1899; *m.* Ellsworth, O., 4 Sept., 1849, John Diehl (*b.* Ellsworth, 21 Mch., 1820; *d.* Southington, 20 Jany., 1892). *Issue:** (All *b.* Southington, O.)

i. Ira[8] (Diehl) *b.* 22 June, 1851; *d.* 20 June, 1855.
ii. Lois A.[8] (Diehl) *b.* 8 Nov., 1853.[a]
iii. Homer[8] (Diehl) *b.* 16 Oct., 1856; *d.* 21 Jany., 1864.
iv. Ella[8] (Diehl) *b.* 23 Aug., 1859; *d.* 11 Feby., 1864.
v. Ammi E.[8] (Diehl) *b.* 25 Aug., 1861.[b]

m. (2)† 11 Jany., 1827, Jane Packard (*d.* 23 Sept., 1841).

Children:

317 V. Harriet Eleanor[7]‡ *b.* 13 June, 1829; *m.* Waverly, Ia., 11 Jany., 1870, William, *s.* John and Margaret (Tarr) Husband (*b.* Westmoreland Co., Pa., 12 Jany., 1827; *d.* Sumner, Ia., 11 Dec., 1886). *Issue:* [*Colebrook, Asht. Co., O.*

i. Ernest Willford[9] (Husband) *b.* 30 Mch., 1871; *d.* 14 Aug., 1871.

318 VI. Rachel Adaline[7]‡ *b.* 10 Sept., 1831; *m.* Gustavus, O., 18 Feby., 1855, Allison, *s.* Alanson and Angeline

a. Lois A. Diehl *m.* Southington, O., 22 Nov., 1900, Henry Burt *s.* John and Harriet (Ryan) Wortman (*b.* Independence, O., 27 Aug., 1846). *No issue.*‡

b. Ammi E. Diehl, *m.* Southington, O., 18 Apl., 1897, Mrs. Effie (Joy) West, *dau.* Orlin Brenson and Cornelia (Chather) Joy (*b.* Southington, 26 Nov., 1860). *No issue.**

* Fam. Rec. and pers. know., Lois A. Wortman.
† P. and Van E. Fams.
‡ Pers. statement.

(Veits) Taylor (*b.* Fowler, O., 4 Feby., 1832). *Issue:* (All *b.* Wayne Tp., Asht. Co., O.) [*Traverse City, Mich.*

i. Ernest Jay[8] (Taylor) *b.* 11 Oct., 1856.[a]
ii. Forrest Daniel[8] (Taylor) *b.* 15 June, 1859.[b]
iii. Adaline Alice[8] (Taylor) *b.* 30 Mch., 1862;[c] *d.* 24 Feby., 1888.

319 VII. Caroline Esther[7]* *b.* 5 May, 1833; *m.* Mecca, O., 2 Mch., 1856, Byron Ezra, *s.* Rev. Alba and Minerva (Rust) Sanford (*b.* Poultney, Vt., 29 June, 1831). *Issue:* [*Belleville, Kan.*

i. Clarence Parshall[8] (Sanford *b.* 12 Dec., 1857.[d] [*Belleville, Kan.*
ii. Alfred Gee[8] (Sanford) *b.* 11 Oct., 1859[e] [*Southwest City, Mo.*
iii. Charles Henry[8] (Sanford) *b.* 29 Jany., 1862.[f] [*Belleville, Kan.*

a. Earnest J. Taylor *m.* Garfield Tp., Grand Traverse Co., Mich., 16 Sept., 1885, Minnie B. Peart. *Issue:* (All *b.* East Bay Tp., G. T. Co., Mich.) *i.* Agnes Ray[9] (Taylor) *b.* 14 Oct., 1886; *ii.* Alice[9] (Taylor) *b.* 31 Mch., 1888; iii. Edgar B.[9] (Taylor) *b.* 11 Oct., 1898.†

b. Forest Daniel Taylor *m.* East Bay Tp., 27 Oct., 1887, Lillian E. Beach. *Issue:* (All *b.* East Bay Tp.) i. Allison A.[9] (Taylor) *b.* 21 Mch., 1889; ii. Grace[9] (Taylor) *b.* 26 Sept., 1890.†

c. Alice A. Taylor *m.* Wayne Tp., Asht. Co., O., 23 Mch., 18—, Edwin Black. *Issue:* i. John Taylor[9] (Black) *b.* 23 Feby., 1888.†

d. Clarence Parshall Sanford *m.* Graham Co., Kan., 4 Oct., 1886, Clara, *dau.* Rev. ——— Chapman. *Issue:* i. Mabel Pearl[9] *b.* 20 June, 1887; ii. Ethel Blanche[9] *b.* — Sept., 1888; iii. Harry Byron[9] *b.* 30 May, 1890; iv. Clara Lillian[9] *b.* 4 Oct., 1891; v. Alice Grace[9] *b.* — Aug., 1893.‡

e. Alfred Gee Sanford *m.* McDonald Co., Mo., — Aug., 1890, Rebecca Newkirk. *Issue:* *i.* Carrie Maude[9] *b.* — Aug., 1891; *ii.* Nellie Minerva[9] *b.* 8 Dec., 1893; iii. Ethel May[9] *b.* 1898.‡

f. Charles Henry Sanford *m.* — Feby., 1890, Matilda, *dau.* Rev. ——— Chapman. *Issue:* i. Charlotte May[9] *b.* 31 Dec., 1891; ii. Ernest C.[9] *b.* — Feby., 1895.‡

* Pers. statement.
† Pers. know. 318.
‡ Pers. know. 319; Henry Rust and his descendants, 217.

iv. Aloney James[8] (Sanford) *b.* 7 Aug., 1864.
v. Mary Avalene[8] (Sanford) *b.* 4 Nov., 1866.[a]
vi. William Earl[8] (Sanford) *b.* 21 July, 1871.
vii. Newton John[8] (Sanford) *b.* 18 Aug., 1874.[b] [*Belleville, Kan.*
viii. Byron Ezra[8] (Sanford) *b.* 6 Oct., 1876.
ix. Minerva Nancy[8] (Sanford) *b.* 10 May, 1879.

320 VIII. Alfred[7] *b.** 29 Nov., 1834; *m.* Green, Trumbull Co., O., 19 Feby., 1860, Anna, *dau.* Wanton and Clarissa (Underwood) Burlingame (*b.* Attica, N. Y., 2 Dec., 1836). *No issue:* [*Colebrook, Asht. Co., O.*

321 IX. Elisha Daniel[7] *b.* 25 Mch., 1837; *d.* 21 Sept., 1841.

m. (3) Milton, O., 4 Nov., 1840, Elizabeth, *dau.* Joseph Turner (*b.* Orange Co., N. Y., 10 Oct., 1806; *d.* Waverly, Ia., 26 Feby., 1866).

Children:

322 X. Eli Gee[7] *b.* 24 Jany., 1844. FAM. CXXVIII.

FAMILY XLVI.‡

THOMAS[6] [107], (*Samuel*[5] *James*[4] *Israel*[3] *Israel*[2] *James*[1]) *b.* 21 July, 1798; *d.* Shalersville, Port. Co., O., 14 Aug., 1878, *m.* (1) Elizabeth Furgeson. [*Shalersville, Portage Co., O.*

a. Newton John Sanford *m.* Alma, Kan., 22 Mch., 1900, May Anderson.†
———— Keith. *Issue:* i. Carrie May[9] (Keith) *b.* 11 Nov., 1887; ii. Charles Veen[9] (Keith) *b.* 16 Jany., 1891; iii. Glen[9] (Keith) *b.* 30 Jany., 1893; iv. Pansie[9] (Keith) *b.* 6 July, 1896.†

b. Mary Avalene Sanford *m.* 18 Nov., 1883, William Ernest *s.* Rev.

---

* Pers. statement.
‡ P. and Van E. Fams.; Fam. Recs. and pers. know., 718.
† Pers. know. 819.

Children: (All *b.* Shalersville, O.)

323 I. Frederick[7] *b.* 2 Apl., 1825. FAM. CXXIX.

324 II. Sophronia[7]* *b.* 24 Mch., 1830; *d.* Cleveland, O., 16 Nov., 1900; *m.* Freedom, O., 2 Nov., 1857, DeForest, *s.* John and Salome (Parsons) Wheelock (*b.* Freedom, O., 18 June, 1834). *Issue:*

i. Lillian[8] (Wheelock) *b.* 21 Apl., 1861.[a] [*Cleveland, O.*

ii. Clifton Day[8] (Wheelock) *b.* 27 Jany., 1863.

iii. Arden Lincoln[8] (Wheelock) *b.* 24 Mch., 1865.

iv. Clayton DeForest[8] (Wheelock) *b.* 20 Mch., 1868.

m. (2) Mrs. Polly (Bond) Holcomb,[b] *dau.* William and Angelica (————) Bond (*d.* Shalersville, O., 23 June, 1881, age 73 years).

Children:

325 III. Statira[7]† *b.* Shalersville, 1838; *d.* Jockson, Mich., 28 Jany., 1898; *m.* Detroit, Mich., 5 July, 1859, George Esbon,‡ *s.* John B, and Catherine (————) Wright (*b.* Sodus, N. Y., 1 Nov., 1840; *d.* Chelsea, Mich., 2 Feby., 1886). *Issue:* [*Jackson, Mich.*

i. Grace Leida[8] (Wright) *b.* 11 Apl., 1860.[c] [*Jackson, Mich.*

ii. John Thomas[8] (Wright) *b.* 23 Sept., 1861.[d]

a. For record of Lillian Wheelock, see Note *b*, FAM. CXXIX.

b. Polly (Bond) Holcomb, at the time of her marriage to Thomas Parshall, was a widow with two children, viz.: Richard and Harriet Holcomb.†

c. Grace Leida Wright *m.* Chelsea, Mich., 22 Dec., 1881, Charles Mortimer *s.* Ansel and Maria (Morrell) Norton (*b.* Leoni, Mich., 7 Sept., 1848).†

d. John Thomas Wright *m.* 27 Sept., 1884, Maggie Schrum.†

* Fam. Recs. and pers. know. Deforest Wheelock.
† Fam. Recs. and pers. know., Mrs. Grace L. Norton.
‡ Marriage Cert. pos. Grace L. Norton.

*FAMILY XLVII.**

DAVID[6] [108], (*Samuel*[5] *James*[4] *Israel*[3] *Israel*[2] *James*[1]) *b.* 17 Oct., 1800; *d.* 12 Feby., 1842; *m.* Ellsworth, O., Abigail, *dau.* of Nicholos and Nancy (Turner) Gee (*b.* 1805; *d.* Shelbyville, Mo., 11 July, 1860). [*Espyville, Pa.*

Children:

326 I. John Harmon[7] *b.* 1 Aug., 1824. FAM. CXXX.

327 II. Nicholas Morgan[7]† *b.* Berlin, O., 20 Apl., 1827; *d.* Kingsville, O., 29 Feby., 1896; *m.* Espyville, Pa., 9 Sept., 1851, Margaret McKee, (*b.* North Shenango, Pa., 11 Dec., 1825; *d.* North Shenango, Pa., 5 June, 1880). *No issue.*
m. (2) Kingsville, O., 26 Jany., 1881, Melvina A., *dau.* of Erastus and Candace (Fox) Peck (*b.* Kingsville, O., 12 June, 1842). *No issue:*

328 III. William Shreve[7] *b.* 3 Oct., 1832. FAM. CXXXI.

329 IV. Nancy Maria[7]‡ *b.* Berlin, O., 6 Dec., 1833; *m.* North Shenango, Pa., 4 Mch., 1852, *m.* (1) William, *s.* of John and Mary (McCrary) Smith (*b.* Berlin, O., 2 Dec., 1831; *d.* Williamsfield, Asht. Co., O., 5 Apl., 1865). *Issue:* [*Larned, Pawnee Co., Kan.*

i. Charles Herbert[8] (Smith) *b.* 27 Oct., 1856. *unm.* [*Larned, Kan.*

m. (2) Williamsfield, Asht. Co., O., 19 Dec., 1867, James Huntley (*b.* 10 Dec., 1825; *d.* Larned, Kan., 14 Apl., 1890.)

* P. and Van B. Fams.; Fam. Rec. and pers. know., 881.
† Fam. Rec. and pers. know., Wld., 327.
‡ Pers. state.

330 v. Lucy Ann[7]* *b.* Berlin, O., 3 Aug., 1838; *d.* Kingsville, O., 2 Mch., 1900; *m.* (1) Espyville, Pa., Marshall, *s.* Jacob and Maria (Hillman) Coursen (*b.* N. J., 17 Jany., 1833; *d.* Kingsville, O., 25 Aug., 1883).
Issue: [*Kingsville, Asht. Co., O.*

i. Abbie Maria[8] (Coursen).
ii. Alzada Justine[8] (Coursen) *b.* Espyville, Pa., 9 Oct., 1858.[a]
iii. Maria McCoy[8] (Coursen).

m. (2) Kingsville, O., Abraham McDowell.
No issue:

331 vi. David Furman[7] *b.* 13 Sept., 1841. FAM. CXXXII.

FAMILY XLVIII.‡

JACOB[6] [109], (*Samuel*[5] *James*[4] *Israel*[3] *Israel*[2] *James*[1]) *b.* probably Ellsworth, O., 15 Mch., 1803; *d.*
m. Elizabeth Van Etten.

Children:

332 i. Gideon[7] *b.* 11 June, 1826. FAM. CXXXIII.
333 ii. Myron[7].
Probably *daus.*

a. Alzada Justine Coursen, *m.* Kingsville, O., 20 Dec., 1877, Oliver, *s.* Rensselaer and Almira (————) Bugby (*b.* Kingsville, 8 July, 1855). *Issue:* i. Wilson Mason[9] (Bugby); ii. Morris Oliver[9] (Bugby); iii. Grace Abbie[9] (Bugby).†

---

* Fam. Rec. and pers. know., Mrs. Alzada Justine Bugby.
† Pers. statement.
‡ P. and Van E. Fams.; Fam. Rec. and pers. know., 333.

*FAMILY XLIX.**

MOSES[6] [111], *(Samuel James Israel Israel James) b.* Ellsworth, O., 10 Jany., 1810; *d.* Ravenna, O., 16 Aug., 1848; *m.* (1) Nancy McCoy.

Children:

334 I. Samuel N.[7] *unm.* [*Pierce, Neb.*

335 II. Mary J.[7] *m.* William Deniston. *Issue:*

i. Fremont[8] (Deniston). [*Oxford Junc, Ia.*

m. (2) Maria Waty, *dau.* Josiah and Sarah (Sherman) Remington, (*d.* Garrattsville, O., 18 June, 1901).

Children:

336 III. Orlina[7] *b.* Mercer, Pa., 12 Apl., 1847, John J., *s.* John Henry and Sarah (Pike) Campbell (*b.* Hale, Ia., 2 Apl., 1859). *No issue:*† [*Pierce, Neb.*

337 IV. Etta E.[7] *b.* Ravenna, O., 6 Sept., 1848; *m.* (1) Ravenna, O., 8 Jany., 18—, George, *s.* Frederick and Anna Maria (————) Hine (*b.* Charleston, O., 28 June, 1847). *Issue:* (All *b.* Charleston, O.)‡

i. Anna Maria[8] (Hine) *b.* 4 July, 1875.[a] [*Cleveland, O.*

a. Anna Maria Hine *m.* Cleveland, O., 25 June, 1896, Eri *s.* George Hawkins (*b.* Alpena, Mich., 1 Dec., 1874). *Issue: i.* Vivian May[9] (Hawkins); ii. Lillian Etta[9] (Hawkins); iii. Edward George[9] (Hawkins).‡

---

* P. and Van E. Fams. and pers. know., 337.
† Pers. statement.
‡ Pers. know., 337.

ii. Herbert Frederick[8] (Hine) *b.* 8 Feby., 1876.[a]
[*Charleston, O.*

m. (2) Cleveland, O., Frank Whitlock (*b.* 8 Jany., 1863). *No issue:*

---

*FAMILY L.**

ISRAEL[6] [112], (*Israel*[5] *Israel*[4] *Israel*[3] *Israel*[2] *James*[1]) *b.* 1782; *d.* Springwater, N. Y., 13 Jany., 1856; *m.* his cousin Deborah, *dau.* of David and Sarah (Cronover) Parshall (21 Apl., 1788; *d.* 29 Dec., 1876).

Children:

338 I. Nancy Ann[7]† *b.* 11 Nov., 1806; *d.* Geneseo, N. Y., about Apl., 1871; *m.* Comfort Carr, *s.* of Benjamin and Lois (Runnels) Greene (*d.* Plymouth, Wayne Co., Mich., 5 May, 1830). *Issue:* (All *b.* Little Valley, Catt. Co., N. Y.) [*Springwater, N. Y.*

i. Amanda Maria[8] (Greene) *b.* 29 May, 1825.[b]
[*Springwater, N. Y.*

a. Herbert Frederick Hine *m.* Edinburg, O., Emma Seraphina, *dau.* David B. and Mary Anne (McCobb) Shilliday.‡

b. Amanda Maria Greene, *m.* Cochocton, Steuben Co., N. Y., 25 Dec., 1847, James, *s.* Jacob and Philana (Phipp) Hunt (*b.* 21 Oct., 1822; *d.* Springwater, N. Y., 27 Nov., 1880). *Issue:* i. Nancy Philana[9] (Hunt) *b.* 15 Sept., 1851; ii. Unadilla Viola[9] (Hunt) *b.* 14 Jany., 1854; iii. Oravilla Adora[9] (Hunt) *b.* 6 Feby., 1857; *d.* 29 Apl., 1874; iv. Lafayette Montrose[9] (Hunt) *b.* 25 Mch., 1862; *d.* 20 Nov., 1874.†

---

* Fam. Recs. and pers. know., 342 and Mrs. Jane P. Paige.
† Fam. Rec. and pers. know., Charlotte J. Briggs.
‡ Pers. know. 897.

ii. Charlotte Jane^{8} (Greene) *b.* 9 Jany., 1828.[a] [*Fremont, Mich.*

iii. Silas Carr^{8} (Greene) *d.* 18 Nov., 1890.

339 II. Amy Matilda^{7}† *b.* Palmyra, N. Y., 8 Jany., 1811; *d.* Canandaigua, N. Y., 10 Aug., 1886; *m.* North Cohocton, N. Y., 20 Sept., 1827, David Peckens (*b.* 17 Mch., 1797; *d.* Springwater, N. Y., 1 Mch., 1859). *Issue:* [*Springwater, N. Y.*

i. Henry^{8} (Peckens) *b.* 3 June, 1830. [*Wayland, N. Y.*

ii. Lucy^{8} (Peckens) *b.* 30 Jany., 1832.[b] [*Canandaigua, N. Y.*

iii. Laura^{8} (Peckens) *b.* 5 Sept., 1833.[c]

iv. Warren^{8} (Peckens) *b.* 19 Sept., 1839. [*Wayland, N. Y.*

v. Levi^{8} (Peckens) *b.* 12 July, 1841.[d]

vi. Jane^{8} (Peckens) *b.* 18 June, 1845.[e] [*Wayland, N. Y.*

vii. Lewis^{8} (Peckens) *b.* 1 Aug., 1847; *d.* 1 Apl., 1871; *unm.*

a. Charlotte Jane Greene, *m.* Bloods Corners, Steuben Co., N. Y., 25 Dec., 1847, Willard Nelson *s.* Zebadiah Lambert and Betsy (Daggett) Briggs (*b.* Richmond, Ont. Co., N. Y., 11 Aug., 1828; *d.* Fremont, Mich., 8 Mch., 1900). *Issue:* i. Elva Adelle^{9} (Briggs); ii. Willard Riley^{9} (Briggs); iii. Richard Alsop Nelson^{9} (Briggs); iv. Arnold Gray^{9} (Briggs); v. Ella Eliza^{9} (Briggs); vi. Willard Warren^{9} (Briggs); vii. Ira Barzilla^{9} (Briggs); viii. Charles Walter^{9} (Briggs).*

b. Lucy Peckens, *d.* Canandaigua, N. Y., 30 May, 1872; *m.* Canandaigua, 17 Mch., 1859, John Boyd (*b.* Canandaigua, 28 Oct., 1823; *d.* Canandaigua, 4 Feby., 1868). *Issue:* i. Eleanor^{9} (Boyd); ii. Jennie^{9} (Boyd); iii. Harriet^{9} (Boyd); iv. John Henry^{9} (Boyd).†

c. Laura Peckens, *d.* Hopewell, N. Y., 20 Aug., 1854; *m.* Springwater, —— ———, 1848, John McFarlin.†

d. Levi Peckens, *d.* —— July, 1864; *m.* 1863, Julia E. Ranney.†

e. Jane Peckens, *m.* Springwater, 18 Oct., 1871, Cassius, *s.* Alonzo and Myra (Bennett) Paige (*b.* Jasper, Lenawee Co., Mich., 18 Oct., 1850). *No issue.**

* Pers. statement.
† Fam. Rec. and pers. know., Jane Peckens Paige.

340 III. Archibald Galloway[7] *b.* 14 June, 1815. FAM. CXXXIV.

341 IV. Levi Thayer[7] *b.* 5 Sept., 1817. FAM. CXXXV.

342 V. Amanda Malvina[7]* *b.* Springwater, N. Y., 22 Apl., 1820; *m.* Cohocton, N. Y., 17 Sept., 1835, Jesse, *s.* of Eli and Abigail (Brooks) Cole (*b.* Carbondale, Pa., 28 June, 1814; *d.* Woodhull, Shiawassee Co., Mich., 5 Jany., 1845). *Issue:*

[*Springwater, N. Y.*

i. Sylvanus Urial[8] (Cole).

[*Fitchburg, Ingham Co., Mich.*

ii. Clarinda Lurena[8] (Cole) *m.* ——— Briggs.

iii. Maria Jane[8] (Cole) *m.* ——— Nevins.

iv. Rachel Rebecca[8] (Cole) *m.* ——— Jones.

v. Martin Jerome[8] (Cole).

vi. Ransom Sylvester[8] (Cole).

vii. Allen Burnham[8] (Cole).

343 VI. Isaac Ransom.[7] FAM. CXXXVI.

FAMILY LI.†

TERRY[6] [113], (*Israel*[5] *Israel*[4] *Israel*[3] *Israel*[2] *James*[1]) *b.* Chemung Co., N. Y., 29 Jany., 1795; *d.* Woodhull, Shiawassee Co., Mich., 25 Jany., 1864; *m.* (1) Chemung Co., N. Y., 1 May, 1813, Lydia, *dau.* Benjamin and Keziah (Parshall) Hulse (*b.* Chemung Co., N. Y., 6 Mch., 1796; *d.* Woodhull, Mich., 28 Mch., 1845). [*Woodhull, Shiawassee Co., Mich.*

---

* Pers. statement.
† Fam. Recs. and pers. know., 356.

Children:

344 I. John^{7} *b.*
345 II. Diana^{7} *b.*
346 III. Harris^{7} *b.*
347 IV. William T.^{7} *b.*
348 V. Louisa^{7} *m.* ——— Wilmath. [*Lansing, Mich.*
349 VI. Deliverance^{7} *b.*
350 VII. Sophia^{7} *b.*
351 VIII. Mary^{7} *b.*
352 IX. Deborah^{7} *b.*
353 X. Abigail^{7} *b.*
354 XI. Ruth Elizabeth^{7} *m.* ——— Albertson.
[*Trufont, Montcalm Co., Mich.*
355 XII. John H.^{7} *b.* Springwater, N. Y., 18 Sept., 1835.
[*Big Prairie, Newaygo Co., Mich.*
356 XIII. Israel D.^{7} *b.* 24 Oct., 1836. FAM. CXXXVII.

m. (2) ——— ———. *No issue.*
m. (3) ——— ———. *No issue.*
m. (4) ——— ———.

Children:

357 XIV. Terry^{7} *b.*

---

*FAMILY LII.**

IRA^{6} [125], (*David^{5} Israel^{4} Israel^{3} Israel^{2} James^{1}*) *b.* Canandaigua, N. Y., 5 Aug., 1792; *d.* Potter, Yates Co., N. Y., 30 June, 1851; *m.* 6 Feby., 1814, Atta Bradford (*b.* 15 Jany., 1776; *d.* 22 Nov., 1867). [*Potter, Yates Co., N. Y.*

* Bible Rec., 125, and pers. know., 364

Children:

358 I. Polly M.[7] *b.* 14 Mch., 1815; *m.* 11 Mch., 1837.
359 II. Isaac Selector[7] *b.* 25 Aug., 1817; *d.* 25 Oct., 1817.
360 III. Jonathan H.[7] *b.* 1 Oct., 1818; *d.* 21 Sept., 1864.
361 IV. Daniel C.[7] *b.* 21 Oct., 1820.
362 V. A child[7] *b.* 17 June, 1822; *d. inf.*
363 VI. A child[7] *b.* 11 Oct., 1826; *d. inf.*
364 VII. George Bradford[7] *b.* 9 Sept., 1827. FAM. CXXXVIII.
365 VIII. Sarah C.[7] *b.* 17 Nov., 1830.
366 IX. Norman A.[7] *b.* 24 Sept., 1832; *d.* 29 Mch., 1903. [*Chesaning, Mich.*
367 X. Lyman S.[7] *b.* 7 Nov., 1836; *d.* 21 May, 1838.

---

*FAMILY LIII.**

ASA[6] [127], (*David*[5] *Israel*[4] *Israel*[3] *Israel*[2] *James*[1]) *b.* Horseheads, N. Y., 15 May, 1796; *d.* Springwater, N. Y., 15 Oct., 1851; *m.* Canandaigua, N. Y., 10 Nov., 1819, Aurilla, *dau.* of Moses and Molly (Dewey) Hull (*b.* Virshire, Vt., 15 July, 1801; *d.* Springwater, N. Y., 17 July, 1889). [*Springwater, N. Y.*

Children:

368 I. Harriet Almira[7] *b.* Potter, N. Y., 6 Nov., 1820; *d.* Springwater, N. Y., 8 June, 1896; *m.* Springwater, N. Y., 2 May, 1850, Amos Stiles, *s.* of Amos and Lorena (Hale) Root (*b.* Conesus, Liv. Co., N. Y., 16 Aug., 1822; *d.* Springwater, N. Y., 12 Oct., 1875). *Issue:* [*Springwater, N. Y.*

* Fam. Rec. pos., 372.

i. Mark Stiles[8] (Root) *b.* 15 Mch., 1859.[a]

369 II. Emily Miranda[7] *b.* Potter, N. Y., 3 June, 1822; *d.* Springwater, N. Y., 10 May, 1859; *unm.*

370 III. Moses Hull[7] *b.* 13 Feby., 1826. FAM. CXXXIX.

371 IV. Edwin Augustus[7] *b.* Springwater, N. Y., 24 Feby., 1833, *d.* Springwater, N. Y., 20 Jany., 1893; *unm.*

372 V. John Dewey[7]† *b.* Springwater, N. Y., 31 Jany., 1835; *m.* Dansville, N. Y., 3 May, 1900, Eliza Emily, *dau.* of John E. and Mariah (Theel) Lawrence (*b.* Sparta, Liv. Co., N. Y., 28 July, 1838). *No issue.*

---

*FAMILY LIV.**

DAVID[6] [128], (*David[5] Israel[4] Israel[3] Israel[2] James[1]*) *b.* 15 Apl., 1798; *d.* Springwater, N. Y., 20 Dec., 1874; *m.* Maria Boyd (*d.* Springwater, N. Y., 29 July, 1874).

[*Springwater, Liv. Co., N. Y.*

Children: (All *b.* Springwater, N. Y.)

373 I. Henry[7] *b.* 5 July, 1820. FAM. CXL.

374 II. Emma[7] *b.* 2 Aug., 1822; *d.* 2 Apl., 1867; *m.* 11 Sept., 1842, Nathan Robinson. *Issue:*

i. Alva[8] (Robinson). [*Auburn, N. Y.*

ii. Mary[8] (Robinson) *m.* ——— Peabody. [*North Cohocton, N. Y.*

iii. Frances[8] (Robinson) *m.* ——— Doughty.

iv. Agnes[8] (Robinson) *m.* ——— Colgrove. [*Canadice, N. Y.*

a. Mark Stiles Root *b.* Springwater, N. Y., 15 Mch., 1859; *d.* Sprigwater, 24 May, 1893; *m.* Greenwood, Steuben Co., N. Y., 27 Dec. 1882, Elizabeth Stark (*b.* 30 Aug., 1858; *d.* Springwater, 18 Mch., 1897). *Issue:* i. Nellie Elizabeth[9] (Root) *b.* 24 Sept., 1883; ii. Harriet Agnes[9] (Root) *b.* 3 June, 1887; iii. Frank Mark[9] (Root) *b.* 24 Jany., 1890.‡

---

* Fam. Recs. and pers. know., 373 and 834.
† Pers. statement.
‡ Pers. know., 372.

375 III. Hiram W.[7] *b.* 18 May, 1824. FAM. CXLI.
376 IV. Amasa Louis[7] *b.* 28 Apl., 1827. FAM. CXLII.
377 V. Jane[7] *b.* 28 Sept., 1833; *d.* 16 May, 18—.
378 VI. Edward[7] *b.* 28 Sept., 1833; *d.* 24 May, 1854; *unm.*
379 VII. Stephen[7] *b.* 28 Dec., 1835. FAM. CXLIII.

---

*FAMILY LV.**

AMZI[6] [136], (*Asa*[5] *Israel*[4] *Israel*[3] *Israel*[2] *James*[1]) *b.* Chemung, N. Y., 6 June, 1799; *d.* Eldred, Pa., 26 Nov., 1867; *m.* Chemung, N. Y., 16 Nov., 1826, Stella Westbrook (*b.* Chemung, N. Y., 15 Sept., 1805; *d.* 4 Feby., 1847).

Children:

380 I. Harriet[7] *b.* Portage, N. Y., 22 Jany., 1828; *d.* Belfast, N. Y., 1851; *m.* J. W. Eldridge. *Issue:*
i. A son *d. inf.*
381 II. Luke[7] *b.* Portage, N. Y., 2 Mch., 1829; *d.* Harwood Hospital, Washington, D. C., 16 Jany., 1865; *unm.*
382 III. Miles Farquhar[7] *b.* 11 Aug., 1830. FAM. CXLIV.
383 IV. Mark[7] *b.* 29 Mch., 1832; *d.* 21 July, 1833.
384 V. Lot[7] *b.* 15 Dec., 1833. FAM. CXLV.
385 VI. Jane[7]† *b.* Castile, N. Y., 28 Oct., 1836; *m.* 15 Dec., 1859, William Wallace Byrnes (*b.* Belfast, N. Y., 21 June, 1833). *Issue:* [*Belfast, N. Y.*
i. Eugene Alexander[8] (Byrnes).[a] [*Washington, D. C.*
ii. Clarence Parshall[8] (Byrnes) *b.* 16 Dec., 1866.[b]

a. Eugene Alexander Byrnes, *m.* Washington, D. C., 17 Nov. 1892, Alice Stier.‡

b. Clarence Parshall Byrnes, *m.* 6 Jany. 1900, Mary Melvin Barrett, of Pittsburgh, Pa.†

---

* Bible Rec., 136, pos., 385.
† Pers. statement.
‡ Pers. know., 385.

386 VII. Martha[7] *b.* 14 June, 1840; *d.* 16 Aug., 1840.

387 VIII. Olive[7] *b.* Castle, N. Y., 7 Jany., 1842.

388 IX. Arthur[7] *b.* Castile, N. Y., 19 Jany., 1844; killed at the Battle of Spottsylvania, 12 May, 1864.

---

*FAMILY LVI.**

THOMAS KEENEY[6] [140], (*Asa*[5] *Israel*[4] *Israel*[3] *Israel*[2] *James*[1]) *b.* Chemung, N. Y., 24 Mch., 1806; *d.* Oceola, Mich., 17 Nov., 1900; *m.* (1) Chemung, 16 Nov., 1826, Celestia, *dau.* Jeremiah and Elizabeth (Griswold) Cassada (*b.* about 1809; *d.* Oceola, Mich., 21 May, 1857). [*Oceola, Mich.*

Children:

389 I. Lesby Caroline[7] *b.* 16 Sept., 1827; *d.* 22 Aug., 1839.

390 II. Vincent[7] *b.* 16 Nov., 1829. FAM. CXLVI.

391 III. Chester[7] *b.* 27 June, 1832.

392 IV. Chauncey[7] *b.* FAM. CXLVII.

393 V. Sarah Jane[7] *b.* 30 Mch., 1838; *d.* 20 Sept., 1864; *unm.*

394 VI. Timothy Brown[7] *b.* 15 Oct., 1839. FAM. CXLVIII.

395 VII. Asa[7] *b.* 7 Feby., 1844. FAM. CIL.

396 VIII. Zachary Taylor[7] *b.* 25 Apl., 1847. FAM. CL.

397 IX. Mark[7] *b.* Oct., 1849; *d.* 25 Jany., 1851.

m. (2) Hartland, Liv., Co., Mich., 2 Dec., 1857, Clarissa (Waldron) Babcock, *dau.* John and Jenette (Monroe) Waldron (*b.* Syracuse, N. Y., 28 Sept., 1829).

---

* Fam. Recs. and pers. know., 396 and 398.

Children:

398 x. Susannah[7]* *b.* Oceola, Mich., 30 Aug., 1860; *m.* Saginaw, Mich., 3 Apl., 1881, Alen, *s.* Alfred and Lucinda (Shepherd) Ferguson (*b.* Oceola, 24 June, 1850). *Issue:*

i. Herbert[8] (Ferguson) *b.* Saginaw, 10 Feby., 1883.

ii. Clarissa Lucina[8] (Ferguson) *b.* Oceola, 27 June, 1887.

iii. Floyd Keeney[8] (Ferguson) *b.* Wise, Isabella Co., Mich., 2 Jany., 1889; *d.* Wise, 7 June, 1889.

399 xi. Luna Rose[7] *b.* 9 Nov., 1863; *d.* 20 Nov., 1886; *m.* ——— Salmon.

400 xii. Thomas Keeney[7] *b.* 20 June, 1865.

401 xiii. Floyd Ransom[7] *b.* 2 Sept., 1871.

FAMILY LVII.†

RANSOM[6] [141], (*Asa*[5] *Israel*[4] *Israel*[3] *Israel*[2] *James*[1]) *b.* 23 Mch., 1808; *d.* Waverly, N. Y., 12 June, 1893; *m.* 13 Nov., 1828, Phyla, *dau.* Gordon and Sarah (Reynolds) Chapman.

Children:

402 i. Nancy[7] *b.* Chemung, N. Y., 30 Sept., 1829; *d.* Sayre, Pa., 28 Aug., 1891; *m.* 6 Nov., 1847, Charles Church. *Issue:*

---

* Pers. statement.

† Fam. Recs. and pers. know., Mrs. Irving K. Park.

i. Mary[8] (Church) *b.* 27 Aug., 1848.[a]
ii. Catherine Chapman[8] (Church) *b.* 13 Nov., 1851.[a]

403 II. Harvey[7] *b.* 26 Aug., 1831; *d.* 21 Sept., 1832.
404 III. Luther[7] *b.* 4 July, 1833. FAM. CLI.
405 IV. Juliette[7] *b.* 12 Oct., 1835; *m.* 25 Nov., 1854, Byron Bennett. *Issue:*

i. Frank[8] (Bennett).

m. (2) — Sept., 1873, A. D. Kimber. *No issue.*
[*Chicago, Ill.*

406 V. Almon[7] *b.* 19 Mch., 1838. FAM. CLII.
407 VI. John Wesley[7] *b.* 10 Oct., 1840; *d.* 7 Sept., 1842.
408 VII. Albert[7] *b.* 14 Sept., 1843; *d.* 14 Sept., 1845.
409 VIII. Mary[7] *b.* 30 Oct., 1845; *m.* Waverly, N. Y., 17 Aug., 1870, George B. Swan. *Issue:*
[*Prospect Park, Cal.*

i. Clara Booth[8] (Swan) *b.* 16 May, 1873.
[*Prospect Park, Cal.*
ii. Louise M.[8] (Swan) *b.* 16 May, 1876.
[*Prospect Park, Cal.*

410 IX. John Wiley[7] *b.* 16 Dec., 1848. FAM. CLIII.
411 X. Wesley[7] *b.* 16 Dec., 1848. FAM. CLIV.
412 XI. Lucy Ella[7] *b.* 23 Jany., 1851; *m.* Waverly, N. Y., 17 Aug., 1870, Walter Van Atta. *Issue:*
[*Toledo, O.*

a. Mary Church, *m.* Waverly, N. Y., 11 Nov. 1868, Edwin Brooks. After her death, he *m.* Sayre Pa., 30 Oct. 1895, her sister, Catherine Chapman Church.[a]

[a] Pers. statement, Mrs. Edwin Brooks.

i. Bert E.[8] (Van Atta) *b.* Waverly, N. Y., 17 Sept., 1871.
ii. Howard Earl[8] (Van Atta) *b.* Toledo, O., 26 May, 1893.

413 XII. Phyla Adell[7] *b.* Nunda, N. Y., 13 Dec., 1855; *m.* Waverly, N. Y., 19 Mch., 1874, Fred J. Krom. *Issue:* [*Sayre, Pa.*

i. Charles Cummings[8] (Krom) *b.* Towanda, Pa., 19 Dec., 1876.
ii. Anna Chapman[8] (Krom) *b.* 22 Nov., 1879.
iii. Helen Eleanor[8] (Krom) *b.* 27 Jany., 1889.

Ransom Parshall was a highly respected citizen of Waverly, N. Y., and a man whose life was depoted to his fellow men. He was prominent in church work and in the affairs of his native place. His wife, who traced her ancestry to Mary Stuart, Queen of Scots, was a lady of great wit and beauty.

---

*FAMILY LVIII.**

LUTHER[6] [142] (*Asa*[5] *Israel*[4] *Israel*[3] *Israel*[2] *James*[1]) *b.* Chemung, N. Y., 22 Mch., 1810; *d.* Brighton, Mich., 29 Jany., 1870; *m.* Chemung, N. Y., 6 Mch., 1834, Emma, *dau.* William and Mehitabel (————) Roberts (*b.* Chemung, N. Y., 26 Apl., 1814; *d.* Brighton, Mich., 12 Feby., 1872).

Children:

414 I. Susan[7] *d. inf.*
415 II. Sarah Ann.[7]

* Fam. Recs. and pers. know., 419.

416 III. Franklin.[7]

417 IV. Frances.[7]

418 V. Susannah.[7]

419 VI. Ransom N. *b.* Brighton, Liv. Co., Mich., 31 July, 1846; *m.* (1) Fenton, Mich., 4 July, 1868, Ursula [422], *dau.* Israel and Minerva (Cole) Parshall (*b.* Parshallville, Mich., 23 Jany., 1847). *No issue.* *m.* (2) Owosso, Mich., 29 Feby., 1896, Julia, *dau.* George and Barbara (Munsch) Hasford (*b.* Perry, Mich., 28 May, 1871). *No issue.*

---

*FAMILY LIX.**

ISRAEL[6] [144], (*Asa[5] Israel[4] Israel[3] Israel[2] James[1]*) *b.* Chemung, N. Y., 4 May, 1815; *d.* Havana, Saginaw Co., Mich., 25 Aug., 1865; *m.* Parshallville, Liv. Co., Mich., 19 May, 1839, Minerva, *dau.* Joseph and Elizabeth (Wicks) Cole (*b.* 8 Dec., 1823; *d.* Havana, Mich., — Feby., 1899).

Children:

420 I. Lemira[7]† *b.* Oceola, Liv. Co., Mich., 3 July, 1840; *m.* Havana, Mich., 1 Jany., 1857, William Harvey, *s.* William H. and Sleanor (——) Niver (*b.* Orange Co., N. Y., 5 Oct., 1835; *d.* Chesaning, Mich., 8 Nov., 1883). *Issue:* (All *b.* Chesaning.) [*Chesaning, Mich.*

i. Alice Maria[8] (Niver) *b.* 22 Nov., 1857.[a]

a. Alice Maria Niver, *m.* Chesaning, Mich., 7 Jany. 1878, James Lawrence, *s.* Peter and Ann Eliza (Davis) McCauley (*b.* Fremont, O., 30 Sept. 1848). *Issue:* (All *b.* Chesaning, Mich.) *i.* Theodora Inez[9] (McCauley)

---

* Fam. Recs. and pers. know., 421 and 422.

ii. Emeroy Alida[8] (Niver b. 31 July, 1861.[a]
iii. Frank Effie[8] (Niver) *b.* 20 Apl., 1871.

421 II. Merrit[7] *b.* 1 Apl. 1844. FAM. CLV.

422 III. Ursula[7]* *b.* Parshallville, Mich., 23 Jany., 1847; *m.* Fenton, Mich., 4 July, 1868, Ransom N., *s.* of Luther and Emily (Roberts) Parshall (*b.* 31 July, 1847). (See 419.) *No issue.*

[*Perry, Shiawassee Co., Mich.*

423 IV. Milton Chatman[7] *b.* 20 Jany., 1850. FAM. CLVI.

[*Commerce, Mich.*

424 V. Alvira Elizabeth[7]* *b.* Parshallville, Mich., 25 Apl., 1852; *m.* Chesaning, Mich., 6 Feby., 1870, Stewart Daniel, *s.* John and Cynthia (Alba) Linabury (*b.* Clarkston, Mich., 10 Mch., 1840). *Issue:*

[*Corunna, Mich.*

i. Ora Abraham[8] (Linabury) *b.* 15 Aug., 1874.
ii. Hattie Minerva[8] (Linabury) *b.* 31 May, 1889.

425 VI. Millis Lincoln[7] *b.* 25 Dec., 1864. FAM. CLVII.

[*Havana, Mich.*

Israel Parshall removed to Michigan, from Chemung, about 1836. Here, in Oceola Township, Livingston County, he cleared one of the finest farms in the State. From Oceola he removed to Parshallville, about 200 miles distant and opened a grist mill and store. In 1855 he finally settled in Chesaning Township, Saginaw County, Michigan, where he built and operated another

b. 23 June, 1879; *m.* Chesaning, Mich., 21 June, 1900, Homer Ellsworth, *s.* Thomas J. Davis (*b.* St. Louis, Mo., 17 Jany., 1870). *Issue: i. Byron Alan*[10] *(Davis) b.* 28 *Jany.* 1902; *ii.* William Frank[9] (McCauley) *b.* 10 July, 1881.†

a. Emaroy Alida Niver, *m.* Chesaning, Mich., 5 Oct. 1886. Byron G., *s.* Richard C. and Hannah (———) Coryell (*b.* Campbell, Steuben Co., N. Y., 12 May, 1854). *No issue.*†

* Pers. statement.
† Pers. know. 420.

Israel Parshall

grist mill. For several terms he was Commissioner of Highways, an office for which his natural energy and forceful personality pre-eminently fitted him. He was killed by the accidental discharge of his gun while on a hunting excursion. (*See Portrait.*)

---

*FAMILY LX.**

JESSE[6] [156], (*Jesse*[5], *Israel*[4], *Israel*[3], *Israel*[2], *James*[1]) *b.* Chemung, N. Y., 30 Mch., 1822; *d.* Oceola, Mich., 22 July, 1893; *m.* Oceola, Mich., 20 Feby., 1850, Prudence, *dau.* Joseph and Elizabeth (Wickes) Cole (*b.* Tompkins Co., N. Y., 28 Jany., 1830; *d.* Fenton, Mich., 29 Oct., 1900). [*Oceola, Mich.*

Children: (All *b.* Oceola, Mich.)

426 I. Edgar Judson[7] *b.* 30 Apl. 1851; *d.* Oceola, Mich., 11 July, 1851.

427 II. Almon J.[7] *b.* 26 July, 1855; *d.* Oceola, Mich., 21 Sept., 1865.

428 III. Lenora Adell[7]† *b.* 12 Sept., 1866; *m.* Oceola, Mich., 28 Jany., 1890, Walter Myron, *s.* Homer L. and Mary (Scott) Van Camp (*b.* Oceola, Mich., 28 Jany., 1864). *Issue:* [*Fenton, Mich.*

i. Minor Jesse[8] (Van Camp) *b.* Oceola, Mich., 28 Dec., 1890.

429 IV. Milan Grant[7] *b.* 5 June, 1869. FAM. CLVII.

---

* Fam. Rec. pers. know., 429.
† Pers. statement.

*FAMILY LXI.**

ASA[6] [150], *(Asa[5], Israel[4], Israel[3], Israel[2], James[1])* *b.* Chemung, N. Y., 20 Apl., 1825; *m.* Athens, Pa., 1 July, 1858, Salina, *dau.* Hiram and Martha (Lemon) Phelps (*b.* Schoharie Co., N. Y., 15 Jany., 1830; *d.* Chemung, N. Y., 15 May, 1897).

Children: (All *b.* Chemung, N. Y.)

430 I. Judson H.[7] *b.* 1 May, 1861; *d.* Chemung, N. Y., 18 May, 1865.

431 II. Carrie[7] *b.* 7 Feby., 1863; *d.* Chemung, N. Y., 19 Sept., 1890, *unm.*

432 III. Mattie M.[7] *b.* 21 Mch., 1865; *d.* Chemung, N. Y., 29 May, 1889, *unm.*

433 IV. Asa Irving[7] *b.* 22 May, 1868; *m.* Chemung, N. Y., 11 Nov., 1898, Minnie, *dau.* U. W. and Mary (Ruggles) Dewitt (*b.* Chemung, N. Y., — Oct., 1870). *No issue.*

434 V. Susie M.[7] *b.* 14 Nov. 1870; *m.* Chemung, N. Y., 22 June, 1897, Stewart S., *s.* Oliver Tyler and Caroline J. (Duffern) Comfort (*b.* Wellsburg, N. Y., 22 Feby., 1871). *No issue.*

Asa Parshall is a successful farmer at Chemung, N. Y., where he lives, upon the farm which his grandfather, Israel Parshall, purchased more than a century ago. Of a genial and kindly nature, "Uncle Asa" is beloved by all who know him. Well-to-do in this world's goods, his heart and purse are ever open to the wants of his less fortunate fellows. A firm and steadfast friend of this work, he has aided the author on several occasions when aid was necessary. The family owe "Uncle Asa" a debt

* Pers. knowledge, 150.

issa Parshall

of gratitude for the interest he has taken in this work, for without the liberal aid he has given it is certain that it would never have appeared in print. (*See Portrait.*)

---

*FAMILY LXII.**

DANIEL[6] [155], *(Jesse[5], Israel[4], Israel[3], Israel[2], James[1]) b.* abt. 1808; *d.* Canandaigua, N. Y., 1871, aged 63 years; *m.* Canandaigua, N. Y., Nancy, *dau.* Isaac and Harriet (———) Buttles (*b.* abt. 1811; *d.* 31 Sept., 1889, aged 78 years).

Children:

435 I. Elizabeth Gorham[7] *b.* Canandaigua, N. Y., abt. 1837; *m.* Canandaigua, N. Y., 18 Feby., 1860, Jacob, *s.* Henry and Mary (———) Ashley (*b.* N. Y. City, 1 Apl., 1825; *d.* Jasper Co., Mo., 14 May, 1877). *Issue:*

i. Isabelle N.[8] (Ashley).
ii. James Edward[8] (Ashley).
iii. Henry Nearon[8] (Ashley).
iv. Harriet Aryetta[8] (Ashley).
v. Mary Elizabeth[8] (Ashley).
vi. Anna Laura[8] (Ashley).
vii. Centennial Henryetta[8] (Ashley).

436 II. Harriet Aryetta.[7]
437 III. Robert Layton[7] *b.* 29 July, 1849. FAM. CLIX.
438 IV. Isabelle.[7]
439 V. Francis.[7]
440 VI. Isaac B.[7]

---

* Fam. Recs. and pers. know., 437.

*FAMILY LXIII.**

JESSE[6] [156], *(Jesse,[5] Israel,[4] Israel,[3] Israel,[2] James[1]) b.* Ontario Co., N. Y., abt. 1810; *d.* Farmington, Ont. Co., N. Y., abt. 1883; *m. n.* Canandaigua, N. Y., Elizabeth Howard.

Children:

441 I. Nelson Clark[7] *b.* 5 Feby., 1840. FAM. CLX.

FAMILY LXIV.†

ELISHA[6] [157], *(Jesse[5], Israel[4], Israel[3], Israel[2], James[1]) b.* — Oct., 1811; *d.* Cheshire, Ont. Co., N. Y., 9 Feby., 1882; *m.* Canandaigua, N. Y., 5 July, 1836, Sylva, *dau.* Paul and Mary (Meyers) Sanford (*b.* R. I., — June, 1811; *d.* Cheshire, N. Y., 5 Oct., 1889).

Children:

442 I. Jesse[7] *b.* 16 Dec., 1837. FAM. CLXI.

443 II. Mary[7] *b.* 6 May., 1842; *d.* 1872; *m.* John Robson.

444 III. Sarah[7] *b.* 6 May, 1842; *m.* 1875, James Grooms.

445 IV. Paul[7] *b.* 16 Mch., 1844; *d.* 12 Oct., 1845.

---

* Fam. Recs. and pers. know., 441.
† Fam. Rec. and pers. know., 442.

*FAMILY LXV.**

RUFUS^{6} [158], (*Jesse^{5}, Israel^{4}, Israel^{3}, Israel^{2}, James^{1}*) *b.* Canandaigua, N. Y., 2 Nov., 1814; *d.* Oceola, Livingston Co., Mich., 2 May, 1898; *m.* Julia, *dau.* Elijah and Mary (Herrick) Kellogg (*b.* Vt., 12 July, 1817; *d.* Oceola, Mich., 22 Oct., 1891).

Children:

446 i. Henry J.^{7} *b.* 1836; went to California in 1854, and is supposed to have been killed by Spaniards in the fall of 1861.

447 ii. Lyman^{7} *b.* — Apl., 1838. [*Hartland, Liv. Co., Mich.*

448 iii. Richard Elisha^{7} *b.* 1 June, 1840. FAM. CLX.

449 iv. Emeline^{7} *d. inf.*

450 v. Julia^{7} *b.* 4 Feby., 1846. [*Leroy, N. Y.*

451 vi. Caroline Eunice^{7}† *b.* Cheshire, Ontario Co., N. Y., 17 Aug., 1847; *m.* Moscow, Livingston Co., N. Y., 7 May, 1871, Rockwell M., *s.* Stephen V. and Angeline (Randall) Lozier (*b.* Dansville, Liv. Co., N. Y., 1 Aug., 1847). *Issue:* [*Rochester, N. Y.*

- i. Frederick Stanley^{8} (Lozier) *b.* 19 May, 1872.
- ii. William Sherman^{8} (Lozier) *b.* 22 Aug., 1876.
- iii. Grace Angeline^{8} (Lozier) *b.* 14 Jany., 1888.

452 vii. Frances^{7} *m.* Vincent Myers. [*Parshallville, Liv. Co., Mich.*

453 viii. Celia^{7} *m.* John Case. [*Fenton, Genesee Co., Mich.*

454 ix. Charles.^{7} [*Hartland, Liv. Co., Mich.*

455 x. William.^{7}

456 xi. Edward^{7} *d.* inf.

457 xii. Rufus^{7} *d.* inf.

---

* Fam. Recs. and pers. know., 448 and 451.
† Pers. statement.

*FAMILY LXVI.**

JOHN[6] [159], (*Jesse*[5], *Israel*[4], *Israel*[3], *Israel*[2], *James*[1]) *b.* Canandaigua, N. Y., 22 Feby., 1822; *m.* (1) Canandaigua, N. Y., 28 Sept., 1843, Marie, *dau.* John and Jane (Saxton) Pinch (*b.* Geneva N. Y., 28 Aug., 1825; *d.* Canandaigua, N. Y., 20 May, 1849). [*Dunellen, N. J.*

Children:

458 I. John Byron[7]† *b.* Canandaigua, N. Y., 13 May, 1845; *m.* Erie, Pa., 24 Oct., 1882, Julia Ann, *dau.* Adam and Magdalena (Gepford) Grimler (*b.* Erie, Pa., 7 Sept., 1852). *No issue.* [*Erie, Pa.*

459 II. Edward Howell[7]† *b.* 10 July, 1848. FAM. CLXIII.

m. (2) Geneva, N. Y., 20 Mch., 1850, Caroline Louise, *dau.* John and Jane (Saxton) Pinch, (*b.* Geneva, N. Y., Oct., 1829; *d.* Atchinson, Kan., 26 Sept., 1880). [*Waterbury, Ct.*

Children:

460 III. George Washington[7] *b.* 19 Nov., 1851. FAM. CLXIV.

461 IV. Emma Bidwell[7]† *b.* Rochester, N. Y., 7 Jany., 1854; *m.* New York, 20 June, 1873, Harry, *s.* Harry and Lillie (Williams) Earl (*b.* New York, 18 June, 1853; *d.* at sea, 20 June, 1896). *Issue:* [*Dunellen, N. J.*

i. Hazel[8] (Earl) *b.* 18 Oct., 1875.
ii. Dearest May[8] (Earl) *b.* 30 May, 1895.

---

* Pers. knowledge, 159.
† Pers. statement.

462 v. Jennie Wilkinson[7] *b.* 16 Jany., 1860.
463 vi. Julia Heusted[7] *b.* 18 Oct., 1862.
464 vii. Charles Clinton[7] *b.* 20 April, 1865.

---

*FAMILY LXVII.**

OTIS KIMBLE[6] [160], *(Jesse[5], Israel[4], Israel[3], Israel[2], James[1]) b.* Canandaigua, N. Y., 18 Jany., 1823; *d.* Cheshire, Ontario Co., N. Y., 26 Aug., 1868; *m.* Canandaigua, N. Y., 19 Mch., 1844, Lodema Prudence, *dau.* Jonathan and Vincey (Hotchkiss) Smith (*b.* 7 Feby., 1827; *d.* 21 June, 1891). [*Cheshire, Ont. Co., N. Y.*

Children:

465 i. Gideon Edgar[7] *b.* 18 Jany., 1845. Fam. CLXV.
466 ii. Charles Kimble[7] *b.* 15 May, 1847. Fam. CLXVI.
467 iii. Arietta Amanda[7] *b.* 8 Apl., 1849; *m.* 24 Dec., 1868, Noadiah, *s.* Henry and Polly (Livermore) Hutchens (*b.* 5 Feby., 1845). *Issue:* [*Cheshire, N. Y.*

i. Adelphia Amanda[8] (Hutchens) *b.* 20 June, 1870.[a]
ii. Mabel Nettie[8] (Hutchens) *b.* 20 Nov., 1872.

468 iv. Samuel Eugene[7] *b.* 17 July, 1852. Fam. CLXVII.
469 v. Julia[7] *b.* 19 Feby., 1854; *d.* 5 Jany., 1900; *m.* (1), 9 Apl., 1873, Frank Larner (*b.* 1846; d. 3 Jany., 1889). *Issue:*

a. Adelphia Amanda Hutchens, *m.* 15 July, 1893, Edwin C. Hutchens (*b.* 19 July, 1869). *Issue: i.* Gordon Laverne[9] (Hutchens) *b.* 19 July, 1894; *d.* 23 Dec., 1898; *ii.* Helen Laura[9] (Hutchens) *b.* 1 Sept., 1896.

---

* Fam. Recs. and pers. know., 471.

i. Etta Lodema[8] (Larner) *b.* 7 Nov., 1874.[a]
ii. William Frank[8] (Larner) *b.* 20 Feby. 1876.

m. (2), 9 Mch., 1892, Henry Lawrence Hanna. *No issue.*

470 VI. Harvey John[7] *b.* 21 July, 1856. FAM. CLXVIII.
471 VII. Emma Adelia[7] *b.* 23 Jany., 1862; *m.* 4 Mch., 1885, Alanson, *s.* John and Sophia (Tice) Willis (*b.* 15 Dec., 1857). *Issue:* [*Canandaigua, N. Y.*

i. Mabel Dell[8] (Willis) *b.* 4 Sept., 1891.

---

*FAMILY LXVIII.**

BENJAMIN CARLISLE[6] [162], (*Israel*[5], *Benjamin*[4], *Israel*[3], *Israel*[2], *James*[1]) *b.* Plattsburg, N. Y., 17 May, 1803; *d.* New York, 28 Aug., 1838; *m.* New York, 26 May, 1824, Eloise, *dau.* William Lane and Margaret (Paul) Pelsue (*b.* New York, 10 May, 1803; *d.* Elizabethport, N. J., 4 Aug., 1865). [*New York, N. Y.*

Children: (All *b.* New York)

472 I. Benjamin Carlisle[7] *b.* 1 Aug., 1825. FAM. CLXIX.
473 II. Sarah Louise[7] *b.* 3 Nov., 1827; *m.* New York, 4 Oct., 1848, Benjamin, *s.* James and Elizabeth (Harrison) Gregory (*b.* Blackburn, Eng., 22 Oct., 1825). *Issue:* [*Trenton, N. J.*

i. Benjamin Carlisle[8] (Gregory *b.* 5 Aug., 1849.[b] [*Chelsea, Mass.*

a. Etta Lodema Larner, *m.* 29 Oct., 1891, Frank Hale. *Issue:* *i.* Maude[9] (Hale) *b.* 18 Aug., 1892; *ii.* Ethel[9] (Hale) *b.* 11 June, 1894.

b. Benjamin Carlisle Gregory, *m.* New York, 25 May, 1871, Leah, *dau.* Thomas W. and Rachel (McLain) Letson (*b.* New York, 20 Apl., 1853). *No issue.*

* Fam. Recs. and pers. know., 473.

ii. James[8] (Gregory) *b.* 24 Oct., 1851. [*New York, N. Y.*

iii. Christopher[8] (Gregory) *b.* 31 Aug., 1854.

iv. William[8] (Gregory) *b.* 29 Aug., 1858.

v. Sarah Louise[8] (Gregory) *b.* 31 Jany., 1863.

vi. Abraham Lincoln[8] (Gregory) *b.* 26 Apl., 1865.

vii. Alfred Cookman[8] (Gregory) *b.* 26 Mch., 1872. [*Trenton, N. J.*

474 III. Elizabeth[7] *b.* 13 Sept., 1831.

475 IV. William Valentine[7] *b.* 29 Apl., 1833. FAM. CLXX.

476 V. Mary Elizabeth[7] *b.* 28 Aug., 1835.

477 VI. James Carlisle[7] *b.* 9 Jany., 1839. FAM. CLXXI.

---

*FAMILY LXIX.**

GEORGE HOTTO[6] [176], *(Benjamin[5], Benjamin[4], Israel[3], Israel,[2] James[1])* *b.* New York, 16 Oct., 1812; *d.* Jamacia, L. I., N. Y., 28 Sept., 1870; *m.* New York, 26 July, 1840, Louisa Jane, *dau.* Noah and Jane (Van Arsdale) Davis (*b.* Lisle, Broome Co., N. Y., 23 Aug., 1824; d. 27 July, 1901).

Children:

478 I. James Henry[7] *b.* 26 Apl., 1841; *d.* 4 Oct., 1841.

479 II. George Hammond[7] (Dr.) *b.* 23 Apl., 1843. FAM. CLXXII.

480 III. Charles Oscar[7] *b.* 28 Dec., 1845; *d.* 27 July, 1846.

481 IV. Mary Jane[7] *b.* 28 Dec., 1847; *d.* 19 Feby., 1848.

482 V. William James[7] *b.* 1 July, 1849; *d.* 8 June, 1891; *unm.*

483 VI. Edwin[7] *b.* 1 July, 1849; *d.* 1 July, 1849.

* Bible Rec. 176 and Fam. Rec. and pers. know., 479.

484 VII. Mary Louise[7] *b.* Jamaica, L. I., N. Y., 21 Dec., 1854; *m.* Brooklyn, 6 Oct., 1875, John I., *s.* John G. and Phebe (Suydam) Williamson (*b.* 8 Sept., 1852). *Issue:* [*Brooklyn, N. Y.*

i. Alvin Parshall[8] (Williamson) *b.* 5 Sept., 1883.

485 VIII. Joseph Alvin[7] *b.* 24 Jany., 1857; *d.* 7 Jany., 1896; *unm.*

486 IX. Charles[7] *b.* 12 Aug., 1859; *d.* 4 Aug., 1860.

George H. Parshall received a common school education, after which he was put to learn the trade of a shoemaker. After finishing his apprenticeship he opened a shop and store of his own. He subsequently removed to Jamacia, L. I., and followed the business until his death as a successful merchant. The traits of honesty and integrity which had characterized his father were inherited by the son, and won for him the respect and esteem of the community in which he lived.

---

*FAMILY LXX.**

JAMES LAWRENCE[6] [177], (*Benjamin*[5], *Benjamin*[4], *Israel*[3], *Israel*[2], *James*[1]) *b.* New York, 14 Feby., 1815; *d.* New York, 27 May, 1896; *m.* New York, 16 Nov., 1837, Phebe Ann, *dau.* Ephriam and Hannah (Barker) Warren (*b.* New York, 1 July, 1819; *d.* New York, 3 Mch., 1901).

[*New York, N. Y.*

Children: (All *b.* and *d.* New York)

487 I. George Warren[7] *b.* 26 Oct., 1839; *d.* 10 Apl., 1842.

488 II. Mary Louise[7] *b.* 12 Aug., 1842; *d.* 29 Oct., 1843.

* Fam. Bible 177, pos. 479.

489 III. Emma Annie[7] *b.* 8 Sept., 1844; *d.* 19 Apl., 1865; *unm.*

He received a common school education and learned the trade of a japanner of wood and metal. Starting in business for himself after completing his apprenticeship he conducted it so successfully that at 40 years of age he was able to retire with a handsome fortune. Thenceforth he devoted himself to the buying and selling of real estate, at Morrissania, N. Y., until his death. Intelligent, earnest and successful, when in active business life he was one of the most prominent men in Westchester County.

---

*FAMILY LXXI.**

DAVID TERRY[6] (Pershall) [178], (*George*[5], *David*[4], *David*[3], *David*[2], *James*[1]) *b.* Riverhead, Suffolk Co., N. Y., 18 Aug., 1807; *d.* New York, 18 May, 1882; *m.* New York, 17 Nov., 1839, Eliza Ann Tuttle (*b.* Bridgeport, Ct., 24 July, 1821; *d.* New York, 22 Apl., 1844). [*New York, N. Y.*

Children:

490 I. Henry Le Roy[7] *b.* abt. 1840; *m.* Josephine, *dau.* Daniel and Ann Jane (Lowney)[a] Slote. *No issue.* [*Brooklyn, N. Y.*

491 II. David Beck[7] *b.* 4 Mch., 1842. FAM. CLXXIII.

a. Ann Jane Lowney, was *b.* Lurgen, Co. Armagh, Ireland, 12 July, 1800.

* Fam. Recs. and pers. know., 491.

*FAMILY LXXII.**

CALEB HALSEY[6] [179], *(George[5], David[4], David[3], David[2], James[1]) b.* Riverhead, Suffolk Co., N. Y., 21 Aug., 1809; *d.* Farmer, Seneca Co., N. Y., 27 Sept., 1883; *m.* Covert, N. Y., 24 Jany., 1835, Elizabeth Barlow, *dau.* Lyman and Hannah (Treadwell) Bradley (*b.* Trumansburg, N. Y., 13 June, 1818; *d.* Farmer, N. Y., 14 Jany., 1888). [*Farmer, Seneca Co., N. Y.*

Children:

492 I. Hannah Julia[7]* *b.* Trumansburg, N. Y., 18 Nov., 1835; *d.* Racine, Wis., 28 Mch., 1871; *m.* Farmer, N. Y., 16 May, 1867, Charles Lincoln Morris (*b. n.* Boston, abt. 1815; *d.* Racine, Wis., 7 Jany., 1872). *Issue:* [*Racine, Wis.*

i. Julia Louise[8] (Morris). [*Chicago, Ill.*

ii. Mary Augusta[8] (Morris) *b.* 20 Dec., 1869.[a] [*Geneva, Ind.*

493 II. Frances Serepta[7]† *b.* Farmer, N. Y., 20 Aug., 1838; *m.* Farmer, N. Y., 29 Nov., 1866, Thomas Rhodes, *s.* David Rathbone and Lydia (Rhodes) Austin (*b.* North Hector, N. Y., 27 Apl., 1841). *Issue:* [*Neosho, Mo.*

i. George Halsey[8] (Austin) *b.* Cedar Rapids, Ia., 19 Jany., 1869. [*Neosho, Mo.*

a. Mary Augusta Morris, *m.* Chicago, Ill., 9 Oct., 1894, George Langstaff, *s.* George Henry and Ada Charlotte (Miller) Thayer (*b.* Chicago, 9 Oct., 1866). *Issue: i.* George Langstaff[9] (Thayer).†

---

* Bible Rec. 179, and pers. know., 493, 495, and 498.
† Pers. statement.

C. H. Parshall

ii. Anna Julia[8] (Austin) *b.* Cedar Rapids, Ia., 10 Feby., 1871.[a] [*Saginaw, Mo.*

iii. Fannie Louisa[8] (Austin) *b.* 4 Feby., 1873; *d.* 14 Mch., 1874.

494 III. Sarah Louise[7] *b.* Farmer, N. Y., 17 Aug., 1840; *d.* Farmer, N. Y., 14 Oct., 1886; *m.* Farmer, N. Y., 1884, William Willshire Boorom. *No issue.*

495 IV. Mary Elizabeth[7]* *b.* Farmer, N. Y., 11 Sept., 1842; *m.* Farmer, N. Y., 7 July, 1874, Abram Vorhees, *s.* Peter and Catharine (Wyckoff) Miner (*b.* New Hudson, Allegany Co., N. Y., 5 Mch., 1844). *Issue:* (All *b.* Farmer, N. Y.)

i. Halsey Parshall[8] (Miner) *b.* 4 Mch., 1879.

ii. Bessie Wilhelmina[8] (Miner) *b.* Auburn, 24 Jany., 1881.

iii. Henry[8] (Miner) *b.* 1 July, 1882.

iv. Morris[8] (Miner) *b.* 15 Aug., 1886.

496 V. Lyman Bradley[7] *b.* 28 June, 1845. FAM. CLXXIV.

497 VI. George Beck[7] *b.* Farmer, N. Y., 10 July, 1847; *d.* Chicago, Ill., 31 Aug., 1870; *unm.*

498 VII. Thomas Wardle[7] *b.* 25 July, 1849. FAM. CLXXV.

499 VIII. Wilhelmina Schenck[7] *b.* Farmer, N. Y., 13 Dec., 1856; *d.* Farmer, N. Y., 6 Mch., 1877; *unm.*

Caleb Halsey Parshall removed from Long Island to Trumansburg, Tompkins County, N. Y., in 1831. Six years later he went to Farmer Village, Seneca County, N. Y., where he thenceforth made his home. There, in quietness and prosperity,

a. Anna Julia Austin, *m.* Saginaw, Mo., 17 July, 1895, James Jones, *s.* John Calhoun and Sarah Ann (Mercer) Cox (*b.* Joplin, Mo., 7 Apl., 1857). *Issue: i.* Lucile[9] (Cox) b. 25 July, 1897.*

* Pers. statement.

he lived the peaceful, useful life of a studious and intelligent farmer; loving his books and his fields; prudent in management, genial in the social circle, winning the respect and regard of all who knew him. For thirty years he was a member of the Reformed Church of Farmer Village, exemplifying in his life the religion he professed.* *(See Portrait).*

FAMILY LXXIII.†

GEORGE LORENZO[6] [182], *(George[5], David[4], David[3], David[2], James[1]) b.* 1818; *d.* 11 Sept. 1880, aged 62 yrs.; *m.* Elizabeth ——.

Children:

500 I. James L.[7] *b.* abt. Feby., 1852; *d.* Morgan Prairie. Ind., 23 Apl., 1873, aged 21 yrs. 2 mos.; *unm.*

501 II. Abbie[7] *b.* abt. 1855; *d.* Porter Co., Ind., 31 Jany., 1877, aged 22 yrs.; *m.* 10 Nov., 1875, Edgar D. Crumpacker, of Valparaiso, Ind. *No issue.*

FAMILY LXXIV.‡

NATHANIEL[6] [184], *(Elias,[5] Elias,[4] David,[3] David,[2] James[1]) b.* prob. New Jersey, 1 Jany., 1791; *d.* Washington Co., Pa., 18 July, 1862; *m.* (1), 22 Nov., 1815, Ruth Smith (*b.* 26 Nov., 1793; *d.* Lebanon, O., 1 Apl., 1880).

---

* The Ovid Independent, 8 Oct. 1898.
† Fam. Rec. and pers. know., wid. 182.
‡ Bible Rec. 184 pos. 517.

Children: (All *b.* Lebanon, O.)

502 I. Elias[7] *b.* 21 Sept., 1816; *d.* 3 Dec., 1816.

503 II. William Ferguson[7] *b.* 18 Feby., 1818. FAM. CLXXVI.

504 III. Mary Jane[7] *b.* 4 June, 1820; *d.* 5 Apl., 1835.

505 IV. James Lawrence[7] *b.* 20 Mch., 1822; *d.* 7 Mch., 1847; *unm.*

506 V. Oliver Hazard Perry[7] *b.* 13 Mch., 1824. FAM. CLXXVII.

507 VI. Ann Malinda[7]* *b.* 26 Oct., 1826; *d.* Columbus, O., 18 Feby., 1896; *m.* (1), Lebanon, O., 16 July, 1845, Horace Morgan, *s.* Ellis and Hannah (Morgan) Stokes (*d.* Lebanon, O., 12 Sept., 1861). *Issue:*

i. Harry Morgan[8] (Stokes) *b.* 6 May, 1846.[a]

ii. William Parshall[8] (Stokes) *b.* 16 Feby., 1848; *d.* 20 June, 1849.

iii. Ellis Archer[8] (Stokes) *b.* 20 Aug., 1850; d. s. p.

iv. Laura[8] (Stokes) *b.* Lebanon, O., 29 Oct., 18—.[b]

v. Fannie[8] (Stokes) *b.* Lebanon, O., 24 Apl., 1858.[c]

a. Harry Morgan Stokes, *m.* Chicago, 29 June, 1892, Hattie, *dau.* Nathaniel and Sarah (Warman) Leonard (*b.* N. J., 16 Apl., 1856; *d.* Chicago, 31 Dec., 1896). *Issue: i.* Horace Morgan[9] *b.* Chicago, 5 June, 1893.†

b. Laura Stokes, *m.* Columbus, O., 7 Dec., 1881, Thomas, *s.* Abisha Woodward (*b.* Belleview, O.) *No issue.*†

c. Fannie Stokes, *m.* Columbus, O., 25 Sept., 1879, John Prouty, *s.* Jonas and Catherine (Lumley) McCune (*b.* Columbus, O., 1 Jan., 1857). *Issue:* (all *b.* Columbus, O.) *i.* Louise[9] (McCune) *b.* 28 Sept., 1880; *ii.* William Pitt[9] (McCune) *b.* 29 Apl., 1885; *iii.* John Stokes[9] (McCune) *b.* 9 Mch. 1887; *iv.* Dorothy[9] (McCune) *b.* 28 Dec. 1892; *v.* Donald Lumley[9] (McCune) *b.* 24 Nov. 1895.†

---

* Fam. Rec. pos. Nelson Sayler and pers. know., Mrs. Fanny McCune.
† Pers. statement.

vi. Mary[8] (Stokes) b. Lebanon, O., 12 Nov., 1860.[a]

m. (2) 31 Mch., 1869, Thomas Sparrow, of Columbus, O. *No issue.*

508 VII. Sarah Jemima Garrison[7] *b.* 6 Jany., 1829; d. 2 Feby., 1833.

m. (2), Washington Co., Pa., 28 June, 1838, Mary Ann, *dau.* Conrad and Catherine (Hafer) Hass, (*b.* Washington Co., Pa., 4 Sept., 1811; *d.* Washington Co., Pa., 22 June, 1883).

Children:

509 VIII. Catherine Hester[7]* *b.* Fayette Co., Pa., 13 May, 1839; *m.* Washington Co., Pa., 23 Aug., 1857, John, *s.* Malachi and Mary Myers Feaster, (*b.* Wash. Co., Pa., 20 Aug., 1811; *d.* Lippincott, Greene Co., Pa., 8 Aug., 1860). *Issue:*

i. Mary Anabelle[8] (Feaster) *b.* 23 Apl., 1858. [*Swartz, Greene Co., Pa.*
ii. Austin[8] (Feaster) *b.* 23 Apl., 1858; *d.* — June, 1858.
iii. Luretta[8] (Feaster) *b.* 1 Oct., 1859.
iv. Lucinda Jane[8] (Feaster) *b.* 17 Feby., 1861.

510 IX. George Eggy[7] *b.* 23 May, 1840. FAM. CLXXVIII.

511 X. Harriet Newell[7]† *b.* Fayette Co., Pa., 26 Apl., 1842; *d.* Russell, Lucas Co., Ia., 30 Oct., 1881; *m.* Wash.

a. Mary Stokes, *m.* Columbus, O., 17 Apl., 1884, Frank Newell, *s.* John Weller and Sarah Louisa (Wing) Brown (*b.* Columbus, O., 7 Sept., 1857). *Issue: i.* Newel Stokes[9] (Brown) *b.* 25 Dec., 1887; *d.* 22 Apl., 1892; *ii.* Ruth Parshall[9] (Brown) *b.* 9 Nov. 1891.*

* Pers. statement.
† Fam. Rec. and pers. know., Mrs. Mary J. May.

Co., Pa., 11 Feby., 1862, Robert Dougherty, *s.* William and Eunitz *(sic)* Hatfield (*b.* Wash. Co., 28 May, 1840; *d.* 27 Mch., 1886). *Issue:*

i. Mary Jane[8] (Hatfield) *b.* 28 Oct., 1862.[a]
ii. Louisa Virginia[8] (Hatfield) *d. inf.*
iii. Harry Roy[8] (Hatfield) *d. inf.*

iv. Nancy Catherine[8] (Hatfield) *b.* 27 Apl., 1866; *d.* 1 Dec., 1881.
v. Calvin E.[8] (Hatfield) *b.* 8 Oct., 1867.
vi. Howard C.[8] (Hatfield) *d. inf.*
vii. Lyman Forest[8] (Hatfield) *b.* 22 Oct., 1870.
viii. Melvin Austin[8] (Hatfield) *b.* 14 Sept., 1872.

512 XI. Nathaniel Hass[7] *b.* Fayette Co., Pa., 16 Mch., 1844; *d.* Allegheny Co., Pa., 14 May, 1848.
513 XII. Elizabeth Ann[7] *b.* Fayette Co., Pa., 24 Nov., 1846; *d.* Wash. Co., Pa., 14 Dec., 1863.
514 XIII. Elias Seth[7] *b.* Allegheny Co., Pa., 12 Sept., 1849; *d.* Allegheny Co., Pa., 19 Jany., 1851.
515 XIV. Susan Maria[7] *b.* Allegheny Co., Pa., 6 Sept., 1851; *d.* Wash. Co., Pa., 28 Sept., 1855.
516 XV. Levi Penny[7]* *b.* Allegheny Co., Pa., 6 Sept., 1851; *m.* Delphas, Russell Co., Kan., 18 Jany., 1885, Kate Carmon. *No issue.* [*Wheaton, Kan.*
517 XVI. Hannah Jane[7] *b.* Wash. Co., Pa., 12 Jany., 1854. [*Swartz, Greene Co., Pa.*

Nathaniel Parshall was a soldier of the War of 1812, serving one year and six months in Capt. McClelland's Company, Lt.-Col. James B. Ball's Regiment.*

a. Mary Jane Hatfield, *m.* 24 Mch., 1882, J. W. May.†

* Recs. Auditor Genl's Office, Pa.
† Pers. statement.

*FAMILY LXXV.**

JOHN[6] [186], *(Elias[5], Elias[4], David[3], David[2], James[1]) b.* prob. N. J., 2 Nov., 1795; *d.* Wayne Co., Ind., 24 June, 1868; *m.* Fayette Co., Pa., 10 Jany., 1822, Elizabeth Halfhill (*b.* 10 Apl., 1800; *d.* White Water, Wayne Co., Ind., 8 Aug., 1872).
[*Franklin Tp., Wayne Co., Ind.*

Children:

518 I. Thirza[7] *b.* 18 Sept., 1822; *d.* 18 Feby., 1835.
519 II. Benonah[7] *b.* 10 Sept., 1824. FAM. CLXXIX.
520 III. Jane[7]† *b.* Fayette Co., Pa., 6 Oct., 1826; *m.* (1), Richmond, Ind., 1848, William Hunt (*d.* Wayne Co., Ind., 30 Mch., 1885). *Issue:*

i. Elizabeth Elvira[8] (Hunt) *b.* 2 Jany., 1849.
ii. Gala Elma[8] (Hunt) *b.* 3 Feby., 1852.
iii. Sarah Jane[8] (Hunt) *b.* 16 Feby., 1854; *d.* 25 Mch., 1885.

m. (2), Richmond, Ind., 1897, Eben Chenowith. *No issue.*

521 IV. John[7] *b.* 13 Jany., 1828. FAM. CLXXX.
522 V. Henry[7] *b.* 2 Jany., 1832. FAM. CLXXXI.
523 VI. Daniel[7] *b.* 24 Jany., 1835.
524 VII. William Harrison[7] *b.* 14 Jany., 1838.
525 VIII. Anderson Quinn[7] *b.* 1 May, 1841; killed at the Battle of Kingston, N. C., 17 Mch., 1865; *unm.*
526 IX. Nathaniel[7] *b.* 19 Oct., 1843. FAM. CLXXXII.
527 X. Albert Sylvester[7] *b.* 28 July, 1848; killed at Battle Milligan's Bend, Miss., 4 Feby., 1863.

---

* Fam. Recs. and pers. know., 526.
† Pers. statement.

*FAMILY LXXVI.**

ELIAS[6] [188], (*Elias[5] Elias[4] David[3] David[2] James[1]*) *b.* Morris Co., N. J., 3 Aug., 1797; *d.* McClellandtown, Fayette Co., Pa., 4 July, 1882; *m. n.* McClellandtown, Pa., 1817, Hannah Matilda, *dau.* John and Mary (Brown) Grove (*b.* Masontown, Pa., 1 Sept., 1800; *d.* McClellandtown, Pa., 28 Apl., 1881.) [*McClellandtown, Fayette Co., Pa.*

Children: (All *b.* McClellandtown, Fayette Co., Pa.)

528 I. Vincent[7] *b.* 12 Dec., 1817. FAM. CLXXXIII.
529 II. Harvey[7] *b.* 19 July, 1819; *d.* 5 June, 1822.
530 III. William Grove[7] *b.* — Sept., 1821. FAM. CLXXXIV.
531 IV. Reuben[7] *b.* 9 Nov., 1823; *d.* 26 Apl., 1884; *unm.*
532 V. Emily[7]† *b.* 25 Sept., 1825; *d.* Toledo, O., 12 June, 1902; *m.* McClellandtown, Pa., 11 Dec., 1845, John Thomas, *s.* Nicholas and Matilda (O'Dell) Worthington (*b.* Baltimore, Md., 18 Nov., 1818; *d.* Toledo, O., 1 Mch., 1884). *Issue:*

i. Hannah Matilda[8] (Worthington) *b.* Masontown, Pa., 23 Dec., 1849.[a] [*Toledo, O.*

533 VI. Mary[7]† *b.* 30 Aug., 1827; *m.* McClellandtown, Pa., 27 Dec., 1849, Thomas W. *s.* John and Catherine (Burchinal) Lyons (*b.* Gans Sta., Fayette Co., Pa., 22 Oct., 1821; *d.* Uniontown, Pa., 29 Sept., 1883). *Issue:* [*Uniontown, Pa.*

a. Hannah Matilda Worthington, *m.* Toledo, O., 22 Aug. 1883, George Eltweed *s.* George and Helen Augusta (Robinson) Pomeroy (*b.* Clinton, Mich., 27 Nov., 1848). *No issue.*†

---

* Fam. Recs. and pers. know., 533.
† Pers. statement.

i. Oliver[8] (Lyons) *b.* 18 Apl., 1851; *d.* 14 Aug., 1854.
ii. Ella C. (Lyons) *b.* 8 Nov., 1854.[a]
iii. A *dau. d. inf.*
iv. Hannah Matilda[8] (Lyons *b.* 12 May, 1861.[b]
v. Lizzie Lee[8] (Lyons) *d.* inf.
vi. William John[8] (Lyons) *b.* 29 Oct., 1868.[c]

534 VI. James M.[7] *b.* 22 Aug., 1829. FAM. CLXXXV.
535 VII. Maria[7] *b.* 7 May, 1831; *d.* Merrittstown,, Pa., 16 Sept., 1873; *m.* William Porter. *No issue.**
536 VIII. Hamilton[7] *b.* 10 Jany., 1833; *d.* 2 Oct., 1833.
537 IX. Nelson[7] *b.* 22 Feby., 1834; *d.* 2 July, 1834.
538 X. Elizabeth[7]* *b.* 9 Mch., 1836; *m.* German Tp., Fayette Co., Pa., 9 May, 1861, George,*s.* Edward Tiffin and Elizabeth Jane (Wilson) Porter (*b.* Indianapolis, Ind., 24 Oct., 1835). *Issue:*

i. Elizabeth[8] (Porter) *b.* 23 May, 1862.[d]

[*Pittsburg, Pa.*

a. Ella C. Lyons *d. n.* Morris Cross Roads, Fay. Co., Pa., 10 Apl., 1896; *m.* n. Morris Cross Roads, 25 Dec., 1878, Daniel P. s. William and Sarah Ann (Stentz) Morgan (*b.* Gans Sta. Pa., 26 Oct. 1851). *Issue: i.* Alice[9] (Morgan) *b.* 28 Oct., 1879; *ii.* Etta[9] (Morgan) *b.* 23 July, 1881; *iii.* Howard W.[9] (Morgan) *b.* 16 July, 1883; *iv.* Thomas W. Lyons[9] (Morgan) *b.* 29 Sept. 1885; *v.* Daniel S.[9] (Morgan) *b.* 10 June, 1900; *vi.* George Nell[9] (Morgan) *b.* 29 Mch., 1896.†

b. Hannah Matilda Lyons, *m. n.* Morris Cross Roads, Fay. Co., Pa., 3 Sept., 1890, Frank *s.* Col. Joseph and Margaretta (Miller) Snider (*b.* n. Rosedall Monongahela Co., Pa., 26 Feby., 1863). *Issue: i.* Joseph[9] (Snider) *b.* 25 Aug., 1894; *ii.* Mary[9] (Snider) *b.* 20 Dec., 1895; *iii.* Marguerite[9] (Snider) *b.* 20 Dec., 1895; *iv.* Thomas W. Lyons[9] (Snider) *b.* 13 June, 1897; *d.* 24 July, 1898; *v.* Frank[9] (Snider) *b.* 30 Aug., 1898*

c. William John Lyons, *m.* Pittsburg, Pa., 11 July, 1895, Emma J. *dau.* James Lynn. *Issue: i.* A *dau. d. inf.*; *ii.* Mary[9] (Lyons) *b.* 21 June, 1897; *iii.* Ella[9] (Lyons) *b.* 27 Oct., 1898; *iv.* Hannah Matilda[9] *b.* 27 Aug., 1902.†

d. Elizabeth Porter, *m.* German Tp., Fay. Co., Pa., ———— 188—, George Alexander, *s.* George Ewing and Sara (Trever) Hogg (*b.* Tower Hill, Fay. Co. Pa., 2 Feby., 1847). *Issue: i.* George Ewing Porter[9] (Hogg) *b.* 9 Mch., 1889; *ii.* Mildred Elizabeth[9] (Hogg) *b.* 9 Mch. 1891; *iii.* Sara Constance[9] (Hogg), *b.* 23 Feby., 1893; *iv.* Mary Caroline[9] (Hogg), *b.* 26 Mch., 1897; *v.* Trever[9] (Hogg) *b.* Apl., 1899.*

---

* Pers. statement.
† Fam. Recs. and pers. know., 533.

Elias Parshall

ii. Edward Tiffin[8] (Porter) *b.* 3 Apl., 1866.[a]
[*McClellandtown, Pa.*

iii. George[8] (Porter) *b.* 21 Nov., 1875.[b]
[*Uniontown, Pa.*

539 XI. Caroline[7]* *b.* 27 Jany., 1838; *m.* New Salem, Fayette Co., Pa., 9 Apl., 1856, Thomas Newton, *s.* John and Elizabeth (Dunaway) Weltner (*b.* Greene Co., Pa., 27 July, 1836; *d.* McClellandtown, Pa., 10 Aug., 1900). *Issue:* [*McClellandtown, Pa.*

i. John Seaton[8] (Weltner) *b.* 24 Jany., 1856.[c]
ii. Reuben Parshall[8] (Weltner) *b.* 6 Apl., 1859.[d]
iii. Florence[8] (Weltner) *b.* 15 Dec., 1865.[e]
iv. Frank[8] (Weltner) *b.* 15 Sept., 1870.[f]
v. William Worthington[8] (Weltner *b.* 24 Mch., 1873.[g]

a. Edward Tiffin Porter, *m.* German Tp., Fay. Co., Pa., 21 Mch., 1894, Julia Hurst, *dau.* William and Elizabeth (Hurst) McShane, *b.* Fay. Co., Pa., 24 Feby., 1867. *Issue: i.* George[9] (Porter) *b.* 2 Feby., 1896; *ii.* Edward Tiffin[9] (Porter) *b.* Jany., 1900.†

b. George Porter, *m.* Uniontown, Pa., 28 Mch., 1900, Mary *dau.* Aaron and Naomie (Grove) Moore (*b.* German Tp., Pa., 19 Sept., 1877).†

c. John Seaton Weltner, *m.* Uniontown, Pa., 9 Apl., 1878, Cordelia, *dau.* Samuel and Martha (Bashear) Ramage (*b.* High House, 4 Mch. 1860). *Issue: i.* Helen[9] (Weltner: *ii.* Wayne[9] (Weltner).‡

d. Reuben Parshall Weltner, *m.* Uniontown, Pa., 6 Jany., 1881, Lenore, *dau.* James M. and Elizabeth (——————) Allebough (*b.* Masonstown, Pa., 19 Sept., 1859). *Issue: i.* Loretta[9] (Weltner); *ii.* George[9] (Weltner); *iii.* Caroline[9] (Weltner).‡

e. Florence Weltner, *m.* McClellandtown, Pa., ——— ——— 18—, William A., *s.* Harvey and Mary P. (——————) Applegate (*b.* Sunny Side, Pa., 23 Oct., 1862). *Issue: i.* Mary Corinne[9] (Applegate); *ii.* Florence Weltner[9] (Applegate); *iii.* Caroline Parshall[9] (Applegate).‡

f. Frank (Weltner), *m.* Merrittstown, Fay. Co., Pa., 18 Sept., 1895, Jennie, *dau.* John Allen and Margaret (McCormick) McCombs, (*b. n.* New Salem, 3 Aug., 1874). *Issue: i.* Guy Carleton[9] (Weltner) *b.* 22 Dec., 1896; *ii.* Ernest Rupert[9] (Weltner) *b.* 6 June, 1898; *iii.* Clifford[9] (Weltner) *b.* 27 Jany., 1900.‡

g. William Worthington Weltner, *b.* Lisbon, O., 6 Mch., 1893, *m.* Maud Ellen *dau.* Henry Clay and Delia (Burson) Morris (*b.* Columbiana Co., O., 15 Sept., 1871). *Issue: i.* Nina Daisy[9] (Weltner); *ii.* Edgar Pomeroy[9] (Weltner); *iii.* Harold[9] (Weltner).‡

---

* Pers. statement.
† Fam. Recs. and pers. know, 538.
‡ Fam. Recs. and pers. know., 539.

vi. Helen[8] (Weltner) *b.* 14 Apl., 1877.[a]

540 XII. Hannah Matilda[7] *b.* 2 Feby., 1840; *d.* 28 Oct., 1844.

541 XIII. Stephen Calvin[7] *b.* 13 Feby., 1842; *d.* 9 Nov., 1844.

542 XIV. Sarah Helen[7]† *b.* 11 Apl., 1844; *m.* Uniontown, Pa., 4 Jany., 1882, Melancthon J., *s.* Isaac and Nancy (Kendal) Crow (*b.* McClellandtown, Pa., 9 Nov., 1838; *d.* Grand Ridge, Ill., 8 Apl., 1884). *No issue.*

543 XV. Louretta[7]† *b.* 17 Aug., 1845; *m.* McClellandtown, Pa., 14 Nov., 1872, Dr. George Washington *s.* Dr. George Williams and Mary Anne (Rhoads) Neff (*b.* Masontown, Pa., 19 Dec., 1845). *Issue:* (All *b.* Masontown, Pa.) [*Masontown, Pa.*

i. Robley Parshall[8] (Neff) *b.* 21 Jany., 1874; *d.* Masontown, Pa., 6 Aug., 1874.

ii. Hannah Matilda[8] (Neff) *b.* 12 Feby., 1875. [*Masontown, Pa.*

iii. Mary Anne[8] (Neff) *b.* 5 June, 1877. [*Masontown, Pa.*

iv. Louretta Parshall[8] (Neff) *b.* 11 Nov., 1879. [*Masontown, Pa.*

v. Elizabeth Porter[8] (Neff) *b.* 21 Mch., 1882. [*Masontown, Pa.*

Elias Parshall was one of the most respected residents of Fayette county. He was a successful farmer, stock dealer and wool grower, and amassed a large fortune. He was a man of excellent judgment and was immovable when once he had made up his

a. Helen Weltner, *m.* Fairmount, W. Va., 2 Feby., 1899, Samuel Cummins, *s.* William Porter and Elizabeth (———) Gwynne (*b.* Pittsburg, Pa., 3 Nov., 1868).*

* Fam. Recs. and pers. know., 539.
† Pers. statement.

mind. At his spacious mansion near McClellandtown, he dispensed a princely hospitality, which all his friends and acquaintances were privileged to share. He was seldom out of humor and was ever a kind and loving husband and indulgent father. His descendants are among the best and most respected people in Fayette county. (*See portrait.*)

---

*FAMILY LXXVII.**

JAMES[6] [189], (*Elias*[5] *Elias*[4] *David*[3] *David*[2] *James*[1]) *b.* McClellandtown, Pa., 23 Feby., 1800; *d.* Jefferson, Pa., 28 Mch., 1881; *m.* McClellandtown, Pa., 1 Mch., 1821, Hannah Coldron (*d.* 25 Oct., 1882).

Children:

544 1. Mary Jane[7]† *b.* McClellandtown, Pa., 27 Jany., 1822; *d. n.* Waynesburg, Pa., 7 Mch., 1884; *m.* Jefferson, Pa., 1854, James, *s.* John and Mary (Enlow) Patterson (*b. n.* Claysville, Wash. Co., Pa., 6 July, 1812; *d.* Greene Co., Pa., 10 July, 1885). *Issue:*

i. Jesse Coldron[8] (Patterson) *b.* 1855. [*Waverly, Ia.*

ii. James Morgan[8] (Patterson) *b.* 6 Mch., 1859; *d.* 17 Mch., 1859.

iii. Albert Enlow[8] (Patterson) *b.* 14 Mch., 1860.[a] [*Lot, W. Va.*

a. Albert Enlow Patterson, *m.* Uniontown, Pa., 2 Sept., 1886, Elvira, *dau.* Peter and Elizabeth (Haught) Glover, (*b.* Uniontown, Pa., 27 Aug., 1866). *Issue: i.* Royal Edward[9] (Patterson) *b.* Waynesburg, Pa., 27 June, 1888.‡

* Fam. Rec. and pers. know., 553.
† Fam. Recs. and pers. know., Albert E. Patterson.
‡ Pers. statement.

545 II. Nathaniel[7] *b.* 12 Feby., 1824. FAM. CLXXXVI.

546 III. Isaac Coldron *b.* 27 Mch., 1826; *d.* Mt. Carmel, Ind., 9 Nov., 1853.

547 IV. Emily[7] *m.* Thomas Hawkins.

548 V. Sarah Ann[7]* *b. n.* McClellandtown, Pa., 21 July, 1834; *m.* Jefferson, Greene Co., Pa., 10 Dec., 1852, Barnet, *s.* Hugh and Mary (————) Gladden (*b.* Greene Co., Pa., 13 Nov., 1825; *d.* Fredericktown, Pa., 27 Apl., 1899). *Issue:*

- i. Hannah[8] (Gladden) *b.* 22 Feby., 1854; *d.* 11 Nov., 1854.
- ii. Emma[8] (Gladden) *b.* 10 May, 1856.
- iii. Anna Maria[8] (Gladden) *b.* 19 June, 1860.
- iv. Mary Jane[8] (Gladden) *b.* 30 Nov., 1862.
- v. William Parshall[8] (Gladden) *b.* 16 Feby., 1864.
- vi. Sarah Belle[8] (Gladden) *b.* 5 May, 1865.

549 VI. Enos[7] *b.* 19 Aug., 1828; *d.* 4 Feby., 1831.

550 VII. John[7] *b.* 17 Jany., 1831. FAM. CLXXXVII.

551 VIII. William[7] *b.* 14 June, 1839. FAM. CLXXXVIII.

552 IX. James Tisdale[7] *b.* 22 July, 1844. FAM. CLXXXIX.

553 X. Albert[7] *b.* 26 Feby., 1847. FAM. CXC.

554 XI. Jeremiah H.[7]

FAMILY LXXVIII.†

JAMES CARLOW[6] [193], (*David*[5] *Elias*[4] *David*[3] *David*[2] *James*[1]) *b. n.* Morristown, N. J., 24 Sept., 1812; *d.* Wheeling, W. Va., 5 Dec., 1885; *m.* Janesville, O., — Oct., 1838, Mary Elizabeth, *dau.* John and Rachel (Lenfesty) Carlow (*b.* 26 May, 1819; *d.* Wheeling, W. Va., 15 Feby., 1844).

[*Wheeling, W. Va.*

---

* Pers. statement.
† Fam. Rec. and pers. know., 197; and wid., 557.

*Children:**

555 I. Mary Elizabeth[7] *d. inf.*
556 II. Caroline[7] *d. inf.*
557 III. John Carlow[7] *b.* Wheeling, W. Va., 11 Oct., 1839; *d. n.* Wheeling, W. Va., 27 May, 1897; *m.* West Liberty, W. Va., 11 Feby., 1886, Sarah Jane, *dau.* Joseph and Jane (Cox) Hedges (*b.* West Liberty, W. Va., 11 Jany., 1854). *No issue.*
[*Wheeling, W. Va.*

---

*FAMILY LXXIX.**

DAVID YOUNGS[6] [194] (*David*[5] *Elias*[4] *David*[3] *David*[2] *James*[1]) *b.* Uniontown, Pa., — Dec., 1816; *d.* Belmont Co., O., — Dec., 1889; *m.* Belmont Co., O., Jane, *dau.* Gen. William and Nancy (————) Dunn (*d.* 1884)[a] [*Wheeling, W. Va.*

Children: (All *b.* Belmont Co., O.)

558 I. William Dunn[7] *b.* 8 Mch., 1848. FAM. CXCI.
559 II. David Thomas[7] *b.* 28 May, 1852. FAM. CXCII.
560 III. John Alexander (Dr.)[7] *b.* 16 Mch., 1854; *unm.*[b]
[*Cleveland, O.*

a. Gen. William Dunn was of Scotch descent and in his life time was one of the most prominent men in Ohio. He was commissioned Major General and ordered to the front during the Mexican War, but was recalled with his command before reaching the scene of hostilities. He was an influential member of the Ohio Legislature and a man of affairs. His residence was in Belmont county, where he had an estate of 1,000 acres of land. He *d.* in 1868 at the age of 84 years.

b. Dr. Parshall was graduated from the Medical Dept. of the Western Reserve University, 3 Mch., 1886, and has been engaged in active practice since. He is of an exteremely ingenious turn of mind and has patented several very clever inventions.

---

* Fam. Recs. and pers. know., 560 and 561.

561 iv. Mary Virginia[7]* *b.* 27 Dec., 1855; *m.* Martins Ferry, Belmont Co., O., 15 Aug., 1877, William, *s.* William and Jane (Patton) Goodhue (*b.* Martins Ferry, O., 6 Aug., 1850). *Issue:* [*Norwalk, O.*

i. Grace Greenwood[8] (Goodhue) *b.* 13 Oct., 1878.
ii. Ira David[8] (Goodhue) *b.* 8 Jany., 1886.
iii. Frances Jean[8] (Goodhue) *b.* 28 Jany., 1888.
iv. Edna Rose[8] (Goodhue) *b.* 6 Jany., 1890.

562 v. Frances Jane[7] *b.* 1 May, 1861. [*Norwalk, O.*

FAMILY LXXX.†

CLARK D.[6] [201], (*James*[5] *James*[4] *David*[3] *David*[2] *James*[1]) *b.* Middlefield, Otsego Co., N. Y., 12 Sept., 1804; *d.* Middlefield, N. Y., 5 Apl., 1889; *m.* 22 Mch., 1827, Hannah, *dau.* Alden Coats (*b.* Springfield, N. Y.; *d.* Middlefield, N. Y., 5 Oct., 1866). [*Middlefield, N. Y.*

Children:

563 I. Helen Mar[7] *b.* Middlefield, N. Y., 23 Mch., 1828; *m.* (1) 23 June, 1847, Harrison North (*d.* 13 Feby., 1875). *Issue:* [*Utica, N. Y.*

i. Charles D.[8] (North) *b.* 15 Sept., 1857.[a] [*Middlefield, N. Y.*

m. (2) Miles C. Comstock. *No issue.*

a. Charles D. North, *m.* 7 Sept., 1881, Cora L. Allen. *Issue:* i. Helen Mar.*

---

* Pers. statement.
† Fam. Rec. and pers. know., 563.

FAMILY LXXXI.*

MINER CORNWALL[6] [202], (*James*[5] *James*[4] *David*[3] *David*[2] *James*[1]) *b.* Middlefield, Otsego Co., N. Y., 15 Aug., 1806; *d.* Hartwick, Otsego Co., N. Y., 3 Aug., 1873; *m.* Middlefield N. Y., 1 Mch., 1832, Caroline Eliza, *dau.* Jonathan P. and Hannah (Sherman) Coffin (*b.* Middlefield, N. Y., 13 Aug., 1813; *d.* 1876).* [*Hartwick, Otsego Co., N. Y.*

Children: (All *b.* Middlefield, Otsego Co., N. Y.)

564 I. Orestes Horace[7] *b.* 21 July, 1842; *unm.*† [*Detroit, Mich.*

565 II. Charlotte Augusta[7]† *b.* Middlefield, N. Y., 7 Feby., 1836; *m.* Hartwick Seminary, N. Y., 15 Sept., 1858, Morgan Sharpsteen, *s.* William Gould and Anna (Sharpsteen) Northrup (*b.* Washington Tp., Dutchess Co., N. Y., 5 Dec., 1830). *Issue:* [*Mt. Vision, Otsego Co., N. Y.*

i. George Edwin[8] (Northrup) *b.* 18 Oct., 1852.
ii. Isabelle Eliza[8] (Northup) *b.* 28 May, 1856.[a]

566 III. Amanda Perry[7]† *b.* Middlefield, N. Y., 29 June, 1842; *m.* Hartwick, N. Y., 9 Feby., 1863, John Lawyer, *s.* Alvin P. and Roseanna (Mallory) Converse (*b.* Hartwick, N. Y., — Oct., 1841; *d.* Cooperstown, N. Y., 6 July, 1887). *Issue:* [*Cooperstown, N. Y.*

a. Isabella Eliza Northup, *m.* 16 Mch., 1892, Charles Edwin Beekley.†

* Fam. Rec. and pers. know., 566.
† Pers. statement.

i. Robert Ralph[8] (Converse) *b.* 11 Nov., 1863.*

567 IV. Elizabeth Frost[7]* *b.* Middlefield, N. Y., 13 June, 1847; *m.* Seymour Teachout.

FAMILY LXXXII.†

DANIEL SHOVE[6] [203], (*James*[5] *James*[4] *David*[3] *David*[2] *James*[1]) *b.* Middlefield, N. Y., 12 Jany., 1809; *d.* — Oct., 1881; *m.* 15 Jany., 1829, Sarah B, Stockton, of New Jersey.

[*Rochester, N. Y.*

Children:

568 I. Anna V.[7] *b.* 15 Oct., 1829; *d.* 26 Apl., 1900; *m.* Clarksville, Otsego Co., N. Y., 20 Oct., 1849, Theodore Slawson. *Issue:*

569 II. Stockton Thomas[7] *b.* 1833. FAM. CXCIII.

FAMILY LXXXIII.‡

ANSON CORNWALL[6] (Hon.) [205], (*James*[5] *James*[4] *David*[3] *David*[2] *James*[1]) *b.* 1 Aug., 1811; *d.* Binghamton, N. Y., 3 Jany., 1883; *m.* Clarksville, Otsego Co., N. Y., 28 Jany., 1844, Emma Clark, *dau.* John and Eliza (Pinney) Hayden (*b.* Clarksville, N. Y.; *d.* Cooperstown, N. Y., 16 Sept., 1895).

[*Clarksville, Otsego Co., N. Y.*

a. Robert Ralph Converse, *m.* Hartwick, Otsego Co., N. Y., 2 May, 1885, Fanny May, *dau.* John M. and Catherine (Connell) Houch, (*b.* Toddsville, Otsego Co., N. Y., 20 Oct., 18—). *Issue*: *i.* Fannie May[9] (Converse) *b.* 4 Apl., 1889; *ii.* Robert Ralph[9] (Converse), *d. inf.**

---

* Pers. statement.
† Fam. Rec. and pers. know., Theo. Slawson.
‡ Fam. Recs. and per. know., 576.

Children:

570 I. Louise Marie[7] *b.* Clarksville, N. Y., 19 Nov., 1851; *m.* Cooperstown, N. Y., 22 Oct., 1851, Rensselaer, *s.* Rensselaer and Olive (Green(Palmer. *Issue:* [*Cooperstown, N. Y.*

i. Guy Ely[8] (Palmer) *b.* 12 Oct. 1876.

---

*FAMILY LXXXIV.**

ALFRED FORD[6] [208], (*James*[5] *James*[4] *David*[3] *David*[2] *James*[1]) *b.* 19 Apl., 1817; *d.* 5 Apl., 1845; *m.* 26 June, 1839, Harriet Eliza, *dau.* John B. and Henrietta (———) North (*d.* Ilion, N. Y., 1 Sept., 1894).

Children:

571 I. Jane A.[7] *d. inf.*
572 II. John Benjamin[7] *b.* 26 Sept., 1842. FAM. CXCII.
573 III. Alfred Ford.[7]

FAMILY LXXXV.†

JAMES NICHOLS[6] [209], (*James*[5] *James*[4] *David*[3] *David*[2] *James*[1]) *b.* Middlefield, Otsego Co., N. Y., 3 July, 1819; *d.* Cherry Valley, N. Y., 23 Mch., 1878; *m.* Worcester, N. Y., 8 Mch., 1843, Delia Ann, *dau.* Dr. Uriah G. and Henrietta (Barney) Bigelow (*b.* Worcester, N. Y., 9 Mch., 1820; *d.* Milford, N. Y., 15 Aug., 1872). [*Milford, Otsego Co., N. Y.*

* Bible Rec. 73, pers. know., 572.
† Bible Rec. 209; Fam. Rec. and pers. know. 576; Bigelow Gen. 209.

Children:

574 I. Henrietta Maria[7] *b.* Albany, N. Y., 4 July, 1844; *d.* Middlefield, N. Y., 15 Jany., 1851.

575 II. Alfred Gregory[7] *b.* 16 Oct., 1847. FAM. CXCV.

576 III. Lucy Elizabeth[7]* *b.* Middlefield, N. Y., 9 Sept., 1850; *m.* Milford, N. Y., 9 Mch., 1869, Rudolph, *s.* Peter A. and Nancy (Keller) Nellis (*b.* Westville, N. Y., 2 Apl., 1844). *Issue:* [*Cherry Valley, N. Y.*

i. James Peter[8] (Nellis) *b.* 2 Nov., 1872.[a] [*Cherry Valley, N. Y.*

577 IV. Henrietta Olivia[7] *b.* Middlefield, N. Y., 9 Mch., 1855. [*Utica, N. Y.*

578 V. James Ayre[7] *b.* Middlefield, N. Y., 23 Nov., 1857; *d.* Middlefield, N. Y., 9 June, 1858.

FAMILY LXXXVI.†

REVILO FORD[6] (Rev.) [211], (*James*[5] *James*[4] *David*[3] *David*[2] *James*[1]) *b.* Middlefield, N. Y., 30 Aug., 1822; *d.* Chicago, Ill., 23 Feby., 1896; *m.* Cooperstown, N. Y., 25 Aug., 1845, Amanda Minerva, *dau.* Thomas and Clarinda (Ismond) Bailey (*b.* Clarksville, N. Y., 20 July, 1826). [*Chicago, Ill.*

Children:

579 I. Ella Augusta[7] *b.* Westford, Otsego Co., N. Y., 27 Aug., 1846; *m.* Carrollton, Ill., 6 Sept., 1870, Wil-

a. James Peter Nellis, *m.* Cherry Valley, N. Y., 20 Oct., 1897, Nellie C. *dau.* John and Janette (Davidson) Whiteman, (*b.* Cherry Valley, 5 Jany., 1875). *Issue: i.* Charles Willard[9] (Nellis) *b.* 5 Feby., 1900.*

---

* Pers. statement.
† Bible Rec. 73, and Fam. Rec. and pers. know., 579.

R. F. Parshall,

liam Wilson, *s.* John and Eliza (Wilson) Beaty (*b.* Hanover, N. J., 17 Sept., 1841). *Issue:* [*Chicago, Ill.*

i. Tessa LeRoy[8] (Beaty) *b.* 20 Dec., 1871.[a] [*Chicago, Ill.*

580 II. LeRoy Dwight[7] *b.* Sloansville, N. Y., 14 Feby., 1849; *d.* Carrollton, Ill., 24 Dec., 1870.

581 III. Anna Louisa[7] *b.* Sloansville, N. Y., 7 Jany., 1851; *m.* Carrollton, Ill., 6 Sept., 1870, Henry, *s.* Alexander and Amanda (Robinson) Smith. *Issue:* [*Chicago, Ill.*

i. Maud Leroy[8] (Smith) *b.* 18 Sept., 1871; *d.* 27 May, 1885. [*Chicago, Ill.*

ii. Paul Clare[8] (Smith) *b.* 20 Jany., 1874.[b] [*Chicago, Ill.*

iii. Arthur Ford[8] (Smith) *b.* 31 Aug., 1876. [*Chicago, Ill.*

iv. Earl Scott[8] (Smith) *b.* 18 June, 1884.

v. Carl Henry[8] (Smith) *b.* 31 Oct., 1887.

582 IV. Fred Sella[7] *b.* Fort Edward, N. Y., 30 Apl., 1857; *d.* Tomah, Wis., 7 Aug., 1887; *unm.*

Rev. Revilo F. Parshall was the youngest of a family of eleven children, and the ministry was his chosen profession from early youth. He received a common school education and at nineteen years of age entered the Theological Department of Madison

a. Tessa LeRoy Beaty, *m.* Chicago, 3 Oct., 1900, Thaddeus Oscar, *s.* Thaddeus Morehouse and Elizabeth (Edmeston) Bunch, (*b.* Paxton, Ill., 26 Oct., 1874).

b. Paul Clare Smith, *m.* Taylorville, 24 June, 1896, Little, *dau.* Newell Douglas, Ricks (*b.* Taylorville, Ill.) *Issue:* i. Douglas Henry[9] (Smith) *b.* Chicago, 19 Aug., 1899.

University. Finishing the theological course in two years, he was ordained at Westford, Otsego Co., N. Y., shortly after attaining his majority. His first charge was the Westford Baptist church, where he remained three years. The next seven years were spent as pastor of the Sloansville (N. Y.) Baptist church, and the succeeding five years in the Fort Edward (N. Y.) church. Going thence to Wisconsin, he founded the Afton Baptist church and subsequently held charges in West Salem, Sparta, Tomah and New Lisbon, in Wisconsin, and in Carrollton, Ill. Receiving a call to the Oakland (Cal.) Baptist church, he went thither and subsequently filled pulpits at Sacramento, Healdsburg and Valejo, in that State. In 1887, he narrowly escaped death in an accident on the Chicago, Milwaukee and St. Paul Railway, one of his limbs being so badly crushed that amputation became necessary. This terminated his active ministerial career and thenceforth until his death he made his home in Chicago. His career was a remarkable one. He combined shrewd business tact with earnest enthusiasm in the cause of religion. More than 6,000 persons are said to owe their conversion to his efforts. More than two score ministers owed their first start in the profession to his helpful offices. As an exhorter he was earnest and forceful, imparting some of his own enthusiasm to all who heard him. (*See portrait.*)

---

*FAMILY LXXXVII.**

JESSE[6] [212], (*Israel[5] James[4] David[3] David[2] James[1]*) *b.* Middlefield, N. Y., 22 Dec., 1807; *d.* Cooperstown, N. Y., 3 June, 1884; *m.* Cherry Valley, N. Y., 19 Dec., 1835, Harriet Dutcher (*b.* 28 Sept., 1815; *d.* Coldwater, Mich., 11 Feby., 1886). [*Cooperstown, N. Y.*

* Fam. Rec. and pers. know., 583.

Children:

583 I. Helen Mary[7] *b.* Cherry Valley, N. Y., 5 Sept., 1857; *m.* (1) Cooperstown, N. Y., 29 Aug., 1861, Erastus, *s.* Chandler Root, of Cooperstown, N. Y., (*d.* 25 Apl., 1886.) *No issue.*
m. (2) 23 Nov., 1868, Robert K., *s.* William and Susan (————) Stewart, of New York, (*d.* 29 Nov., 1884). *No issue.* [*Coldwater, Mich.*

584 II. Rexeville[7] *d. inf.*

585 III. Ortense[7] *d. inf.*

586 IV. Israel A.[7] *b.* 24 July, 1844. FAM. CXCIV.

587 V. Leroy Lloyd[7] *b.* Westville, Otsego Co., N. Y., 14 May, 1849; *d.* Coldwater, Mich., 18 Apl., 1892; *m.* Coldwater, Mich., 19 July, 1877, Elizabeth A. *dau.* Jacob and Elizabeth C., (————) Bernhardt (*b.* Three Rivers, Wis., 20 Jany., 1849). *No issue.* [*Coldwater, Mich.*

---

*FAMILY LXXXVIII.**

JAMES[6] [215], (*Israel[5] James[4] David[3] David[2] James[1]*) *b.* Otsego Co., N. Y., 19 Dec., 1815; *d.* Springfield, Minn., 6 Jany., 1898; *m.* Cherry Valley, N. Y., 5 May, 1840, Catherine, *dau.* George and Laney (Garlock) Nellis (*b.* Fort Plain, N. Y., 31 Mch., 1823). [*Springfield, Minn.*

Children:

588 I. Clarissa[7]† *b.* Otsego Co., N. Y., 17 June, 1841; *m.* (1) Rock Co., Wis., 21 Apl., 1858, Albert, *s.* Garrett and Catherine (————) Smith (*b.* Herk. Co., N. Y., 28 June, 1836; *d.* 7 Oct., 1871). *Issue:* [*Mt. Vernon, Ill.*

---

* Fam. Rec. and pers. know., 589 and Wld. 215.
† Pers. statement.

i. Ida May[8] (Smith) *b.* 8 June, 1860.
ii. George Albert[8] (Smith) *b.* 21 Apl., 1861.
iii. Clarke[8] (Smith) *b.* 25 Nov., 1866.
iv. Charles Henry[8] (Smith) *b.* 25 Mch., 1868; *d.* 19 Feby., 1893.
v. Stephen Jefferson[8] (Smith) *b.* 5 May, 1871.

m. (2) Worthington, Minn., 29 Mch., 1874, Gamaliel, *s.* Thomas and Mary Ann (Burgess) Scutt (*b.* Columbia, N. Y., 12 June, 1837). *Issue*:

vi. James Thomas[8] (Scutt) *b.* 15 Mch., 1875.
vii. Garfield[8] (Scutt) *b.* 12 Oct., 1882.

589 II. Rexeville[7]* *b.* Otsego Co., N. Y., 15 May, 1843; *m.* Big Grove, Benton Co., Ia., 26 Nov., 1868, Julius J., *s.* John H. and Eliza (Gardner) Westinghouse (*b.* 11 Dec., 1844). *Issue:* [*Springfield, Minn.*

i. John H.[8] (Westinghouse) *b.* 16 Feby., 1871; *d.* 26 Feby., 1871.
ii. Hattie E.[8] (Westinghouse) *b.* 10 Jany., 1872; *d.* 26 May, 1877.
iii. Violetta[8] (Westinghouse) *b.* 13 Aug., 1874; *d.* 14 Aug., 1881.
iv. Bert[8] (Westinghouse) *b.* 18 Feby., 1879.
v. Gertrude[8] (Westinghouse) *b.* 25 Aug., 1881.

590 III. Jonas Israel[7] *b.* 1 Nov., 1845. FAM. CXCVII.

591 IV. Mary Elizabeth[7]* *b.* Cherry Valley, N. Y., 30 Dec., 1846; *m.* Vinton, Benton Co., Ia., 3 Jany., 1866, Henry T., *s.*, Cornelius and Susanna (Adams) Lauderbaugh (*b.* Waynesboro, Pa., 20 Nov., 1842). *Issue:* [*Chattanooga, Tenn.*

* Pers. statement.

i. Annie[8] (Lauderbaugh) *b.* 8 May, 1867; *d.* 1 Sept., 1867.

ii. John D.[8] (Lauderbaugh) *b.* 14 Sept., 1869. *Unm.* [*Highland Park, Tenn.*

iii. James B.[8] (Lauderbaugh) *b.* 11 Oct., 1871.[a]

592 v. James[7] *b.* Otsego Co., N. Y., 21 Aug., 1848.

593 vi. George[7] *b.* 10 Dec., 1850. Fam. CXCVIII.

594 vii. William[7] *b.* Otsego Co., N. Y., 5 May, 1852; *d.* 15 Nov., 1852.

595 viii. Adelmar[7] *b.* Otsego Co., N. Y., 1 Apl., 1856.

596 ix. Estella[7]* *b.* Rock Co., Wis., 28 Jany., 1859; *m.* 24 July, 1859, William Elijah, *s.* Fred and Mary Ann (Roby) Bloom (*b.* Green Co., Wis., 19 Oct., 1860). *Issue:* [*Worthington, Minn.*

i. Clarinda Ethel[8] (Bloom) *b.* 21 Aug., 1882.

ii. George Luther[8] (Bloom) *b.* 14 June, 1885.

iii. Harry Edlow[8] (Bloom) *b.* 1 Feby., 1887.

iv. John William[8] (Bloom) *b.* 16 Jany., 1893.

v. Barbara Catherine[8] (Bloom) *b.* 2 Oct., 1898.

597 x. Dewitt Clinton[7] *b.* 19 June, 1861. Fam. CIC.

FAMILY LXXXIX.†

JOHN ABEL[6] [219], (*Miner*[5] *James*[4] *David*[3] *David*[2] *James*[1]) *b.* Pierstown, Otsego Co., N. Y., 25 Sept., 1818; *d.* Delhi, N. Y., 27 Apl., 1899; *m.* Delhi, N. Y., 4 June, 1844, Juliette, *dau.* Ferdinand and Dorothy (McLean) Thurber (*b.* Delhi, N. Y., 8 Aug., 1824). [*Delhi, N. Y.*

a. James B. Lauderbaugh, *m.* Chattanooga, Tenn., Elizabeth, *dau.* Jean and Elizabeth (Rickaby) Michel, (*b.* New Orleans, 15 Aug., 1876).*

---

* Pers. statement.
† Fam. Recs. and pers. know., 598.

Children: (All *b.* Delhi, N. Y.)

598 I. Elizabeth[7]* *b.* 28 Dec., 1845; *m.* Delhi, N. Y., 16 Aug., 1866, William R., *s.* William and Mary (Barry) Hull (*b.* New York, 12 Jany., 1843; *d.* Litchfield, Conn., 3 May, 1879). *Issue:* [*Delhi, N. Y.*

i. Elizabeth[8] (Hull) *b.* 8 July, 1867; *d.* 8 Sept., 1868.

ii. Wallace Parshall[8] (Hull) *b.* 17 Feby., 1871; *d.* 5 Dec., 1887.

iii. Mary Barry[8] (Hull) *b.* 5 Dec., 1872; *unm.* [*Delhi, N. Y.*

599 II. William Ambrose[7] *b.* 23 May, 1848; *d.* New York, 21 Dec., 1892; *unm.* [*New York, N. Y.*

John A. Parshall was a printer for more than sixty years, and a man loved and respected by all who knew him. In the course of his long life, he served the people of Delhi as President of the Village, Trustee, Clerk of the Board of Trustees, Fire Commissioner and in fact in every office within the gift of his fellow townsmen. It is said that he occupied the same case, in the same office, at the same window for more than fifty years, and that he "set" birth, death and marriage notices for three generations of his neighbors. (*See portrait.*)

FAMILY XC.†

ROBERT ASAHEL[6] [220], (*Miner,*[5] *James,*[4] *David,*[3] *David, James*[1]) *b.* Pierstown, Otsego Co., N. Y., 14 July, 1820; *d.* Cooperstown, N. Y., 7 Oct., 1900; *m.* Roseboom, Otsego Co., N. Y., 14 Jany., 1852, Catherine, *dau.* Asa and Elizabeth (Lough) Howland (*b.* Roseboom, N. Y., 23 Mch., 1834). [*Cooperstown, N. Y.*

* Pers. statement.
† Fam. Recs. and pers. know., Wid., 220.

John A. Fairchild.

Children:

600 I. Elizabeth Huldah[7]* *b.* Pierstown, N. Y., 16 Feby., 1853; *m.* Pierstown, N. Y., 25 Dec., 1873, Irvin, *s.* Almon and Emeline (Boyce) Grover. *Issue:* [*Cooperstown, N. Y.*

i. William A.[8] (Grover) *b.* 19 Oct., 1874; *unm.* [*Cooperstown, N. Y.*

ii. Alice M.[8] (Grover) *b.* 24 Mch., 1882.

iii. Mabel E.[8] (Grover) *b.* 18 June, 1886.

601 II. Ambrose[7] *b.* 26 June, 1856; *d.* 19 Dec., 1861.

602 III. Flora[7] *b.* 4 Mch., 1859; *d.* 14 Nov., 1861.

603 IV. Ten Eyck C.[7]* *b.* 16 June, 1862; *m.* Springfield Centre, N. Y., (Mrs.) Minnie L. Tunnicliff. *No issue.* *m.* (2) Stone Arabia, Otsego Co., N. Y., 23 Aug., 1889, Belle [628], *dau* Adriel and Louise (Dutcher) Parshall (*b.* 26 Aug., 1860). *No issue.* [*Fort Plain, N. Y.*

604 V. Emory Upton[7]* *b.* 16 July, 1864; *m.* Pierstown, N. Y., 17 Dec., 1890, Augusta M., *dau.* Deacon W. Kendrick and Jeanette M. (Miller) Warren. *No issue.* [*Cooperstown, N. Y.*

605 VI. Nellie[7]* *b.* 7 June, 1869; *m.* Richfield Springs, N. Y., 12 Oct., 1892, Thomas O., *s.* William and Mary (Rentole) McDonald. *Issue:* [*Pittsburg, Pa.*

i. Lee Parshall[8] (McDonald) *b.* 23 May, 1893.

ii. Jessie F.[8] (McDonald) *b.* 12 Mch., 1895; *d.* 19 Feby., 1896.

iii. Firman A.[8] (McDonald) *b.* 28 Feby., 1899.

606 VII. Lee[7] *b.* 17 Oct., 1871. FAM. CC.

† Pers. statement.

*FAMILY XCI.**

WILLIAM[6] [222], (*Miner*[5] *James*[4] *David*[3] *David*[2] *James*[1]) *b.* Pierstown, Otsego Co., N. Y., 7 Nov., 1823; *d.* Syracuse, N. Y., 5 June, 1892; *m.* Syracuse, N. Y., 1 Sept., 1858, Elizabeth, *dau.* William and Esther Riggs (Orton) Barker† (*b.* Manlius, Onondago Co., N. Y., 11 Sept., 1836). [*Syracuse, N. Y.*

Children: (All *b.* Syracuse, N. Y.)

607 I. James Clark[7] *b.* 30 June, 1859. FAM. CCI.
608 II. Helen Esther[7] *b.* 15 Dec., 1860; *unm.* [*Syracuse, N. Y.*
609 III. William Barker[7] *b.* 12 Sept., 1862. FAM. CCII.
610 IV. Fanny Hall[7]‡ *b.* 15 July, 1864; *m.* Syracuse, N. Y., 28 Oct., 1880, James, *s.* Hon. James and Elizabeth (Caldwell) Noxon (*b.* Syracuse, N. Y., 3 May, 1857). *Issue:* (All *b.* Winona, Minn.) [*Syracuse, N. Y.*

i. Elizabeth[8] (Noxon) *b.* 1 Nov., 1887.
ii. James Alan[8] (Noxon) *b.* 14 June, 1890.

611 V. John Miner[7] *d. inf.*
612 VI. Caroline Elizabeth[7] *b.* 29 Mch., 1871; *unm.* [*Syracuse, N. Y.*
613 VII. Mary Louise[7]‡ *b.* 15 Jany., 1875; *m.* Syracuse, N. Y., 26 Apl., 1900, Henry Monroe, *s.* Henry Elisha and Ellen (Lewis) Ford (*b.* Syracuse, N. Y., 17 Aug., 1865). *Issue:* [*Syracuse, N. Y.*

i. Dorothy Lewis[8] (Ford) *b.* 4 Feby., 1901.

---

* Fam. Rec. and pers. know., 607.
† Marriage cert. pos., 607.
‡ Pers. statement.

Wm Parshall

William Parshall left home when a boy of fourteen to seek his fortune. Going to Rochester, N. Y., he spent the years 1838 and 1839, working in a dry goods store. At the end of that time he returned to Cooperstown, where he was employed in a hardware store. In 1848, he came to Syracuse, and on April 5th of that year, entered the employ of Norton, Hall & Co., the largest hardware dealers in that part of the State. Two years later, in 1850, he bought out the interest of Mr. Hall, and the firm subsequently became Norton, Bradley & Co., Bradley, Parshall & Co., and Parshall & Searl. In all these firms Mr. Parshall was the practical hardware man of the concern and was noted as a shrewd and careful buyer and conservative business man. In 1890, having accumulated a fortune, he retired from business. Close and economical in business matters, in his family he was liberal to a fault, and no wish of his children was ever too extravagant for him to gratify. Though not a member of the church, he was always interested in its welfare and contributed liberally to religious work. He was a member of the Board of Trustees of the Park Central Presbyterian church of Syracuse for more than forty years, and was Chairman of the Board for nearly that length of time. A business man of the "old school," his *word* was always better than another man's *bond*. Honest and upright himself, he ever sought to instill sentiments of honor and honesty into his children, his servants and his clerks. Few men have left behind them such a reputation for integrity as he. Honored and respected in the community where he lived, loved by his family, as few fathers are, he met death with the serene fortitude with which he had met every crisis of his life. (*See portrait.*)

*FAMILY XCII.**

PETER[6] [227], (*George*[5] *James*[4] *David*[3] *David*[2] *James*[1]) *b.* Middlefield, Otsego Co., N. Y., 24 Nov., 1827; *m.* Middlefield, N. Y., 29 May, 1855, Ordelia, *dau.* Benjamin and Catherine (Shiels) Pitts (*b.* 29 Oct., 1835; *d.* Whitesville, Allegany Co., N. Y., 24 July, 1880). [*Cooperstown, N. Y.*,

Children: (All *b.* Middlefield, N. Y.)

614 I. Latonus J.[7] *b.* 17 Nov., 1860. FAM. CCIII.
615 II. Lulu[7] *b.* 17 Apl., 1865; *m.* Cooperstown, N. Y., 17 Oct., 1889, Charles H., *s.* Norman L. and Jennie (Huntington) Mason (*b.* Middlefield Center, N. Y., 26 Aug., 1861). *Issue:* [*Cooperstown, N. Y.*

i. Jennie Ordelia[8] (Mason) *b.* 23 May, 1892.

FAMILY XCIII.†

DANIEL[6] [229], (*George*[5], *James*[4], *David*[3], *David*[2], *James*[1]) *b.* Middlefield, Otsego Co., N. Y., 24 Apl., 1833; *m.* Westford, Otsego Co., N. Y., 28 Oct., 1868, Estelle C., *dau.* John A. and Mahala (Bates) Snyder (*b.* Westville, Otsego Co., N. Y., 28 Oct., 1848). *Issue:* [*Cooperstown, N. Y.*

Children: (All *b.* Middlefield, N. Y.)

616 I. Floyd B.[7] *b.* 1 Nov., 1872; *unm.* [*Middlefield, N. Y.*

---

* Fam. Recs. and pers. know., 615.
† Fam. Recs. and pers. know., 617.

G W Parshall

617 II. Grace L.[7] *b.* 13 Apl., 1876; *m.* Cooperstown, N. Y., 30 Apl., 1896, Dr. Bennett W., *s.* John F. and ——— (Bennett) Dewar (*b.* Oneonta, N. Y., 2 Mch., 1871). *No issue.* [*Cooperstown, N. Y.*

---

*FAMILY XCIV.**

GEORGE WASHINGTON[6] [230], (*George*[5], *James*[4], *David*[3], *David*[2], *James*[1]) *b.* Middlefield, Otsego Co., N. Y., 4 Apl., 1837; *m.* Middlefield, N. Y., 11 Feby., 1865, Harriet I., *dau.* Charles G. and Priscilla (Wiltse) Coffin (*b.* Middlefield, N. Y., 27 July, 1842; *d.* Middlefield, N. Y., 22 Feby., 1900). [*Cooperstown, N. Y.*

Children: (All *b.* Middlefield, N. Y.)

618 I. Charles Henry[7] *b.* 12 Jany., 1866. FAM. CCIV.
619 II. Lynn George[7] *b.* 14 July, 1870. FAM. CCV.
620 III. Karl Alfred[7] *b.* 4 Aug., 1877.[a] [*New York.*

Received a common school education. Left home when sixteen years of age and learned the trade of a wagonmaker, which he followed for ten years. When twenty-six years of age he bought a farm and followed the calling of a farmer until 1895. He was one of the largest hop growers in the State, as high as 20,000 pounds having been raised by him in a single year. In 1898, was elected Supervisor of the Town of Middlefield, and re-elected for several terms. Was president of the Otsego County Agricultural Society in 1899. (*See portrait.*)

a. Karl Alfred Parshall was a graduate of the Cooperstown High School and of the Albany Medical College and a licensed practitioner. He was formerly a member of the staff of the Saratoga (N. Y.) hospital, and is now in general practice in New York City.

* Fam. Rec. and pers. know., 230.

*FAMILY XCV.**

FARRAND COFFIN[6] [234], *(Gilbert[5], James[4], David[3], David[2], James[1])* *b.* Middlefield, Otsego Co., N. Y., 12 Dec., 1828; *d.* Cooperstown, N. Y., 26 Mch., 1892; *m.* Portlandville, Otsego Co., N. Y., 23 Oct., 1851, Jane Hoff, *dau.* Lewis and Catherine Hoff (Covert) Barnum (*b.* Middlefield, N. Y., 22 June, 1834). [*Cooperstown, N. Y.*

Children:

621 I. Estelle Ann[7] *d. inf.*
622 II. Mary L.[7] *b.* Middlefield, N. Y., 19 Oct., 1855. [*Glens Falls, N. Y.*
623 III. Louis Gilbert[7] *d. inf.*
624 IV. Grace Belle[7] *b.* Cooperstown, N. Y., 6 Sept., 1869. [*Glens Falls, N. Y.*

FAMILY XCVI.†

JAMES GILES[6] [235], *(Gilbert[5], James[4], David[3], David[2], James)* *b.* Middlefield, Otsego Co., N. Y., 7 Feby., 1830; *d.* Cooperstown, N. Y., 19 Apl., 1903; *m.* (1), Springfield, Otsego Co., N. Y., 23 Nov., 1853, Mary E., *dau.* Abram B. and Elvira (Pier) Van Horne (*b.* Otsego Co., N. Y., 17 Oct., 1832; *d.* Springfield, N. Y., 17 Oct., 1855). [*Cooperstown, N. Y.*

Children:

625 I. Willie Gilbert[7] *d. inf.*

---

* Fam. Recs. and pers. know., 622.
† Pers. statement.

m. (2) 11 Oct., 1859, Cornelia E., *dau.* Abram B. and Elvira (Pier) Van Horne (*b.* Otsego Co., N. Y., — Apl., 1838; *d.* 16 Apl., 1863).

Children:

626 II. Cornelia Maria[7] *b.* Utica, N. Y., 13 Apl., 1863; *d.* Utica, N. Y., 8 Dec., 1892; *m.* Bridgewater, Oneida Co., N. Y., — Aug., 1887, Dr. David Slade, *s.* John and Esther E. (Williams) Eynor (*b.* Utica, N. Y., 30 Mch., 1863; *d.* Utica, N. Y., 22 Mch., 1897). *Issue:* [*Utica, N. Y.*

i. John Stewart[8] (Eynor) *b.* Bridgewater, N. Y., 26 Apl., 1889. [*New York, N. Y.*

m. (3) Fort Plain, N. Y., 11 June, 1879, Kate R., *dau.* Parks and Sarah Ann (Young) Baird (*b.* Wayne Co., Pa., 22 May, 1837). *No issue.*

---

*FAMILY XCVII.**

ADRIEL[6] [236], *(Gilbert[5], James[4], David[3], David[2], James[1])* *b.* Middlefield, Otsego Co., N. Y., 13 Sept., 1831; *d.* Whig Corners, Otsego Co., N. Y., 1 Oct., 1896; *m.* Springfield, Otsego Co., N. Y., 31 Dec., 1855, Louise, *dau.* John and Laura (Burlingame) Dutcher (*b.* Springfield, N. Y., 17 July, 1833). [*Whig Corners, Otsego Co., N. Y.*

Children:

627 I. Adelbert[7] *b.* 24 Apl., 1857. FAM. CCVI.

---

* Fam. Recs. and pers. know., 628.

628 II. Belle[7] *b.* Springfield, N. Y., 26 Aug., 1860; *m.* (1) Whig Corners, N. Y., 15 Oct., 1879, Curtis, *s.* Abijah and Laura S. (Pierce) Barnum (*b.* Cooperstown, N. Y., 7 May, 1857). *Issue:* [*Fort Plain, N. Y.*

i. Harold A.[8] (Barnum) *b.* 10 Jany., 1882.
ii. Laura P.[8] (Barnum) *b.* 9 Dec., 1886.

m. (2) Stone Arabia, Otsego Co., N. Y., 23 Aug., 1899, Ten Eyck [603], *s.* Robert Asahel and Catherine (Howland) Parshall (*b.* 16 June, 1862). *No issue.*

629 III. Claude Monroe[7] *b.* Middlefield, N. Y., 9 Oct., 1874; *m.* Phoenix Mills, Otsego Co., N. Y., 20 Mch., 1895, Lulu, *dau.* Theodore and Eliza (Cahoon) Snedecker (*b.* Phoenix Mills, N. Y., 12 Sept., 1877). *No issue.*

---

*FAMILY XCVIII.**

ALBERT ORLANDO[6] [238], (*Gilbert*[5], *James*[4], *David*[3], *David*[2], *James*[1]) *b.* Middlefield, Otsego Co., N. Y., 17 Apl., 1835; *m.* Westford, Otsego Co., N. Y., 26 Oct., 1859, Matilda A., *dau.* Bela J. and Maria (Bailey) Kaple (*b.* Middlefield, N. Y., 12 Mch., 1835). [*Cooperstown, N. Y.*

Children:

630 I. Irving B.[7] *d. inf.*
631 II. Ada M.[7] *d. inf.*
632 III. Gilbert[7] *b.* Middlefield, N. Y., 17 Jany., 1866. [*Middlefield, N. Y.*
633 IV. Carrie M.[7] *b.* Middlefield, N. Y., 23 July, 1869; *m.* Middlefield, N. Y., 18 Oct., 1899, Howard, *s.* Viree and Albertine (Keller) Clark. *No issue.* [*Middlefield, N. Y.*

---

* Fam. Recs. and pers. know., 634.

634 v. Frederick Carlton[7] *b.* Cooperstown, N. Y., 7 July, 1871. [*Plattsburgh, N. Y.*

---

*FAMILY IC.**

HENRY CLAY[6] [240], *(Gilbert[5], James[4], David[3], David[2], James[1]) b.* Middlefield, Otsego Co., N. Y., 19 Aug., 1844; *d.* Middletown, N. Y., 17 July, 1890; *m.* 22 Sept., 1870, Ann J. Richmond (*b.* 15 Aug., 1851; *d.* Middletown, N. Y., 17 July, 1890). [*Oneonta, N. Y.*

Children:

635 i. Cassius Clay[7] *b.* Hamilton City, Butler Co., O., 17 Oct., 1871. [*Oneonta, N. Y.*
636 ii. Maud Luella[7] *b.* New Lisbon, O., 12 May, 1873. [*Cooperstown, N. Y.*
637 iii. Frank Karl[7] *b.* New Lisbon, O., 30 May, 1880. [*Oneonta, N. Y.*
638 iv. Raymond Curtis[7] *b.* New Lisbon, O., 21 June, 1882. [*Oneonta, N. Y.*

FAMILY C.†

GILBERT[6] [245], *(David[5], James[4], David[3], David[2], James[1]) b.* Middlefield, Otsego Co., N. Y., 30 Aug., 1835; *m.* Owego, N. Y., 24 Dec., 1862, Sophronia, *dau.* Ira and Ann (Vasbinder) Brooks (*b.* Tioga Center, N. Y., 25 Feby., 1839; *d.* Danby, N. Y., 1 Aug., 1874). [*West Danby, Tompkins Co., N. Y.*

---

* Fam. Recs. and pers. know., 237.
† Pers. statement.

Children: (All *b.* Danby, N. Y.)

639 I. Fred[7] *b.* 29 Oct., 1864. [*West Danby, N. Y.*

640 II. Minnie[7] *b.* 9 July, 1867; *m.* Tioga Center, N. Y., William Moses, *s.* Samuel and Mary (Everhart) Dawes (*b.* Danby, N. Y., 26 Nov., 1858). *Issue:* (All *b.* Danby, N. Y.) [*Spencer, Tioga Co., N. Y.*

i. Leo H.[8] (Dawes) *b.* 4 Nov., 1887.
ii. Laton Gilbert[8] (Dawes) *b.* 16 Oct., 1897.

641 III. Dollie[7] *b.* 24 Aug., 1869; *m.* Ithaca, N. Y., 21 Nov., 1896, Raymond A., *s.* Marcus L. and Mary (Sabin) Cowles (*b.* Spencer, N. Y., 29 Oct., 1877). *Issue:* [*West Danby, N. Y.*

i. Lillian Mary[8] (Cowles) *b.* 22 Apl., 1899.

Gilbert removed to Danby with his parents when a mere child. He still owns and cultivates the farm which his father cleared at that time. "He is a lively little man, full of stories." He is an advanced farmer, believing fully in the truth of the old maxim, that "What is worth doing at all is worth doing well." His farm is said to present the best appearance of any in his township. Possessing the racial characteristics of diminutive stature, in his youth he was of Herculean strength. Small, wiry, strong, of rugged constitution, he might well stand as a type of our family.

---

*FAMILY CI.**

ELEPHAS[6] [246], (*David*[5], *James*[4], *David*[3], *David*[2], *James*[1]) *b.* Danby, Tompkins Co., N. Y., 15 Mch., 1839; *m.* Danby,

* Pers. statement.

N. Y., 18 Nov., 1863, Orcelia, *dau.* William Henry and Abigail (Gunn) Green (*b.* Danby, N. Y., 4 Aug., 1847).
[*West Danby, Tioga Co., N. Y.*

Children: (All *b.* Danby, N. Y.)

642 I. Edward L.[7] *b.* 13 Apl., 1868; *m.* Spencer, N. Y., 24 Jany., 1893, Nancy Elizabeth, *dau.* Cornelius and Eliza D. (Carpenter) Davis (*b.* Van Etten, N. Y., 4 Oct., 1868). *No issue.* [*Elmira Heights, N. Y.*

643 II. Ada[7] *b.* 22 May, 1873; *d.* Danby, N. Y., 11 Feby., 1894.

644 III. Mildred[7] *b.* 13 Nov., 1883; *m.* — Apl., 1902, Burr Loomis. [*West Danby, N. Y.*

A farmer like his father and elder brother, Elephas is also a mason and follows both occupations. He built with his own hands the house in which he resides and many others in the neighborhood. The stone work of many of the bridges in his township is his handiwork. A lover of music, he is an adept at the violin. Somewhat reserved, to those who have succeeded in winning his confidence he is guide, mentor and friend. Open-handed and charitable, he is always ready to extend a helping hand to the unfortunate.

---

*FAMILY CII.**

DAVID SIDNEY[6] [248], *(Mehitabel[5], John[4], David[3], David[2], James[1])* *b.* 14 Apl., 1814; *d.* Somerset, Niag. Co., N. Y., 6 Feby., 1849; *m.* Somerset, N. Y., 30 Sept., 1839, Elizaette Hoag (*b.* Lawrence, Otsego Co., N. Y., 14 Dec., 1819).
[*Somerset, Niag. Co., N. Y.*

* Bible Rec. 38, and Fam. Recs. and pers. know., Mrs. Rosamond Barry.

Children: (All *b.* Somerset, N. Y.)

645 I. Sarah Hortense[7] *b.* 10 Sept., 1840; *d.* Somerset, N. Y., 28 Feby., 1849.

646 II. Hannah Maria[7] *b.* 1 Mch., 1842; *m.* 16 Apl., 1862, George Horsfall, (*d.* 16 July, 1864). *No issue.* *m.* (2) Middleport, N. Y., 6 Jany., 1873, William Henry, *s.* John and Elizabeth (———) Horsfall (*b.* Somerset, N. Y., 18 June, 1839). *Issue:* [*Scotts, Mich.*

- i. Emeline[8] (Horsfall).
- ii. Walter Sidney[8] (Horsfall).
- iii. Hattie Belle[8] (Horsfall).
- iv. Alonzo Delos[8] (Horsfall).
- v. Mary Etta[8] (Horsfall).

647 III. Amanda Malvina[7] *b.* 5 Oct., 1844; *d.* Somerset, N. Y., 29 Jany., 1879; *m.* Wilson, Niag. Co., N. Y., 25 Feby., 1863, John Jacob, *s.* David Wilber and Sarah (Barker) Haight (*b.* Somerset, N. Y., 4 Feby., 1840). *Issue:*

- i. Mary Rosamond[8] (Haight) *b.* 15 June, 1864.* [*Lockport, N. Y.*

648 IV. Phebe Ann[7] *b.* 16 Nov., 1846; *m.*—Dec., 1872, Alonzo Scranton. [*Sandusky, O.*

a. Rosamond Haight, *m.* Somerset, Niag. Co., N. Y., 16 Mch., 1886, William Henry, *s.* Samuel and Fidelia Elsie (Frost) Barry (*b.* Somerset, N. Y., 4 Oct., 1860). *Issue:* *i.* Raymond Samuel[9] (Barry) *b.* 2 Nov., 1886; *ii.* Leah Elsie[9] (Barry) *b.* 7 June, 1888; *iii.* Maude Amanda[9] (Barry) *b.* 9 Apl., 1890; *iv.* John Lewis[9] (Barry) *b.* 12 Nov., 1893; *d.* 20 Dec., 1893; *v.* Forrest William[9] (Barry) *b.* 6 Mch., 1896; *vi.* Beulah Rosamond[9] (Barry) *b.* 11 Dec., 1897; *vii.* Blanche Louise[9] (Barry) *b.* 31 Oct., 1900.*

---

* Pers. statement.

A Marshall

*FAMILY CIII.**

JAMES EVERETTE[6] [251], *(Elias[5], John[4], David[3], David[2], James[1]) b.* Middlefield, Otsego Co., N. Y., 2 Aug., 1839; *m.* (1) Toddsville, Otsego Co., N. Y., 30 June, 1861, Phoeba Ann, *dau.* Riley and Ada (———) Field (*b.* Toddsville, N. Y., 21 Aug., 1836; *d.* Milford, Otsego Co., N. Y., 31 Jany., 1899).
[*Milford, Otsego Co., N. Y.*

Children:

649 I. Frank James[7] *d. inf.*
650 II. Horace Field[7] *b.* 9 Sept., 1865.[a] [*London, Eng.*

m. (2) 26 Apl., 1900, Mimi Blackstock. *No. issue.*

James E. Parshall is a successful lawyer at Milford, N. Y., and occupies a high rank at the Otsego County bar. He is a recognized authority on real estate law and in Surrogate's Court practice. He has one of the finest private law libraries in New York State. (*See portrait.*)

a. Horace Field Parshall, *m.* 20 Dec., 1894, Annie M., *dau.* R. P. and A. (Montgomery) Rogers (*b.* Halifax, Nova Scotia, 4 July, 1873.) *No issue.** Mr. Parshall is a member of the Institution of Civil Engineers, member of the Institution of Electrical Engineers, of Great Britain, and member of the Institute of Mechanical Engineers, member of the Institute of Electrical Engineers of America, born September 9th, 1865, at Milford, New York, U. S. A., educated at Hartwick Seminary, New York; Cornell University, Ithaca, New York; Lehigh University, South Bethlehem, Pennsylvania. Subsequently he had experience in the Sprague Electric Railway and Motor Co., first as designing engineer of stationary motors and subsequently as designing engineer of railway motors. He afterwards occupied the position of Chief Engineer to the Wenstrom Dynamo & Motor Co., of Baltimore, in which position he developed the 4-pole Slow Speed Single Reduction Steel Railway Motor now used in the United States. He afterwards acted as Chief Designing Engineer to the Edison General Electric Co., and subsequent to the consolidation of that Company with the Thomson-Houston Co., occupied the same position with the General Electric Co. of America. During this period the type of apparatus at present in use was developed and standardized, notably large

* Pers. statement.

*FAMILY CIV.**

HENRY E.[6] [253], (*Elias*[5], *John*[4], *David*[3], *David*[2], *James*[1]) *b.* Cooperstown, N. Y., 26 Nov., 1850; *m.* Warren, Herk. Co., N. Y., 8 Mch., 1876, Ella, *dau.* Ira and Minerva (Millington) Whiter (*b.* Warren, N. Y., 23 Feby., 1854).

[*Cooperstown, N. Y.*

Children: (All *b.* Cooperstown, N. Y.)

651 I. Elias I.[7] b. 1 Jany., 1877.
652 II. Earl R.[7] *b.* 17 Nov., 1884.

FAMILY CV.†

JOHN[6] [255], (*David Jefferson*[5], *John*[4], *David*[3], *David*[2], *James*[1]) *b.* probably Otsego Co., N. Y., 24 May, 1829; *d.* Lake

railway generators, three-phase generators, rotary converters, railway motors and the electrical equipment of motor cars and locomotives. Since the year 1895 he has been in practice as a Consulting Engineer in Great Britain, and has carried out many important installations, amongst these being, The Dublin United Tramways, Bristol Tramways, London United Tramways, Glasgow Corporation Tramways, Isle of Thanet Tramways, and is the originator of the system used on the Central London Railway, to which Company he is permanent Consulting Engineer. Mr. Parshall has also visited upper Egypt to report upon a Power Transmission Scheme. He was for some time lecturer on dynamo design at the Massachusetts Institute of Technology, and is joint author with Mr. H. M. Hobart of a treatise on Armature Windings and a book on the Design of Electrical Generators, which were well received by the technical press, and which have a large sale both in Great Britain and America. Mr. Parshall is also the author of a number of technical papers relating to the design of electric tramways and railway installations and apparatus, and in 1896 gained the Crampton Prize awarded by the Institution of Civil Engineers for a paper read before that Institution entitled "Magnetic Data of Iron and Steel," and in 1898 gained a premium awarded by the Institution of Electrical Engineers for a paper entitled "Earth Return for Electric Tramways." (*See portrait.*)

---

* Pers. statement.
† Fam. Recs. and pers. know., 659.

J. Parshall

Geneva, Wis., 17 May, 1896; *m.* Lake Geneva, Wis., 3 July, 1856, Olive Octavia, *dau.* Horace and Jane (———) Marshall (*b.* 20 May, 1836; *d.* Lake Geneva, Wis., 27 Mch., 1891). (*See portrait.*) [*Lake Geneva, Wis.*

Children: (All *b.* Lake Geneva, Wis.)

653 I. Willard De Forest[7] *b.* 30 June, 1857; *d.* Lake Geneva, Wis., 7 Nov., 1865.

654 II. Charles Henry[7] *b.* 7 Nov., 1860; *d.* Lake Geneva, Wis., 14 Jany., 1862.

655 III. Cora Mabel[7] *b.* 25 Dec., 1863; *unm.* [*Elkhorn, Wis.*

656 IV. John Frank[7] *b.* 11 May, 1865. FAM. CCVII.

657 V. Albert Justin[7] *b.* 2 Mch., 1867; *d.* Lake Geneva, Wis., 11 Dec., 1867.

658 VI. George Francis[7] *b.* 11 Apl., 1870; *d.* Lake Geneva, Wis., 12 Mch., 1872.

659 VII. Mary Blanche[7]* *b.* 26 July, 1872; *m.* Lake Geneva, Wis., 26 July, 1893, William Percy, *s.* Thomas and Annie Elizabeth (Dunn) Longland (*b.* Yardley, Hastings, Northamptonshire, Eng., 7 Mch., 1870). *Issue:*

i. Albert Percy[8] (Longland) *b.* 10 Nov., 1895. [*Chicago, Ill.*

ii. Frank Thomas[8] (Longland) *b.* 26 Apl., 1897).

660 VIII. Elbert Lewis[7] *b.* 28 Sept., 1874; *unm.* [*Wheaton, Ill.*

661 IX. Harry Clyde[7] *b.* 25 Dec., 1878; *m.* Lake Geneva, Wis., 20 Jany., 1901, Mary Rachel, *dau.* Eugene and Carrie (Campbell) Lenon (*b.* Lyons, Wis., 14 July, 1880). [*Lake Geneva, Wis.*

---

* Pers. statement.

FAMILY CVI. *

JOHN[6] [258], (*James*[5] *Jonathan*[4] *Jonathan*[3] *David*[2] *James*[1]) *b.* Little Britain, Orange Co., N. Y., 15 Oct., 1789; *d.* Mendon, Mich., 5 Oct., 1858; *m.* Palmyra, N. Y., Persis, *dau.* Caleb and Elizabeth (Williams) Hopkinson (*b.* Manlius, Onon. Co., N. Y., 28 Nov., 1794; *d.* Mendon, Mich., 1881). [*Mendon, Mich.*

Children:

662 I. Harriet[7]† *b.* Palmyra, N. Y., 10 Dec., 1812; *d.* Detroit, Mich., 24 Mch., 1897; *m.* Royal Oak, Mich., 1 June, 1834, Henry Christy, *s.* Allen and Philena (Gunn) Gaylord (*b.* Ohio, 23 Jany., 1811; *d.* Detroit, Mich., 18 Jany., 1854). *Issue:* (All *b.* Detroit, Mich.) [*Detroit, Mich.*

- i. Charles Henry[8] (Gaylord) *b.* 15 Sept., 1838.
- ii. John Allen[8] (Gaylord) *b.* 27 Jany., 1841; *d.* Detroit, Mich., 13 Jany., 1876.
- iii. Adrian Frank[8] (Gaylord) *b.* 15 Mch., 1843; *d.* Detroit, Mich., — June, 1844.
- iv. James Inglis[8] (Gaylord) *b.* 28 Jany., 1845.
- v. Hattie Lavinia[8] (Gaylord) *b.* 28 Jany., 1845.[a]
- vi. Emma Virginia[8] (Gaylord) *b.* 30 May, 1847.
- vii. Frank Adrian[8] (Gaylord) *b.* 23 Aug., 1849.

663 II. Julia Ann[7]‡ *b.* Palmyra, N. Y., 25 Oct., 1814; *m.* Royal Oak, Mich., 17 Mch., 1836, Edwin Wells, *s.*

a. Hattie Lavinia Gaylord, *m.* 17 Aug., 1867, James S. Booth (*d.* 10 Feby., 1874). *No issue. m.* 2d, Detroit, 27 Aug., 1879, Lucian Hayden *s.* Charles A. and Julia Ann (Benedict) Fex (*b.* Pa., 4 May, 1836). *No issue.*‡

---

* Fam. Recs. and pers. know., 663, 666, and 667.
† Fam. Recs. and pers. know. Mrs. Hattie L. Fox.
‡ Pers. statement.

Samuel and Anna Maria (Bean) Bakewell (*b.* Wellsburg, W. Va., 20 July, 1812). *Issue:*
[*Carbondale, Ill.*

i. Campbell Newton[8] (Bakewell) *b.* Bethany, W. Va., 14 July, 1837.
ii. Irving Howard[8] (Bakewell) *b.* Bethany, W. Va., 31 Dec., 1838.
iii. Albert Melvin[8] (Bakewell) *b.* Bethany, W. Va., 17 Oct., 1840; *d.* Sibley, Ill., 11 July, 1881.
iv. Olivia Overton[8] (Bakewell) *b.* Bethany, W. Va., 22 Feby., 1845; *d.* Bloomington, Ill., 22 Mch., 1847.
v. Selina Huntington (Bakewell) *b.* Bloomington, Ill., 10 Dec., 1847.
vi. Louisa May[8] (Bakewell) *b.* Bloomington, Ill., 30 Nov., 1855; *m.* James Dawson.

664 III. Sarah Ann[7]* *b.* Palmyra, N. Y., 29 June, 1816; *d.* Chagrin Falls, O., 6 Nov., 1887; *m.* Pontiac, Mich., 11 May, 1834, Jedediah, *s.* Jedediah and Hannah (Turner) Hubbell (*b.* Warrensville, O., 22 Feby., 1813; *d.* Chagrin Falls, O., 7 Dec., 1877). *Issue:*
[*Chagrin Falls, O.*

i. Charles Harold[8] (Hubbell) *b.* Warrensville, O., 16 Nov., 1836. [*Chagrin Falls, O.*
ii. Alice Lovina[8] (Hubbell) *b.* Warrensville, O., 8 Sept., 1838; *m.* ——— King.
[*Monteagle, Tenn.*
iii. James Emerson[8] (Hubbell) *b.* Chagrin Falls, O., 22 July, 1846; *d.* Chagrin Falls, O., 7 Mch., 1876.

* Fam. Recs. and pers. know., Chas H. Hubbell; Hist Hubbell Fam. 315.

iv. Julia Rosalie[8] (Hubbell) *b.* Chagrin Falls, O., 2 Dec., 1849; *m.* ——— Worley. [*Detroit, Mich.*

v. Frances Eliza[8] (Hubbell) *b.* Chagrin Falls, O., 31 Dec., 1858; *m.* ——— Rogers. [*Detroit, Mich.*

665 IV. Elizabeth[7] *b.* Palmyra, N. Y., 8 June, 1868; *d.* Mendon, Mich., 12 Feby., 1882; *m.* Mendon, Mich., 4 Oct., 1857, John Goodaker (*b.* Lincolnshire, Eng., 1818). *Issue:*

i. A child[8] *d. inf.*

666 V. Priscilla[7]* *b.* Pontiac, Mich., 7 July, 1837; *m.* Detroit, Mich., 23 Oct., 1856, John Thornton, *s.* Edmund H. and Mildred Woodford (Gregory) Didlake (*b.* Winchester, Ky., 29 Oct., 1833). *Issue:*

i. William Parshall[8] (Didlake) *b.* 15 Mch., 1858; *m.* Emma Fletcher. [*Alton, Ill.*

ii. Mildred Gregory[8] (Didlake) *b.* 28 Feby., 1861. [*Bloomington, Ill.*

iii. Charles Dexter[8] (Didlake) *b.* 13 Apl., 1864. [*Denison, Texas.*

iv. James Sidney[8] (Didlake) *b.* 5 Oct., 1865; *d.* 19 Feby., 1872.

v. Julia Virginia[8] (Didlake) *b.* 21 Mch., 1869.[a] [*Fort Smith, Kan.*

vi. Mary Poston[8] (Didlake) *b.* 12 Jany., 1871.[b] [*Litchfield, Ill.*

a. Julia Virginia Didlake, *m.* Hepler, Kan., 17 Oct., 1894, Frederick Deitrich Tonney.†

b. Mary Poston Didlake, *m.* Hepler, Kan., 17 Oct., 1894, Frank Marion Thomas.†

---

* Pers. statement.

† Pers. know., 666.

vii. John Woodford[8] (Didlake) *b.* 4 June, 1854.[a]
viii. Edmund Hockaday[8] (Didlake) *b.* 5 Apl., 1877; *d.* 6 Sept., 1877.
ix. Harriet Louise[8] (Didlake) *b.* 21 Dec., 1879.

667 VI. James Judson[7] *b.* 23 Feby., 1820. FAM. CCVIII.
668 VII. Rebecca[7]* *b.* Palmyra, N. Y., 22 Jany., 1822; *d.* Mendon, Mich., 15 May, 1891; *m.* Royal Oak, Mich., John Harkness Aldrich (*d.* Mendon, Mich., 5 Feby., 1895). *Issue:*
i. Fred J.[8] (Aldrich) *b.* 20 July, 1854.[b] [*Maples, Allen Co., Ind.*
ii. Edward Aaron[8] (Aldrich) *b.* 17 Jany., 1863.[c] [*Terre Haute, Ind.*

669 VIII. John Melvin[7] *b.* 21 Mch., 1828. FAM. CCIX.
670 IX. Charles Henry[7] *b.* 11 Aug., 1830. FAM. CCX.

FAMILY CVII.‡

JOSEPH[6] [259], (*James[5] Jonathan[4] Jonathan[3] David[2] James[1]*) *b.* probably Palmyra, N. Y., 8 May, 1791; *d.* Waterford, Oakland Co., Mich., 17 Feby., 1867; *m.* Palmyra, N. Y., 2 May, 1816, Clarissa Moon (*b.* Rutland, Vt., 28 Dec., 1795; *d.* Detroit, Mich., 2 July, 1887). [*Waterford, Oakland Co., Mich.*

a. John Woodford Didlake, *m.* Fort Scott, Kan., 16 Jany., 1901, Catherine Devero.†

b. Fred J. Aldrich, *m.* Maples, Ind., 20 Dec., 1881, Lydia, *dau.* Robert and Mary (————) Mooney. *Issue*: *i.* Melvin H.[9] (Aldrich); *ii.* Hattie M.[9] (Aldrich); *iii.* Allie L.[9] (Aldrich); *iv.* Aldon D.[9] (Aldrich); *v.* Luther J.[9] (Aldrich).§

c. Edward Aaron Aldrich, *m.* Chicago, 19 Dec., 1898, Carrie, *dau.* Aquilla and Lizzie (Mitchell) Branham. *No issue.**

---

* Fam. Recs. and pers. know., Fred J. Aldrich.
† Pers. know., 666.
‡ Fam. Recs. and pers. know., 676, 678 and 679.
§ Pers. statement.

671 I. Ira Selby[7] *b.* 10 Mch., 1817; *d.* 30 Dec., 1893; *unm.*

672 II. Arloe[7] *b.* 27 July, 1818; *d.* 15 July, 1864; *unm.*

673 III. Chester Spaulding[7] *b.* 9 Dec., 1821. [*Waterford, Mich.*

674 IV. Dyantha[7] *b.* 12 June, 1826; *d.* — Sept., 1856; *m.* ——— Letts.

675 V. Joseph Preston[7] *b.* 2 Aug., 1820. FAM. CCXI.

676 VI. Clarissa Cornelia[7]* *b.* Drayton Plains, Mich., 18 Oct., 1824; *m.* (1) Detroit, Mich., 19 Nov., 1854, Marlin, *s.* Loren and Elizabeth (Preston) Hobart (*b.* Harmony, N. Y., 28 July, 1826; *d.* Harmony, N. Y., 6 Mch., 1858). *Issue:* [*Detroit, Mich.*

i. Alice[8] (Hobart) *b.* Drayton Plains, Mich., 4 Oct., 1855.

ii. Agnes[8] (Hobart) *b.* Drayton Plains, 4 Oct., 1855; *d.* 29 Apl., 1856.

iii. Mary[8] (Hobart) *b.* Owosso, Mich., 5 Jany., 1858.[a]

m. (2) 15 Mch., 1860, Nelson L., *s.* Solomon and Esther (Barber) Goodrich (*b.* 13 Oct., 1810; *d.* Blissfield, Mich., 30 Nov., 1876). *Issue:*

iv. Joseph Parshall[8] (Goodrich) *b.* 26 June, 1864. [*Detroit, Mich.*

677 VII. Cullen Foster[7] *b.* 25 Mch., 1828; *d.* 22 Apl., 1883; *unm.*

a. Mary Hobart, *m.* Blissfield, Lena Co., 20 Oct., 1880, Charles Edwin, *s.* Edwin W. and Abbie (Ellis) Freese (*b.* 22 Apl., 1854; *d.* Clinton, Mich., 12 June, 1881). *Issue: i.* Charles Edwin[9] (Freese) *b.* Blissfield, Mich., 28 Oct., 1881; *m.* 2d, Detroit, 3 Dec., 1884, Julius Austin, *s.* Waterman Phillips and Elizabeth (Hackett) Grow (*b.* 19 Jany., 1857). *Issue: i.* Austin Hobart[9] (Grow) *b.* 3 Mch., 1886; *d.* Detroit, 3 May, 1887; *ii.* Julius Alfred[9] (Grow) *b.* 5 Dec., 1887; *iii.* Hobart[9] (Grow) *b.* 19 July, 1890; *iv.* Russell Waterman[9] (Grow) *b.* 13 Nov., 1892; *v.* Lillian Irene[9] (Grow) *b.* 10 Sept., 1894; *vi.* Mary Gertrude[9] (Grow) *b.* 20 Apl., 1899.

* Fam. Recs. and pers. know., 676; Hist. Goodrich Fam., 87.

678 VIII. James[7] *b.* 9 May, 1830. FAM. CCXII.

679 IX. Sarah Jane[7]* *b.* 21 Feby., 1832; *m.* Detroit, Mich., 6 June, 1855, John Francis, *s.* John and Freelove (Spink) Antisdel (*b.* Oneida County, N. Y., 13 June, 1829; *d.* Detroit, Mich., 15 May, 1900). *Issue:*

i. James Francis[8] (Antisdel) *b.* 29 Apl., 1856.[a]
ii. Emma[8] (Antisdel) *b.* 8 May, 1858; *d.* 10 Aug., 1859.
iii. John Parshall[8] (Antisdel) *b.* Jany., 1861
iv. Edward[8] (Antisdel) *b.* 14 Feby., 1862; *d.* 15 Feby., 1862.
v. Ella Marie[8] (Antisdel) *b.* 7 Feby., 1863.
vi. Clara Freelove[8] (Antisdel) *b.* 5 Apl., 1865; *d.* 15 Nov., 1865.
vii. Winne Blanche[8] (Antisdel) *b.* 1 Dec., 1868.

680 X. Silas Norman[7] *b.* 12 Aug., 1835; *d.* 25 Apl., 1857; *unm.*

681 XI. Celestia[7]* *b.* 3 Sept., 1838; *m.* Detroit, Mich., 15 Oct., 1868, Arthur, *s.* Stephen and Lucy (Clifford) Tredway (*b.* Beaconsfield, Beecks, Eng., 16 Oct., 1833). *Issue:* [*Detroit, Mich.*

i. Lucy Clara[8] (Tredway) *b.* 3 Aug., 1870; *d.* 14 Nov., 1876.
ii. Arthur Clifford[8] (Tredway) *b.* 26 Aug., 1872.
iii. Norman Parshall[8] (Tredway) *b.* 11 Aug., 1875; *d.* 22 Feby., 1879.

682 XII. Rebecca[7] *b.* 31 Aug., 1840; *m.* M. C. Marr. [*Detroit, Mich.*

a. James Francis Antisdel, *m.* Jessie Lindell Baker. *Issue:* *i.* James; *ii.* Jessie Gladys; *iii.* Esther.†

---

* Pers. statement.
† Pers. know., 679.

*FAMILY CVIII.**

DEWITT[6] (Hon.) [264], *(Nathan[5] Jonathan[4] Jonathan[3] David[2] James[1]) b.* Palmyra, N. Y., 23 Mch., 1812; *d.* Lyons, 12 May, 1880; *m.* Lyons, N. Y., 25 Apl., 1838, Susan, *dau.* Samuel and Susan (Stafford) Hecox (*b.* Lyons, N. Y., 22 June, 1819). [*Lyons, N. Y.*

Children:

683 I. William Henry[7] *b.* 14 Feby., 1839. FAM. CCXIII.

684 II. DeWitt[7] *b.* 30 July, 1841; *d.* Lyons, N. Y., 29 Sept., 1866; *unm.*

685 III. Katharine[7] *b.* 13 Oct., 1843; *m.* Lyons, N. Y., 16 Oct., 1867, Dwight Scott, *s.* Timothy Dwight and Julia (Wheeler) Chamberlain (*b.* Litchfield, Ct., 22 Feby., 1839). *Issue:* [*Lyons, N. Y.*

i. Dwight Parshall[8] (Chamberlain) *b.* 1 Mch., 1869.[a]

ii. Frederick William[8] (Chamberlain) *b.* 3 Jany., 1871.[b]

iii. Grace Stafford[8] (Chamberlain) *b.* 15 June, 1896.[c]

a. Dwight Parshall Chamberlain, *m.* 5 June, 1895, Margaret E., *dau.* Henry and Mary A. (Hance) Russell (*b.* 28 Mch., 1871). *Issue: i.* Dwight Russell[9] *b.* 10 Oct., 1896.†

b. Frederick William Chamberlain, *m.* Brooklyn, 11 June, 1895, Anne Elizabeth, *dau.* Frederick and Mary (Nix) Eckel (*b.* Hempstead, N. Y., 1872). *Issue, all b. Lyons: i.* Frederick Parshall[9], *b.* 14 Mch., 1896; *ii.* Katharine[9] *b.* 2 Aug., 1900.*

c. Grace Stafford Chamberlain, *m.* Lyons, N. Y., 15 June, 1898, John, *s.* William Glen and Sarah (Taft) David (*b.* Lyons, 29 Nov., 1860). *No issue.**

* Fam. Rec. and pers. know., 1079.
† Fam. Rec.; Dwight Gen. 510; Hamlin Fam. 230.

DeWitt Parshall received his education at the Canandaigua Academy, where he was for several terms a classmate and roommate of Stephen A. Douglass. Choosing the law as a profession, he entered the office of the late Gen. William H. Adams, at Lyons, where he industriously prosecuted his studies and was admitted to the bar in 1838, having, since leaving his father's house, entirely supported himself by his own exertion—teaching, surveying, copying law papers in the County Clerk's Office, etc. He opened his first law office at Lyons, but in 1839, having formed a co-partnership with the late Judge Theron R. Strong, he moved to Palmyra, but feeling that there was a better field for his activities at the County seat, the partnership was dissolved at his own request and he returned to Lyons, where he continued to reside for the remainder of his life. In addition to his law practice he became extensively engaged in real estate transactions and continued until his death the most extensive dealer in and owner of real estate in the county. The Village of Lyons owes much of its prosperity to his enterprise and public spirit. In 1852, he established the Palmyra Bank, of Lyons, the name of which was changed to the Lyons Bank two years later and again in 1865, it was converted into the Lyons National Bank, under which name it has ever since enjoyed an unexampled prosperity. He served as Supervisor of his town several terms, and later was President of the Village of Lyons. In 1868, he was elected to the Legislature of New York State, where he served one term. A man of sterling worth, upright and honorable in every walk of life, devoted to his family and friends, he won the esteem of all who knew him. (*See portrait.*)

---

*FAMILY CIX.**

HENDEE[6] [265], (*Nathan*[5] *Jonathan*[4] *Jonathan*[3] *David*[2] *James*[1]) *b.* Palmyra, N. Y., 8 Dec., 1814; *d.* Palmyra, N. Y.,

* Fam. Recs. and pers. know., 690.

6 Dec., 1890; *m.* Palmyra, N. Y., 27 Dec., 1838, Sarah Ann, *dau.* Stephen B. and Maria (Rossman) Jordan (*b.* 7 Dec., 1821 *d.* Palmyra, N. Y., 22 Oct., 1891). [*Palmyra, N. Y.*

Children: (All *b.* Palmyra, N. Y.)

686 I. Edwin[7] *b.* 27 Jany., 1840; *d.* Palmyra, N. Y., 14 Jany., 1864.
687 II. Rossman Jordan[7] *b.* 18 Nov., 1844. FAM. CCXIV.
688 III. William Allen[7] *b.* 13 Jany., 1850; *d.* Palmyra, N. Y., 22 Apl., 1865.
689 IV. John Snook[7] *b.* 19 Sept., 1851; *d.* Palmyra, N. Y., 21 Apl., 1855.
690 V. George Hendee[7] *b.* 3 Mch., 1859.
691 VI. Charles[7] *b.* 9 Sept., 1862; *d.* Palmyra, N. Y., 26 June, 1878.

---

*FAMILY CX.**

SCHUYLER[6] [267], (*Nathan[5] Jonathan[4] Jonathan[3] David[2] James[1]*) *b.* Palmyra, Wayne Co., N. Y., 27 July, 1819; *d.* Tuscumbia, Ala., 28 Oct., 1890; *m.* 9 Oct., 1839, Mary Griffin, *dau.* ——— and Mary (Bennet) Perkins. [*Tuscumbia, Ala.*

Children:

692 I. Charles Wallace.[7a] [*Oberlin, Kan.*
693 II. Emma Richmond.[7] [*Oberlin, Kan.*
694 III. Mary Elizabeth[7]† *m.* Denison J., *s.* VanRensselaer and Emma Amelia (Denison) Richmond. *Issue:* [*Syracuse, N. Y.*

a. Charles Wallace Parshall, *m.* Iowa City, Ia., 12 Oct., 1865, Mary E., *dau.* James and Martha (Pringle) Guniken.†

---

* Fam. Recs. and pers. know., 692.
† Pers. statement.

i. Mary Parshall[8] (Richmond) *d.* 26 July, 1874.
ii. VanRensselaer[8] (Richmond).
iii. Denison[8] (Richmond).
iv. Schuyler Parshall[8] (Richmond).

---

*FAMILY CXI.**

EZRA K.[6] [269], (*Jesse*[5] *Jonathan*[4] *Jonathan*[3] *David*[2] *James*[1]) *d.* Pontiac, Mich., 29 Mch., 1888.

Children:

695 I. Margery[7] *d. inf.*

696 II. Darwin.[7a]

---

*FAMILY CXII**

JOHN B.[6] [270], (*Jesse*[5] *Jonathan*[4] *Jonathan*[3] *David*[2] *James*[1]) *b.* 28 Oct., 1808; *d.* Palmyra, N. Y., 22 Jany., 1888; *m.* Detroit, Mich., 1857, Mary Jane, *dau.* Charles and Lydia (Griffith) Goldsmith (*b.* Palmyra, N. Y., 28 Nov., 1832; *d.* Palmyra, N. Y., 25 Sept., 1884).

Children: (All *b.* Palmyra, N. Y.)

a. Darwin left home on reaching his majority and was never afterward heard from.

---

* Fam. Recs. pos. 690.
† Fam. Recs. and pers. know. 697.

697 I. Emma Jane[7]* *b.* 17 Mch., 1858; *m.* Palmyra, N. Y., 20 Mch., 1878, John Blodgett, *s.* David and Dighton (Johnson) Shear (*b.* Perrinton, Monroe Co., N. Y., 6 Nov., 1852). *Issue:* (*b.* E. Palmyra, N. Y.)

i. Jay Parshall (Shear) *b.* 26 Jany., 1888.

FAMILY CXIII.†

CHARLES HUMPHREY[6] [270], (*Jesse*[5] *Jonathan*[4] *Jonathan*[3] *David*[2] *James*[1]) *b.* Orange Co., N. Y., 2 Mch., 1814; *d.* Seneca Castle, Seneca Co., N. Y., 13 Apl., 1898; *m.* Seneca Castle, N. Y., 11 Dec., 1845, Cornelia A., *dau.* Luther and Hannah L. (Smalley) Whitney (*b.* Seneca Castle, N. Y., 11 Dec., 1829). [*Seneca Castle, Seneca Co., N. Y.*

Children:

699 I. Frank Luther[7] *b.* Seneca Castle, N. Y., 18 Nov., 1856. [*Seneca Castle, N. Y.*

FAMILY CXIV.‡

JAMES MILTON[6] [279], (*David*[5] *David*[4] *Jonathan*[3] *David*[2] *James*[1]) *b.* Little Britain, Orange Co., N. Y., 11 Apl., 1813; *d.* Alhambra, Cal., 23 Aug., 1900; *m.* Rushford, N. Y., 5 June, 1848, Mehitabel, *dau.* George and Sally (Lyon) Smith (*b.* Nelson, N. Y., 20 Jany., 1818). [*Alhambra, Cal.*

700 I. Mary Ella[7] *b.* 10 Feby., 1855; *unm.* [*Alhambra, Cal.*

---

* Pers. statement.
† Fam. Recs. and pers. know., 699; Whitney Gen. 413.
‡ Fam. Recs. and pers. know., 700.

FAMILY CXV.*

CALEB[6] [280], (*David[5] David[4] Jonathan[3] David[2] James[1]*) *b.* Little Britain, Orange Co., N. Y., 24 Nov., 1815; *d.* Port Jervis, N. Y., 28 Feby., 1886; *m.* Fire Place, Suff. Co., N. Y., 5 Jany., 1848, Jerusha K., *dau.* Dr. Nathaniel and Sarah (Havens) Miller (*b.* Fire Place, N. Y., 4 Nov., 1822). [*Port Jervis, N. Y.*

Children: (All *b.* Walden, N. Y.)

701 I. Caroline M.[7] *b.* 7 July, 1849; *unm.*
702 II. Sarah N.[7] *b.* 4 May, 1853; *unm.*
703 III. William Andrews[7] *b.* 9 Dec., 1865. FAM. CCXV.

Caleb Parshall resided on the farm formerly belonging to his father for many years. On the construction of the Walkill Valley Railroad, he was one of the Commissioners appointed by the Supreme Court to appraise the damages for lands taken by that corporation for railroad purposes. In Sept., 1869, he removed to Port Jervis, N. Y., and engaged in the construction of the Port Jervis, Monticello and New York Railroad, after the completion of which he retired from active life, but continued to make his home in Port Jervis until his death.

FAMILY CXVI.†

DAVID BAYARD[6] [284], (*David[5] David[4] Jonathan[3] David[2] James[1]*) *b.* Walden, Orange Co., N. Y., 11 Aug., 1826; *m.* Walden, N. Y., 11 Oct., 1860, Susan, *dau.* David G. and Hannah (Dill) Bogert (*b.* Walden, N. Y., 23 Nov., 1833).
[*Montgomery, Orange Co., N. Y.*

* Fam. Recs. and pers. know., 703; Mallman's Shelter Island.
† Pers. statement.

Children: (All *b.* Walden, N. Y.)

704 I. David Bogert[7] *b.* 7 Aug., 1862; *unm.*

705 II. Isabella Dill[7] *b.* 17 Dec., 1865; *m.* Walden, N. Y., 10 Feby., 1886, William S., *s.* James Arnole and Phebe M. (Shafer) Hanlon (*b.* Montgomery, N. Y., 23 July, 1857). *Issue:* [*Montgomery, N. Y.*

- i. William Bayard[8] (Hanlon) *b.* 9 Nov., 1886.
- ii. Alice Isabella[8] (Hanlon) *b.* 9 Jany., 1889.
- iii. James Raymond[8] (Hanlon) *b.* 2 Sept., 1890.
- iv. Susan Grace[8] (Hanlon) *b.* 8 June, 1892.
- v. Ruth[8] (Hanlon) *b.* 25 Nov., 1894.
- vi. Earl Bogert[8] (Hanlon) *b.* 20 Dec., 1896.
- vii. Ralph[8] (Hanlon) *b.* 21 Dec., 1898.

706 III. Alice[7] *b.* 2 July, 1872; *unm.*

The Seventh Generation.

*FAMILY CXVII.**

SAMUEL[7] [287], (*James[6] Samuel[5] James[4] Israel[3] Israel[2] James[1]*) *b.* Poland, O., 15 Apl., 1805; *d.* Braceville, O., 29 July, 1894; *m.* Milton, O., 17 Nov., 1834, Jane, *dau.* Samuel and Margaret (Craig) Linton (*b.* Downingtown, Westchester Co., Pa., 1 May, 1807; *d.* Braceville, O., 8 Mch., 1884).
[*Braceville, Trumbull Co., O.*

Children:

707 1. Margaret[8]† *b.* Milton, O., 23 Oct., 1837; *m.* Warren, O., 1 Jany., 1863, Thomas Parker, *s.* Stephen and Magdalene (Forshee) Benjamin (*b.* Marlboro, N. Y., 20 Feby., 1838; *d.* Sioux City, Ia., 8 May, 1899). *Issue:* [*Phalanx Sta., O.*

i. Jennie[9] (Benjamin) *b.* Ravenna, O., 28 June, 1865.[a] [*Farmington, O.*
ii. Burke[9] (Benjamin) *b.* Newton Falls, O., 30 Dec., 1873.[b] [*Pittsburg, O.*

a. Jennie Benjamin, *m.* Warren, O., 11 Dec., 1897, Densmore Daniel, *s.* Daniel F. and Catherine (Albert) Bower (*b.* Farmington, O., 24 Oct., 1851).‡
b. Dr. Burke Benjamin, *m.* Pittsburgh, Pa., 20 Apl., 1897, Cecelia, *dau.* Thomas and Mary (Poland) Lomax, (*b.* Shawnee, Franklin Co., O., 1 Jany., 1878).‡

---

* Fam. Recs. and pers. know., 707; P. and Van B. Fams.
† Pers. state.; Cool Gen. 201.
‡ Pers. know., 707.

iii. Lemoyne[9] (Benjamin) *b.* Braceville, O., 19 Jany., 1880. [*Phalanx Sta., O.*

FAMILY CXVIII.

JACOB[7]* [288], (*James[6] Samuel[5] James[4] Israel[3] Israel[2] James[1]*) *b.* Milton, O., 20 June., 1806; *d.* Milton, O., 19 Dec., 1865; *m.* Milton, O., 5 July, 1832, Annie Crays (*b.* Milton, O., 16 Jany., 1816; *d.* Atwater Center, O., 25 June, 1877).
[*Milton, O.*

Children: (All *b.* Milton, O.)

708 I. Joseph[8] *b.* 12 Apl., 1833.[a] [*Yale, O.*

709 II. Elizabeth[8]† *b.* 15 Nov., 1835; *m.* Milton, O., 6 Apl., 1854, Daniel, *s.* Jacob and Mary Agnes (Shafter) Floor (*b.* Springfield, O., 1 Apl., 1834). *Issue:*

i. Harriet Celeste[9] (Floor) *b.* Berlin, O., 23 Feby., 1855.[b]

ii. Anna Ennis[9] (Floor) *b.* Berlin, O., 30 Dec., 1856.[c]

a. Joseph Parshall, *m.* Milton, O., 29 Jany., 1857, Lovina, *dau.* Eben and Abigail (Headly) Coburn, (*b.* Bazetta, O., 9 Apl., 1827). *Issue:* 1085 *i.* Armine Cazzad[9] *b.* Milton, O., 22 Oct., 1857, *unm.*; 1086. *ii.* Wallace Jacob[9] *b.* Lordstown, O., 20 June, 1865, *unm.*‡

b. Harriet Celeste Floor, *m.* Warren, O., 1 Apl., 1872, James Edward, *s.* Clayton and Nancy (Taylor) Keeler (*b.* Berlin, O., abt. 1853). *Issue:* *i.* Nora[10] (Keeler) *b.* 4 Sept., 1875; *ii.* Charles[10] (Keeler) *b.* Sept., 1877; *iii.* *Ola[10] (Keeler) b 2 Sept., 1879; iv. John[10] (Keeler)* *b.* 6 *Jany.*, *1886.*‡

c. Anna Ennis Floor, *m.* Salem, O., 2 May, 1873, Llewellyn Earl, *s.* James and Laura (Ormsby) Jordan (*b.* Jackson, O., 26 Sept., 1854; *d.* Buffalo, N. Y., 30 Jany., 1901). *Issue:* *i.* Hubert Eugene[10] (Jordan) *b.* 26 Sept., 1878; *ii.* Aubrey Loyal[10] (Jordan) *b.* 1 Aug., 1883.‡

---

* Bible Rec. 228, pos., wid. 711; P. and Van E. Fams.
† Pers. statement.
‡ Fam. Recs. and pers. know., 709.

iii. Olive Serepta[9] (Floor) *b.* Jackson, O., 10 Feby., 1863.[a]

iv. Charles Grant[9] (Floor) *b.* 1 Oct., 1865; *d.* 13 Oct., 1865.

v. Birdie Agnes[9] (Floor) *b.* Berlin, O., 30 Sept., 1870.[b]

vi. Vincent Rienzi[9] (Floor) *b.* Berlin, O., 14 Feby., 1875.[c]

710 III. Lemuel[8] *b.* 9 Sept., 1840. Left home about 1874, and never since been heard from.

711 IV. Walling[8] *b.* 19 May, 1844.[d]

712 V. Alonzo Ferrill[8] *b.* 31 Mch., 1850. Left home about 1874, and never since heard from.

FAMILY CXIX.‡

ISAAC[7] [293], *(James[6], Samuel[5], James[4], Israel[3], Israel[2], James[1])* *b.* Milton, O., 16 Dec., 1819; *d.* Milton, 1 Aug., 1884;

a. Olive Serepta Floor, *m.* Middlefield, O., 6 Oct., 1897, Cyrus Solon, *s.* Martin and Mary (Curtis) Bundy (*b.* West Farmington, O., 15 Nov., 1852).

b. Birdie Anges Floor, *m.* Berlin, O., 27 Mch., 1889, William Sylvester, *s.* Sylvester and Lydia (Harshman) Bowles (*b.* Mich., 7 Apl., 1869). *Issue: i.* Earl Algērnon[10] (Bowles) *b.* 7 Aug., 1891; *ii.* Josephine Lyda[10] (Bowles) *b.* 3 June, 1894; *iii.* Zora Elizabeth[10] (Bowles) *b.* May, May, 1897.*

c. Vincent Rienzi Floor, *m.* Canfield, O., 23 Dec., 1892, Margaret *dau.* Christ and Christina (————) Dustman. *No issue.**

d. Walling Parshall, *d.* Atwater, Portage Co., O., 1 Apl., 1892; *m.* Canfield, O., 7 Oct., 1869, Hannah Christenia, *dau.* John B. and Mary Ann (Baker) Felnogle, (*b.* Berlin, O., 25 Aug., 1846) *ch.* (all *b.* Atwater, O.) 1087: Jetta Blanche[9] *b.* 18 Sept., 1870; *m.* Portage Co., O., 9 Feby., 1893, Hansel James, *s.* James Hansel and Sarah Elizabeth (Cleverly) Green (*b.* Deerfield, O., 16 Oct., 1867). *Issue: i. Lamont Oscar*[10] *(Green) b. 30 June, 1898;* 1088: *ii.* Edwin Ellis[9] *b.* 1 Apl., 1874; *d.* 23 Mch., 1877; 1089. *iii.* Margaret Pearl[9] *b.* Jany., 1878; *m.* Ravenna, O., 3 Oct., 1899, Frank Herbert, *s.* Frank and Sarah (Linge) Clapsaddle (*b.* Marlboro, O., 6 Apl., 1875). *Issue: i. Ralph Herbert*[10] *(Clapsaddle) b. 19 Oct.*, 1900.†

---

* Fam. Recs. and pers. know., 709.
† Fam. Recs. and pers. know., wid., 711.
‡ Bible Rec. 293, pos. Clifford Crays, Diamond, O.

m. Milton, 24 Dec., 1846, Sophia, *dau.* Martin and Catherine (Kimmer) Kale (*b.* Milton, O., 28 Mch., 1826; *d.* Milton, 11 May, 1902).

Children: (All *b.* Milton, O.)

713 I. Alrenia Ann[8] *b.* 4 Nov., 1848.
714 II. Martin James[8] *b.* 23 Jany., 1849; *d.* 17 Nov., 1849.
715 III. Mary Catherine[8] *b.* 23 Nov., 1851.
716 IV. Margaret Alice[8] *b.* 25 Apl., 1854.
717 V. Serena Triphena[8] *b.* 2 Apl., 1856.
718 VI. Orlando Gilmore[8] *b.* 11 Mch., 1858.
719 VII. Seymour Walter[8] *b.* 16 Apl., 1868.

---

*FAMILY CXX.**

JOHN MUNNELL[7]* [299], (*Samuel[6], Samuel[5], James[4], Israel,[3] Israel,[2] James[1]*) *b.* prob. Orange Co., N. Y., 23 Feby., 1809; *d.* Tryonville, Pa., 6 Nov., 1889; *m.* Tidioute, Pa., abt. 1829, Alice, *dau.* Samuel and Charity (Gilson) McGuire (*b.* Tidioute, Pa., 10 Nov., 1811; *d. n.* Titusville, Pa., —— Apl., 1898). [*Tryonville, Pa.*

Children: (All *b.* Tidioute, Pa.)

720 I. Samuel[8] *b.* 1830; *d. s. p.**
721 II. Rhoda[8] *b.* 24 Apl., 1832; *m.* —— Sterling.*
722 III. Matilda[8] *b.* 15 Feby., 1835; *m.* —— Abbey.*
723 IV. Elizabeth W.[8] *b.* 1836; *unm.**
724 V. Lucinda Marion[8]† *b.* 5 Dec., 1838; *m.* Tidioute, Pa., 10 Nov., 1853, John, *s.* Samuel and Sarah (Shields) Matchette (*b.* Cork, Ireland, 25 Dec., 1828; *d.* Black River Falls, Wis., 16 Nov., 1891). *Issue:* [*Black River Falls, Wis.*

---

* Fam. Recs. and pers. know., 726 and 728; P. and Van E. Fams.
† Pers. statement.

i. John Leonard[9] (Matchette) *b.* 10 Aug., 1854.
ii. Ella[9] (Matchette) *b.* 4 May, 1856.[a] [*Portage, Wis.*
iii. Cordelia Marion[9] (Matchette) *b.* 28 Mch., 1858.[b] [*Chippewa Falls, Wis.*
iv. William Henry[9] (Matchette) *b.* 28 Apl., 1860.[c]
v. Franklin James[9] (Matchette) *b.* 24 Feby., 1863.[d] [*Milwaukee, Wis.*
vi. Jessie Maude[9] (Matchette) *b.* 22 Oct., 1869.[e] [*Black River Falls, Wis.*
vii. Louis Dudley[9] (Matchette) *b.* 23 Dec., 1874. [*Black River Falls, Wis.*

725 VI. William Henry Harrison[8] *b.* 30 Oct., 1840.[f]
726 VII. Hugh McGuire[8g] *b.* 23 July, 1842.
727 VIII. Nancy M.[8*] *b.* 21 Oct., 1844; *m.* Sheldon, Huston Co., Minn., 7 May, 1863, George Washington, *s.* James H. and Lavina (————) Cooper (*b.* Green Co., O., 28 Dec., 1842). *Issue:* [*Gilmantown, Buffalo Co., Wis.*

a. Ella Matchette, *m.* ———— Apl., 1878, Theodore, *s.* Benjamin and Catherine (————) Holbrook.†

b. Cordelia Marion Matchette, *m.* 11 May, 1876, Frank C., *s.* Harvey and Electa (Bixby) Allen.†

c. William Henry Matchette, *m.* 1897, Therese Woodward.†

d. Franklin James Matchette, *m.* 24 Sept., 1885, Nellie, *dau.* Thomas and Lois (————) Smith.†

e. Jessie Maude Matchette, *m.* ———— Nov., 1894, G. Merlin Hull.†

f. William Henry Horace Parshall, *m.* Julia Ann Fischer, ch.; 1090; Frank William[9] *b.* Pa., 8 Sept., 1867; *d.* La Crosse, Wis., 27 Jany., 1890 *unm.*; 1091. *ii.* Frederick Lincoln[9] *b.* Hokah, Minn., 14 Apl., 1870; *m.* (1) ———— ———— *Issue:* 1274 *i. Frederick Wilbur*[10] *b. St. Paul, Minn., 14 May, 1893, m.* (2) St. Paul, 8 Nov., 1898, Helen, *dau.* John Walter and Mary Ann (————) O'Grady (*b.* 15 Dec., 1875). *No Issue;* 1092. *iii.* Caroline May[9] *b.* La Crosse, Wis., 17 Oct., 1872; *m.* Hudson, Wis., ——— Dec., 1891, Charles W. Rodman. *No issue;* 1093. *iv.* Herbert Henry[9] *b.* La Crosse, Wis., 16 July, 1875; 1094. *v.* Pearl Pearless[9] *b.* La Crosse, Wis., 10 Mch., 1877; *d.* St. Paul, 2 Nov., 1895; 1095. *vi.* Jessie Dorothy[9] *b.* La Crosse, Wis., 26 Nov., 1882.‡

g. Hugh McGuire Parshall, *m.* Erie, Pa., 18 Apl., 1866, Sara, *dau.* Spencer and Susannah (Morgan) West (*b.* Harbor Creek, Pa., 14 Feb., 1846) Ch.; 1096.

* Pers. statement.
† Pers. know., 724.
‡ Pers. know., 724 and 1091.

i. Hugh Lincoln[9] (Cooper) *b.* 28 Apl., 1865.*
[*Sao Paulo, Brazil.*

ii. Lillian Alice[9] (Cooper) *b.* 8 July, 1868.*
[*Sheffield, Mass.*

iii. Maude Lavina[9] (Cooper) *b.* 1 Apl., 1874.*
[*La Crosse, Wis.*

iv. Dexter Parshall[9] (Cooper) *b.* 10 July, 1880.
[*Sao Paulo, Brazil.*

728 ix. John Munnell[8] *b.* 15 Nov., 1846.*

FAMILY CXXI.‡

SAMUEL[7] [302], *(Samuel[6], Samuel[5], James[4], Israel[3], Israel[2], James[1])* *b.* Trumbull Co., O., 14 Nov., 1814; *d.* Pleasantville, Pa., 4 Feby., 1901; *m.* Pleasantville, Pa., 8 July, 1854, Lucy Ann, *dau.* David and Jane (Watson) Henderson (*b.* Pleasantville, Pa., 11 July, 1830; *d.* Pleasantville, Pa., 6 Feby., 1901).
[*Pleasantville, Pa*

i. Harriet May[9] *b.* Corry, Pa., 3 Feby., 1867; 1097. *ii.* Frank West[9] *b.* Corry, Pa., 19 July, 1868; *d.* Harbor Creek, Pa., 19 Mch., 1870; 1098. *iii.* Edward Everette[9] *b.* Harbor Creek, Pa., 16 Apl., 1871; *d.* Parkersburg, W. Va., 10 Feby., 1897; 1099. *iv.* Alan West[9] *b.* Tidioute, Pa., 31 Dec., 1876; *d.* Tidioute, 17 Feby., 1877; 1100. *v.* Hugh Raymond[9] *b.* Tidioute, Pa., 17 Apl., 1878; *m.* Sheffield, Pa., 12 June, 1901, Ellen Jane Kraeer; 1101. *vi.* Florence[9] *b.* Tidioute, Pa., 30 Sept., 1881.*

a. Hugh Lincoln Cooper, *m.* Rochester, Minn., 8 Oct., 1892, Frances Marion, *dau.* Albert and —— (Bliss) Graves. *Issue:* *i.* Agnes Lillian[10]; *ii.* Hugh L.[10]†

b. Lillian Alice Cooper, *m.* Black River Falls, Wis., 14 Sept., 1893, Rollin Satterlee. *Issue:* *i.* Hugh Wendell[10], (Satterlee).†

c. Maude Lavina Cooper, *m.* Black River Falls, Wis., 9 June, 1898, William B. Batchelder.†

d. John Munnell Parshall, *m.* Greenville, Pa., 21 Mch., 1869, Elizabeth, *dau.* Jonathan D. and Jane (Walton) Hogan (*b.* Venango Co., Pa., 2 May, 1846). Ch. (all *b.* Tidioute, Pa.); 1102. *i.* Frank Carlton[9] *b.* 30 Aug., 1873, *m.* Estella, *dau* Samuel and Elizabeth (————) Jobson; 1103. *ii.* Alice

---

* Pers. statement.
† Pers. know., 727.
‡ Fam. Recs. pos. 730.

Children: (All *b.* Pleasantville, Pa.)

729 I. Samuel Chapin[8] *b.* 16 June, 1855.[a] [*Wellsville, N. Y.*
730 II. David Newton[8] *b.* 11 Oct., 1858.[b] [*Pleasantville, Pa.*
731 III. Vernon Elmer[8] *b.* 21 Nov., 1860.[c]
[*Ridgeway, Elk Co., Pa.*
732 IV. William Everette[8] *b.* 4 Apl., 1866.[d]
[*Pleasantville, Pa.*

FAMILY CXXII.†

GEORGE STRANAHAN[7] [304], (*Samuel*[6], *Samuel*[5], *James*[4], *Israel*[3], *Israel*[2], *James*[1]) *b.* Pulaski, O., 14 Jany., 1820; *d.* Pleasantville, Pa., 27 Nov., 1865; *m.* Deerfield Tp., Warren Co.,

Genevieve[9] *b.* 25 Apl., 1876, *m.* Erie, Pa., 25 Oct., 1900, Dr. Charles C., *s.* Dr. Charles Kemble; 1104. *iii.* Winifred[9] *b.* 6 May, 1878; 1105. *iv.* Charles Deforest[9] *b.* 18 Aug., 1880; 1106. *v.* Ernest Chapin[9] *b.* 19 Sept., 1885. John M. Parshall enlisted in Co. D. 145th Pa. Vols., 10 Aug., 1862, and served until the war closed, being discharged with the rank of sargeant, at Erie, Pa., June, 1865. He attended Edinboro (Pa.) State Normal School for two years and has been in active merchantile life since 1871. He is a member of the M. E. church, and has been a member of Temple Lodge, No. 412 A. Y. M. of Tidioute since 1877.*

a. Samuel Chapin Parshall, *m.* Tidioute, Pa., 1876, Anna Savilla McClusky (*b.* Pa., 9 Apl., 1859) *Ch.;* 1107. *i.* Maude Elizabeth[9] *b.* 16 Aug., 1877; 1108. *ii.* Hugh Chapin[9] *b.* 24 Nov., 1880; 1109. *iii.* Vera Pearl[9] *b.* 22 Nov., 1882.*

b. David Newton Parshall, *m.* Pleasantville, Pa., 25 July., 1889, Lilla Maude, *dau.* Lott L. and Marinda (House) Nye (*b.* Fabius, Onon. Co., N. Y., 10 June, 1866) *Ch.;* 1110. *i.* Claude Coleman[9] *b.* 4 June, 1891.*

c. Vernon Elmer Parshall, *m.* Sugar Grove, Warren Co., Pa., 20 Sept., 1883, Carrie Luzerne, *dau.* Hosea Southwick and Sally Jane (Ashley) Densmore (*b.* Guys Mills, Crawf. Co., Pa., 24 Dec., 1858) *Ch.;* 1111. *i.* Hubert Earl[9] *b.* 24 Aug., 1884; *d.* 24 Aug., 1885; 1112. *ii.* Roger Aubrey[9] *b.* 24 Mch., 1889; 1113. *iii.* Charlotte Marie[9] *b.* 15 Feby., 1897.*

d. William Everette Parshall, *m.* Jamestown, N. Y., 25 June, 1888, Clara Leona, *dau.* John D. and Eleanor Canada (Barr) Holeman (*b.* New Richmond, Pa., 25 Sept., 1867) *Ch.;* (all *b.* Pleasantbille, Pa.); 1114. *i.* Samuel Dale[9] *b.* 12 May, 1889; 1115. *ii.* Kate[9] *b.* 25 Apl., 1892; *d.* 26 Aug., 1892; 1116. *iii.* Helen Christene[9] *b.* 9 Oct., 1894; 1117. *iv.* Nellie M.[9] *b.* 21 Jany., 1901.*

---

* Pers. statement.
† P. and Van E. Fams., and pers. know., 736 and 737.

Pa., 22 Dec., 1842, Flora, *dau.* Samuel and Margaret (Vanalstine) Thompson (*b.* Deerfield Tp., Warren Co., Pa., 12 Oct., 1824). [*Tidioute, Pa.*

Children:

733 I. Edwin W.[8] *b.* Deerfield Tp., Warren Co., Pa., 14 Oct., 1846.[a] [*Warren, Pa.*

734 II. Martha E.[8] *b.* Tidioute, Pa., 19 June, 1847. [*Warren, Pa.*

735 III. James W.[8] *b.* 26 Apl., 1851; *d.* Pleasantville, Pa., 24 Dec., 1891; *unm.*

736 IV. Wesley Warren[8] *b.* 19 July, 1855.[b] [*Rico, Colo.*

737 V. George Sherman[8] *b.* Pleasantville, Pa., 20 Apl., 1863.[c] [*Pittsburg, Pa.*

FAMILY CXXIII.†

JAMES[7] [306], (*Samuel*[6], *Samuel*[5], *James*[4], *Israel*[3], *Israel*[2], *James*[1]) *b.* 19 Sept., 1827; *d.* Geneva, O., 30 Aug., 1896; *m.* (1), Tidioute, Pa., 25 Dec., 1854, Henrietta L., *dau.* John W. and Catherine (McCabe) Shugart (*b.* Franklin, Pa., 7 Nov., 1838; *d.* Tidioute, Pa., 10 Nov., 1881). [*Titusville, Pa.*

a. Edwin W. Parshall, *m.* Warren, Pa., 5 Feby., 1872, Belle, *dau.* Myron Waters (*b.* Warren, Pa., 23 Apl., 1848; *d.* Warren, Pa., 15 Feby., 1897); *Children*, 1118. *i.* Clarabelle[9] *b.* Pleasantville, Pa., 5 Feby., 1873, *m.* Warren, Pa., 5 Apl., 1899, Carl, *s.* Isaac Norton and Isabel (Stoutenberg) Gildersleeve (*b.* Cochocton, N. Y., 29 Sept., 1872). *Issues i. John Marshall*[10] *(Gildersleeve) b. 4 Mch., 1900; ii. Stanley Parshall*[10] *(Gildersleeve) b. 25 Apl., 1902;* 1119. *ii.* Marshall Curtis[9] *b.* Pleasantville, Pa., 27 Aug., 1877.*

b. Wesley Warren Parshall, *m.* Rochester, N. Y., 18 June, 1882, Ida Gertrude, *dau.* Edward and Mary (———) Palmer (*b.* Rochester, N. Y., 23 Jany., 1860) *Ch. (all b. Rico, Colo.)* 1120. *i.* Harold Christie[9] *b.* 7 Nov., 1882; 1121. *ii.* Wesley Warren[9] *b.* 6 Sept., 1893.*

c. George Sherman Parshall, *m.* Olean, N. Y., 7 Oct., 1886, Emma, *dau.* Milton and Mary (Aults) Means (*b.* Ia., 3 Dec., 1866) *Ch.;* 1122. *i.* Flora[9] *b.* Olean, N. Y., 20 June, 1887; 1123. *ii.* George Sherman[9] *b.* Rico, Colo., 19 Jany., 1894.*

---

* Pers. statement.

† Fam. Recs. and pers. know., 738 and 739.

Children:

738 I. Samuel Wilson[8] *b.* Tidioute, Pa., 11 May, 1856.[a]
[*Akron, O.*

739 II. Maude Ellen[8] *b.* Tidioute, Pa., 23 Jany., 1870.
[*Titusville, Pa.*

m. (2)† Pleasantville, Pa., 3 May, 1883, Mrs. Adah (Meade) James, *dau.* Abyrom Parke and Margaret Webb (Campbell) Meade (*b.* Keokuk, Ia.).

Children:

740 III. James Jay[8] *b.* Titusville, Pa., 17 May, 1885.†
[*Cleveland, O.*

FAMILY CXXIV.‡

JACOB COOK[7] [307], (*John*[6], *Samuel*[5], *James*[4], *Israel*[3], *Israel*[2], *James*[1]) *b.* Ellsworth, Mahoning Co., O., 16 Dec., 1812; *d.* Faribault, Minn., 15 Mch., 1890; *m.* Butler Co., Pa., 11 June, 1834, Sarah Maria, *dau.* James Cratty (*b.* Butler Co., Pa., 19 Aug., 1811; *d.* Faribault, Minn., 6 Oct., 1892).
[*Faribault, Minn.*

a. Samuel Wilson Parshall, *m.* Akron, O., 5 Feby., 1880, Harriet Evaline, *dau.* William Eyles and Helen Sophia (Dickey) Pardee (*b.* Nebraska City, Neb., 29 July, 1858) *Ch.;* 1124. *i.* Inez[9] *b.* Titusville, Pa., 19 Jany., 1881; 1125. *ii.* Gladys[9] *b.* Titusville, 11 Oct., 1882; 1126. *iii.* Edward Pardee[9] *b.* Akron, O., 12 July, 1884; 1127. *iv.* Wallace Dickey[9] *b.* Akron, 14 Mch., 1889; *d.* Mentor, O., 20 Oct., 1893; 1128. *v.* Samuel Wilson[9] *b.* Akron, 1 Sept., 1890; *d.* Mentor, 14 Oct., 1893; 1129. *vi.* Don Aaron[9] *b.* Akron, 3 Oct., 1893; 1130; *vii.* Henrietta[9] *b.* Akron, O., 3 July, 1895; *d.* Akron, O., 7 July, 1895.*

---

* Pers. statement.
† Pers. know., wid. 206.
‡ Fam. Recs. and pers. know., 741 and 745.

Children:

741 I. John R.[8] *b.* Newton Falls, O., 17 May, 1835.[a] [*Faribault, Minn.*

742 II. James Wallace[8] *b.* New Lyme, O., 10 Dec., 1842.[b] [*Faribault, Minn.*

743 III. William Dennis[8] *b.* Lyme, O., 17 May, 1848.[b] [*Williston, S. Dak.*

a. Hon. John R. Parshall, *d.* Fairbault, Minn., 10 Sept., 1902; *m.* New Lyme, O., 3 Oct., 1866, Francenia M. *dau.* Zopher and Aurelia (Moses) Gee, (*b.* New Lyme, O., 21 Mch., 1848) *Children:* 1131: *i.* Lottie Irene, *b.* 17 Oct., 1867; *d.* 23 Apl., 1868; 1132. *ii.* Bernice A.[9] *b.* Faribault, Minn., 21 Apl., 1869; 1133. iii. Eloise[9] *b.* Faribault, 8 June, 1876; *d.* Faribault, 21 Jany., 1885.* He was educated in the public schools of New Lyme O., and at Kingsville (O) Academy; followed mercantile business, farming and school teaching at different places for several years. Enlisted Aug., 1861, in Co. A, 6th Ohio Vol. Cavalry. Served in W. Va., and in the Army of the Potomac. Was mustered out as 1st Lieut., Nov., 1864, by reason of the expiration of his term of service. Returning to Faribault, Minn., he engaged in the grocery business, and in 1869, was elected Registrar of Deeds, for Rice Co., Minn., and served six years. Engaged in book and stationery business, and was elected Mayor of Faribault, 1878. Was appointed Postmaster in 1885, and served in that capacity four years. In 1889, was appointed Trustee of the Minnesota Soldiers' Home, and in 1892, was elected Fiscal Agent and Steward of the Minnesota Institute for Defectives, which last two positions he held at his death. He has been Master of Faribault Lodge, F. & A. M., Commander of Faribault Commandry, Commander of Mitchell Cook Post, G. A. R., and Vestryman of Cathedral Parish for many years.*

b. James Wallace Parshall, *b.* New Lyme, O., 10 Dec., 1842; *m.* Faribault, Minn., 11 Feby., 1865, Sarah A., *dau.* Heman G. and Maria (Bitley) Crossett (*b.* Troy, N. Y., 1 Sept., 1846). *Children:* (All *b.* Faribault, Minn.) 1134. *i.* William Walter[9] *b.* 30 Sept., 1866; *m.* Currie, Minn., 10 Jany., 1893, Margaret, *dau.* Michael and Mary (Rice) Stiern (*b.* Germany, 17 Feby., 1874). *Children:* 1275. *i. Marie Amelia*[10] *b. 5 Nov., 1893;* 1276. *ii. Arthur John*[10] *b. 5 July, 1896; d. 10 Oct., 1898;* 1277. *iii. George Clarence*[10] *b. 11 May, 1900;* 1135. *ii.* Heman Franklin[9] (Rev.) *b.* 27 Sept., 1867; *m.* Faribault, Minn., 31 May, 1884, Minta Nell, *dau.* James Jasper and Matilda (Crane) Gilmer (*b.* Faribault, 8 Mch., 1867). *Children:* 1278. *i. Margaret Gilmer*[10] *b. Faribault, 10 Mch., 1895;* 1279. *ii. Catherine Crane*[10] *b. St. Cloud, Minn., 16 Oct., 1898; d. ¼ Nov., 1898;* 1280. *iii. Eleanor Crossett*[10] *b. St Cloud, 8 July, 1900.* 1136. *iii.* Mary Maria[9] *b.* Faribault, 23 Nov., 1868; *m.* Scovell, Minn., 8 Dec., 1886, Thomas Francis, *s.* Thomas and Sarah (Butler) Robinson (*b.* Mazomanie, Wis., 29 July, 1858) *Issue: i. Sarah Alice*[10] *(Robinson) b. 30 Oct., 1887; ii. Frank Parshall*[10] *(Robinson) b. 15 June, 1889; iii. Madge*[10] *(Robinson) b. 16 July, 1891.* 1137. *iv.* Alice Gertrude[9] *b.* Faribault, 13 Feby., 1870; *m.* Slayton, Minn., 30 May, 1891,

* Pers. statement.

744 IV. Mary Emily[8] *b.* New Lyme, O., 15 Sept., 1853.[*] [*Boyd, Ore.*

FAMILY CXXV.†

JOSEPH[7] [309], (*William*[6], *Samuel*[5], *James*[4], *Israel*[3], *Israel*[2], *James*[1]) *b.* Butler Co., Pa., 17 Aug., 1821; *d.* Virginia City, Nev., 14 Nov., 1876; *m.* Mercer Co., Pa., 15 Mch., 1842, Elizabeth, *dau.* William and Sarah (Harlan) Wilkin.

Children: (All *b.* Leesburg, Pa.)

745 I. Jennie E.[8] *b.* 11 Aug., 1843; *m.* Leesburg, 2 Mch., 1865, William Adam, *s.* Adam and Mary (Risher) Munnel (*b.* New Wilmington, Pa., 25 Apl., 1840). *Issue:*

i. Bessie Maude[9] (Munnel) *b.* 4 Aug., 1868.[b]

Benjamin Delaney, *s.* Christian and Mary Ann (Brown) Stine (*b.* Omaha, Neb., 19 Feby., 1863). *Issue:* (All *b.* Omaha, Neb.) *i. Glenn Parshall*[10] *(Stine) b. 26 May, 1892; ii. Ruth Alice*[10] *b. 23 Dec., 1897;* 1138. *v.* Arthur Edgar[9] *b.* Faribault, 18 June, 1872; *m.* Faribault, 17 Feby., 1901, Bessie Arvilla, *dau.* Charles Edward and Frances (Lewis) Smith (*b.* Toledo, O., 17 Feby., 1876); 1139. *vi.* Dana Herman[9] *b.* Faribault, 13 July, 1874; 1140. *vii.* James Telliff[9] *b.* Cameron, Minn., 15 Sept., 1880; *d.* Cameron, 21 Oct., 1883.*

a. Mary Emily Parshall b. 20 Sept., 1853; *m.* Faribault, 4 Sept., 1878, John Alexander, *s.* Angus, and Annie (McKinie) Bethune (*b.* Charlottenberg, Ont., Canada, 13 Sept., 1848). *Issue: i.* Joseph Youngman[9] (Bethune) *b.* Red Wing, Minn., 9 June, 1879; *ii.* Maude Alice[9] (Bethune) *b.* Faribault, Minn., 30 June, 1883; *iii.* James Angus[9] (Bethune) *b.* Eau Claire, Wis., 29 May, 1886.‡

b. Bessie Maude Munnell *d.* Banbury, Pa., 8 Apl., 1898; *m.* Rich Hill, Pa., — Sept., 1888, William Hudsbeth, *s.* James and Anna (Sager) Harrison (*b.* Pittsburg, Pa., 11 Oct., 1862). *Issue: i.* William Munnell[10] (Harrison) *b.* 25 June, 1889; *ii.* James Richard[10] (Harrison) *b.* 8 Jany., 1891; *ii.* Bessie Hazel[10] (Harrison) *b.* 19 Aug., 1893; *iv.* Edward Seager[10] (Harrison) *b.* 19 May, 1895.†

---

* Fam. Recs. and pers. know., 1136.
† Fam. Recs. and pers. know., 745.
‡ Pers. statement.

ii. Nettie[9] (Munnel) *b.* 2 Dec., 1870.
iii. Mary Blanche[9] (Munnel) *b.* 27 Sept., 1872.[a]
iv. William Boyd[9] (Munnel) *b.* 22 Feby., 1876.[b]
v. Olive Estella[9] (Munnel) *b.* 25 May, 1878.

746 II. Sarah[8] *b.* 11 Oct., 1845; *d.* Volant, Pa., 14 Feby., 1900; *m.* Mercer Co., Pa., 7 Oct., 1863, Isaac Donaldson, *s.* James Young and Martha (Donaldson) Kirk (*b.* Indian Run, Pa., 19 Nov., 1841). *Issue:*

i. Olive Estella[9] (Kirk) *b.* 4 July, 1864.
ii. James Parshall[9] (Kirk) *b.* 11 Oct., 1867.

747 III. Mary[8] *b.* 28 Aug., 1847; *d.* 26 May, 1886.
748 IV. William[8] *b.* 26 June, 1849.[c]
749 V. Jonathan Wilkin[8] *b.* 24 July, 1851.[d]
750 VI. Dorcas[8] *b.* 31 Dec., 1854; *d.* Indian Run, Pa., 2 Oct., 1897; *m.* New Wilmington, Pa., 20 Aug., 1878, William, *s.* Mathias and Margaret (McBride) Edeburn (*b.* Volant, Pa., 24 Jany., 1859). *Issue:*

a. Mary Blanche Munnel *m.* New Castle, Pa., 14 Feby., 1900, Guy L., *s.* William E. and Margaret (Parker) Lockhart (*b.* New Castle, 28 June, 1869). *Issue:* *i.* William Glenn[10] (Lockhart) *b.* 22 Dec., 1900.[*]

b. William Boyd Munnel *m.* Rich Hill, Pa., 3 July, 1902, Sarah Edna, *dau.* Wilbur and Ella (Reed) Minich.[*]

c. William Parshall *m.* New Castle, Pa., 22 Feby., 1874, Eliza Jane, *dau.* John and Elizabeth (Daniels) Nelson (*b.* 1 Nov., 1853). *Children:* 1141. *i.* Mary Elizabeth[9] *b.* 1 Aug., 1875; 1142. *ii.* Beriah Gibson[9] *b.* 22 July, 1878; 1143. *iii.* Clark Munnel[9] *b.* 8 Aug., 1879; 1144. *iv.* Etta Jane[9] *b.* 22 Jany., 1882.[*]

d. Jonathan Wilkin Parshall *m.* Black Town, Pa., Matilda Jane, *dau.* Henry and Christena (Baughman) Rodawald (*b.* Clarksville, Pa., 23 Aug., 1851). *Children:* 1145. *i.* Clide William[9] *b.* 23 Sept., 1872; 1146. *ii.* Charles Boyd[9] *b.* 1 Feby., 1875; 1147. *iii.* Emma[9] *b.* 23 Feby., 1877; 1148. *iv.* Louis Melville[9] *b.* 9 May, 1879; 1149. *v.* Carrie May[9] *b.* 5 Sept., 1882; 1150. *vi.* Olive Helen[9] *b.* 4 Sept., 1884; 1151. *vii.* Mabel Christena[9] *b.* 26 Mch., 1887; 1152. *viii.* Earl Jonathan[9] *b.* 3 Nov., 1890; 1153. *ix.* Ellen Maria[9] *b.* 12 Sept., 1894.[*]

[*] Fam. Recs. and pers. know., 745.

i. Joseph Oscar[9] (Edeburn) *b.* 21 Nov., 1878.
ii. Mary Luella[9] (Edeburn) *b.* 26 Jany., 1882.
iii. Carrie Ethel[9] (Edeburn) *b.* 4 May, 1884.
iv. Clark Parshall[9] (Edeburn) *b.* 18 Apl., 1886.

751 VII. Clark[8] *b.* 22 Mch., 1858.[a]
752 VIII. John Rudolph[8] *b.* 6 May, 1860.

---

*FAMILY CXXVI.**

SAMUEL[7] [310], *(William[6], Samuel[5], James[4], Israel[3], Israel[2], James[1]) b.* Centerville, Pa., 27 Oct., 1824; *d.* West Middlesex, Pa., 14 June, 1889; *m.* West Middlesex, Pa., 26 Oct., 1848, Rebecca, *dau.* John and Elizabeth (McBride) Newkirk (*b.* Darlington, Pa., 14 Mch., 1824).

Children:

753 I. Emma[8] *b.* 9 July, 18—; *m.* 20 June, 1887, W. J. Davidson. [*Beaver Falls, Pa.*
754 II. Harry Alfred[8] *b.* 27 Feby., 1862.[b] [*West Middlesex, Pa.*

FAMILY CXXVII.‡

JAMES ALEXANDER[7] [311], *(William[6], Samuel[5], James[4], Israel[3], Israel[2], James[1]) b.* Centerville, Butler Co., Pa., 11 Dec.,

a. Clark Parshall *m.* Adda McGinnis. *No issue.*
b. Harry Alfred Parshall *m.* Sandy Lake, Pa., 25 June, 1902, Ella, *dau.* Robert Hugh and Martha (Baird) McCullough (*b.* Sandy Lake, 20 June, 1877).†

---

* Fam. Recs. and pers. know. 754.
† Pers. statement.
‡ Fam. Recs. and pers. know., 756 and 757.

1827; *d.* Neshannock Falls, Pa., 16 Dec., 1885; *m.* Centerville, Pa., 20 May, 1848, Maria, *dau.* of James Rodgers (*b.* Centerville, 3 Oct., 1832; *d.* Neshannock Falls, 3 Aug., 1895).

Children:

755 I. Ida[8] *b.* 24 Apl., 1852; *d. inf.*

756 II. William L.[8] *b.* Mercer, Pa., 3 Oct., 1854.[a] [*St. Marys, W. Va.*

757 III. Francis Rudolph[8] *b.* Mercer, Pa., 4 May, 1858.[b] [*Allegheny City, Pa.*

758 IV. Clara Jane[8] *b.* Leesburg, Pa., 22 Nov., 1862.

759 V. Mary Ada[8] *b.* Leesburg, Pa., 28 Feby., 1867.

760 VI. Melvin C.[8] *b.* Leesburg, Pa., 22 Mch., 1872.

---

*FAMILY CXXVIII.**

ELI GEE[7] [322], *(Daniel[6], Samuel[5], James[4], Israel[3], Israel[2], James[1]) b.* Milton, O., 24 Jany., 1844; *m.* Independence, Ia., 6 Jany., 1870, Adelia, *dau.* John and Catherine (Trainer) Callahan (*b.* Columbus, Wis., 25 Dec., 1847). [*Cuba, Mo.*

a. William L. Parshall *m.* Latrobe, Westmoreland Co., Pa., 19 May, 1897, Harriet, *dau.* John and Hannah (———) Wright (*b.* Pennsville, Fayette Co., Pa., 9 June, 1872). *Children:* 1154. *i.* Helen[9] *b.* Pennsyllle, Pa., 9 July, 1898; 1155. *ii.* Arthur LeRoy[9] *b.* Pennsville, 14 June, 1901.*

b. Franklin Rudolph Parshall *m.* Leesburg, Pa., — Apl., 1888, Margaret Sophia, *dau.* Charles and Harriet (———) Banfield (*b.* England, 18 Apl., 1863). *Children:* 1156. *i.* Stanley Banfield[9] *b.* New Castle, Pa., 27 Oct., 1899; 1157. *ii.* Sydney Gardner[9] *b.* New Castle, Pa., 4 Sept., 1892; 1158. *iii.* Paul B.[9] *b.* Franklin, Pa., 14 Mch., 1890; *d.* 16 Mch., 1890.*

---

* Pers. statement.

Children:

761 I. Frank G.[8] *b.* New Hampton, Ia., 12 Nov., 1871.[a] [*New Hampton, Ia.*

762 II. Mary Elizabeth[8] *b.* Lawler, Ia., 11 Jany., 1875; *d.* Sumner, Ia., 3 Apl., 1876.

763 III. Catherine Grace[8] *b.* Sumner, Ia., 23 Apl., 1877; *d.* Sumner, Ia., 23 Apl., 1879. [*Sumner, Ia.*

764 IV. Etta Gertrude[8] *b.* Chickasaw Co., Ia., 6 Mch., 1880.

765 V. May Catherine[8] *b.* New Hampton, Ia., 29 May, 1882.

766 VI. LeVinnie Rose[8] *b.* Dresden, Ia., 6 Nov., 1884.

767 VII. Philip Alfred[8] *b.* Sumner, Ia., 28 Jany., 1887.

768 VIII. Arthur John[8] *b.* Sumner, Ia., 26 May, 1890.

FAMILY CXXIX.†

FREDERICK[7] [323], (*Thomas*[6], *Samuel*[5], *James*[4], *Israel*[3], *Israel*[2], *James*[1]) *b.* Ravenna, O., 2 Apl., 1825; *d.* Sharlersville, Portage Co., O., 14 Oct., 1885; *m.* 27 Apl., 1855, Eliza, *dau.* Daniel and Susan (———) Depue (*b.* 4 Apl., 1835; *d.* Shalersville, O., 25 Feby., 1901). [*Shalersville, Portage Co., O.*

Children: (All *b.* Shalersville, O.)

769 I. Willie Ernest[8] *b.* 19 Mch., 1859.[b]

770 II. Luna Eugenia[8] *b.* 20 Mch., 1861.[c]

a. Frank G. Parshall *m.* Elma, Ia., 6 Feby., 1901, Mattie, *dau.* George Pittinger (*b.* North Washington, Ia., 20 Feby., 1880).*

b. Willie Ernest Parshall *d.* Shalersville, O., 20 Feby., 1901; *m.* Detroit, Mich., 6 Sept., 1888, Lillian, *dau.* Deforest and Sophronia (Parshall) [———] Wheelock (*b.* Freedom, O., 21 Apl., 1861). *Children:* 1159. *i.* Clayton Deforest.[9]†

c. Luna Eugenia Parshall *m.* Akron, O., 2 Oct., 1884, George, *s.* Henry and Mary (Hall) Corl (*b.* Mogadore, O., 14 Jany., 1861). *Issue:* *i.* Fred[9] (Corl.)†

---

* Pers. statement.
† Fam. Recs. and pers. know., 771.

771 III. Friend Luman[8] *b.* 27 Nov., 1868.[a]

772 IV. Pearlie James[8] *b.* 10 Feby., 1872; *d.* Shalersville, O., 31 Dec., 1876.

FAMILY CXX.†

JOHN HARMON[7], Dr., [326], *(David[6], Samuel[5], James[4], Israel[3], Israel[2], James[1])* *b.* Ellsworth, Mahoning Co., O., 1 Aug., 1824; *d.* Kingsville, O., 24 Dec., 1883; *m.* 20 Sept., 1849, Susan B., *dau.* Thomas and Nancy (Miller) Van Winkle (*b.* Linesville, Pa., 6 June, 1831; *d.* Kingsville, O., 6 Apl., 1884).
[*Kingsville, Ashtabula Co., O.*

Children: (All *b.* Linesville, Pa.)

773 I. Abbie Winifred[8]‡ *b.* 15 June, 1850; *d.* Geneva, O., 10 June, 1889; *m.* Kingsville, O., 3 July, 1871, Worthy T., *s.* Lorenzo Solon and Harriet (Taylor) Bull (*b.* Solon, O., 17 Oct., 1843). *No issue.*
[*Kingsville, O.*

774 II. Herbert Morgan[8] *b.* 10 Oct., 1858.[b]

a. Friend Luman Parshall *m.* Ravenna, O., 6 Nov., 1889, Addie Irene, *dau.* John and Ella (Baxter) Brown (*b.* Franklin, O., 24 Jany., 1873). *Children:* Kankakee, Ill., 23 Oct., 1862). *No issue.**

b. Herbert Morgan Parshall *b.* 10 Oct., 1858; *m.* Topeka, Kan., 15 Aug., 1889, Hannah E., *dau.* Joel Harrison and Sarah Jane (Swan) Bledsoe (*b.* Kankakee, Ill., 23 Oct., 1862). *No issue.*

---

* Pers. statement.
† P. and Van E. Fams.; Fam. Recs. and pers. know., 774.
‡ P. and Van E. Fams., and pers. know. Worthy T. Bull.

*FAMILY CXXXI.**

WILLIAM SHREVE[7] [328], (*David*[6], *Samuel*[5], *James*[4], *Israel*[3], *Israel*[2], *James*[1]) *b.* Trumbull Co., O., 3 Oct., 1832; *m.* Trumbull Co., O., 28 Oct., 1852, Mary A., *dau.* John and Jane (McCrary) Smith (*b.* Trumbull Co., O., 27 Mch., 1834; *d.* Dows, Ia., 26 Dec., 1900). [*Dows, Wright Co., Ia.*

Children:

775 I. Ruth Athalia[8] *b.* Trumbull Co., O., 28 June, 1853. [*Eagle Grove, Wright Co., Ia.*

776 II. Ida Adelaide[8] *b.* Trumbull Co., O., 28 Mch., 1856; *d.* Jamestown, N. Dak., 28 Dec., 1886; *m.* Cedar Rapids, Ia., 3 Mch., 1884, Henry, *s.* John and ——— (Scott) Wheeler (*b.* Wis., 2 Sept., 1855). *Issue:*

i. Alta May[9] (Wheeler) *b.* 22 Feby., 1885.

777 III. Alice D.[8] *b.* Shelby Co., Mo., 1 Jany., 1861; *m.* Webster City, Ia., 1 Jany., 1880, William H., *s.* David and Sarah (Green) Inman (*b.* Ohio). *Issue:* [*Eagle Grove, Ia.*

i. Jessie Floss Clendina[9] (Inman).
ii. Grace Vivian[9] (Inman).
iii. William Shreve[9] (Inman).
iv. Alice Sophronia[9] (Inman).
v. Firman Gee[9] (Inman).

778 IV. Florence Abbie[8] *b.* Richmond, Wash. Co., Ia., 29 Mch., 1862; *m.* Webster City, Ia., 28 Sept., 1881,

* Compiled from Fam. Recs. by 783.

William, *s.* Robert and Christena (Hendry) Bain (*b.* Canada, 19 Oct., 1861). *Issue:*

[*Waldeck, Atkin Co., Minn.*

i. Earl[9] (Bain) *b.* 28 May, 1882; *d.* 8 Mch., 1886.
ii. Florence Edna[9] (Bain) *b.* 4 Aug., 1884.
iii. Jessie Mary[9] (Bain) *b.* 11 June, 1886.
iv. Wilmer J.[9] (Bain) *b.* 14 Aug., 1888.
v. Windle G.[9] (Bain) *b.* 14 Aug., 1888.
vi. Etta May[9] (Bain) *b.* 18 June, 1890.
vii. Mary Ida[9] (Bain) *b.* 30 Nov., 1895.
viii. William[9] (Bain) *b.* 23 Dec., 1897.

779 v. John Harmon[8] *b.* Richmond, Ia., 6 Apl., 1864; *d.* Richmond, Ia., 20 Sept., 1865.

780 vi. Margaret May[8] *b.* Richmond, Ia., 26 Jany., 1867; *m.* Blairsburg, Ia., 28 May, 1889, Fred S., *s.* Amos and Mary (Swarts) Bailey (*b.* Webster City, Ia., 26 Nov., 1866). *Issue:* [*Webster City, Ia.*

i. Amos F.[9] (Bailey) *b.* 18 May, 1893.
ii. Ralph William[9] (Bailey) *b.* 20 June, 1897; *d.* 11 Apl., 1898.

781 vii. Mary Adelia[8] *b.* Richmond, Ia., 6 Apl., 1869; *d.* Richmond, Ia., 25 July, 1870.

782 viii. Blanche Adelia[8] *b.* Richmond, Ia., 21 May, 1871.

783 ix. Mary Etta[8] *b.* Webster City, Ia., 12 July, 1874.

---

*FAMILY CXXXII.**

DAVID FURMAN[7] [331], *(David[6], Samuel[5], James[4], Israel[3], Israel[2], James[1])* *b.* Berlin, Mahoning Co., O., 13 Sept., 1841; *m.*

* Pers. statement.

Espyville, Crawford Co., Pa., 4 May, 1864, Sarah Elizabeth, *dau.* Joseph and Hannah (Stinson) Gibson (*b.* Espyville, Pa., 27 Nov., 1846). [*Denmark, Lee Co., Ia.*

Children:

784 I. Fred Gibson[8] *b.* 18 Feby., 1865.[a]

785 II. Emma Julia[8] *b.* Danville, Des Moines Co., Ia., 23 Mch., 1868; *m.* Fort Madison, Ia., 26 Nov., 1890, Thomas Roach, *s.* Reuben Adams and Mary (Tinsley) Smith (*b.* Bardolph, Ill., 23 July, 1856). *Issue:*

i. Frank Parshall[9] (Smith) *b.* 10 Sept., 1891.

786 III. Herbert[8] *b.* 14 Feby., 1874.[b]

787 IV. Frank[8] *b.* Denmark, Ia., 17 Dec., 1877; d. 11 Feby., 1880.

788 V. Lizzie Florence[8] *b.* Denmark, Ia., 4 Sept., 1880; *m.* Denmark, Ia., 5 Oct., 1898, Charles E., *s.* Daniel and Margaret (Bazel) Purcell (*b.* Burlington, Ia., 22 Feby., 1866). *Issue:*

i. Bessie Julia[9] (Purcell) *b.* 16 Aug., 1900. [*Fort Madison, Ia.*

789 VI. Alta Lucy[8] *b.* Denmark, Ia., 1 June, 1883.

a. Fred Gibson Parshall *m.* New London, Ia., 18 Jany., 1888, Florence, *dau.* Joseph and Lucretia (Cramner) Miller (*b.* Quincy, Ill., 6 Oct., 1867). *Children:* 1161. *i.* Furman Clark[9] *b.* Denmark, Ia., 26 May, 1893; 1162. *ii.* Frank Miller[9] *b.* Mt. Pleasant, Ia., 28 Dec., 1900.*

b. Herbert Parshall *m.* Ft. Madison, Ia.; 15 Feb., 1898, Cora Dell, *dau.* John W. and Elizabeth (Seager) Baker (*b.* Denmark, Ia., 14 Apl., 1880). *Children:* (All *b.* Denmark.) 1163. *i.* Earl Baker[9] *b.* 17 June, 1898; 1164. *ii.* Hazel Esther[9] *b.* 27 Oct., 1899.*

---

* Pers. statement.

*FAMILY CXXXIII.**

GIDEON[7] [332], *(Jacob[6], Samuel[5], James[4], Israel[3], Israel[2], James[1]) b.* Mahoning Co., O., 11 June, 1826; *m.* Milton Center, O., 12 Aug., 1847, Hannah, *dau.* Isaac and Elizabeth (De Long) Winans (*b.* Newton Tp., O., 30 Nov., 1827; *d.* Pipestone, Mich., 13 Oct., 1895). [*Pipestone, Mich.*

Children: (All *b.* Pa.)

790 I. Albert.[8]
791 II. Isaac H.[8] *b.* 9 July, 1851.[a]
792 III. Daniel.[8]
793 IV. Celoy.[8]
794 V. Grant[8] *b.* 17 June, 1863.[b]

FAMILY CXXXIV.†

ARCHIBALD GALLOWAY[7] [340], *(Israel[6], Israel[5], Israel[4], Israel[3], Israel[2] James[1]) b.* Albion, N. Y., 14 June, 1815; *d.* East Springwater, N. Y., 23 Aug., 1899; *m.* East Springwater, 31 Dec., 1836, Emeline, *dau.* John and Lucy (Howard) Andrews (*b.* Union, Broome Co., N. Y., 20 Nov., 1816; *d.* East Springwater, 7 July, 1888).

a. Isaac H. Parshall *m.* Benton Harbor, Mich., — May, 1873, Jennie, *dau.* Frank and Amelia (Bushey) Pryne. *Children:* 1165. *i.* Alma.[9]*

b. Grant Parshall *m.* (1) Berrien Springs, Mich., 18 Sept., 1884, Agnes, *dau.* Harley and Mary Jane (Maddox) Dana (*b.* Pipestone, Mich., 29 July, 1866; *d.* ———) *Children:* 1166. *i.* Glenn J.[9] *b.* 20 June, 1887, *m.* (2) Dowegiac, Mich., 4 Nov., 1895, Catherine, *dau.* Lord Smith (*b.* 1860). *No issue.**

---

* Pers. statement.
† Fam. Recs. and pers. know., 795.

Children:

795 I. Lucy Howard[8]* *b.* East Springwater, 10 June, 1838; *m.* Springwater, 23 Sept., 1866, Ira Leet, *s.* Elijah and Polly (Arnold) Wetmore, (*b.* East Springwater, 28 Feby., 1842). *Issue:*

i. Zoe[9] (Wetmore) *b.* 2 Dec., 1869; *m.* ——— Bowles.
ii. Emma[9] (Wetmore) *b.* 14 July, 1872; *m.* ——— Hosley.
iii. Wirt E.[9] (Wetmore) *b.* 23 Aug., 1874.
iv. Archibald Galloway[9] (Wetmore) *b.* 25 Dec., 1877.
v. Daisy L.[9] (Wetmore) *b.* 1 Feby., 1882.

796 II. Alice[8] *b.* 4 July, 1840; *d.* — Mch., 1842.
797 III. Ellen Charlotte[8] *b.* 19 Aug., 1842; *d.* 5 Feby., 1883; *m.* ——— Coykendall.
798 IV. Harriet Adelma[8] *b.* 4 Jany., 1846; *d.* 20 Nov. 1875. *m.* ——— Fuller.
799 V. Emily Amelia[8] *b.* 13 May, 1848; *d.* — Mch., 1874;
800 VI. John Lever[8] *b.* 23 July, 1852.

FAMILY CXXXV.†

LEVI THAYER[7] [341], *(Israel*[6]*, Israel*[5]*, Israel*[4]*, Israel*[3]*, Israel*[2]*, James*[1]*)* *b.* Springwater, N. Y., 5 Sept., 1817; *d.* Waterford Mills, Ind., 27 Dec., 1860; *m.* Columbia City, Ind., 21 Sept., 1845, Lydia, *dau.* Peter and Polly (Birch) Mosher (*b.* Hannibal, N. Y., 25 Dec., 1820; *d.* 27 Apl., 1860).

[*Waterford Mills, Ind.*

---

* Pers. statement.
† Fam. Recs. and pers. know., 302.

Children:

801 I. Arthur James[8] *b.* Columbia City, Ind., 27 Sept., 1846.[a] [*Mitchell, S. Dak.*

802 II. Israel Peter[8] *b.* 22 Feby., 1849.[b] [*Coldwater, Mich.*

803 III. Archibald Galloway[8] *b.* 18 July, 1851; *d.* 26 Jany., 1857.

804 IV. Deborah Alfaretta[8] *b.* 26 July, 1853; *d.* Collamer, Ind., 14 Oct., 1854.

805 V. Charles Lewis[8] *b.* 2 Aug., 1857.[c]

806 VI. Jennie Jeanette[8] *b.* 25 Nov., 1859.

a. Hon. Arthur James Parshall *m.* Chicago, Ill., 19 Sept., 1865, Mary Vanness, *dau.* William P. and Eliza Nevil (Jacques) Carney (*b.* Chicago, 15 Nov., 1847). *Children:* 1167. *i.* Leon M.[9] *b.* Chicago, 13 Sept., 1866; *d.* Voncouver, Wash., 9 Jany., 1898; *m.* Oregon City, Ore., 14 July, 1892, ——— ———; 1168. *ii.* Lumas Arthur[9] *b.* Chicago, 20 Jany., 1869; *d.* Chicago, 19 Aug., 1870; 1169. *iii.* Jennie Elizabeth Lydia[9] *b.* Chicago, 23 Aug., 1872; 1170. *iv.* Fannie Violette Rose[9] *b.* Rockport, So. Dak., 7 Sept., 1873; 1171. *v.* Edward Louis[9] *b.* Rosedale, So. Dak., 13 Aug., 1875; 1172. *vi.* Frank Pettigrew[9] *b.* Rosedale, So. Dak., 20 May, 1881; *d.* Alexandrina, So. Dak., 25 Sept., 1890; 1173. *vii.* Harry Raymond[9] *b.* Alexandrina, So. Dak., 14 Dec., 1883. Arthur J. Parshall enlisted in an Ind. Regt. at 16 years of age and served until the close of the War. Located at Chicago and studied law. Was burned out during the great fire of 1871, and removed to Dakota Territory in 1872. Helped organize Hansen County and was its first prosecuting attorney. Afterwards Register of Deeds and Ex-officio County Clerk for eight years. Elected to the Territorial Legislature, he served one term. Has since devoted himself to journalism and is now (1902) Editor of the Parkstown, (So. Dak.) Advance.*

b. Israel Peter Parshall *m.* Rosedale, So. Dak., 19 Sept., 1880, Mary Stevenson (*b.* Seneca Falls, N. Y., 1 Aug., 1862). *Children:* 1174. *i.* Rosaline May[9] *b.* Mitchell, So. Dak., 14 Dec., 1881; 1175. *ii.* Thayer Peter[9] *b.* So. Whitley, Ind., 27 Oct., 1887; 1176. *iii.* Althea Julia[9] *b.* So. Whitley, 20 Oct., 1889; 1177. *iv.* Bessie Fern[9] *b.* So. Whitley, 27 Nov., 1891.*

c. Charles Lewis Parshall *m.* Morehead, Ia., 31 Mch., 1881, Nancy Martin, *dau.* Martin and Mary (Shaw) Potter. *Children:* 1178. *i.* Lucy Ann[9] *b.* Little Sious, Ia., 18 Sept., 1882.*

* Pers. statement.

*FAMILY CXXXVI.**

ISAAC RANSOM[7] [343], (*Israel*[6] *Israel*[5] *Israel*[4] *Israel*[3] *Israel*[2] *James*[1]) *b.* Springwater, Liv. Co., N. Y., 6 Dec., 1823; *d.* Fremont, Mich., 4 Mch., 1879; *m.* Bloods Corners, Steuben Co., N. Y., 5 Sept., 1848, Rowena Belinda, *dau.* Zebadiah and Betsey (Dagget) Briggs, (*b.* Cattaraugus Co., N. Y., 8 Mch., 1832). [*Fremont, Mich.*

Children:

807 I. Mary[8] *b.* Springwater, N. Y., 27 Feby., 1850; *m.* Fremont, Mich., 8 Jany., 1868, Wilford Denis, *s.* Benjamin Bowin and Miranda (Terry) Briggs (*b.* Richmond, Ont. Co., N. Y., 6 Jany., 1844). *Issue:* [*Fremont, Mich.*

i. Francis Orval[9] (Briggs) *b.* 9 Mch., 1869.
ii. Benjamin James[9] (Briggs) *b.* 7 Feby., 1871.
iii. Dollie May[9] (Briggs) *b.* 26 Apl., 1874.
iv. Joshua Irvin[9] (Briggs) *b.* 16 Mch., 1880.
v. Edith Melvina[9] (Briggs) *b.* 15 July, 1883.
vi. Norman Brazilla[9] (Briggs) *b.* 28 Oct., 1885.

808 II. Julia[8] *b.* 20 Nov., 1851; *d.* 11 Oct., 1852.
809 III. Brazilla Waterman[8] *b.* Springwater, N. Y., 23 Oct., 1853; *unm.* [*Fremont, Mich.*
810 IV. Deborah Elizabeth[8] *b.* 23 Mch., 1856; *d.* 16 Aug., 1878; *m.* William Friend. *Issue:*

i. Mary Elizabeth[9] (Friend) *b.* 9 June, 1874.

---

* Fam. Rec. and pers. know. 812.

ii. ——— (Friend) *b.* 13 Oct., 1876; *d.* 27 July, 1877.

iii. Maude[9] (Friend) *b.* 30 Apl., 1878; *d.* 11 Oct., 1878.

811 v. George Ransom[8] *b.* 1 Aug., 1862; *d.* 1 Oct., 1881.

812 vi. Phebe Melissa[8] *b.* Kalamazoo, Mich., 19 Aug., 1867; *m.* Fremont, Mich., 31 Aug., 1885, Albert Henry, *s.* David Lewis and Elizabeth (Marks) Reed (*b.* Kalamazoo, Mich., 17 June, 1861). *No issue:* [*Fremont, Mich.*

---

*FAMILY CXXXVII.**

ISRAEL D.[7] [356], (*Terry*[6] *Israel*[5] *Israel*[4] *Israel*[3] *Israel*[2] *James*[1]) *b.* Springwater, Livingston Co., N. Y., 24 Oct., 1836; *m.* Sciota Tp., Shiawassee Co., Mich., 16 July, 1865, Margaret Jane, *dau.* Jacob Birch and Rebecca Matilda (Coryell) Haviland (*b.* Iosco, Liv. Co., Mich., 25 Aug., 1848). [*Laingsburg, Shiawassee Co., Mich.*

Children: (All *b.* and *d.* Woodhull, Mich.)

813 i. Annie V.[8] *b.* 4 July, 1867; *d.* 28 Jany., 1876.

814 ii. Mark J.[8] *b.* 9 July, 1869; *d.* 13 May, 1875.

815 iii. Terry E.[8] *b.* 16 Feby., 1872; *d.* 13 May, 1873.

816 iv. Charles B.[8] *b.* 4 Sept., 1873; *d.* 4 Feby., 1874.

817 v. Bruce[8] *b.* 6 June, 1882.

* Pers. statement.

*FAMILY CXXXVIII.**

GEORGE BRADFORD[7] [364], (*Ira*[6] *David*[5] *Israel*[4] *Israel*[3] *Israel*[2] *James*[1]) *b.* Potter, Yates Co., N. Y., 16 Sept., 1827; *m.* Potter, N. Y., 10 Nov., 1853, Ann Elizabeth, *dau.* John and Nancy (Gage) Saunders (*b.* Potter, N. Y., 30 Mch., 1831; *d.* Potter, 1 Mch., 1902). [*Potter, Yates Co., N. Y.*

Children:

818 I. Rosalie Van Tyle[8]† *b.* Grass Lake, Mch., 13 Sept., 1854; *m.* Benton Center, Yates Co., N. Y., 26 May, 1878, Levi, *s.* Ira and Harriet (Horde) Pressler (*b.* Ferguson Corners, N. Y., 29 July, 1850). *Issue.* [*Potter, Yates Co., N. Y.*

i. Fred Wellington[9] (Pressler) *b.* 10 Apl., 1879.
ii. Ellen Victoria[9] (Pressler) *b.* 7 May, 1883.

819 II. Ira John[8] *b.* Rushville, Yates Co., N. Y., 23 May, 1858.[a]

820 III. William Albert[8] *b.* 16 Mch., 1862.[b] [*Laport City, Ia.*

a. Ira John Parshall *d.* Atlanta, Steuben Co., N. Y., 6 Nov., 1881; *m.* North Cohocton, Steuben Co., N. Y., 20 Feby., 1878, Nettie, *dau.* Daniel and Elizabeth (Jones) Stephenson (*b.* Naples, Ont. Co., N. Y., 8 Oct., 1859). *Children:* 1179. *i.* Charles Augustus[9] *b.* Naples, 26 Nov., 1878; *m.* Rochester, N. Y,. 4 Apl., 1901, Zada M., *dau.* Elias Almond and Emily Ida (Rankin) Lapp (*b.* Belleville, Ont., 4 Apl., 1883). *Children:* 1281. *i. Ira John*[10] *b. 21 Apl., 1902;* 1180. *ii.* Minnie[9] *b.* Rushville, N. Y., 23 Feby., 1880. The widow of Ira J. Parshall *m.* (2) 1 Dec., 1886, Charles J. Coons and had issue: *i.* Floyd Lorentus (Coons) *b.* 23 Sept., 1888; *ii.* George Bradford (Coons) *b.* 17 June, 1891.‡

b. William Albert Parshall *m.* Independence, Ia., 16 Mch., 1892, Ruby Annette, *dau.* Orson Tarbell and Sarah Ann (Graves) Conery (*b.* Delmar, Ia., 7 Apl., 1867). *Children:* 1181. *i.* Effie Tabor[9] *b.* Independence, Ia., 21 June, 1895.†

---

* Fam. Recs. and pers. know., 364.
† Pers. statement.
‡ Fam. Recs. and pers. know., wid., 819.

821 iv. Edward Delos[8] *b.* 17 Apl., 1869.[a]
[*Rushville, Yates Co., N. Y.*

*FAMILY CXXXIX.**

MOSES HULL[7] [370], (*Asa*[6] *David*[5] *Israel*[4] *Israel*[3] *Israel*[2] *James*[1]) *b.* Potter, Yates Co., N. Y., 13 Feby., 1826; *d.* Springwater, N. Y., 25 Sept., 1855; *m.* Springwater, N. Y., 18 Feby., 1853, Sophia, *dau.* Ethan Grover. [*Springwater, N. Y.*

Children:

822 I. Julia Estella[8] *b.* Springwater, N. Y., 9 Dec., 1853; *m.* South Lima, N. Y., Isadore A. Stacey. *Issue:*
[*Rochester, N. Y.*

i. Maude Elizabeth[9] (Stacey) *b.* 31 Mch., 1875.
ii. Isadore Mabel[9] (Stacey) *b.* 7 July, 1877.
iii. Frederick Grant[9] (Stacey) *b.* 24 Dec., 1878.
iv. Nettie[9] (Stacey) *b.* 31 Dec., 1880.
v. Harriet A.[9] (Stacey) *b.* 6 Oct., 1884.

FAMILY CXL.†

HENRY[7] [373] (*David*[6] *David*[5] *Israel*[4] *Israel*[3] *Israel*[2] *James*[1]) *b.* Springwater, N. Y., 5 July, 1820; *m.* Springwater, N. Y., 15 Mch., 1843, Lucina, *dau.* Amos and Rowena (Hale) Root (*b.* Springwater, N. Y., 16 Mch., 1825; *d.* Oakley, Mich., 29 Jany., 1892). [*Oakley, Saginaw Co., Mich.*

a. Edward Delos Parshall *m.* Potter Center, N. Y., 12 Feby., 1898, Nettie *dau.* John and Susan (Elwell) Brandon (*b.* Italy, N. Y., 23 Aug., 1880). *Children:* 1182. *i.* Frances Leone[9] *b.* Potter, N. Y., 12 July, 1901.†

* Fam. Recs. and pers. know. 372.
† Fam. Rec. and pers. know., 373 and pers. know., 837.

Children: (All *b.* Springwater, N. Y.)

823 I. Franklin Stephen[8] *d. s. p.*

824 II. Louisa Manetie[8] *d.* — Aug., 1863; *unm.*

825 III. Rowena[8]* *b.* 18 Dec., 1849; *m.* Oakley, Mich., 16 Oct., 1870, Llewellyn, *s.* Lemuel and Elizabeth (Shutt) Homer (*b.* Pa., 27 Mch., 1850). *Issue:* [*Chesaning, Mich.*

i. Harry L.[9] (Homer) *b.* 8 Dec., 1880.

826 IV. Amos Root[8] *b.* 19 Mch., 1852.[a] [*Oakley, Mich.*

827 V. Maria[8]* *b.* 8 July, 1855; *m.* Chesaning, Mich., 20 Dec., 1874, Charles, *s.* Benjamin and Nancy (Acethorp) Washburn (*b.* Fort Ann, N. Y., 16 Apl., 1842). *Issue:* [*Oakley, Mich.*

i. Charles Henry[9] (Washburn) *b.* 13 Oct., 1875.
ii. Elnora Maria[9] (Washburn) *b.* 7 Nov., 1877.
iii. Benjamin Francis[9] (Washburn) *b.* 21 Mch., 1880.
iv. Alta May[9] (Washburn) *b.* 8 Jany., 1882.
v. Mary Elma[9] (Washburn) *b.* 26 Apl., 1884.
vi. Mattie Ellena[9] (Washburn) *b.* 23 July, 1887.
vii. Louisa Rowena[9] (Washburn) *b.* 19 Nov., 1891; *d.* 19 Nov., 1891.
viii. Lucina Hazel[9] (Washburn) *b.* 24 July, 1893.

828 VI. Addie May[8] *b.* 11 Oct., 1863; *m.* ——— Merrill. [*Oakley, Mich.*

a. Amos Root Parshall *m.* Oakley, Sag. Co., Mich., 31 Jany., 1875, Elizabeth, *dau.* John and Mary J. (Knapp) Crambell (*b.* Cayuga, N. Y., 2 Sept., 1854). *Children:* 1183. *i.* Alice J.[9] *b.* 10 Dec., 1876; 1184. *ii.* John Henry[9] *b.* 20 Jany., 1878; 1185. *iii.* Arthur Parker[9] *b.* 22 Sept., 1881; 1186. *iv.* Fred Earl[9] *b.* 18 Apl., 1885†

* Pers. statement.
† Fam. Recs. and pers. know., 1186.

FAMILY CXLI.*

HIRAM WILLARD[7] [375], (*David[6] David[5] Israel[4] Israel[3] Israel[2] James[1]*) *b.* 18 May, 1824; *d.* Springwater, N. Y., 1 Nov., 1896; *m.* 1 Jany., 1850, Jane N., *dau.* Ezra and Harriet (Stewart) Walker (*b.* Springwater, 24 July, 1827; *d.* Springwater, 12 Oct., 1900). [*Springwater, N. Y.*

Children: (All *b.* Springwater, N. Y.)

829 I. Alice E.[8] *b.* 30 May, 1853; *m.* Springwater, 12 Jany., 1876, Lyman, *s.* John Smith (*d.* Buffalo, N. Y., 1 July, 1884). *Issue:* [*Eddytown, Yates Co., N. Y.*

i. Effie E.[9] (Smith) *b.* 2 Jany., 1877; *d.* 29 Jany., 1889.
ii. Ernest E.[9] (Smith) *b.* 27 July, 1878.
iii. Albertis[9] (Smith) *b.* 2 Oct., 1879.
iv. Wayne McV.[9] (Smith) *b.* 28 June, 1881.

830 II. Mary E.[8] *b.* 17 June, 1857; *m.* Springwater, 1 May, 1878, Richmond, *s.* John and Hannah (Bishop) Ray. *No issue.* [*Springwater, N. Y.*

831 III. Rozedna[8] *b.* 24 Feby., 1858. [*Springwater, N. Y.*

FAMILY CXLII.†

AMASA LOUIS[7] [376], (*David[6] David[5] Israel[4] Israel[3] Israel[2] James[1]*) *b.* Springwater, Livingston Co., N. Y., 28 Apl., 1827; *d.* 26 Apl., 1854; *m.* 8 Aug., 1848, Mary E. Bristol.

---

* Fam. Recs. and pers. know., 831; Walker Mem. 265.
† Fam. Recs. and pers. know., 831.

Children:

832 I. Ellen L.[8] *b.* 2 July, 1850; *d.* 30 Mch., 1855.
833 II. M. Addie[8] *b.* 24 July, 1853; *m.* ——— Burgette. [*Red House, Catt. Co., N. Y.*

*FAMILY CXLIII.**

STEPHEN[7] [379], (*David*[6] *David*[5] *Israel*[4] *Israel*[3] *Israel*[2] *James*[1]) *b.* Springwater, Livingston Co., N. Y., 28 Dec., 1835; *d.* Canadice, Ontario Co., N. Y., 18 May, 1891; *m.* Springwater, N. Y., 6 Jany., 1858, Esther, *dau.* Elisha and Elizabeth (Fletcher) Bailey (*b.* Canadice, N. Y., 6 Jany., 1842; *d.* Canadice, N. Y., 19 Sept., 1898). [*Springwater, Liv. Co., N. Y.*

Children:

834 I. Andolia May[8] *b.* Springwater, N. Y., 17 Mch., 1868; *m.* Springwater, N. Y., 10 Feby., 1887, John Sylvester, *s.* James W. and Alida (McGrossen) Capron (*b.* Springwater, N. Y., 31 Oct., 1866). *Issue:* [*Canadice, Ont. Co., N. Y.*

i. Earl Stephen[9] (Capron) *b.* 6 Nov., 1895; *d.* 9 Mch., 1899.

ii. Russell James[9] (Capron) *b.* 5 Feby., 1900.

835 II. Alla[8] *b.* 22 Apl., 1875; *d.* 18 Jany., 1876.

* Fam. Recs. and pers. know. 834.

*FAMILY CXLIV.**

MILES FARQUHAR[7] [382], (*Amzi[6] Asa[5] Israel[4] Israel[3] Israel[2] James[1]*) *b.* Portage, N. Y., 11 Aug., 1830; *m.* Mt. Morris, N. Y., 16 Nov., 1852, Lydia Emily, *dau.* Isaac and Lydia (Bidlack) Lamkin (*b.* Mt. Morris, Liv. Co., N. Y., 28 Apl., 1835). [*Albuquerque, N. M.*

Children:

836 I. Alden Wallace[8] *b.* 5 Sept., 1856; *d.* Eldred, Pa., 22 Mch., 1864.

837 II. Arthur Lamkin[8] *b.* 1 Sept., 1862. [*Albuquerque, N. M.*

838 III. Mary Geneva[8]* *b.* Eldred Pa., 13 Mch., 1865; *m.* Albuquerque, N. M., 17 Sept., 1885, Joseph T., *s.* William and Elizabeth (Cowan) Johnson (*b.* Prince Edward's Island, Canada, 17 Sept., 1855). *Issue:* [*Albuquerque, N. M.*

i. Willard Parshall[9] (Johnson) *b.* 26 June, 1886.

ii. Nellie McCabe[9] (Johnson) *b.* 2 Aug., 1892.

Is much interested in church work, having served as Superintendent of the Sabbath School of the M. E. church in St. Helena, Wyoming Co., N. Y., for three years. Has also served as Superintendent, Class Leader and Trustee in the M. E. churches at Eldred, McKean Co., Pa., Belfast, Allegany Co., N. Y., Witchita, Kan., and in Albuquerque, N. M.

* Pers. statement.

*FAMILY CXLV.**

LOT[7] [384], (*Amzi*[6] *Asa*[5] *Israel*[4] *Israel*[3] *Israel*[2] *James*[1]) *b.* Portage, N. Y., 15 Dec., 1833; *m.* Belfast, N. Y., 31 Dec., 1863, Lydia Maria, *dau.* Abel and Nancy (————) Parker (*b.* Seneca Falls, N. Y., 30 Mch., 1839; *d.* Ringgold, Ga., 19 Dec., 1886).

Children:

839 I. Mabel[8] *b.* 7 Feby., 1865; *d.* Alleghany Bridge, Pa., 23 Jany., 1866.

840 II. William Klein[8] *b.* 12 Dec., 1866; *d.* Chemung, N. Y., 19 Feby., 1867.

841 III. Frank Charles[8] *b.* Elmira, N. Y., 9 Apl., 1867.[a] [*Atlanta, Ga.*

842 IV. Frederick Arthur[8] *b.* 6 July, 1868. [*Corning, Ark.*

843 V. Harry Abel[8] *b.* 26 Aug., 1871. [*Atlanta, Ga.*

844 VI. Walter Byrnes[8] *b.* 29 July, 1874.

845 VII. George Baldwin[8] *b.* 1 June, 1878. [*Philadelphia, Pa.*

FAMILY CXLVI.†

VINCENT[7] [390], (*Thos. K.*[6] *Asa*[5] *Israel*[4] *Israel*[3] *Israel*[2] *James*[1]) *b.* Chemung, N. Y., 16 Nov., 1829; *m.* Oceola, Mich., 13 Apl., 1851, Caroline, *dau.* Jonathan and Mary (Wells) Roberts (*b.* Chemung Co., N. Y., 18 Dec., 1826).

a. Frank Charles Parshall is an adopted son; surname not known; took name of Parshall; *m.* Atlanta, Ga., 6 Sept., 1891, Emma E., *dau.* Felix and Clara (Maroney) Webb (*b.* Polk Co., Tenn., 31 Jany., 1871). *Children:* 1187. *i.* Lottie Bell.[9]

---

* Pers. state. 384

† Fam. Recs. and pers. know., 846.

Children:

846 I. Chester A.[8] *b.* Oceola Tp., Mich., 27 June, 1852.[a]

---

*FAMILY CXLVII.**

CHAUNCEY[7] [392], (*Thomas K.*[6] *Asa*[5] *Israel*[4] *Israel*[3] *Israel*[2] *James*[1]) *b.* Chemung, N. Y., 2 Oct., 1834; *d.* Oceola, Mich., 7 July, 1902; *m.* Mary Jane, *dau.* Daniel and Susan (————) Van Syckle (*b.* Liv. Co., Mich., 26 June, 1837).
[*Oceola, Mich.*

Children:

847 I. Estella[8] *b.* Everett Tp., Newaygo Co., Mich., 30 Sept., 1860; *m.* 22 Dec., 1880, William Armstrong.
848 II. William R.[8] *b.* Oceola, Mich., 9 Feby., 1863.[b]
849 III. Jesse B.[8] *b.* Oceola, Mich., 11 Apl., 1867.[c]

FAMILY CXLVIII.†

TIMOTHY BROWN[7] [394], (*Thomas K.*[6] *Asa*[5] *Israel*[4] *Israel*[3] *Israel*[2] *James*[1]) *b.* Oceola, Liv. Co., Mich., 15 Oct., 1839; *d.* 18 Mch., 1864; *m.* Corunna, Mich., Harriet M., *dau.* Michael and Cynthia (————) Alliton (*b.* Petersburg, Mich., 13 Aug., 1839).
[*Parshallville, Liv. Co., Mich.*

a. Chester A. Parshall *m.* Parshallville, Mich., 20 May, 1874, Ella Estelle, *dau.* Jacob Snell and Esther (Mason) Griswold (*b.* Parshallville, Mich., 19 Dec., 1853). *Children:* 1188. *i.* Caroline Esther[9] *b.* 5 Apl., 1875; 1189. *ii.* Pearl[9] *b.* 27 June, 1877; 1190. *iii.* Beulah Josephine[9] *b.* 22 May, 1885.*
b. William R. Parshall, *m.* 22 Feby., 1880, Emma C. Smith.
c. Jesse B. Parshall, *m.* 30 May, 1889, Maggie Hardy.

---

* Pers. statement.
† Fam. Recs. and pers. know., 350.

Children:

850 I. Ella Jane[8]* *b.* New Haven, Shia. Co., Mich., 17 Oct., 1861; *m.* Chesaning, Mich., 14 June, 1884, Alpheus Cecil, *s.* Hiram B. and Hannah (Larkin) Josselyn (*b.* Buffalo, N. Y., 3 Oct., 1858). *Issue:* [*Owosso, Mich.*

i. Mabel H.[9] (Josselyn) *b.* 3 Aug., 1885.
ii. Leon Alliton[9] (Josselyn) *b.* 18 June, 1888.

851 II. Mina Anne[8] *b.* Shiawassee Co., Mich., 23 Mch., 1863; *m.* Owosso, Mich., 15 Mch., 1894, George Springer. *Issue:* [*Owosso, Mich.*

i. Irene[9] (Springer) *b.* 9 Feby., 1897.

---

*FAMILY CIL.**

ASA[7] [395], (*Thomas K.*[6] *Asa*[5] *Israel*[4] *Israel*[3] *Israel*[2] *James*[1]) *b.* Oceola, Liv. Co., Mich., 7 Feby., 1844; *m.* Fenton, Genesee Co., Mich., 3 Oct., 1867, Mary J., *dau* Joseph and Ann (Munerly) Blinton (*b.* Erie Co., N. Y., 19 Oct., 1845). [*Howell, Liv. Co., Mich.*

Children:

852 I. William V.[8]
853 II. L. Celestia.[8]

---

* Pers. statement.

*FAMILY CL.**

ZACHARY TAYLOR[7] [396], (*Thomas K.*[6] *Asa*[5] *Israel*[4] *Israel*[3] *Israel*[2] *James*[1]) *b.* Oceola, Liv. Co., Mich., 25 Apl., 1847; *m.* (1) 16 Dec., 1870, Harriet, *dau.* Henry W. Roberts. [*St. Louis, Mo.*

Children:

854 I. Atha[8] *b.* Oceola, Mich., 20 Feby., 1871.

m. (2) St. Louis, Mo., 3 July, 1890, Elizabeth S., *dau.* Samuel and Sarah (Tarbell) Downs (*b.* East St. Louis, Ill., 2 Oct., 1868). *No issue.*

FAMILY CLI.†

LUTHER[7] [404], (*Ransom*[6] *Asa*[5] *Israel*[4] *Israel*[3] *Israel*[2] *James*[1]) *b.* Portage, N. Y., 4 July, 1833; *d.* Rutherford, N. J., 17 Oct., 1899; *m.* Dansville, N. Y., 8 Sept., 1863, Emily, *dau.* Frederick and Mary (Pratt) Stanley. [*Rutherford, N. J.*

Children:

855 I. Cordie Stanley[8] *b.* Richburg, N. Y., 16 Aug., 1864; *m.* Waverly, N. Y., 25 Aug., 1893, Irving K., *s.* Dana Park, of Athens, Pa. [*Athens, Pa.*

856 II. Jennie Elizabeth[8] *b.* 19 Feby., 1869.

---

* Pers. statement.
† Fam. Recs. and pers. know., 855.

857 III. Frederick Ransom[8] *b.* 19 Nov., 1871; *d.* 11 June, 1898.[a]

---

*FAMILY CLII.**

ALMON[7] [406], (*Ransom*[6] *Asa*[5] *Israel*[4] *Israel*[3] *Israel*[2] *James*[1]) *b.* 19 Mch., 1838; *m.* Agnes Martin. [*Covington, Ky.*

Children:

858 I. Clifford.[8]

859 II. Almon Howard[8] *b.* Louisville, Ky., 1 Mch., 1867.[b]

860 III. Amy.[8]

a. Frederick Ransom Parshall, while yet a boy, developed an interest in the organ that never flagged to the close of his brief life. After six lessons from a local teacher, he assumed the organ bench. In the fall of 1890, he went to Brooklyn and studied under the famous Dr. Dudley Buck, with whom he made rapid progress. He served as organist in St. John's and St. Mathew's churches, of Brooklyn; Christ church, in Elizabeth, N. J., and Zion and St. Timothy's churches of Manhattan Borough. As an organist, he was singularly clever in manipulation of registers, in accuracy, and in clearness of phrasing. The works of Bach, Widos and Merkel, and the host of other organ classics were to him open and familiar; the fugue and the sonata were his daily exercises. Cut down in almost the beginning of his career, his life was of singular purity and devotion to his profession.

b. Almon Howard Parshall, *m.* Covington, Ky., 24 Nov., 1886, Ann Elizabeth, *dau.* Jeremiah and Myra (Adderly) Holloway (*b.* Irondale, O., 1 Jany., 1868) *Ch.*, 1191. *i.* Howard Percival[9]; 1192, *ii.* Agnes Myra[9]; 1193. *iii.* Edna Adderly[9]. Received a common school education, supplemented by a two years' course in the Queen City Commercial College. Learned watch case engraving and subsequently carriage making. Is now superintendent of a large carriage factory at Elkhart, Ind†.

---

* Fam. Recs. pos. 859.
† Pers. statement.

*FAMILY CLIII.**

JOHN WILEY[7] [410], (*Ransom*[6] *Asa*[5] *Israel*[4] *Israel*[3] *Israel*[2] *James*[1]) *b.* 16 Dec., 1848; *d.* 1 Sept., 1896; *m.* (1) Halsey Valley, N. Y., — Feby., 1870, Ruth Cashady, *No issue.*

m. (2) Knoxville, Pa., 21 Jany., 1883, Emma, *dau.* Gabriel and Mary Elizabeth (Mansfield) Williams (*b.* Waverly, N. Y., 3 Dec., 1861). [*Waverly, N. Y.*

Children:

861 I. Grace[8] *b.* 20 Nov., 1883.
862 II. Fay[8] *b.* 1 Sept., 1886.
863 III. Hazel[8] *b.* 5 Sept., 1888.

FAMILY CLIV.†

WESLEY[7] [411], (*Ransom*[6] *Asa*[5] *Israel*[4] *Israel*[3] *Israel*[2] *James*[1]) *b.* Portage, N. Y., 16 Dec., 1848; *m.* Chemung, N. Y., 1 Nov., 1876, Georgiana, *dau.* Charles and Elizabeth (Warren) Swain (*b.* Chemung, N. Y., 10 Nov., 1850). [*Waverly, N. Y.*

Children:

864 I. Clifford[8] *b.* 19 Oct., 1877. [*Waverly, N. Y.*
865 II. Mary[8] *b.* 26 Oct., 1893.

* Fam. Rec. and pers. know., wid., 410.
† Pers. statement.

*FAMILY CLV.**

MERRIT^{7} [421], (*Israel^{6} Asa^{5} Israel^{4} Israel^{3} Israel^{2} James^{1}*) *b.* Oceola, Liv. Co., Mich., 1 Apl., 1844; *m.* Chesaning, Mich., 21 July, 1867, Adaline S., *dau.* James C. and Sarah H. (Whipple) Fuller (*b.* Chesaning, Mich., 18 Aug., 1850).
[*Chesaning, Mich.*

Children: (All *b.* Chesaning, Mich.)

866 i. Flora M.^{8} *b.* 20 May, 1868; *d.* Chesaning, Mich., 13 June, 1868.
867 ii. James Grant^{8} *b.* 17 Aug., 1869.^{a} [*Chesaning, Mich.*
868 iii. Floyd Merrit^{8} *b.* 11 Aug., 1872.^{b}

FAMILY CLVI.‡

MILTON CHATMAN^{7} [423], (*Israel^{6} Asa^{5} Israel^{4} Israel^{3} Israel^{2} James^{1}*) *b.* Parshallville, Liv. Co., Mich., 20 Jany., 1850; *m.* Havana, Sag. Co., Mich., 3 July, 1870, Charlotte Ann, *dau.* Eli Rickerson and Lourein (May) Ismond (*b.* Grimsby, Wentworth Co., Ont., 12 May, 1851). [*Commerce, Mich.*

a. James Grant Parshall *b.* 17 Aug., 1869; *m.* Durand, Mich., 3 Oct., 1896, Emma H., *dau.* Nathan R. and Harriet E. (Townsend) Jersey (*b.* Romeo, Mich., 2 Dec., 1864). *Children:* (All *b.* Chesaning, Mich.) 1194. *i.* Floyd Frank^{9} *b.* 29 Oct., 1897; 1195. *ii.* Grant Loyal^{9} *b.* 1 Jany., 1898; 1196. *iii.* Merrit Maurice^{9} *b.* 2 Apl., 1900.†

b. Floyd Merrit *b.* 11 Aug., 1872; *d.* Philadelphia, Pa., 1 Jany., 1897; *m.* Camden, N. J., 9 Nov., 1896, May, *dau.* John and Anna (———) Kotzwinkle (*b.* Scranton, Pa., 3 Oct., 1874). *No issue.**

---

* Fam. Recs. and pers. know. 421.
† Pers. statement.
‡ Fam. Recs. and pers. know., 423.

Children:

869 I. Israel Jay.[8]
870 II. Eli Judd.[8]

---

*FAMILY CLVII.**

MILLIS LINCOLN[7] [425], (*Israel[6] Asa[5] Israel[4] Israel[3] Israel[2] James[1]*) *b.* Havana, Sag. Co., Mich., 25 Dec., 1864; *m.* Chesaning, Mich., 12 Sept., 1887, Delphine, *dau.* James V. and Persis (Sanson) Judd (*b.* Maple Grove, Sag. Co., Mich., 12 Sept., 1868). [*Havana, Sag. Co., Mich.*

Children:

871 I. Lynne J.[8]
872 II. Dale Ivan.[8]
873 III. Emeroy Merle.[8]
874 IV. Millis Vincent.[8]

---

*FAMILY CLVIII.**

MILAN GRANT[7] [429], (*Jesse[6] Asa[5] Israel[4] Israel[3] Israel[2] James[1]*) *b.* Oceola, Liv. Co., Mich., 5 June, 1869; *m.* Tyrone, Mich., 13 Apl., 1893, Matie E., *dau.* Andrew Jackson and Mary (Slover) Wolverton (*b.* Tyrone, Mich., 8 Nov., 1872). [*Parshallville, Liv. Co., Mich.*

Children: (*b.* Tyrone, Mich.)

875 I. Raymon D.[8] *b.* 5 Mch., 1894.

---

* Pers. statement.

*FAMILY CLIX.**

ROBERT LAYTON[7] [437], (*Daniel[6] Jesse[5] Israel[4] Israel[3] Israel[2] James[1]*) *b.* Canandaigua, N. Y., 29 July, 1849; *m.* Penn Yan, N. Y., 17 Nov., 1874, Marietta, *dau.* Henry Baker and Sarah (Sutton) Gardner (*b.* Wayland, N. Y., 31 May, 1855).
[*West Henrietta, N. Y.*

Children:

876 I. Henry Daniel[8] *b.* 26 Jany., 1876.[a]
[*Rochester, N. Y.*

877 II. Bessie Belle[8] *b.* 9 Feby., 1878.

878 III. Edith Leonora[8] *b.* 10 Dec., 1887.

879 IV. Jean Lois[8] *b.* 27 July, 1890.

880 V. Ernest Robert[8] *b.* 26 Dec., 1892; *d.* 4 Mch., 1898.

---

*FAMILY CLX.**

NELSON CLARKE[7] [441], (*Jesse[6] Jesse[5] Israel[4] Israel[3] Israel[2] James[1]*) *b.* Canandaigua, N. Y., 5 Feby., 1840; *m.* Geneseo, Liv. Co., N. Y., 12 July, 1877, Ida Mary, *dau.* Jerme and Mary Anne (Windsor) Allen (*b.* Dubuque, Ia., 15 Jany., 1857).
[*Brooklyn, N. Y.*

Children:

881 I. Percival Windsor[8] *b.* Geneseo, N. Y., 14 Sept., 1878.
[*Brooklyn, N. Y.*

a. Henry Daniel Parshall *b.* Glenora, Yates Co., N. Y., 26 Jany., 1876; *m.* Hilton, N. Y., 23 Jany., 1898, Georgia Coral, *dau.* John and Mary (Nash) Bell (*b.* N. Greece, N. Y., 10 Jany., 1878.)*

---

* Pers. statement.

Educated at Canandaigua Academy, and subsequently a teacher in that institution. Enlisted at Canandaigua, 12 May, 1863. Served in the Army of the Potomac, passing through the various grades of non-commissioned officer. Was commissioned 2d Lieut. after the Battle of the Wilderness, and subsequently for gallant conduct at Reames Station, near Petersburg, Va., was made 1st Lieut. and appointed on the staff of Maj. Gen. Hancock, commanding the 2d Army Corps, where he served until nearly the close of the War. Was Adjutant of the 15th N. Y. Vol. Engineers, when mustered out of the service in 1865. Studied law at Yale University, 1866-7, and was admitted to the bar at Rochester, in July, 1868. Subsequently withdrew from practice and was appointed Principal of Wadsworth Grammar School, at Rochester, where he remained eighteen years. Is the author of several school text books and is now a recognized authority on food adulteration, food values and cognate subjects. In Masonry he is a K. T., and a Past Grand Master of Odd Fellows.

---

*FAMILY CLXI.**

JESSE[7] [442], *(Elisha[6], Jesse[5], Israel[4], Israel[3] Israel[2], James[1])* *b.* Canandaigua, N. Y., 16 Dec., 1837; *m.* (1), Canandaigua, 30 July, 1858, Charity, *dau.* Peter and Phebe (Prouty) Brandon (*b.* Canandaigua, 8 Dec., 1837; *d.* Canandaigua, 29 June, 1890). [*Cheshire, Ont. Co., N. Y.*

Children:

882 i. Truman T.[8] *b.* 30 May, 1865.[a] [*Detroit, Mich.*

a. Truman T. Parshall *m.* Windsor, Canada, 14 Aug., 1893, Lizzie, *dau.* William and Hilda (————) Fox. *Children:* 1197. *i.* Edna[9] *b.* 25 Apl., 1894; 1198. *ii.* Doshia[9] *b.* 16 Feby., 1896. Left home when a boy of four-

* Fam. Rec. and pers. know. 442.

883 II. Josephine[8] *b.* 1 Aug., 1866; *m.* Cheshire, N. Y., 1881, Frank M. Stiles (*b.* 1838). *Issue:* [*Detroit, Mich.*

i. Lester Leroy[9] (Stiles) *b.* 21 Oct., 1891.

884 III. Lizzie[8] *b.* Cheshire, N. Y., 9 Aug., 1868; *m.* Cheshire, 25 Dec., 1884, John Moshier (*b.* 1850). *Issue:*

i. Elmer[9] (Moshier).
ii. Maude[9] (Moshier).
iii. William[9] (Moshier).
iv. Harry[9] (Moshier) *b.* 25 Nov., 1890.
v. Ida May[9] (Moshier) *b.* 2 Aug., 1898.

885 IV. Fred[8] *b.* Canandaigua, 12 July, 1870. [*Canandaigua, N. Y.*

886 V. Florence[8] *b.* Cheshire, 2 June, 1872; *m.* Canandaigua, 1892, Daniel, *s.* William McGinnis (*b.* 1854).

887 VI. Paul[8] *b.* 24 Dec., 1874.

888 VII. Lucius[8] *b.* 13 July, 1879.

889 VIII. Lewis[8] *b.* 12 Mch., 1881.

m. (2), Canandaigua, 26 Feby., 1891, Frances, *dau.* Philetus and Hannah (Richardson) Jones (*b.* Italy, Yates Co., N. Y., 10 Aug., 1856).

Children:

890 IX. Charles Henry[8] *b.* 22 Dec., 1891.

891 X. Ernest Vogel[8] *b.* 12 Sept., 1893.

892 XI. Hazel Frances[8] *b.* 14 Oct., 1894.

teen. Was employed as brakeman and conductor on several Western railroads. In 1889, entered the employ of the Michigan Central Railroad, promoted to conductor in 1893, which position he still holds. Is a member of Division 48, Order of Railway Conductors and has been a delegate to several important conventions of the order.*

* Pers. statement.

Jesse Parshall served in the Civil War as a private in the 18 N. Y. Vols; discharged for disability after a year and a half, he enlisted in the Navy and served on U. S. S. Ceres, until the close of the war. He is now a member of Charles R. Little Post, No. 303, G. A. R., and a U. S. pensioner. His son, Paul, is serving in the U. S. Navy, having enlisted in 1899 for four years.

---

*FAMILY CLXII.**

RICHARD ELISHA[7] [448], *(Rufus[6], Jesse[5], Israel[4], Israel[3], Israel[2], James[1])* *b.* Canandaigua, N. Y., 1 June, 1840; *m.* Le Roy, N. Y., 14 Dec., 1859, Caroline A., *dau.* Jacob and Anna (George) Salmon (*b.* Shaggarberry, Wyo. Co., N. Y., 25 Jany., 1839). [*Howell, Liv. Co., Mich.*

Children: (*b.* Hartland, Mich).

893 I. Henry Elmer[8] *b.* 8 Mch., 1862.[a] [*Honey Grove, Tex.*

Richard E. Parshall enlisted in the War of the Rebellion and met with some exciting experiences while in the service. On the 28th of March, 1864, while a member of Co. A, 6th Regt.,

a. Henry Elmer Parshall *b.* Hartland, Mich., 8 Mch., 1862; *m.* Williamston, Mich., 27 Nov., 1883, Nora Bell, *dau.* Hiram J. and Alice (Barnes) Dana. *Children:* 1199. *i.* Alma[9] *b.* Williamston, Mich., 11, June, 1885.
m. (2) Howell, Mich., ———— 188—, Sarah Ann, *dau.* Gabriel and Anna Adasha (Mcianis) McPhee *b.* Shipka, P. O., O. N. T., 4 May, 1868. *Children:* 1200. *ii.* Richard Gabriel[9] *b.* White Cloud, Mich., 6 Feby., 1888; 1201. *iii.* William Royal[9], *b.* Lenox, Mich., 12 Feby., 1889; 1202. *iv.* Harry Elmer[9] *b.* Auburn June, 23 Jany., 1891; 1203. *v.* Hazel Marie[9] *b.* St. Louis, Mich., 19 Sept., 1895; 1204. *vi.* Flossie Anna May[9] *b.* Gainesville, Tex., 1 Feby., 1899; 1205. *vii.* Nellie Lindall[9] *b.* Honey Grove, Tex., 6 Jany., 1901.*

---

* Pers. statement.

Michigan Cavalry, Gen. Kilpatrick learning of his ability and desperate courage detailed him as a scout. While on this duty he was captured within the rebel line, near Richards Ferry, Va., wearing a Confederate uniform and was tried, convicted and sentenced to be hanged as a spy, on the 27th day of April, 1864. On that day the death warrant was read to him in his cell and he was carried to the place of execution, but by the timely interference of Gen. Kilpatrick his life was saved. He was sent to Libby Prison and from thence to Pemberton Prison, from which place he finally succeeded in making his escape after suffering all the miseries and horrors of a rebel hell. After returning to his command he was sent West to fight Indians. Was recommended to Gen. Sheridan as a scout and served under him in that capacity for nearly a year. He was discharged at Fort Leavenworth, Kan., on the expiration of his term of enlistment, 15 July, 1865, and returned to Michigan, where he has since resided.

---

*FAMILY CLXIII.**

EDWARD HOWELL[7] [459], (*John*[6], *Jesse*[5], *Israel*[4], *Israel*[3], *Israel*[2], *James*[1]) *b.* Canandaigua, N. Y., 10 July, 1848; *m.* Cross River, N. J., Nettie W., *dau.* William H. and Clarissa (———) Shelley (*b.* Cross River, N. J., 5 Oct., 1871). [*Waterbury, Ct.*

Children: (*b.* So. Norwalk, Ct.)

894 1. Willie H.[8] *b.* 10 May, 1895.

* Pers. statement.

*FAMILY CLXIV.**

GEORGE WASHINGTON[7] [460], *(John[6], Jesse[5], Israel[4], Israel[3], Israel[2], James[1])* *b.* Canandaigua, N. Y., 19 Nov., 1850; *m.* Rochester, N. Y., 11 Dec., 1877, Lily A., *dau.* William and Charlotte (Harvey) Dyer (*b.* Rochester, N. Y., 8 May, 1861). [*South Norwalk, Ct.*

Children:

895 I. George Gregor.[8] [*Rochester, N. Y.*
896 II. Charlotte Lillian.[8] [*Rochester, N. Y.*

---

*FAMILY CLXV.**

GIDEON EDGAR[7] [465], *(Otis K.[6], Jesse[5], Israel[4], Israel[3], Israel[2], James[1])* *b.* 18 Jany., 1845; *m.* 1 July, 1876, Maggie E., *dau.* William and Melissa (Johnson) Corner (*b.* 15 May, 1856).

Children:

897 I. Clarence W.[8] *b.* 15 Aug., 1876.
898 II. Maude L.[8] *b.* 2 Dec., 1879; *m.* 2 June, 1901, Harry Stout (*b.* 8 Nov., 1887.
899 III. Nettie M.[8] *b.* 7 Mch., 1884.
900 IV. Eugenie E.[8] *b.* 8 Nov., 1887.

* Pers. statement.

*FAMILY CLXVI.**

CHARLES KIMBLE[7] [466], *(Otis K.*[6], *Jesse*[5], *Israel*[4], *Israel*[3], *Israel*[2], *James*[1]*)* *b.* Canandaigua, N. Y., 15 May, 1857; *m.* 2 Sept., 1872, Imogene, *dau.* Stephen and Samantha (Sauer) Stiles (*b.* 3 Feby., 1854).

Children:

901 I. Belmont[8] *b.* 29 June, 1874.[a]

---

*FAMILY CLXVII.**

SAMUEL EUGENE[7] [468], *(Otis Kimble*[6], *Jesse*[5], *Israel*[4], *Israel*[3], *Israel*[2], *James*[1]*)* *b.* 17 July, 1852; *m.* 4 Mch., 1872, Jennie Lucy, *dau.* Thomas and Rebecca (Keller) O'Dell (*b.* 22 June, 1853). [*Shortsville, Ont. Co., N. Y.*

Children:

902 I. Frank Otis.[8b]

903 II. Archibald Eugene[8] *b.* 12 Apl., 1894.

a. Belmont Parshall *m.* 12 Aug., 1896, Edith Townsend (*b.* 18 Aug., 1877). *Issue:* 1206. *i.* Mildred[9] *b.* 1 June, 1897.

b. Frank Otis Parshall *m.* 28 Nov., 1894, Catherine Gertrude Curran (*b.* 1 Sept., 1873). *Children:* 1207. *i.* Harold[9] *b.* 18 Nov., 1895.

---

* Fam. Recs. and pers. know. 471.

FAMILY CLXVIII.*

HARVEY JOHN[7] [470], *(Otis K.[6], Jesse[5], Israel[4], Israel[3], Israel[2], James[1]) b.* 21 July, 1856; *m.* 16 Sept., 1884, Nancy Jane, *dau.* James and Emeline (Dewey) Williams (*b.* 14 Oct., 1857). [*Detroit, Mich.*

Children:

904 I. Harvey James[8] *b.* 23 Oct., 1886.

FAMILY CLXIX.†

BENJAMIN CARLISLE[7] [472], *(Benj. Carlisle[6], Israel[5], Benjamin[4], Israel[3], Israel[2], James[1]) b.* New York, 1 Aug., 1825; *d.* New York, 4 June, 1865; *m.* New York, Fall of 1844, Margaret, *dau.* Jeremiah and Prudence (Dutcher) Anderson (*d.* New York, — Feby., 1868). [*New York, N. Y.*

Children: (All *b.* New York)

905 I. Benj. Carlisle[8] *d. inf.*
906 II. Sarah Ellen[8] *d. inf.*
907 III. Prudence Louise[8] *b.* 20 Aug., 1857; *m.* Mt. Vernon, N. Y., 21 Feby., 1886, John Joseph Masterson (*b.* Dublin, Ireland, 6 Apl., 1865). *No issue.*† [*Mt. Vernon, N. Y.*
908 IV. George Washington[8] *b.* 13 July, 1854.[a]

a. George Washington Parshall, *m.* Brooklyn, 20 Aug., 1880, Ella, *dau.* John and Johanna (Butler) Coffey (*b.* New York, 1 Nov., 1857). *No issue.*‡

* Fam. Recs. and pers. know., 471.
† Fam. Recs. pos. 908.
‡ Pers. statement.

FAMILY CLXXI.‡

WILLIAM VALENTINE[7] [475], *(Benj. Carlisle*[6]*, Israel*[5]*, Benjamin*[4]*, Israel*[3]*, Israel*[2]*, James*[1]*)* *b.* New York, 29 Apl., 1833; *d.* New York, 1 Feby., 1895; *m.* New York, — Oct., 1858, Margaret Ann Hauche, *dau.* Hampden and Catherine Eliza (Rooke) Green (*b.* New York, 24 Dec., 1835).

[*New York, N. Y.*

Children: (All *b.* New York)

909 I. Sarah Louise[8] *b.* 24 Feby., 1860; *d.* — Aug., 1860.
910 II. Catherine Eliza[8] *b.* 1 Mch., 1861. [*Mt. Vernon, N. Y.*
911 III. William Valentine[8] *b.* 12 Feby., 1863.[a] [*New York, N. Y.*
912 IV. James Henry[8] *b.* 26 Aug., 1865; *d.* 18 July, 1866.
913 V. Benjamin Carlisle[8] *b.* 29 July, 1895.[b]
914 VI. Grace Butterfield[8] *b.* 5 May, 1869; *d.* — Aug., 1869.

---

*FAMILY CLXXI.**

JAMES CARLISLE[7] [477], *(Benj. Carlisle*[6]*, Israel*[5]*, Benj.*[4]*, Israel*[3]*, Israel*[2]*, James*[1]*)* *b.* New York — —— ——; *d.* New York, 12 Aug., 1872; *m.* New York, 15 Sept., 1861, Elizabeth,

a. William Valentine Parshall *m.* New York, 4 Sept., 1889, Sophia, *dau.* Christian and Caroline (Pelgmann) Oelker (*b.* New York, 9 Apl., 1868). *Children:* (All *b.* New York.) 1208. *i.* Sophia Elizabeth[9] *b.* 26 July, 1890; 1209. *ii.* Grace Caroline[9] *b.* 12 Mch., 1892; 1210. *iii.* Lillian Margaret[9] *b.* 19 May, 1894; 1211. *iv.* Edna May[9] *b.* 13 Mch., 1896.†

b. Benjamin Carlisle Parshall *m.* New York, 5 Mch., 1895, Emma, *dau.* John Gottlieb and Donhera Runft (*b.* New York, 1 Oct., 1874). *Children:* 1212. Benjamin Carlisle[9] *b.* Mt. Vernon, N. Y., 21 Jany., 1896.†

---

* Fam. Recs. and pers. know., wid., 475 and 912.
† Pers. statement.
‡ Fam. Recs. and pers. know., 915.

dau. William and Mary (McGlade) Brown (*b.* Dublin, Ireland, 10 July, 1842). [*New York, N. Y.*

Children:

915 I. Eloise Pelso[8] *b.* New York, 8 Sept., 1867; *m.* Brooklyn, 11 Apl., 1894, Joseph Thompson, *s.* William Henry and Eliza (Shaw) Shearer (*b.* Brooklyn, 26 Jany., 1866). *Issue*:

i. Jennie Marguerite[9] (Shearer) *b.* 27 June, 1895; *d.* 24 July, 1896.

ii. William Henry[9] (Shearer) *b.* 10 Jany., 1902.†

916 II. A son, *d. inf.*

917 III. A daughter, *d. inf.*

918 IV. A daughter, *d. inf.*

---

*FAMILY CLXXII.**

GEORGE HAMMOND[7] (Dr.), (Hon.), [479], (*George Hotto*[6], *Benjamin*[5], *Benjamin*[4], *Israel*[3], *Israel*[2], *James*[1]) *b.* Jamaica, (L. I.), N. Y., 23 Apl., 1843; *m.* Orange, N. J., 5 Dec., 1871, Ada Augusta, *dau.* Charles and Maria (Westerfield) Carter (*b.* Brooklyn, N. Y., 8 Feby., 1849). [*Brooklyn, N. Y.*

Children: (All *b.* Brooklyn, N. Y.)

919 I. Emma Louise[8] *b.* 18 Apl., 1873; *m.* Brooklyn, N. Y., 10 Feby., 1892, Cassius Dwight Baker (*b.* 21 Sept., 1873). *Issue*: (All *b.* Brooklyn, N. Y.) [*Brooklyn, N. Y.*

i. Ada Louise[9] (Baker) *b.* 16 Feby., 1893. *Issue:*

* Pers. statement.

George H. Dorshall M.D.

ii. Rollin Dwight[9] (Baker) *b.* 26 Jany., 1895.
iii. George Parshall[9] (Baker) *b.* 25 Feby., 1900.

920 II. George Frederick[8] *b.* 13 Sept., 1874.[a]

921 III. Ernest Van Arsdale[8] *b.* 15 Nov., 1876.

922 IV. Florence May[8] *b.* 9 Sept., 1880; *d.* 19 Dec., 1881.

923 V. James Charles[8] *b.* 8 July, 1883; *d.* 31 July, 1901.

924 VI. Phoebe Ada[8] *b.* 20 Oct., 1888.

Educated at Union Hall Academy, Jamaica, L. I., N. Y. Physician, graduate of L. I. College Hospital, Class '84. Member of the Emprie State Society Sons of the American Revolution and of F. & A. M. Has been prominent in local politics. Served as delegate to several State Conventions. Republican member of Assembly (N. Y.), 7th Ass. Dist., Kings Co., 1897. Was the Republican candidate for State Senator, 5th Senatorial Dist., N. Y., 1900. Appointed Examining Surveyor in the Bureau of Pensions by Commissioner Henry Clay Evans, from which he resigned. Is now Physician in the Federal Service, attached to the Postoffice. (*See portrait.*)

---

*FAMILY CLXXIII.**

DAVID BECK[7] (Pershall) [491], (*David Terry[6] George[5] David[4] David[3] David[2] James[1]*) *b.* New York, 4 Mch., 1842; *m.* Walden, Orange Co., N. Y., 6 Aug., 1863, Ellen Lucinda, *dau.* William D. and Ellen (Crans) Decker (*b.* Walden, N. Y., 17 Sept., 1844; *d.* New York, 5 Apl., 1900). [*New York, N. Y.*

a. George Frederick Parshall *m.* 23 May, 1903, Ellen Gertrude, *dau.* Edward and Louise (Frankcohl) Fanning (*b.* Brooklyn, 5 Oct., 1884).

* Pers. statement.

Children: (All *b.* New York.)

924 I. Anna Hadley[8] *b.* 22 Sept., 1864; *m.* (1) New York, 24 Feby., 1885, George Underhill, *s.* Joseph A. and Elizabeth (Underhill) Dixon (*b.* New York, 29 May, 1860; *d.* New York, 24 Dec., 1895). *Issue:* [*Troy, N. Y.*

i. Clifford Pershall[9] (Dixon) *b.* 21 Dec., 1888; *d.* 2 July, 1889.

m. (2) New York, 20 Oct., 1897, George Andrew, *s.* George and Wealthy (Morss) Bradbury (*b.* Guilford, N. Y., 28 Dec., 1857). *No issue.*

925 II. Ellen Louise[8] *b.* 24 Sept., 1869; *m.* New York, Robert Mortimer, *s.* Edwin Mortimer and Marie Louise (Davis) Dunn (*b.* New York, 16 Apl., 1857). *Issue:* [*Brooklyn, N. Y.*

i. Ellen Pershall[9] (Dunn).
ii. George Mortimer[9] (Dunn).

926 III. Agnes Estelle[8] *b.* 28 Nov., 1872; *m.* New York, 9 Feby., 1892, George, *s.* James and Eliza Ann (Irwin) Lawyer (*b.* Middleburg, Scho. Co., N. Y., 24 Sept., 1864). *Issue:* [*Albany, N. Y.*

i. James Pershall[9] (Lawyer).
ii. George Irwin[9] (Lawyer).
iii. David Buchanan[9] (Lawyer).

927 IV. Henry LeRoy[8] *b.* 20 Mch., 1874.

928 V. Josephine Slote[8] *b.* 14 July, 1876; *m.* New York, 14 July, 1896, Stewart Courtlandt, *s.* Clarence Edward

* Fam. Recs. compiled by Mrs. Anna Hadley Bradbury.

and Carrie Virginia (Courtlandt) Alger (*b.* Flushing (L. I.), N. Y., 1 Dec., 1871). [*New York, N. Y.*

i. Marjorie Pershall[9] (Alger).

---

*FAMILY CLXXIV.**

LYMAN BRADLEY[7] [496], (*Caleb Halsey*[6] *George*[5] *David*[4] *David*[3] *David*[2] *James*[1]) *b.* Farmer, Seneca Co., N. Y., 28 June, 1845; *m.* Cedar Rapids, Ia., 24 July, 1884, Ella Smith. [*Canton, Jackson Co., Ia.*

Children:

929 I. Genevieve.[8]
930 II. Wilhelmina.[8]

FAMILY CLXXV.†

THOMAS WARDLE[7] [498], (*Caleb Halsey*[6] *George*[5] *David*[4] *David*[3] *David*[2] *James*[1]) *b.* Farmer, Seneca Co., N. Y., 4 June, 1873, Susan A., *dau.* William D. and Ellen J. (Crans) Decker (*b.* Walden, Orange Co., N. Y., 10 Jany., 1850). [*Chicago, Ill.*

Children:

931 I. Henry August[8] *b.* 14 Feby., 1874.
932 II. Adalyn Estelle[8] *b.* 7 Sept., 1876.

---

* Fam. Bible of Caleb Halsey Parshall and pers. know., 498.
† Fam. Bible 179, and pers. state., 498.

*FAMILY CLXXVI.**

WILLIAM FERGUSON[7] [503], (*Nathaniel[6] Elias[5] Elias[4] David[3] David[2] James[1]*) *b.* Lebanon, O., 18 Feby., 1818; *d.* Lebanon, O., 17 Dec., 1893; *m.* Lebanon, O., 31 Aug., 1841, Henrietta, *dau.* John Ely and Sarah (Mount) Dey (*b.* Lebanon, O., 17 May, 1821; *d.* Lebanon, O., 4 Nov., 1872). [*Lebanon, O.*

Children: (All *b.* Lebanon, O.)

933 I. Laura[8] *b.* 22 Sept., 1842; *d.* Home City, Ham. Co., O., 9 Aug., 1891; *m.* Lebanon, O., 25 Dec., 1862, Nelson, *s.* John and Catherine (Riner) Sayler (*b.* Lewisburgh, Preble Co., O., 17 Apl., 1834). *Issue:* [*Cincinnati, O.*

i. Maud[9] (Sayler) *b.* 26 Feby., 1864; *d.* Lebanon, O., 7 Aug., 1867.

ii. Frank[9] (Sayler) *b.* 21 July, 1865; *d.* 6 Dec., 1884.

iii. Arthur[9] (Sayler) *b.* 19 Oct., 1867. [*Dos Cabezos, Ariz.*

iv. Helen[9] (Sayler) *b.* 14 Aug., 1869; *d.* Tallahassee, Fla., 1 Feby., 1890.

v. Milton[9] (Sayler) *b.* 9 Aug., 1871.

vi. Nelson[9] (Sayler) *b.* 29 Sept., 1873; *d.* Fort Springs, W. Va., 18 Aug., 1880.

vii. Edith[9] (Sayler) *b.* 16 Nov., 1875. [*Cincinnati, O.*

viii. Alice[9] (Sayler) *b.* 16 Nov., 1875. [*Cincinnati, O.*

* Bible Rec. 503, and pers. know. Nelson Sayler.

ix. Katharine Riner[9] (Sayler) *b.* 28 Jany., 1880; *d.* 4 June, 1880.

x. Henrietta[9] (Sayler) *b.* 28 Jany., 1880. [*Cincinnati, O.*

xi. Marjorie Riner[9] (Sayler) *b.* 5 Dec., 1884. [*Cincinnati, O.*

934 II. William Henry[8] *b.* 25 Feby., 1845.[a]

935 III. John Morrison[8] *b.* 6 Oct., 1846.[b]

---

*FAMILY CLXXVII.**

OLIVER HAZARD PERRY[7] [504], (*Nathaniel*[6] *Elias*[5] *Elias*[4] *David*[3] *David*[2] *James*[1]) *b.* 13 Mch., 1824; killed at the Battle of Chickamauga, Ga., 19 Sept., 1863; *m.* 3 Apl., 1849, Belle Howell.

Children:

936 I. Imogene[8] *m.* H. Percy Smith. *Issue:*

i. Helen[9] (Smith).

a. William Henry Parshall *m.* Brooklyn, N. Y., 25 Feby., 1881, Harriet, *dau.* Elisha and Hannah Eliza (Brower) Davis (*b.* Brooklyn, N. Y., 7 Aug., 1856; *d.* Brooklyn, 17 June, 1901). *Children:* 1213. *i.* William Henry[9] *b.* 5 Jany., 1882; 1214. *ii.* Henrietta Dey[9] *b.* 3 Feby., 1883; 1215. *iii.* Dora Marcia[9] *b.* 3 Mch., 1900. Enlisted in 1862, at the age of 17 years, in the 84th Regt. O. Infantry, for three months. Discharged at the expiration of his term of service, he re-enlisted, in 1863, for six months, in the 4th Independent Battalion, O. Vol. Cavalry. Discharged at the exipration of this term, he again re-enlisted for three years, serving under Gen. Sherman, and following that great commander in his famous march "From Atlanta to the Sea," was honorably discharged at the close of the War. Is a member of Rankin Post, No. 10, G. A. R., of Brooklyn. Is employed in the Water Department of the Borough of Brooklyn, N. Y.†

b. John Morrison Parshall *d.* Tallahassee, Fla., 4 Feby., 1894; *m.* 13 Oct., 1843, Medorah Lester. *No issue.* Served during the Civil War in Co. A, 146th Regt., O. V. Infantry, as Corporal. Term of service 100 days.*

---

* Fam. Recs. and per know., Nelson Sayler.

† Pers. statement.

*FAMILY CLXXVIII.**

GEORGE EGGY[7] [510], (*Nathaniel*[6] *Elias*[5] *Elias*[4] *David*[3] *David*[2] *James*[1]) *b.* Fayette Co., Pa., 23 May, 1840; *d.* Canonsburg, Wash. Co., Pa., 20 Feby., 1872; *m.* Wash., Pa., 4 June, 1867, Sophia Ann, *dau.* Levi and Rozanna (Teagarden) Hallam (*b.* Wash. Co., Pa.)

Children: (All *b.* Washington Co., Pa.)

937 I. Gertrude Deane[8] *b.* 13 Apl., 1868; *m.* Washington, Pa., 5 May, 1888, John Lentz, *s.* Robert and Sarah (Sutton) Morrow (*b.* Tidioute, Pa., 5 Apl., 1862). *Issue:*(All *b.* Wash., Pa.) [*Washington, Pa.*

- i. Robert Kelley[9] (Morrow) *b.* 10 Feby., 1889.
- ii. Joseph Hallam[9] (Morrow) *b.* 30 Nov., 1891.
- iii. John Adair (Morrow) *b.* 1 Jany., 1902.

237½ II. Boyd Crumrine[8] *b.* 15 Apl., 1869.[a]
938 III. Lewanna[8] *b.* 7 Mch., 1871.

FAMILY CLXXIX.‡

BENONAH[7] [519], (*John*[6], *Elias*[5], *Elias*[4], *David*[3], *David*[2], *James*[1]) *b.* Fayette Co., Pa., 10 Sept. 1824; *m.* Wayne Co., Ind., 31 Dec., 1850, Sarah Jane, *dau.* Ockey and Maria (———)

a. Boyd Crumrine Parshall, *m.* Cumberland, Md., 7 Nov., 1898, Minnie Merelda, *dau.* Samuel Foster and Sara Lucinda (Cosgrove) McCaulley (*b.* Bradford, Pa., 31 July, 1878). *Children:* 1216. *i.* Boyd Fremont[9] *b.* Washington, Pa., 17 Sept., 1899.†

* Fam. Recs. and pers. know. 937.
† Pers. statement.
‡ Fam. Recs. and pers. statement, 519.

Lancaster (*b.* Wayne Co., Ind., 17 Oct., 1827; *d.* Wayne Co., Ind., 25 Oct., 1889). [*Richmond, Ind.*

Children: (All *b.* Wayne Co., Ind.)

939 I. Cora Estelle[8] *b.* 8 Oct., 1851; *m.* Richmond, Ind., 19 June, 1881, John Lewis, *s.* George and Naomi (Barnes) Williams (*b.* Md., 13 June, 1840; *d.* Billingsville, Union Co., Ind., 24 July, 1888). *Issue:* [*Richmond, Ind.*

i. Lemuel Blaine[9] (Williams) *b.* 8 June, 1884; *d.* 8 Sept., 1884.
ii. Oran Everette[9] (Williams) *b.* 16 July, 1885.
iii. George Forrest[9] (Williams) *b.* 18 Sept., 1886; *d.* Richmond, Ind., 8 May, 1889.

940 II. Eva Maria[8] *b.* 16 Apl., 1854; *unm.* [*Richmond, Ind.*

941 III. Marcellus[8] *b.* 2 May, 1857; *unm.* [*Richmond, Ind.*

942 IV. Edward Everette[8] *b.* 19 Nov., 1859.[a] [*Richmond, Ind.*

943 V. William Elmer Ellsworth[8] *b.* 17 Apl., 1862; *unm.* [*Richmond, Ind.*

944 VI. Albert Wesley[8] *b.* 26 Nov., 1864; *unm.* [*Richmond, Ind.*

945 VII. Alta Nevada[8] *b.* 15 Apl., 1867; *d.* Wayne Co., Ind., 7 Apl., 1896.

946 VIII. Thirza Lovena[8] *b.* 21 Dec., 1869; *d.* Wayne Co., Ind., 3 Sept., 1894.

a. Edward Everette Parshall *m.* Centreville, Ind., 22 Feby., 1893, Mary Elizabeth, *dau.* Harlan and Mary Ann (Finder) Robbins (*b.* Wayne Co., Ind., 1 May, 1873) *Children:* (All *b.* Wayne Co., Ind.) 1217. *i.* Benonah Harlan[9] *b.* 12 Feby., 1895; 1218. *ii.* Mary Jane[9] *b.* 19 Oct., 1897.[*]

[*] Pers. statement.

*FAMILY CLXXX.**

JOHN[7] [521], *(John[6], Elias[5], Elias[4], David[3], David[2], James[1])* *b.* Pa., 13 Jany., 1828; *d.* Indianapolis, Ind., 17 Mch., 1897; *m.* (1), ——— ———

Children:

947 I. William.[8]

m. (2), Indianapolis, Ind., 28 Sept., 1878, Mrs. Sarah J. (Thompson) Swallow, *dau.* John and Jane (———) Thompson (*b.* Connorsville, Ind., 16 Nov., 1829). *No issue.* [*Indianapolis, Ind.*

The following from a Chicago paper relates to John Parshall:

"INDIANAPOLIS, IND., March 17.—John Parshall, an ex-soldier, died very suddenly to-day of heart failure.

"Parshall was one of the six men intrusted with the final disposition of the body of John Wilkes Booth, the assassin of Lincoln, all of whom registered an oath never to reveal Booth's last resting place.

"Five of these soldiers are now dead and the secret so far has been religiously kept.

"Parshall was a member of the Alexander expedition sent to Utah to compel Brigham Young to vacate his office."

FAMILY CLXXXI.†

HENRY[7] [522], *(John[6], Elias[5], Elias[4], David[3], David[2], James[1])* *b.* Fayette Co., Pa., 12 Jany., 1832; *m.* Wayne Co., Ind., 2 Sept., 1852, Nancy Jane, *dau.* Jesse and Elizabeth (———) Burke (*b.* Clinton Co., Ind.; *d.* Wayne Co., Ind., 13 May, 1877). [*Richmond, Ind.*

---

* Fam. Bible 186, and state. wid., 521.
† Pers. statement.

Vincent Parshall.

Children:

948 I. John William.[8]
949 II. Elizabeth Ann.[8]
950 III. Elsie Marie.[8]
951 IV. Jessie Locke.[8]
952 V. Mary Jane.[8]
953 VI. Anderson Quinn.[8]
954 VII. Charles S.[8]
955 VIII. Sarah Maria.[8]

---

*FAMILY CLXXXII.**

NATHANIEL[7] [526], *(John[6], Elias[5], Elias[4], David[3], David[2], James[1])* *b.* Wayne Co., Ind., 19 Oct., 1843; *m. n.* Madison, Darke Co., O., 2 Dec., 1867, Antoinette, *dau.* Benjamin Franklin and Mary (Payne) Gray (*b.* Darke Co., O., 30 Sept., 1847). [*Richmond, Ind.*

Children:

956 I. Ulysses[8] *b.* 13 Sept., 1868; *unm.* [*Richmond, Ind.*
957 II. Clara Jane[8] *b.* 8 Sept., 1870; *unm.* [*Richmond, Ind.*
958 III. Charles Ernest[8] *b.* 1874. [*Richmond, Ind.*
959 IV. Evalenia[8] *b.* 30 Aug., 1876; *m.* Eaton, Preble Co., O., 27 Aug., 1898, James, *s.* James and Elizabeth (———) Taggart. *Issue:* [*Richmond, Ind.*

i. Marie[9] (Taggart) *b.* 21 Nov., 1899.

960 V. William Edgar[8] *b.* 13 Oct., 1881. [*Richmond, Ind.*

* Pers. statement.

*FAMILY CLXXXIII.**

VINCENT[7] [528], *(Elias[6], Elias[5], Elias[4], David[3], David[2], James[1]) b.* McClellandtown, Fayette Co., Pa., 12 Dec., 1817; *d.* Berryville, Va., 25 May, 1898; *m.* McClellandtown, Pa., 23 Feby., 1843, Eliza Ann, *dau.* Isaac and Nancy (Kendall) Crow (*b. n.* Uniontown, Pa., 1797; *d.* McClellandtown, Pa., 6 June, 1872). [*Berryville, Va.*

Children: (All *b.* McClellandtown, Pa.)

961 I. H. Matilda[8] *b.* 14 May, 1844. [*Berryville, Va.*
962 II. Laura[8] *b.* 10 May, 1846; *m.* Berryville, Va., 23 Feby., 1885, Silas Franklin Baughman. [*Berryville, Va.*
963 III. N. Louise[8] *b.* 16 June, 1847. [*Berryville, Va.*
964 IV. Elias Calvin[8] *b.* 15 Oct., 1849; *d.* Berryville, Va., 16 Dec., 1901.
965 V. Isaac Hamilton[8] *b.* 22 Sept., 1851.[a] [*Grand Ridge, Ill.*
966 VI. Mary Elizabeth[8] *b.* 22 June, 1855. [*Berryville, Va.*
967 VII. James Worthington[8] (Dr.) *b.* 4 Nov., 1862. [*Uniontown, Pa.*

Upon reaching his majority Vincent Parshall immediately took an active interest in the business affairs of Fayette County. He aided in the development of the extensive coal deposits in that part of the State, which proved extremely profitable. During

a. Isaac Hamilton Parshall *m.* Grand Ridge, Ill., 7 Feby., 1878, Frances A., *dau.* Ransom Palmer (*b.* Grand Ridge, Ill., 22 Sept., 1854). *Children:* 1219. *i.* Ralph Ransom[9] *b.* Girard, Kan., 10 Sept., 1878; 1220. *ii.* Vernon Vincent[9]; 1221. *iii.* Leo Irwin[9] *d.* 29 Dec., 1898; 1222. *iv.* Mabel Louise[9]; 1223. *v.* Blanche Marie[9]; 1224. *vi.* Raymond Palmer.[9]†

* Fam. Recs. and pers. know., 961 and 966.
† Fam. Recs. and pers. know., 1219.

the Civil War he held several important government positions. In 1878 he purchased an estate of 618 acres in the beautiful Shenandoah Valley, in Virginia, and thither he immediately removed with his family. He was a man of broad and catholic mind; well informed, and of pleasing manners. A loving husband, a kind and indulgent father, a good neighbor and an honest, earnest, upright man, he won the respect and esteem of all who knew him. (*See portrait*).

---

*FAMILY CLXXXIV.**

WILLIAM GROVE[7] [530], *(Elias[6], Elias[5], Elias[4], David[3], David[2], James[1]) b.* McClellandtown, Pa., — Sept., 1821; *d.* Uniontown, Pa., 4 July, 1883; *m.* — Apl., 1864, Martha A., *dau.* Jonathan and Clarissa (Pease) Hawks (*b.* 14 Feby., 1835). [*Uniontown, Pa.*

Children: (All *b.* Nicholson Tp., Fay. Co., Pa.)

968 I. William Worthington[8] *b.* 18 June, 1866.[a]
969 II. Louisa P.[8] *d. inf.*
970 III. Delafield[8] *d. inf.*
971 IV. Emily[8]† *b.* 8 Nov., 1875; *m.* McClellandtown, Pa., 11 Oct., 1899, Frank R., *s.* Josiah B. and Elizabeth (McCombs) Crow (*b.* McClellandtown, 1 June, 1874). *No issue.* [*McClellandtown, Pa.*
972 V. Vesta[8] *d. inf.*

a. William W. Parshall *m.* Springfield, O., 11 June, 1902, Amelia, *dau.* Henry and Maria (Dawson) Baldwin. A graduate of Cornell University, he afterwards studied law and was admitted to the bar. He is now practicing his profession with much success at Uniontown, Pa.† (*See portrait.*)

---

* Bible Rec. 188, and Fam. Recs. and pers. know. 533 and 968.
† Pers. statement.

William G. Parshall was a citizen well known in legal and political circles in Fayette County. He graduated at Jefferson College, and afterward studied law, being admitted to the bar in 1844. While practicing law he also engaged in agricultural pursuits, to which he was ever strongly attracted. He was a delegate to several State Conventions and his voice was often heard there. He was a man of great vigor, both of mind and body, and was well read in various lines of thought. Having acquired a competency he was preparing to retire from active life when stricken by death. (*See portrait*).

---

*FAMILY CLXXXV.**

JAMES M.[7] [534], *(Elias[6], Elias[5], Elias[4], David[3], David[2], James[1]) b.* McClellandtown, Fayette Co., Pa., 22 Aug., 1829; *d.* Uniontown, Pa., 11 Feby., 1903; *m.* Redstone Tp., Fayette Co., Pa., 22 Dec., 1865, Mary, *dau.* James Cowden and Rachel (Brown) Higginbotham (*b.* New Geneva, Fayette Co., Pa., 20 Mch., 1840). (*See portrait.*) [*McClellandtown, Pa.*

Children:

973 I. William James[8] *b.* Brownsville, Pa., 22 June, 1867.[a] [*McClellandtown, Pa.*

974 II. Robert Vincent[8] (Dr.) *b.* Nicholson Tp., Fay. Co., Pa., 24 Nov., 1869.[b] [*Lundy's Lane, Pa.*

a. William James Parshall, *m.* Brownsville, Pa., 11 Oct., 1888, Mary Ella, *dau.* Capt. Michael and Mary Ella (Krepps) Cox (*b.* Brownsville, Pa., 9 Oct., 1866) *Ch.*, 1225. *i.* James M.[9] *b.* 15 Mch., 1890; 1226. *ii.* Mary[9] *b.* 14 Feby., 1892; 1227. *iii.* Michael A. Cox[9] *b.* 13 Aug., 1894.* (*See portrait.*)

b. Dr. Robert Vincent Parshall, *m.* Steubenville, O., 21 Mch., 1898, Carrie Edith, *dau.* Sylvanus Lathrop and Mary Baily (Strubble) McCain (*b.* Castle Shannon, Alleghany Co., Pa., 26 Sept., 1876) *Ch.*, 1228. *i.* Robert Vincent[9] *b.* Lundy's Lane, Pa., 7 Feby., 1900.*

---

* Pers. statement.

James M Parshall

*FAMILY CLXXXVI.**

NATHANIEL[7] [545], *(James[6], Elias[5], Elias[4], David[3], David[2], James[1])* *b.* Fayette Co., Pa., 12 Feby., 1824; *d.* Greene Co., Pa., 26 Mch., 1881; *m.* Greene Co., Pa., 31 Jany., 1858, Priscilla, *dau.* Alpheus Augustus and Elizabeth (Tate) Delancy (*b.* Greene Co., Pa., 27 June, 1834; *d.* Greene Co., Pa., 11 Mch., 1900).

Children: (All *b.* Greene Co., Pa.)

975 I. Charles Tilton[8] *b.* 24 Sept., 1859.[a]
[*Hunter's Cave, Pa.*

976 II. Elizabeth[8] *b.* 9 Feby., 1861; *d.* 22 Apl., 1863.

977 III. Hannah[8]† *b.* 15 Nov., 1862; *m.* Greene Co., Pa., 30 Sept., 1882, Elmer, *s.* Stephen and Evaline (Tuttle) Kinnan (*b.* W. Va., 30 Apl., 1859). *Issue:*
[*Waynesburg, Greene Co., Pa.*

- i. Guy Ringnol[9] (Kinnan) *b.* 4 Apl., 1883.
- ii. Gertrude[9] (Kinnan) *b.* 30 Oct., 1885.
- iii. Priscilla[9] (Kinnan) *b.* 10 Sept., 1887; *d.* 19 May, 1888.
- iv. Eva[9] (Kinnan) *b.* 10 Sept., 1887; *d.* 2 June, 1888.
- v. Jesse[9] (Kinnan) *b.* 15 May, 1889.
- vi. Dora[9] (Kinnan) *b.* 10 July, 1891.

a. Charles Tilton Parshall, *m.* Waynesburg, Pa., 24 Sept., 1885, Mary Ellen, dau. Richard (*d.* 30 May, 1894) and Hester (Morris) Aukrom *d.* 20 Mch., 1890, *b.* Jefferson, Pa., 21 May, 1858) *Ch.*, 1229. *i.* Charles Nathaniel[9] *b.* Sycamore, Pa., 24 Jany., 1887; 1230. *ii.* Jessie Milton[9] *b.* Wash. Tp., Greene Co., Pa., 5 Sept., 1888; 1231. *iii.* Ivia Lillian[9] *b.* Wash. Tp., 14 Nov., 1892.†

* Fam. Bible 545, pos. 975; Bates Hist. Green Co., Pa., p. 689.
† Pers. statement.

Wm. H. Parshall

vii. Slater Franklin[9] (Kinnan) *b.* 25 Mch., 1894; *d.* 19 Oct., 1894.
viii. Mary Ellen[9] (Kinnan) *b.* 11 Sept., 1895.
ix. Charles Nathaniel[9] (Kinnan) *b.* 8 Sept., 1899.

978 IV. Sarah Belle[8]* *b.* 17 June, 1865; *m.* Waynesburg, Pa., 19 Dec., 1884, Joseph, *s.* Peter and Eleanor (Freeland) Mason. *Issue:*

i. Agnes Lusetta[9] (Mason) *b.* 6 July, 1886.
ii. John Slater[9] (Mason) *b.* 20 Sept., 1889.
iii. William Franklin[9] (Mason) *b.* 1896.

979 V. Alpheus Augustus[8] *b.* 13 May, 1867.[a]
980 VI. William[8] *b.* 29 Jany., 1869; *d.* 29 Jany., 1869.
981 VII. Isaac Slater[8] *b.* 6 May, 1871.[b] [*Waynesburg, Pa.*

FAMILY CLXXXVII.†

JOHN[7] [550], (*James[6], Elias[5], Elias[4], David[3], David[2], James[1]*) *b.* Fayette Co., Pa., 17 Jany., 1831; *m.* Greene Co., Pa., 15 Mch., 1855, Phebe, *dau.* James and Julia Ann (Quick) Patterson (*b.* Greene Co., Pa., 13 Aug., 1836).
[*Kansas City, Kan.*

a. Alpheus Augustus Parshall, *m.* Waynesburg, Pa., 14 Nov., 1891, Sarah Elizabeth, *dau.* Enoch and Charlotte (Morris) Rush (*b.* Green Co., Pa., 14 Nov. 1871; *d.* Greene Co., 13 Jany., 1893). *No issue. m.* 2d. Dean, Wetzel Co., W. Va., 3 Jany., 1895, Mary Elizabeth, *dau.* Jesse and Rhoda (Morris) Mason *b.* Wetzel Co., W. Va., 12 May, 1877). *No issue.**

b. Isaac Slater Parshall, *m.* Greene Co., Pa., 20 Dec., 1899, Eva E., *dau.* David and ——— (Jones) Shull, *Ch.*, 1232. *i.* Ralph Shull[9] *b.* 14 Apl., 1901; *d.* 31 May, 1901.*

---

* Pers. statement.
† Fam. Recs. and pers. know., 550.

Wm. H. Parshall.

Children:

982 I. Hannah Julia[8] *m.* ——— McVay. [*Washington, Pa.*

983 II. James Patterson.[8] [*Claysville, Pa.*

984 III. Sarah Ann[8]* *b.* Greene Co., Pa., 6 Sept., 1863; *m.* Washington, Pa., 15 Dec., 1892, William, *s.* Anthony and Nancy (Mull) Palett (*b.* Wash. Co., Pa., 20 Jany., 1851). *Issue:* [*Washington, Pa.*

i. Anthony Owen[9] (Palett) *b.* 14 Sept., 1893.

ii. John William[9] (Palett) *b.* 6 Jany., 1895.

985 IV. Isaac Randolph[8] *b.* 15 Apl., 1860.[a] [*Claysville, Pa.*

986 V. William Thomas.[8] [*Waynesburg, Pa.*

987 VI. Ida Belle[8]* *b.* 6 Mch., 1875; *m.* Wash. Co., Pa., 26 Feby., 1895, William, *s.* Elisha and Minerva (Black) Crouch (*b.* Fayette Co., Pa., 5 Aug., 1875). *Issue:* [*Washington, Pa.*

i. Clyde Huston[9] (Crouch).

ii. William Ray[9] (Crouch).

iii. Harry Baker[9] (Crouch).

a. Isaac Randolph Parshall, *m.* Wheeling, W. Va., 29 Nov., 1888, Margaret Thompson, *dau.* Peter Hill and Cecelia Catherine (———) Leighton (*b.* Wheeling, W. Va., 25 Jany., 1859) *Ch.*, 1233. *i.* Phebe Patterson[9] *b.* Washington, Pa., 7 May, 1889; 1234. *ii.* Cecelia[9] *b.* Washington, Pa., 7 May, 1889; 1235. *iii.* John Randolph Hill[9] *b.* Washington, Pa., 22 Mch., 1891; 1236. *iv.* Jessie May[9] *b.* Claysville, Pa., 17 Aug., 1892; 1237. *v.* Margaret Elizabeth[9] *b.* 8 July, 1894; 1238. *vi.* Beulah Thelma[9] *b.* Claysville, Pa., 27 Apl., 1896.*

* Pers. statement.

FAMILY CLXXXVIII.*

WILLIAM[7] [551], (*James*[6], *Elias*[5], *Elias*[4], *David*[3], *David*[2], *James*[1]) b. Fayette Co., Pa., 19 June, 1839; *m.* 1867, Mary Coffee. [*Woodland Park, Colo.*

Children:

988 I. Christian Gass.[8]

FAMILY CLXXXIX.†

JAMES TISDALE[7] [552], (*James*[6], *Elias*[5], *Elias*[4], *David*[3], *David*[2], *James*[1]) *b.* Fayette Co., Pa., 22 July, 1844; *m.* Jefferson, Pa., 17 June, 1866, Jennie Kline (*b.* Jefferson, Pa.; *d.* Jefferson, Pa., 17 July, 1867). [*Lathrop, Mo.*

Children:

989 I. Isaac Enos Coldron *b.* — July, 1867; *d.* 27 July, 1867.

m. (2) Plattsville, Ia., 5 Sept., 1869, Mary Ellen, *dau.* William and Mary Ann (White) Huggins (*b.* Garrett's Fort, Greene Co., Pa., 1 Jany., 1844).

Children:

990 II. Louisa[8] *b.* 19 Aug., 1870; *d.* Plattsville, Ia., 12 Nov., 1870.

991 III. Maud[8] *b.* 11 Oct., 1871; *m.* Lathrop, Mo., 1888, William Staples. *Issue:* [*Kansas City, Mo.*

---

* Pers. statement.
† Fam. Recs. and pers. statement 552.

i. Rena[9] (Staples).
ii. James Thomas[9] (Staples).
iii. Gretchen[9] (Staples).
iv. Aletha[9] (Staples).

992 IV. Ichabod King[8] *b.* 9 Nov., 1873. [*St. Louis, Mo.*

993 V. Edna[8] *b.* 7 Nov., 1875; *d.* McKeesport, Pa., 17 Sept., 1876.

994 VI. Lena[8] *b.* 31 May, 1877; *d.* Lathrop, Mo., 24 Aug., 1878.

995 VII. Ethel[8] *b.* 19 Feby., 1879; *m.* Lathrop, Mo., 17 Jany., 1900, Fulton, *s.* George Washington and Margaret (Brooks) Nicholas (*b.* 17 Nov., 1873). *Issue:* [*Lathrop, Mo.*

i. Ona Maud[9] (Nicholas) *b.* 4 Oct., 1900.

996 VIII. Jimmie Ellen[8] *b.* 7 Mch., 1882. [*Lathrop, Mo.*

---

*FAMILY CXC.**

ALBERT[7] [557], *(James[6], Elias[5], Elias[4], David[3], David[2], James[1]) b.* Fayette Co., Pa., 26 Feby., 1847; *m.* Centre Tp., Greene Co., Pa., 23 Jany., 1866, Mary Ann, *dau.* George and Ann (McCann) Rush (*b.* Centre Tp., Pa., 27 Feby., 1847; *d.* New Freeport, Pa., 7 Aug., 1899). [*Waynesburg, Pa.*

Children: (All *b.* Greene Co., Pa.)

997 I. Annie May[8] *b.* 21 Mch., 1867.

998 II. Hannah Jane[8] *b.* 4 May, 1868; *m.* Greene Co., Pa., 26 Sept., 1887, John Longdon, *s.* Isaac Newton and Sarah Ann (Longdon) Clutter (*b.* Wash. Co., Pa., 6 Jany., 1859). *Issue:* [*Bealsville, Wash Co., Pa.*

---

* Fam. Recs. and pers. know. 557.

i. Albert Newton[9] (Clutter) *b.* 20 Oct., 1888.
ii. Ola Vann[9] (Clutter) *b.* 22 Feby., 1890.
iii. Paul George[9] (Clutter) *b.* 18 Dec., 1894.

999 III. George Rush[8] *b.* 5 Nov., 1869; *d.* Sistersville, W. Va., 25 Mch., 1895.
1000 IV. William Reed[8] *b.* 8 Nov., 1871.[a]
1001 V. James T.[8] *b.* 20 Sept., 1873.
1002 VI. Jesse Coldren[8] *b.* 25 Aug., 1878.[b]
1003 VII. Robert Frank[8] *b.* 3 Dec., 1880.
1004 VIII. A son *b.* 5 Apl., 1882; *d.* 11 Apl., 1882.
1005 IX. Violet Blanche[8] *b.* 21 Jany., 1889.

---

*FAMILY CXCI.**

WILLIAM DUNN[7] [558], *(David Youngs[6], David[5], Elias[4], David[3], David[2], James[1])* *b.* Belmont Co., O., 8 Mch., 1848; *m.* Wichita, Kan., 14 Nov., 1892, Fannie Hilton, *dau.* Charles and Anna Caroline (Moody) Schultz (*b.* 10 Apl., 1849).
[*Wichita, Kan.*

Children:

1006 I. Burton William.[8]

a. **William Reed Parshall, *m.* Waynesburg, Pa., 10 Apl., 1898, Margaret, *dau.* William and Nancy (Phillips) Gidley (*b.* Greene Co., Pa., 23 June, 1881) *Children,* 1239. *i.* Nell[9] *b.* 1 Feby., 1899.***

b. **Jesse Coldren Parshall *b.* 25 Aug., 1878; *m.* Waynesburgh, Pa., 17 Apl., 1901, Della, *dau.* William and Martha Jane (————) Gibbons (*b.* Greene Co., Pa., 5 Apl., 1876.***

* **Pers. statement.**

W. J. Parshall

*FAMILY CXCII.**

DAVID THOMAS[7] [559], (*David Youngs*[6], *David*[5], *Elias*[4], *David*[3], *David*[2], *James*[1]) *b.* Belmont Co., O., 28 May, 1852; *m.* (1), Martin's Ferry, O., 10 Sept., 1878, Jennie Ellison, *dau.* John and Elizabeth (Ellison) Leach (*b.* Berry, Eng.; *d. n.* Hamilton, O., — Jany., 1891. [*Pittsburg, Pa.*

Children:

1007 I. Jennie Maude[8] *b.* 21 July, 1880.
1008 II. Hazel Dunn[8] *b.* 30 June, 1884.

m. (2), Jennie May, *dau.* William T. and Jane (Ent) Morris (*b.* Millville, O., 10 Sept., 1871).

Children:

1009 III. Hazel Marie[8] *b.* 27 Nov., 1893.
1010 IV. Clover Morris[8] *b.* 23 Jany., 1895.

FAMILY CXCIII.†

STOCKTON THOMAS[7] [569], (*Daniel Shove*[6], *James*[5], *James*[4], *David*[3], *David*[2], *James*[1]) *b.* 1833; *m.* (1), Sterling, Oswego Co., N. Y., Antoinette Sanford (*d.* — Feby., 1858). [*Rochester, N. Y.*

Children:

1011 I. Clarence Stockton *b.* — Feby., 1858. [*Rochester, N. Y.*

m. (2), Mary Horton.

---

* Fam. Recs. and pers. know., 1897.
† Fam. Recs. and pers. know., Theo. Slawson, Rochester, N. Y.

Children:

1012 II. Chester Winn *b.* — Dec., 1863. [*U. S. Army.*

m. (3), ——— ———. *No issue.*

---

*FAMILY CXCIV.**

JOHN BENJAMIN[7] [572], (*Alfred Ford*[6], *James*[5], *James*[4], *David*[3], *David*[2], *James*[1]) *b. n.* Cooperstown, N. Y., 26 Sept., 1842; *m.* St. Louis, Mo., 5 Aug., 1872, Ellen, *dau.* David and Elizabeth Ann (Nasmith) Steel (*b.* Cran Bourne, Eng., 2 Apl., 1851). [*St. Louis, Mo.*

Children: (All *b.* St. Louis, Mo.)

1013 I. Burton Watson[8] *b.* 29 Oct., 1875. [*St. Louis, Mo.*
1014 II. John Benjamin[8] *b.* 21 July, 1877. [*St. Louis, Mo.*
1015 III. Harriet Elizabeth[8] *b.* 4 Oct., 1879; *m.* Clayton, Mo., 6 June, 1900, William Peter, *s.* James Joseph and Mary Ellen (Querk) McCabe (*b.* Co. Wicklow, Ireland, 23 Oct., 1876). [*St. Louis, Mo.*
1016 IV. Ellen Lina[8] *b.* 25 Sept., 1889.
1017 V. David Steel[8] *b.* 5 Mch., 1890.

FAMILY CXCV.†

ALFRED GREGORY[7] [575], (*James Nichols*[6], *James*[5], *James*[4], *David*[3], *David*[2], *James*[1],) *b.* Albany, N. Y., 16 Oct., 1847; *m.* Cobleskill, N. Y., 18 Feby., 1868, Carrie, *dau.* William

* Fam. Recs. and pers. know. 572.
† Fam. Recs. and pers. know., 576, and 1021.

and Margaret (———) Bunn (*b.* West Fulton, Scho. Co., N. Y., 15 June, 1848).

Children:

1018 I. Alfred A.[8] *b.* W. Fulton, N. Y., — Mch., 1869; *d.* Jersey City, N. J., 15 Jany., 1883.

1019 II. Arthur Bunn[8] *b.* 26 June, 1870.[a] [*Deerfield, Oneida Co., N. Y.*

1020 III. Anson Charles[8] *b.* 25 Oct., 1871.[b] [*Frankfort, Herk. Co., N. Y.*

1021 IV. Amos David Everette Frederick[8] *b.* 25 Apl., 1873.[c] [*Frankfort, N. Y.*

1022 V. William Henry[8] *b.* Sharon Springs, N. Y., 13 Nov., 1876.[d] [*Albany, N. Y.*

1023 VI. Olivia Adelia[8] *b.* Ilion, N. Y., 8 Dec., 1880; *m.* Albany, N. Y., 22 Jany., 1902, Warren W., *s.* Charles and Betsey (Clark) Denslow (*b.* Frankfort, N. Y., 4 Sept., 1864).* [*Deerfield, Oneida Co., N. Y.*

a. Arthur Bunn Parshall, *m.* Herkimer, N. Y., 4 Nov., 1892, Elizabeth Brunette, *dau.* George Henry and Mary Ann (Mowers) Stroup (*b.* Boonville, N. Y., 27 Sept., 1869) *Ch.*, 1240. *i.* Warren Miles[9] *b.* Ravenna, Alb. Co., N. Y., 4 Mch., 1894; 1241. *ii.* Ruth May[9] *b.* Utica, N. Y., 16 June, 1895; 1242. *iii.* Stanley Bigelow[9] *b.* Utica, 20 Feby., 1897; 1243. *iv.* Ada Elizabeth[9] *b.* Frankfort, N. Y., 7 Apl., 1898; 1244. *v.* Howard Arthur[9] *b.* Frankfort, 27 Nov., 1899; 1245. *vi.* Earl LeRoy[9] *b.* Deerfield, Oneida Co., N. Y., 8 Nov., 1901.*

b. Anson Charles Parshall, *m.* New Hartford, Oneida Co., N. Y., 25 Dec., 1895, Etho Pearl, *dau.* George and Mary Jane (Marks) Culver (*b.* Ilion, N. Y., 12 Sept., 1878).*

c. Amos David Everette Frederick Parshall, *m.* Frankfort, N. Y., 10 July, 1895, Mayme Elizabeth, *dau.* John Lenord and Sarah Anna (Ashby) Renk (*b.* Frankfort, N. Y., 2 Feby., 1874) *Ch.*, (all *b.* Frankfort, N. Y., 1246. *i.* Glenwood Renk[9] *b.* 15 Aug., 1896; 1247. *ii.* Nellie Raymond[9] *b.* 1 Sept., 1898; 1248. *iii.* Isabelle Edith[9] *b.* 10 Dec., 1899.*

d. William Henry Parshall, *m.* Albany, N. Y., 28 Feby., 1896, Harriet, *dau.* J. K. Swaney (*b.* Lynchburg, W. Va., 16 Aug., 1876) *Ch.*, 1249. *i.* John Henry[9] *b.* Albany, N. Y., 7 Mch., 1897.*

---

* Pers. statement.

FAMILY CXCVI.*

ISRAEL A.[7] [586], *(Jesse[6], Israel[5], James[4], David[3], David[2], James[1]) b.* Middlefield, Otsego Co., N. Y., 24 July, 1844; *d.* Cooperstown, N. Y., 3 June, 1884; *m.* Cooperstown, N. Y., 14 Dec., 1870, Allie D., *dau.* Gilbert H. and Hannah N. (Eckler) Cole (*b.* Pierstown, Otsego Co., N. Y., 29 Nov., 1853).

[*Cooperstown, N. Y.*

Children: (All *b.* Cooperstown, N. Y.)

1024 I. Frank G.[8] *b.* 4 July, 1872.[a] [*Cooperstown, N. Y.*

1025 II. Charles Hartson[8] *b.* 2 July, 1875.

[*Cooperstown, N. Y.*

FAMILY CXCVII.†

JONAS ISRAEL[7] [590], *(James[6], Israel[5], James[4], David[3], David[2], James[1]) b.* Cherry Valley, N. Y., 1 Nov., 1845; *m.* Vinton, Ia., 1 July, 1868, Casandra Belle, *dau.* James Henry and Christiana (Westcott) Dummett (*b.* Pittsburg, Pa., 11 Sept., 1851). [*Butte, Boyd Co., Neb.*

a. Frank G. Parshall, *m.* Cooperstown, N. Y., 1 Oct., 1892, Elizabeth M. *dau.* Lewis and Mary Ann (Griffiths) Edwards (*b.* Blenavon, Monmouthshire, Wales, 2 Jany., 1872) *Ch.*, 1250. *i.* Helen L.[9]

* Fam. Recs. and pers. know. 1024 and wid., 586.
† Fam. Recs. and pers. know., 590.

Children:

1026 I. James Henry[8] *b.* Vinton, Ia., 17 Sept., 1869.[a]

1027 II. Nellie May[8] *b.* Worthington, Minn., 18 Apl., 1872; *m.* Butte, Neb., 14 Feby., 1893, Frank Russel, *s.* Andrew and Etta Belle (Russel) Smith (*b.* Beaver Dam, Wis., 8 Sept., 1869). *Issue:* (All *b.* Butte, Neb). [*Butte, Neb.*

- i. Euda Winnifred[9] (Smith) *b.* 23 July, 1893.
- ii. Earl Russel[9] (Smith) *b.* 29 Mch., 1896.
- iii. Frank Edward[9] (Smith) *b.* 14 Oct., 1899.

1028 III. Jonas Alvin[8] *b.* 17 June, 1875; *d.* Worthington, Minn., 10 May, 1878.

1029 IV. William Clinton[8] *b.* 14 May, 1877; *d.* Worthington, Minn., 9 Apl., 1880.

1030 V. Joseph Eaden[8] *b.* Fulda, Minn., 29 May, 1879.

1031 VI. Mary Kate[8] *b.* Blue Springs, Neb., 14 Dec., 1881.

1032 VII. Julius Earl[8] *b.* Carns, Neb., 5 Apl., 1885; *d.* Carns, Neb., 4 May, 1889.

1033 VIII. Pearl Estella[8] *b.* Carns, Neb., 11 July, 1890.

1034 IX. Frank Israel[8] *b.* Butte, Neb., 26 Sept., 1893.

---

*FAMILY CXCVIII.**

GEORGE[7] [593], (*James*[6], *Israel*[5], *James*[4], *David*[3], *David*[2], *James*[1]) *b.* Cooperstown, N. Y., 10 Dec., 1850; *m.* Cleveland, Minn., 13 Jany., 1878, Emma Delsina, *dau.* Andrew Jackson

a. James Henry Parshall, *m.* Butte, Neb., 22 Mch., 1894, Claribel, *dau.* Andrew and Etta Belle (Russel) Smith (*b.* Beaver Dam, Wis., 23 Apl., 1876, *Ch.*, (all *b.* Butte, Neb.) 1251. *i.* Julia May[9] *b.* 6 Apl., 1896; 1252; *ii.* Edith Belle[9] *b.* 4 June, 1897.†

* Fam. Recs. and pers. know. 593.
† Pers. statement.

and Mary Elizabeth (Sebree) Burk (*b.* Hinckley, Ill., 1 Oct., 1858). [*Phoenix, Holt Co., Neb.*

Children:

1035 I. Gilbert Andrew James[8] *b.* Long Pine, Neb., 30 Mch., 1883.
1036 II. Le Roy[8] *b.* Worthington, Minn., 18 May, 1890.
1037 III. Floyd Arthur[8] *b.* Butte, Neb., 26 Feby., 1893.

---

*FAMILY CXCIX.**

DEWITT CLINTON[7] [595], *(James[6], Israel[5], James[4], David[3], David[2], James[1])* *b.* Laporte, Ind., 19 June, 1861; *m.* Highland Park, *n.* Chattanooga, Tenn., 16 Aug., 1899, Gussie Belle, *dau.* James Snyder and Sarah Green (Bryden) Duke (*b.* Farmington, Ill., 22 Jany., 1876). [*Fairmount, Tenn.*

Children:

1038 I. Eva Belle *d.* 6 Feby., 1901.

---

*FAMILY CC.**

LEE[7] [606], *(Robert Asahel[6], Miner[5], James[4], David[3], David[2], James[1])* *b.* Cooperstown, N. Y., 17 Nov., 1871; *m.* Fort Plain, N. Y., 28 Dec., 1893, Elenora, *dau.* Herman and Agnes (——) Hime.

Children:

1039 I. TenEyck[8] *b.* 18 July, 1895.

---

* Pers. statement.

The Author's Children

*FAMILY CCI.**

JAMES CLARK[7] [607], *(William[6], Miner[5], James[4], David[3], David[2], James[1])* *b.* Syracuse, N. Y., 30 June, 1859; *m.* Syracuse, 16 Apl., 1887, Frances Gertrude Forster (*b.* Oneida Valley, Madison Co., N. Y., 9 Apl. 1869). [*Syracuse, N. Y.*

Children:

1040 I. William[8] *b.* Syracuse, N. Y., 14 Mch., 1888.
1041 II. Marguerite[8] *b.* Middletown, N. Y., 6 Oct., 1895.

James Clark Parshall, the author of this work, was educated in several of the public and private schools of Syracuse, graduating from the Syracuse Classical School and Syracuse High School. Entered into business with his father, but becoming dissatisfied with a mercantile life, withdrew after three years and commenced the study of law. Admitted to the bar at Rochester, N. Y., 6 Oct., 1882, he practiced successfully at Syracuse until 1885, when owing to ill health he retired from active practice. Was a resident of Middletown, N. Y., from 1891 to 1897, where he engaged in newspaper work. Returned to Syracuse, 1897, where he has since resided. Is much interested in genealogical studies and is the author of several works on the subject. Is a member of the Society of the Sons of the American Revolution. (*See frontispiece.*)

FAMILY CCII.†

WILLIAM BARKER[7] [609], *(William[6], Miner[5], James[4], David[3], David[2], James[1])* *b.* Syracuse, N. Y., 12 Sept., 1862; *m.*

---

* Fam. Recs. and pers. know., 607; Bruce's Hist. of Syracuse, N. Y.
† Bible Rec. 223, and pers. state., 609.

Syracuse, N. Y., 20 Dec., 1888, Kate Louise, *dau.* Daniel Lee, and Sarah Williams (Terry) Fry (*b.* Syracuse N. Y., 25 Sept., 1865). [*Philadelphia, Pa.*

Children:

1042 I. Esther[8] *b.* Winona, Minn., 29 Dec., 1893.

William B. Parshall was educated in the public schools of Syracuse, N. Y. Entered business with his father where he remained several years. Removed 1884 to Winona, Minn., where he engaged in the hardware business for a number of years. Is now (1903) Secretary and Treasurer of the Franklin Fountain Pen Co., of Philadelphia, Pa. *(See portrait).*

---

*FAMILY CCIII.**

LATONUS J.[7] [614], *(Peter[6], George[5], James[4], David[3], David[2], James[1]) b.* Middlefield, Otsego Co., N. Y., 17 Nov., 1860; *m.* Middlefield, N. Y., 4 Jany., 1882, Ida H., *dau.* Silas and Hattie (Moore) Derrick (*b.* New York, 17 Oct., 1861). [*Middlefield, N. Y.*

Children:

1043 I. Helen Ordelia[8] *m.* Frederick E. Hopkins.
1044 II. Harry Latonus.[8]
1045 III. Florence Irene.[8]
1046 IV. Guy Clinton[8] *b.* 26 Oct., 1891; *d.* 23 Feby., 1893.

---

* Pers. statement.

William B. Paxhall

FAMILY CCIV.*

CHARLES HENRY[7] [618], (*George Washington[6] George[5] James[4] David[3] David[2] James[1]*) *b.* Middlefield, Otsego Co., N. Y., 12 Jany., 1866; *m.* Ithaca, N. Y., 3 Jany., 1894, Jennie, *dau.* Holmes and Lucy R. (Rightmire) Hollister (*b.* Ithaca, N. Y., 28 May, 1867). [*Cooperstown, N. Y.*

Children:

1047 I. Holmes Hollister.[8] *b.* 13 Oct., 1894.

A graduate of Cooperstown High School and of Cornell University. Subsequently took a two years' course in the Law School of Cornell University, and was admitted to the bar in 1891. Was elected School Commissioner of the First Commissioner District of Otsego County in 1893. Is now one of the Editors of the Otsego Farmer, published at Cooperstown, N. Y. (*See Portrait*).

FAMILY CCV.*

LYNN GEORGE[7] [619], (*George Washington[6] George[5] James[4] David[3] David[2] James[1]*) *b.* Middlefield, Otsego Co., N. Y., 14 July, 1870; *m.* Middlefield, N. Y., 13 Dec., 1892, Nellie, *dau.* Silas L. and Hattie (Moore) Derrick (*b.* Erie, Pa., 23 Aug., 1872). [*Cooperstown, N. Y.*

Children:

1048 I. Edna Elizabeth.[8]

---

* Pers. statement.

A graduate of Cooperstown High School, he subsequently took a special course in surveying and is now following the profession of Civil Engineer and Surveyor.

---

*FAMILY CCVI.**

ADELBERT[7] [627], (*Adriel[6] Gilbert[5] James[4] David[3] David[2] James[1]*) *b.* Springfield Center, Otsego Co., N. Y., 24 Apl., 1857; *m.* West Burlington, Otsego Co., N. Y., 31 Oct., 1883, Olive, *dau.* Caleb and Thirza (Knapp) Clark (*b.* Otsego Co., N. Y., 25 June, 1854). [*West Burlington, N. Y.*

Children: (All *b.* Otsego Co., N. Y.)

1049 I. Thirza[8] *b.* 13 Oct., 1885.
1050 II. Dora Louise[8] *b.* 16 May, 1887.
1051 III. Lena Belle[8] *b.* 11 July, 1888; *d.* 18 Apl., 1896.
1052 IV. Alphonzo Clark[8] *b.* 25 Aug., 1889.
1053 V. Dutcher[8] *b.* 24 Apl., 1891.

---

*FAMILY CCVII.**

JOHN FRANK[7] [656], (*John[6] David Jefferson[5] John[4] David[3] David[2] James[1]*) *b.* Lake Geneva, Wis., 11 May, 1865; *m.* Lake Geneva, Wis., 27 Oct., 1895, Elizabeth, *dau.* John Hagan. [*Robinson, Walworth Co., Wis.*

Children: (All *b.* Lynn, Walworth Co., Wis.)

1054 I. Nina Hazel[8] *b.* 8 Jany., 1898.
1055 II. Merton Elwood[8] *b.* 5 Aug., 1900.

---

* Pers. statement.

Charles H. Parshall

*FAMILY CCVIII.**

JAMES JUDSON[7] [667], (*John*[6] *James*[5] *Jonathan*[4] *Jonathan*[3] *David*[2] *James*[1]) *b.* Palmyra, N. Y., 23 Feby., 1820; *m.* (1) Detroit, Mich., 1 Jany., 1845, Esther, *dau.* John and Betsy (Smith) McFarlin (*b.* Rush, Monroe Co., N. Y., 1 Sept., 1822; *d.* Royal Oak, Mich., 26 Oct., 1856). (*See portrait.*) [*Ann Arbor, Mich.*

Children: (All *b.* Ann Arbor, Mich.)

1056 I. Julian Grenville[8] *b.* 18 Aug., 1847.[a] [*Lafayette, Ind.*

1057 II. Adrain Jefferson[8] *b.* 24 May, 1849.[b] [*Cheyenne, Wyo.*

1058 III. Florence Alta[8] *b.* 22 Aug., 1852; *m.* Ann Arbor, Mich., 23 Oct., 1879, Charles Roswell, *s.* John and Sevilla (Roswell) Henry (*b.* Macon, Mich., 29 Dec., 1856). *Issue:* [*Alpena, Mich.*

i. Guy DeVere[9] (Henry).
ii. Carl R.[9] (Henry).

a. Julian Grenville Parshall *b.* 18 Aug., 1847, *m.* La Fayette, Ind.,—— 1878, Ella, *dau.* Samuel and Ella (Bixler) Iddings, ch., 1253. *i.* Samuel James[9].*

b. Adrian Jefferson Parshall, *m.* Cheyenne, Wyo., 21 Dec., 1879, Annie Florence, *dau.* Dr. George Henry and Ann Pettibone (Simons) Kilbourne (*b.* Lewiston, Mich., 23 June, 1855) *Ch.*, 1254. *i.* Amalia[9] *b.* Deadwood, S. Dak., 2 Nov., 1880; 1255. *ii.* Florence[9] *b.* Cheyenne, Wyo., 3 May, 1866; *d.* Cheyenne, 12 Aug., 1886. Graduated at Michigan University in 1871 with degree of C. E. Moved to Wyoming in 1872; was draughtsman in the office of the Surveyor General in 1872-4 and chief clerk in 1875. Moved to Deadwood, Dak., in 1876 and returned to Cheyenne, Wyo., in 1883. Was clerk of State Board of Land Commissioners 1895 to 1898 since which time he has been Asst. State Engineer and Resident Hydographer of the U. S. Geological Survey for Wyoming. Is an active member in masonic Circles. A member of Wyoming Consistory No. 1. A. A. S. R.-32°. Was Grand Commander of Knights Templar of Wyoming in 1896-7.* (*See portrait.*)

* Pers. statement.

m. (2) 19 Mch., 1857, Christiana Elizabeth, *dau.* John and Mary (Goheen) Culbertson (*b.* Groveland, N. Y., 10 Sept., 1828; *d.* Ann Arbor, Mich., 1 Mch., 1869).

Children:

1059 IV. Charles Theodore[8] *b.* 3 Mch., 1859.[a]

[*Ann Arbor, Mich.*

m. (3) 16 Nov., 1870, Sarah Ann, *dau.* John and Ellen (Molyneaux) Twamley (*b.* Lydon, Mich., 25 Sept., 1836; *d.* Ann Arbor, Mich., 14 Dec., 1897).

Children:

1060 V. Lena May[8] *b.* 3 Mch., 1874.

[*Ann Arbor, Mich.*

FAMILY CCIX.†

JOHN MELVIN[7] [666], (*John[6] James[5] Jonathan[4] Jonathan[3] David[2] James[1]*) *b.* Newbury, O., 28 Mch., 1828; *d.* Jackson, Mich., 2 Jany., 1900; *m.* Detroit, Mich., 2 Oct., 1857, Cynthia, *dau.* Joseph and Sara (Macomber) Cole (*b.* Saratoga, N. Y., 1 June, 1831). [*Jackson, Mich.*

Children:

1061 I. Gage LeGrand[8] *b.* 30 July, 1858.[b]

1062 II. A *dau. d. inf.*

a. Charles Theodore Parshall *b.* 3 Mch., 1859, *m.* Fairfield, Ia., 1 Jany., 1883, Anna Maria, *dau.* Nathan and Maria (Porter) White (*b.* Ann Arbor, Mich., 9 Jany., 1860) *Ch.*, 1256. *i.* Roy Nathan[9]; 1257. *ii.* Olive Louise[9]*

b. Gage LeGrand Parshall, *m.* East Saginaw, Mich., 30 Oct., 1884, Louisa, *dau.* John Campbell and Martha (Mayfield) Valentine, *Ch.*, 1258. *i.* John Melvin[9] *b.* Bay City, Mich., 14 Aug., 1885; 1259. *ii.* Bessie Louise[9]; 1260. *iii.* Luella May[9]; 1261. *iv.* Gage LeGrand[9].*

---

* Pers. statement.

† Fam. Recs. and pers. know., 1061.

James J Parshall

*FAMILY CCX.**

CHARLES HENRY^{7} [670], (*John^{6} James^{5} Jonathan^{4} Jonathan^{3} David^{2} James^{1}*) *b.* Newbury, O., 11 Aug., 1830; *m.* Detroit, Mich., 2 Dec., 1851, Ellen Louise, *dau.* James Houston and Ellen (Ryan) D'Arcy (*b.* Isle LaMotte, Lake Champlain, 28 Jany., 1832; *d.* Detroit, Mich., 25 Mch., 1884).
[*New York, N. Y.*

Children:

1063 I. Frank D'Arcy^{8} *b.* 21 Feby., 1853.[a] [*Chicago, Ill.*

1064 II. Minnie Estelle^{8} *b.* Wyandotte, Mich., 11 June, 1857; *m.* Detroit, Mich., 17 Nov., 1880, Charles Francis, *s.* Joseph and Mary Catherine (Ling) Swan (*b.* Detroit, 28 Nov., 1850). *Issue:* (All *b.* Detroit, Mich.)
[*Detroit, Mich.*

- i. Ellen Louise^{9} (Swan) *b.* 19 Aug., 1881; *d. inf.*
- ii. Harry Bennett^{9} (Swan) *b.* 9 Mch., 1885.
- iii. Louis Parshall^{9} (Swan) *b.* 8 Dec., 1887; *d.* 19 May, 1888.
- iv. Ellwood Paul^{9} (Swan) *b.* 14 May, 1893.

1065 III. Charles Henry^{8} *b.* 15 Oct., 1861.[b] [*St. Louis, Mo.*

1066 IV. John Harry^{8} *b.* 13 Feby., 1866.[c] [*Detroit, Mich.*

a. Frank D'Arcy Parshall, *m.* Chicago, Ill., 7 Nov., 1879, Annie Louise, *dau.* Frederick and Anna (Powell) Smith (*b.* Milwaukee, Wis., 8 Dec., 1857).†

b. Charles Henry Parshall, Jr., *m.* Detroit, Mich., 18 Jany., 1882, Cynthia Catherine, *dau.* James and Nancy (Burdette) Grooms (*b.* Shannonville, Ont., Canada, 29 May, 1857).†

c. John Harry Parshall, *m.* Pontiac, Mich., 4 Oct., 1888, Flora, *dau.* Emanuel and Jane (German) Newman (*b.* Pontiac, Mich., 27 Oct., 1865) *Ch.*, 1262. *i.* Helen Louise^{9} *b.* Detroit, 11 May, 1890; 1263. *ii.* Newman Ames^{9} *b.* Detroit, 22 Oct., 1891; *d.* Trenton, Mich., 8 May, 1892; 1264. *iii.* Dorothy Jeanette^{9} *b.* Trenton, Mich., 28 July, 1894; 1265. *iv.* Louis Henry^{9} *b.* 22 Aug., 1899.†

---

* Fam. Recs. and pers. know., 670, 1064 and 1068.

† Pers. statement.

1067 v. William Smith[8] *b.* 8 Jany., 1868.[a]

1068 vi. Louis Ayers[8] *b.* 21 Jany., 1870.[b] [*Detroit, Mich.*

Charles Henry Parshall is the inventor and patentee of many ingenious contrivances, among the more important of which may be mentioned an atmospheric Ice machine, which produces a temperature of 256° below zero, Fahrenheit, by the compression and expansion of air. This invention was the result of more than six years' continuous labor. It is now in use on all U. S. Battleships and Cruisers for cooling the powder magazines and for other purposes. Mr. Parshall is also the inventor of the Sight Feed Lubricator, a contrivance in use in every civilized country on the globe and from which he has realized a large fortune. (*See portrait.*)

---

*FAMILY CCXI.**

JOSEPH PRESTON[7] [675], (*Joseph*[6] *James*[5] *Jonathan*[4] *Jonathan*[3] *David*[2] *James*[1]) *b.* Palmyra, N. Y., 6 Aug., 1820; *d.* Canton, Wayne Co., Mich., 21 Aug., 1890; *m.* Canton, Mich., 18 Nov., 1847, Margaret, *dau.* William and Fanny (Britten) Hannan (*b.* Florida, Mont. Co., N. Y., 10 Feby., 1824). [*Canton, Mich.*

a. William Smith Parshall, *d.* Detroit, 3 Jany., 1899; *m.* Detroit, 3 Oct., 1889, Emma, *dau.* John Ward (*b.* London, Eng., 25 June, 1868; *d.* Detroit, 2 Oct., 1893) ch., 1266. *i.* Ward[9] *b.* 2 Oct., 1893; *d.* 3 Oct., 1893.‡

b. Louis Ayers Parshall, *m.* Monroe, Mich., 13 Sept., 1892, Lizette Annie, *dau.* Frank Brighton and Josephine Chaubert (MacBride) Clarke (*b.* Monroe, Mich., 3 Feby., 1873; *d.*, Detroit, 27 July, 1899) *Ch.*, 1267. *i.* Van Miller[9] *b.* 23 Apl., 1894.†

---

* Fam. Recs. pers. know. 1071.
† Pers. statement.
‡ Fam. Recs. and pers. know. 1068.

C. H. Parshall

Children: (All *b.* Canton, Wayne Co., Mich.)

1069 I. Dewitt Henry[8] *b.* 4 June, 1849.[a]

1070 II. Clarissa Cornelia[8] *b.* 23 Nov., 1850.

1071 III. Esther Arloe[8]* *b.* 9 Feby., 1852; *m.* Canton, Mich., 28 Oct., 1873, John Cyrus, *s.* Nelson L. and Ruth (Pease) Goodrich (*b.* Blissfield, Mich., 19 Oct., 1848). *Issue:* [*Detroit, Mich.*

i. Flora E.[9] (Goodrich) *b.* 5 Sept., 1874.
ii. John N.[9] Goodrich) *b.* 30 Aug., 1876.
iii. Alvin P.[9] (Goodrich) *b.* 3 Mch., 1879.
iv. Ira J.[9] (Goodrich) *b.* 30 June, 1881.

1072 IV. Fanny Lurene[8]† *b.* 28 Feby., 1854; *m.* Canton, Mich., 4 Dec., 1896, Martin, *s.* Oscar and Cornelia (Miller) Leonard (*b.* Elba, Genesee Co., N. Y., 9 May, 1855). *No issue.* [*Plymouth, Mich.*

1073 V. Diantha M.[8]† *b.* 3 Nov., 1856; *m.* Canton, Mich., 20 Dec., 1881, Charles Henry, *s.* Henry and Mary Ann (McKinny) Jones (*b.* Detroit, Mich., 11 Nov., 1857). *Issue:* [*Wayne, Wayne Co., Mich.*

i. Charles LeRoy[9] (Jones).
ii. Violet Leetta[9] (Jones).

1074 VI. James Norman[8] *b.* 1 Mch., 1860; *d.* 6 Aug., 1860.

1075 VII. Joseph Preston[8] *b.* 10 Oct., 1862.[b]

a. Dewitt Henry Parshall, *b.* 4 June, 1849, *m.* Wayne, Mich., 19 Oct., 1881, Belle, *dau.* Edward H. and Calista (Walker) Seeley (*b.* Novi, Oakland Co., Mich., 3 Sept., 1859) *Ch.*, 1268. *i.* Dewey[9] *b.* 29 Jany., 1887; 1269. *ii.* Florence[9] *b.* 13 Jany., 1893.†

b. Joseph Preston Parshall, *b.* 10 Oct., 1862; *m.* Ann Arbor, Mich., 1 Feby., 1888, Mary Louise, *dau.* Samuel G. and Elozia (Clough) Benham (*b.* Ithaca, N. Y., 8 Nov., 1860). *No issue.*†

* Pers. statement; Goodrich Fam. 147.
† Pers. statement.

*FAMILY CCXII.**

JAMES[7] [678], (*Joseph[6] James[5] Jonathan[4] Jonathan[3] David[2] James[1]*) *b.* Palmyra, N. Y., 9 May, 1830; *m.* Redford, Mich., 24 Dec., 1857, Caroline, *dau.* Thomas and Hepzibah (Shattuck) Finney (*b.* Redford, Mich., 7 Feby., 1836). (*See portrait.*) [*Pontiac, Mich.*

Children:

1076 I. Sarah Warner[8] *b.* 2 Jany., 1860; *d.* 2 May, 1863.
1077 II. James Joseph[8] *b.* 19 Jany., 1863; *d.* 25 July, 1864.
1078 III. Homer Ellsworth[8] *b.* 4 Dec., 1864.[a] [*Detroit, Mich.*

FAMILY CCXIII.†

WILLIAM HENRY[7] [683], (*DeWitt[6] Nathan[5] Jonathan[4] Jonathan[3] David[2] James[1]*) *b.* Lyons, Wayne Co., N. Y., 14 Feby., 1839; *d.* Lyons, 17 Mch., 1871; *m.* Lyons, N. Y., — Sept., 1859, Lisette, *dau.* Hiram Gilbert and Mary Williams (Ashley) Hotchkiss (*b.* Lyons, 7 Feby., 1840). [*Lyons, N. Y.*

Children:

1079 I. Lisette[8] *b.* Lyons, N. Y., 3 Feby., 1862. [*Lyons, N. Y.*

a. **Homer Ellsworth Parshall *b.* Detroit, Mich., 4 Dec., 1864; *m.* Stutgart, Germany, 7 Nov., 1894, Caroline Pauline, *dau.* Johann and Caroline Pauline (Lustnauer) Eitel (*b.* Friedrichshafen am Bodensee, Wurternberg, Germany, 23 May, 1866) *Ch.*, 1270. *i.* James Eitel[9] *b.* Berlin, 3 Mch., 1896; 1271. *ii* Homer Hans[9] *b.* Berlin, 30 May, 1897; 1272. *iii.* Dorothy[9] *b.* Berlin, 23 Apl., 1901.***

---

* Pers. statement.
† Fam. Recs. and pers. know., 1079.

1080 II. DeWitt[8] *b.* Buffalo, N. Y., 2 Aug., 1864.[a]
1081 III. Annie Hotchkiss[8] *b.* Buffalo, N. Y., 17 Sept., 1866; *m.* Lyons, N. Y., 20 Oct., 1898, Christopher H. R. Woodward. [*Morristown, N. J.*

*FAMILY CCXIV.**

ROSSMAN JORDAN[7] [687], (*Hendee[6] Nathan[5] Jonathan[4] Jonathan[3] David[2] James[1]*) *b.* Palmyra, Wayne Co., N. Y., 18 Nov., 1844; *m.* (1) Palmyra, N. Y., Kate Evaline Thurber. [*Lyons, N. Y.*

Children:

1082 I. Rossman Thurber[8] *b.* 4 July, 1876. [*Chicago, Ill.*

m. (2) 10 Sept., 1895, Emma Lee Blakely.

Children:

1083 II. Lamont Blakely[8] *b.* 3 Dec., 1897.

FAMILY CCXV.†

WILLIAM ANDREWS[7] [703], (*Caleb[6] David[5] David[4] Jonathan[3] David[2] James[1]*) *b.* Walden, Orange Co., N. Y., 9 Dec., 1865; *m.* Port Jervis, N. Y., 1 June, 1893, Christine, *dau.* Lewis E. and Florence (Corwin) Senger (*b.* Port Jervis, N. Y., 3 May, 1868). [*Port Jervis, N. Y.*

a. Dewitt Parshall, *m.* New York City, 2 Nov., 1895, Carrie, *dau.* John Newton and Jennie K. (Storel) Ewell, ch., 1173. *i.* Douglas Ewell[9] *b.* 19 Nov., 1899.

* Fam. Recs. and pers. know., 690 and 1079.
† Pers. statement; Mallman's Hist. of Shelter Island.

Children:

1084 I. Walter Corwin[8] *b.* Port Jervis, N. Y., 19 July, 1895.

William Andrews Parshall graduated from the Port Jervis (N. Y.) Academy in 1883, and from the Academic Dept., of Yale University, in 1889. He then entered the Albany Law School, from which he was graduated in 1889. In 1890, he was admitted to the bar and has since practiced his profession in Port Jervis. On Oct. 1st, 1890, he formed a co-partnership with Hon. O. P. Howell and R. E. Schofield, Esq., under the style of Howell, Parshall & Schofield, from which he withdrew in Sept., 1893, to become local attorney for the Erie Railroad Co. He has served one term as Town Clerk of Deerpark, and seven terms as corporation counsel for the Village of Port Jervis. He is now attorney for the New York, Lake Erie & Western R. R., the Port Jervis, Monticello and New York R. R., and several local corporations, including the National Bank of Port Jervis, of which he is also a director. He has been Master of Port Jervis Lodge, No. 328, F. & A. M.; High Priest of Neversink Lodge, No. 186, R. A. M.; Commander of Delaware Commandery, No. 44, Knights Templar, and is now District Deputy Grand Master of the Thirteenth Masonic Dictrict of the State of New York. (*See portrait.*)

Wm. P. Marshall

Unconnected Families.

*FAMILY CCXVI.**

JOHN HICKEY[1] [1282] *b.* Pa., 18 Apl., 1897; *d.* Lockbourne, O., 13 May, 1852; *m.* (1) 1 Aug., 1822, Sarah Gilbert (*b.* 22 May, 1803; *d.* Lockbourne, O., 9 Apl., 1837.*

Children:

1283 I. Catherine Maria[2]† *b.* N. Y., 1 Mch., 1823; *d.* 1 Apl., 1880; *m.* Groveport, Franklin Co., O., John Hamler (*d.* Newburn, N. C., — Apl., 1865). *Issue:*

- i. Jonathan Norman[3] (Hamler) *b.* Union Co., O., 15 Apl., 1851.[a] [*Wellington, O.*
- ii. Emanuel[3] (Hamler).
- iii. Jacob[3] (Hamler).
- iv. Isaac[3] (Hamler).
- v. William Henry[3] (Hamler).
- vi. Sarah Mariah[3] (Hamler).
- vii. Elsie Ann[3] (Hamler).
- viii. Eliza Lucretia[3] (Hamler).

a. Jonathan Norman Hamler, *m.* West Salem, Ashland Co., O., 12 Feby., 1883, Mary Elizabeth, *dau.* Abraham and Caroline Creath (Arbogast) Ober (*b.* Plain Tp., Wayne Co., O., 14 Nov., 1854; *d.* Wellington, Loraine Co., O., 16 Sept., 1893). *Issue:* *i.* Carrie Caroline[4] *b.* 14 Sept., 1883. *ii.* May Creath[4] *b.* 9 Beby., 1886. *iii.* Roy Abraham[4] *b.* 9 Feby., 1886†

---

* Fam. Rec. and pers. know., 1284.

† Fam. Rec. and pers. know., Jonathan N. Hamler.

1284 II. Jonathan Knapp[2] *b.* 13 Mch., 1825. FAM. CCXVII.

1285 III. Lydia Elmira[2]* *b.* 18 June, 1827; *m.* South Bloomfield, O., 17 Nov., 1847, George Birley (*b.* 8 May, 1823; *d.* Ind., 21 Jany., 1873). *Issue:* [*Terre Haute, Ind.*

- i. Henry Theodore[3] (Birley) *b.* 20 Nov., 1857.
- ii. Gustavus Adolphus[3] (Birley).
- iii. Charles Edward[3] (Birley) *b.* 17 Feby., 1858.
- iv. Emma Amelia[3] (Birley) *b.* 22 Jany., 1859.
- v. Hannah Elsie[3] (Birley) *b.* 12 July, 1861.
- vi. George[3] (Birley) *b.* 19 Apl., 1863; *d.* Nov., 1863.
- vii. Jessie[3] (Birley) *b.* 3 May, 1867.

1286 IV. Hannah Lovina[2]* *b.* 20 Jany., 1829; *m.* (1) Bloomfield, O., 8 Nov., 1859, Jacob McClain (*d.* 18 Sept., 1877). *No issue.*
m. (2) 14 Apl., 1879, Horace Jacobs (*d.* Lewis, Cass Co., Ia., 28 June, 1888). *No issue.* [*Lewis, Cass Co., Ia.*

1287 V. Elsie Ann[2]* *b.* Pa., 8 Mch., 1833; *m.* Pickaway Co., O., 11 Jany., 1860, Silas, *s.* John and Mary (Klor) Brinker. *Issue:* [*Obed, Shelby Co., Ill.*

- i. Alfred Eugene[3] (Brinker) *b.* 19 Feby., 1862.
- ii. Arthur Jacob[3] (Brinker) *b.* 21 Feby., 1866.
- iii. David Lewis[3] (Brinker) *d.* Aetna, Neb., 16 Oct., 1894.[a]

a. David Lewis Brinker, *m.* 30 Mch., 1894, Cynthia Hill (*b.* 5 Nov., 1863). *Issue:* *i.* Clara Maude[4] *b.* 12 Sept., 1887. *ii.* Elsie Ann[4] *b.* 17 July, 1890. *iii.* Charlotte Irene[4] *b.* 30 May, 1892, *iv.* Mary Ellen[4] *b.* 27 Aug., 1894.†

---

* Pers. statement.
† Pers. know., 1287.

m. (2) 4 Sept., 1840, Elizabeth Hamter (*b.* 22 May, 1793; *d.* 6 May, 1847). *No issue.*

m. (3) Annie Quince. *No issue.*

Mr. Jonathan K. Parshall, the sole living male representative of this family, writing of his father, says: "My earliest recollection is that my father moved from the State of New York to Western Pennsylvania, and from there to Lockbourne, O., where my mother died. We children were placed in different families. In time my father married again, but the family was never re-united. * * * I remember two of my father's brothers, William, who moved with us, with his family, from Pennsylvania to Lockbourne, which place he left soon after. Then there was Uncle Reuben, whom I only knew by name, and a sister, Hannah, who *m.* Dennis Larkin, lived in Pennslyvania, and brought up a large family of children, who, in time, came to Indiana and Illinois." I have never been able to gain the slightest clue to the paternity of John Hickey Parshall, nor have I found in any family a "John" unaccounted for, who could by any possibility be the one in question.

---

*FAMILY CCXVII.**

JONATHAN KNAPP[2] [1284], (*John Hickey*[1]) *b.* 13 Mch., 1825; *m.* Columbus, O., 28 Feby., 1860, Mary A. McDonald, of Delaware Co., O.

Children:

1288 1. Emma[3] *b.* 11 Sept., 1862.

---

* Pers. statement.

*FAMILY CCXVIII.**

DAVID[2] [1289], (*Elias*[1]) *b.* Muttontown, Pa., 11 Mch., 1805; *d.* Zanesville, O., 6 Dec., 1893; *m.* Zanesville, 22 Feby., 1826, Elizabeth, *dau.* ——— and Diana (Ford) Allen (*b. n.* Manchester, Eng., 28 Feby., 1809; *d.* Zanesville, 30 July, 1890).

Children:

1290 I. David[3] killed in a railroad accident in 1852.
1291 II. John Allen[3] *b.* 1 Jany., 1829. FAM. CCXIX.
1292 III. William[3] *d. inf.*
1293 IV. Elizabeth[3] *d.; m.* ——— Martin.
1294 V. Reuben Jones[3] *d.; m.* ——— ———.
1295 VI. Mary.[3]
1296 VII. Caroline[3] *b.* Zanesville, O., 6 Apl., 1843; *m.* Zanesville, 11 May, 1864, Robert, *s.* Daniel and Anna (Woodward) Price (*b.* Zanesville, 22 July, 1833). *No issue.* [*Zanesville, O.*
1297 VIII. Elias[3] *d.; m. Issue:* one *dau.*
1298 IX. Robert Soffard.[3] [*Zanesville, O.*
1299 X. Edith[3] *d. inf.*
1300 XI. Goodsel Buckingham.[3] [*Chicago, Ill.*

In reference to this family, Mr. Robert Price, of Zanesville, O., President of the Muskingum County Pioneer and Historical Society, himself a genealogist and antiquarian of no mean pretentions, wrote me as follows: "My wife (Caroline[3] Parshall) says her father (David[2]) had a brother, who, she thinks, lived near Uniontown, Fayette Co., Pa. His name was Elias, and her father visited 'Uncle Elias' when she was a girl. * * *

* Fam. Recs. and pers. know., 1896.

John[3] says his father (David[2]) had a brother John, who was a physician in Cincinnati, O., and another brother, William, a lawyer, residence unknown." This would seem to connect the family with the descendants of Elias[5] of Fayette Co., Pa., but I have very complete records of that family and none is unaccounted for; moreover, all the members of that line to whom I have written on the subject disclaim all knowledge of this Zanesville family.

---

*FAMILY CCXIX.**

JOHN ALLEN[3] [1291], (*David[2] Elias[1]*) *b.* Zanesville, O., 1 Jany., 1829; *m.* (1) Fultonham, O., 12 Aug., 1852, Sarah Risley (*b.* Fultonham, 7 Feby., 1829; *d.* Zanesville, 10 Apl., 1891). [*Zanesville, O.*

Children:

1301 I. Charles Gibson[4] *b.* 1 June, 1855. FAM. CCXX.
1302 II. Edward Stewart[4] *b.* 12 Mch., 1858. FAM. CCXXI. [*Zanesville, O.*
1303 III. Alice Belle.[4]
1304 IV. Carrie Amelia[4] *m.* ——— Fleming. [*Zanesville, O.*

m. (2) Sarah Catherine ——— (*d.* Zanesville, 28 Aug., 1901). *No issue.*

FAMILY CCXX.†

CHARLES GIBSON[4] [1301], (*John Allen[3] David[2] Elias[1]*) *b.* Zanesville, O., 1 June, 1855; *d.* Zanesville, 20 Aug., 1883; *m.* Zanesville, 28 Nov., 1887, Ella, *dau.* Isaac and Emily (Moore) Piersol (*b.* Zanesville, O., 29 Dec., 1855).

---

* Pers. statement
† Fam. Rec. and pers. know., wid. 1901.

Children: (All *b.* Zanesville, O.)

1305 I. Edna May[5] *b.* 6 Nov., 1880; *d.* Zanesville, 20 Aug., 1881.

1306 II. Harry Gibson[5] *b.* 24 Feby., 1882. [*New York, N. Y.*

---

*FAMILY CCXXI.**

EDWARD STEWART[4] [1302] (*John Allen*[3] *David*[2] *Elias*[1]) *b.* Zanesville, O., 12 Mch., 1858; *m.* Zanesville, 16 Oct., 1879, Mary ———.

Children:

1307 I. William Allen.[5]

1308 II. Bessie Belle.[5]

FAMILY CCXXII.†

PETER CROSS[2] [1309] (*James*[1a]) *b.* Sacketts Harbor, N. Y., 30 Dec., 1812; *d.* Penn Yan, Yates Co., N. Y., 17 Sept., 1885; *m.* Julia Loverna Hill.

a. James Parshall, the father of Peter, was twice married, and had sixteen children. By one wife he had Stephen, Peter Cross and Elizabeth; by the other William and Sarah. The names of the others are not known. It seems strange that so large a family could leave so little trace of its existence. I have been able to discover only Peter, Cross and William, though relatives of James are said to have lived in Sharpsburg and Pittsburg, Pa., a number of years ago.

---

* Fam. Rec. and pers. know., 1291.
† Fam. Rec. and pers. know., 1310.

Children:

1310 i. Helen Elizabeth[3]* *b.* Byron, Genesee Co., N. Y., 1 May, 1837; *m.* Penn Yan, 11 June, 1855, George, *s.* Joshua and Phebe (Briggs) Wells (*b.* Penn Yan, 17 May, 1831). *Issue:* (All *b.* Penn Yan, N. Y.) [*Penn Yan, N. Y.*

i. Hiram Alonzo[4] (Wells) *b.* 2 May, 1856; *d.* 24 Aug., 1856.

ii. William Andrus[4] (Wells) *b.* 29 Apl., 1858.[a] [*Penn Yan, N. Y.*

iii. George Washington[4] (Wells) *b.* 7 Apl., 1861.[b] [*Monterey, N. Y.*

iv. Rosetta Julian[4] (Wells) *b.* 8 June, 1864; *d.* 24 June, 1866.

v. Eugene Fred[4] (Wells) *b.* 11 Apl., 1867.[c] [*Rochester, N. Y.*

vi. Mary Isadora[4] (Wells) *b.* 19 Mch., 1870.[d]

a. William Andrus Wells, *m.* Yatesville, N. Y., 6 Mch., 1878, Emma J. *dau.* Benjamin and Martha (Smith) Kennerson (*b.* Copaxe Flats, Catt. Co., N. Y., 18 Oct., 1858). *Issue: i.* Fred R.[5] *b.* 7 Aug., 1879. *ii.* Frank[5] *b.* 17 June, 1884. *iii.* Charles J.[4] *b.* 2 May, 1887. *iv.* Margaret L.[5] *b.* 6 Apl., 1889. *v.* Leslie[5] *b.* 9 Mch., 1892. *vi.* Irena[5] *b.* 14 Mch., 1897. *vii.* Martha[5] *b.* 27 May, 1899.†

b. George Washington Wells, *m.* Penn Yan, N. Y., 1 Jany., 1884, Mary H. *dau.* Stephen and——— (Coryell) Wood (*b.* 9 Aug., 1863).†

c. Eugene Fred Wells, *m.* Penn Yan, 18 Aug., 1886, Kate, *dau.* George and Catherine (Thomas) Holloway (*b.* Wales, 1 Aug., 1867). *Issue: i.* George Eugene[5] *b.* 17 Sept., 1887. *ii.* Arthur Vincent[5] *b.* 11 Apl., 1890; *d.* 20 Apl., 1890. *iii.* Catherine Mae[5] *b.* 22 Apl., 1893. *iv.* Helen Lettie[5] *b.* 20 Sept., 1894; *d.* 4 Oct., 1894.†

d. Mary Isadora Wells, *m.* Penn Yan, 19 Mch., 1889, Hiram, *s.* Charles and Julia Ann (Miller) Graves (*b.* Roadesport, Chemung Co., N. Y., 24 Jany., 1867). *Issue: i.* Nellie May[5] (Graves) *b.* 27 Feby., 1892. *ii.* Clarence Eugene[5] (Graves) *b.* 28 May, 1894. *iii.* Idah Luella[5] (Graves) *b.* 3 Mch., 1899.†

* Pers. statement.
† Pers. knowledge 1310.

vii. Retta Sarah[4] (Wells) *b.* 20 Sept., 1872.[a] [*Potter, Yates Co., N. Y.*

m. (2) Elizabeth Frost.

Children:

1311 II. Irene Matilda[3] *m.* ——— Davis.
1312 III. Francis Albert.[3] [*Penn Yan, N. Y.*
1313 IV. Georgetta Minerva[3] *b.* Lockport, N. Y., 4 May, 1857; *m.* 5 Sept., 1886, George E. Calkins, (*b.* Starkey, Yates Co., N. Y.) [*Penn Yan, N. Y.*
1314 V. John Stephen.[3]

---

*FAMILY CCXXIII.**

WILLIAM[2] [1315], (*James*[1]) *b.* ———; *d.* ———; *m.* Margaret, *dau.* of ——— and Ruth (Applegate) Scobey (*b.* about 1805; *d.* Edinboro, Pa., 14 Feby., 1898.)

Children:

1316 I. Laomi.[3]
1317 II. Harriet.[3]
1318 III. Mary.[3]
1319 IV. William Henry[3] *b.* 30 Jany., 1837. FAM. CCXXIV.

William Parshall lived at times in New York State and Pennsylvania, and in Dayton, Toledo and Newark, O. He finally joined the Mormons and is believed to have been killed at

a. Retta Sarah Wells, *m.* Penn Yan, 24 July, 1892, Charles G., *s.* Oliver and Rachel (Fredenburgh) McCann (*b.* Yatesville, N. Y., 17 Oct., 1871). *Issue:* *i.* Sarah Elizabeth[5] (McCann) *b.* 23 May, 1897; *ii.* Lestie Edward[5] (McCann) *b.* 13 June, 1901.†

---

* Fam. Rec. and pers. know., 1819.
† Pers. knowledge 1810.

Nauvoo, Ill., during the troubles there. His *daus.* Naomi and Harriet are said to have been adopted by a physician at Newark, O., and all trace of them has been lost.

---

*FAMILY CCXXIV.**

WILLIAM HENRY[3] [1319], (*William*[2] *James*[1]) *b.* Dayton, O., 30 Jany., 1837; *m.* (1) Edinboro, Pa., 5 Jany., 1859, Martha Sheffield, *dau.* John and Rebecca (Holloway) Card (*b.* Providence, R. I., 6 Mch., 1836; *d.* Fond du Lac, Wis., 25 Nov., 1876). [*Edinboro, Erie Co., Pa.*

Children: (All *b.* Edinboro, Pa.)

1320 I. Margaret Rebecca[4] *b.* 13 Oct., 1861; *m.* (1) Lincoln, Neb., 7 Sept., 1887, Sidney F. Maxwell. *Issue:*

i. Florence Hilda[5] (Maxwell) *b.* Edinboro, Pa., 6 Nov., 1888.

m. (2) Girard, Pa., 20 Apl., 1895, Nathan Russell Grafton. *No issue.* [*Edinboro, Pa.*

1321 II. William Hazard[4] *b.* 24 Feby., 1864. FAM. CCXXV.

1322 III. John F.[4] *b.* 2 Dec., 1867. [*Edinboro, Pa.*

1323 IV. Charles Franklin[4] *b.* 9 Oct., 1870; *d.* 16 May, 1878.

1324 V. Elmer Spellman[4] *b.* 9 Feby., 1874. [*Edinboro, Pa.*

m. (2) Edinboro, Pa., 12 Jany., 1881, Anna Stewart Campbell. *No issue.*

---

† Pers. know., 1810.

*FAMILY CCXXV.**

WILLIAM HAZARD[4] [1321], (*William Henry*[3] *William*[2] *James*[1]) *b.* Edinboro, Pa., 24 Feby., 1864; *m.* Lincoln, Neb., 28 May, 1886, Anna, *dau.* John and Anne (————) Haylen (*b.* England, 7 Nov., 1863). [*Davey, Lancaster Co., Neb.*

Children:

1325 I. William J.[5] *b.* 5 May, 1888.
1326 II. James C.[5] *b.* 13 Nov., 1890.
1327 III. Edward E.[5] *b.* 11 Jany., 1892.
1328 IV. Harry T.[5] *b.* 11 May, 1894.
1329 V. Mark F.[5] *b.* 5 Oct., 1896.
1330 VI. Margaret[5] *b.* 20 July, 1898.
1331 VII. Myrtle[5] *b.* 20 July, 1898.
1332 VIII. Eugene[5] *b.* 20 June, 1900.

* Pers. statement.

Marriages

Marriages

Marriages

Marriages

Births

Births

Births

Births

Deaths

Deaths

Deaths

Deaths

Index.

Every surname upon a page is indexed at least once, but to avoid repetition and confusion all christian names are not given. Any christian name in the book may be found by looking up its appropriate surname.

INDEX

Printed in the USA
CPSIA information can be obtained
at www.ICGtesting.com
LVHW081536280124
770077LV00001B/271